To four generations of women: my grandmother Audrey, my mother, Margaret, my wife, Junya, and my daughter, Sarah. —R. B.

To my sisters, the ones who came to me through the women's movement and the three I started out with: Frieda, Toni, and Sydelle. —L. S. R.

CONTENTS

PREFACE

A $4 billion per year tourist industry is the linchpin of the modernization process called the "Thai Economic Miracle." And the linchpin of that industry is sex. Young women are lured to Bangkok to staff the teeming brothels, massage parlors, and sex bars that cater to male tourists from the United States, Western Europe, Japan, Australia, the Gulf States, Malaysia, and Singapore. *Night Market* traces the historical, cultural, material, and textual traditions that have combined in unique and complex ways to establish sex tourism as an integral part of the developing Thai economy. It explores international sex tourism from the perspectives of economic development planning, forced labor market choices, international sexual alienation, and textual traditions that have constructed sexual Other cultures in the Western imagination.

The introductory chapter, "Points of Departure: Catalysts and Contexts," contains three separate sections. The first provides anecdotes relating how each of us became interested in the project personally and professionally. Besides addressing that thing called subject position, these anecdotes inductively invoke specific issues taken up in the book. Following the anecdotes is a revised version of an article Robinson published in 1993 that is the nucleus of this project. Finally, we explain the construction of the text and the methods deployed to address a topic so intimately linking globalization processes and individual experience. Chapter 2, "Naming the Problem," examines representations of Thai tourism in discursive realms as diverse as academic research and popular media. Of particular import is how sex tourism emerged as a "problem" in the late 1980s and early 1990s, but only in reference to AIDS and child prostitution.

The third chapter, "Languages of Tourism," considers the multiple discursive practices, both inside and outside the country, intended to promote and generate tourism; these range from government documents and promotional material to travel brochures and guidebooks. Integral to both Chapters 2 and 3 is the role of economics as it pertains to international and national strategies of modernization and development.

Chapter 4, "A Very Political Economy," provides a political economic analysis of the role tourism has played in Thai development within a global context. In it we read academic analyses and government documents reporting on the industry but curiously eliding the fuel that drives the machine: sex. Sex and its multiple representations in the writings of explorers, travelers, philosophers, and novelists become the focus of Chapter 5, "Imagining Sexual Others," which examines the discursive and material genealogies of these constructions. In essence, these texts present other cultures as qualitatively and quantitatively different with regard to sexual practices and mores. The chapter explores how the long textual tradition of so representing "exotic" cultures provides the context, and possibly the pretext, for contemporary sex tourists' interactions with the natives and how contemporary writers reinscribe the tropes that manifest themselves in this textual genealogy. "The Bar Scene," Chapter 6, provides ethnographic accounts of the sexual subjectivities alienated enough to travel halfway around the world to purchase the realization of their fantasies. The chapter includes voices of sex clients, sex workers, and others professionally involved in the industry.

Despite the pervasiveness of the sex industry in international public discourse about Thailand and its tangible pervasiveness in the daily lives of many Thais and tourists, the subject itself is almost completely missing from national public discourse; what is unspeakable in Thai culture is that which is most egregiously speakable elsewhere about that culture. Chapter 7, "The Unspeakable," explores the general functions of unspeakability within a given culture and its specific operation in the tightly constrained discourse of modernization in Thailand's recent history. The final chapter, "Sexual Theory and Its Discontents," attempts to fill in an understanding of the sexual nature of the product being sold in this industry, in light of contemporary sexual theory and the gaps in it. The chapter thus attempts to provide a political economy of sexuality.

This is what the book does address. Vast as that is, what it does not address is equally vast. Primarily absent from or significantly underrepresented is material related to gay sex workers and gay sex tourism, Japanese sex tourism (which has superseded West European and North American tourism in terms of sheer buying power), and the massive indigenous sex industry. The reasons for these omissions are theoretical, pragmatic, and ethical: theoretical because we wanted our focus to be on the acts of our own nation and its citizens on the historical global stage, pragmatic because access to the sites in which these other forms of sex work occur is difficult, and ethical because we hoped to limit our critique as much as possible to cultural processes and practices in which we are directly implicated.

In the composition of what we do address in this text, there has been a relatively clear division of labor. We assigned primary responsibility for five of the chapters to one of us individually to take best advantage of individual theoretical strengths and interests. Each one, then, would produce a draft to be examined by the other, who intervened on levels as broad as the conceptual and as specific as the lexical. Ryan Bishop had primary responsibility for "Imagining Sexual Others," "The Bar Scene," and "The Unspeakable"; Lillian Robinson for "A Very Political Economy" and "Sexual Theory and Its Discontents." The remaining chapters were coauthored, each of us taking primary responsibility for specific sections and then both of us weaving the sections together.

As to authorial voice, most of the text is written in a kind of omniscient third person that occasionally identifies itself in the first person plural, regardless of who wrote what. But in some places this voice became difficult, if not downright silly, to maintain, especially Robinson's history within the feminist movement, women's studies, and sexual theory, and Bishop's fieldwork research with sex clients, sex workers, and others related to the industry. We likewise deploy the first person singular in Chapter 1 to illustrate how each of us individually became interested in and then involved in this project.

Another problem was how best to reference Thai names in English. In Thailand a person's given name is commonly the one used in speaking about him or her—we were called Dr. Ryan and Dr. Lillian during our respective sojourns in the kingdom—but the difficulty of so referring to Thai academics and authors in an English text is obvious. We therefore decided to follow a convention by which we referred to Thais living, writing, and working in Thailand and in the Thai language the way Thais would: thus, Sanitsuda Ekechai is called Sanitsuda. For Thais living in English-speaking environments or writing in English, we use English-language conventions: Thongchai Winichakul, therefore, is referred to as Winichakul. In either case, however, we use the surname of a given author for in-text citations.

The problem of names, however, is minor compared with the problems of transliteration in general. Thai script and Thai pronunciation have led to a wide variety of chirographic representations of lexical items, especially proper nouns, in English. In general, our rule has been to follow the most common English spelling of a term in our own prose but to retain that used in any given text we quote or reference.

Although many people and institutions have provided help and support for both of us, the majority did so for one of us. Most of those who assisted us jointly show up in one of our individual lists. But we would both like to be on record as acknowledging our initial editor, Cecilia Cancellero; Bill Germano of Routledge; Alex Giardino and T. J. Mancini also at Routledge; Patricia Sterling, our copy editor; Jonathan Arac; Sue and John Leonard and Molly Rauch at the *Nation*; Mike Albert at *Z Magazine*; Nerida Cook of the University of Tasmania and Peter Jackson at Australian National University, coordinators of the Canberra conference on Gender and Sexuality in Modern Thailand and editors of the forthcoming volume on that topic; and the many Thai academics, intellectuals, friends, activists, and sex workers, as well as *farang* colleagues and expats, too numerous to mention individually.

Books may be written in isolation, but they are never written alone, so Ryan thanks all those who helped in infinite ways with the completion of this book. For providing lecture venues that allowed an opportunity to explore and discuss ideas used in this text, I thank George Marcus at Rice University, Chris Palmer at La Trobe University in Melbourne, and Stephen Hood in the Department of Religious Studies at Rice University; for travel and research funding, Narayan Bhat and the Office of Faculty Research at Southern Methodist University, and Robert Hunter and the Department of English, also at SMU. Many people gave me intellectual and emotional support during this project, especially Stephen A. Tyler, George Marcus, Michael M. J. Fischer, Jyotsna Singh, Walter Spitz, Bruce Levy, Anindyo Roy, John Erni, Sharon Traweek, Herb Smith, and Dennis Foster. I am indebted also to my dear friends and early mentors Heather Hardy and John Crow. My students helped and encouraged me in ways they may never truly know. I thank my family, extended and far-flung, as well as direct and close by, for their love, care, humor, and patience. Jeff Petry deserves very special gratitude for all his logistical help, multiple readings and suggestions, on-the-ground knowledge, and intellectual concern, without which much of my contribution to this book might not have been possible. And finally, for all her linguistic, cultural, and intellectual insight and constant love, to my wife, Junya, who gave me the courage to pursue this project, I owe more than I can say.

Lillian's ideas were tested, challenged, and enriched through the experience of presenting lectures and papers on the issues discussed in this study. My thanks to those whose invitations made this possible: Françoise Lionnet who asked me to take part in an MLA Forum; the Virginia Tech English Department which sponsored my spring 1994 Garvin Lecture, and the Women's Studies fall 1994 lecture series; Marie Farr who arranged for me to keynote the 1994 Southeastern Women's Studies Association Conference; Mark van Wienen (Roanoke College); Linda Wagner-Martin and Jane Burns (University of North Carolina, Chapel Hill); Ellen Cronan Rose (University of Nevada, Las Vegas); Susan Fraiman and Eric Lott (University of Virginia); and Liz Kennedy (the State University of New York, Buffalo). For support in getting related work into print, I am grateful to Elsa Dixler, Katha Pollit, and JoAnn Wypijewski at the *Nation*; Ellen Cantarow and Linda Gardiner at *Women's Review of Books*; and Nan Bauer Maglin and Donna Perry, editors of *"Bad Girls"/"Good Girls."* Invaluable materials and information were provided by Rick Berg, Elizabeth Bounds, Rhoda Channing, Mary DeShazer, Terri Ebert, David Gilden, H. Kermit Leggett III, Douglas Michael Massing, Ellen Cronan Rose, Saul Slapikoff, Michael Squires and Lynn Talbot, Mihoko Suzuki, Emily Toth, Eleanor Ty, and Kazuko Watanabe. At my SUNY, Buffalo, lecture Hester Eisenstein asked the right question at the right moment, a question that helped me define my project as creating a political economy of sexuality.

Many of my ideas were worked out with undergraduate students in two Women's Studies courses: "Sex and Strategy in Contemporary Feminist Debate" at Virginia Tech, and "Sexual Revolutions" at East Carolina University. East Carolina began its material support of this project even before I joined its faculty: the English Department, through head Don Palumbo, provided travel money that allowed me to attend the conference in Canberra. ECU also gave me a full semester's research leave through the College of Arts and Sciences Research Award, a Summer Research Grant, and travel funds for work meetings with my collaborator in San Francisco and Dallas. Hospitality during research and writing trips was generously provided by Marilyn and Irvin Yalom, Toni and Ed Robinson, and Greg Robinson and Heng Gun Ngo. My assistants, Dale Williamson and Mel De Jesus, supplied nurturance and humor. The late Constance Coiner, Shelley Fisher Fishkin, Louis Kampf, Paul Lauter, Jane Marcus, Michael Massing, Tillie Olsen, and Greg Robinson join my ECU colleagues Marie Farr, Julie Fay, Jeff Franklin, Bruce McComiskey, Robin Martin, Cynthia Ryan, McKay Sundwall, Rick Taylor, Gay Wilentz, and Jeff Williams on the list of those who help me believe that the work I do is worthwhile. My son, Alex Robinson-Gilden, daily convinces me of it.

1

POINTS OF DEPARTURE
Catalysts and Contexts

Much of the impetus for my writing this book stemmed from my own ignorance. I had been to Thailand several times, always with my wife, who is Thai, to visit her family—the first time for the wedding itself. When I arrived to teach on the Fulbright, I traveled up country to visit a friend conducting field research there. When he mentioned Patpong, the infamous sex tourist area of Bangkok, I asked him what he was talking about. He replied with some bemusement, "You're probably the only white guy in Thailand who doesn't know what Patpong is!"

Although I was initially ignorant of international sex tourism, my inheritance as a North American male traveling the country with a Thai woman became increasingly apparent. No matter where we went, regardless of the fact that my wife dresses in a way that marks her as being of a particular class and that she speaks in a way that indicates an educational level not attained by the vast majority of sex workers, the assumption by all we met in all situations was that she was a hooker. And, of course, for 95 percent of similar couples, the assumption would most likely be correct. In neighborhood restaurants, where everyone knew who we were, Thai men eating and drinking at nearby tables would make loud, condescending remarks about the two of us and the lucre my wife was undoubtedly carting away by selling her body to foreigners. Not even my rebukes in Thai could silence their tongues. In all our daily activities, vendors, merchants, taxi drivers, passers by, manual laborers—everyone—commented on the assumed nature of our relationship. (It was impossible for them to imagine the reality of the situation: that her family was wealthier than mine could ever dream of being.) Even when we traveled under Fulbright auspices, with our hotel reserva-tions made by the local university where I gave lectures or seminars, the staff would treat my wife like a sex worker. One time, the clerks in a hotel gift shop chided her for not agreeing to pay inflated prices for postcards; they accused her of making money off me and not allowing them to do the same.

I'd been invited to Thailand to keynote a conference on "Changing Directions in the Study of American Literature," emphasizing the introduction of multicultural and feminist approaches into the curriculum. In the taxi en route to the Austin airport, this was how I answered the cabby's question about the purpose of my trip. But the driver was a Vietnam vet with a pragmatic sense of just who sends one to Southeast Asia and what their agenda is, so he asked, "How come they're sending you to Thailand to talk about feminism when the whole economy over there depends on prostitution?" My answer, flipped off the top of my head was, "Because they think that what academics say doesn't matter."

That's why, 40-some hours later and 8000 miles away, jet lag still ringing in my ears, when I sat next to Ryan Bishop at a dinner party my first evening in Bangkok and his first private words to me were, "I want to take you to the sex shows," I was ready for the utter seriousness of his invitation. At a lighter moment in the evening, though, I pointed out that there's something exceedingly peculiar about being a professor of cultural studies at this moment in history. "In the real world," I told him, gesturing across the table at Professor Jonathan Arac, who had also come to address the conference, "you, as the resident American male, would take *Jonathan* aside and offer to show him the town."

"Well, Jonathan can come if he likes, but you're the one I want to take. It's important for your feminist work." *Important for my feminist work.* In my mind, that came to stand—as a possibility, at least—against "What academics say doesn't matter."

As a Fulbright Lecturer, I taught a survey course in poetry to help prepare gradu-ate students for their comprehensive exams. William Blake's "London" was fea-tured on the syllabus. I hoped that students would find many parallels between Blake's London in the latter part of the eighteenth century and their own Bangkok in the latter part of the twentieth. Like Blake's London, my students' Bangkok had recently become an overrun, swollen urban site, the locus of a massive population shift from rural to urban areas, of economic shifts from agrarian to industrially driven economies, of an increase in landless urban poor, of rapidly changing socioeconomic relations caused by globalization processes and development strategies, of fundamental transformation of values and mores predicated primarily on theological beliefs to those informed by secular and mercantile institutions.

Before we addressed the broad brushstrokes of historical parallels, however, we began our discussion inductively, moving from specifics in the text to specifics in the reading context. May 1992 had seen the violent suppression of student protests against the unconstitutional ascension to the prime minister's office of a general involved in a bloodless coup a few years before. Students and merchants, opposition politicians and disenchanted civil servants took to the streets in protest. The crowds were met with a show of force not seen since the 1970s, and the country once again witnessed the military firing on the populace it supposedly protected. As in past coups, government censorship attempted to control the flow and dissemination of information. Thus, for my students, Blake's invocation of "marks of weakness, marks of woe," his cries of fear, his bans and "mind-forg'd manacles," his "hapless" soldiers and blood-stained palace walls conjured up images and actions hauntingly familiar and temporally close.

Yet perhaps the eeriest evocations occurred in the final stanza. The Prasanmitr campus of Srinakharinwirot University, where we sat in my air-conditioned office/classroom, stands at the end of soi 21. At the mouth of the narrow street is the entry to Soi Cowboy: a miniature, block-long version of the city's (in)famous Patpong area. The majority of the students passed Soi Cowboy as they exited buses and walked to the campus grounds. On their daily walk to class, they had to pass by what has become an international and national incubator for AIDS, a site where rural women take part in the nation's rapid economic expansion in ways unavailable to them—with regard to wage-earning potential—anywhere else in the country, and the goal of many a tourist's journey. Thus, Soi Cowboy was one of the most concentrated sites for the students to interact with foreigners and to witness aspects of their American Studies program materialize beyond their classroom walls. Like Patpong, Soi Cowboy constitutes a synecdoche of Thailand's highly touted economic growth, which is due in part to international tourism. As a result of physical and cognitive proximity, Blake's dirge of harlots' curses that result in plagues and marriage hearses struck multiply resonant chords for the students.[1]

On a flight from Sydney in the summer of 1995, I met an Australian businessman who initiated the usual polite airplane chat. "What's your destination? London?" he asked.

"Nope, Bangkok," I replied.

His face lit up with interest: "Me, too, you naughty boy," he said, giving me a knowing wink. When I told him that the purpose of my trip was research and the focus of my research was the international sex industry, he showed a different kind of interest, questioning me about the many reports he'd heard regarding the AIDS epidemic and infection rates among sex workers. As I cited the statistics I knew, his expression grew increasingly grim. "So," he asked, "you wouldn't advise anyone using the services of one of these women, eh?"

"I wouldn't advise it whether or not AIDS were in the picture, but that's my own opinion."

After I said this, his expression became even more dour. "Thanks for the chat," he said and added, "Thanks for ruining my holiday."

On the way to the American literature conference in Pattaya, Dr. A., a Thai professor in her forties, told me that the conference hotel there was very pleasant, and, unlike a number of the resorts, welcomed Thai guests. At least, she hastened to add, respectable academics like herself and the other conference participants. "But they would never admit a—a *certain kind of woman.*"

Like practically every pool I've ever been in, the one at the hotel in Pattaya had a couple of young girls in it, shrieking, splashing, clambering onto their boyfriends' shoulders. If I'd even registered it consciously, I would have defined it as International Adolescent Horseplay, Watersports Division. Ryan was telling me about racism within Thailand, which entails both regional and color prejudice. "You mean, those two beautiful girls over there would have trouble making good marriages because of their skin color?"

"Er, Lillian, I think they'd have more trouble because of their profession."

"They're prostitutes? But how can you tell?"

"The revealing bathing suits. And Thai women wouldn't usually fool around like that in the pool."

"Well, but Dr. A. told me just yesterday that there were no prostitutes at this hotel."

"It's what I told you: the sex industry is like the racism—something that's unspeakable in public."

"I guess it's supposed to be invisible, too."

At the American Studies conference in Pattaya, a highly placed academic from an elite Thai university assailed the current university curricula in Thai history. "The problem," he said, "is that it stops just before the modern era. Students do not learn, for example, how come the city where we are having this conference is filled with prostitutes. They are ignorant of the historical forces that led to this situation." Only the language of this conference (English) and its subject matter (critique of national practices within U.S. universities) allowed him to make this observation without the public censure that would usually follow his raising in public and before foreigners a topic usually off limits to social discourse: the sex industry.

In early November of 1992, a prostitute named Phassarawara Samrit, age twenty-four, fled the brothel where she worked, in the southern province of Songkhla, trying to get to her home in Chiang Mai. On 3 November 1992 at 5:30 A.M., Phassarawara was found with her throat cut a mere three meters from the Songkhla city hall. The death of a prostitute in a country teeming with sex industry workers is rarely newsworthy. However, this case occurred during the administration of Chuan Leekpai, who as prime minister had pushed the issue of child prostitution into public discourse. An article in the 31 December 1993 issue of *The Nation* (Bangkok) reported the sentencing of two policemen who were found guilty in the death of the runaway prostitute. What *is* newsworthy is that this story made it into the newspaper. Such occurrences usually disappear into the informal social silence that surrounds unspeakable topics.

In the fall of 1992 the English-language press in Thailand reported the success of government crackdowns on prostitution encouraged by the Chuan government. One precinct captain in Bangkok claimed to have shut down all of the brothels in his jurisdiction. The next day the chief of police for the entire city, who obviously was not on the same page as the national government, issued an official statement charging that the precinct captain had misspoken; according him, there *were* no brothels in Bangkok.

A Japanese feminist friend has a male compatriot, a journalist, who admitted that when he visits Thailand, he takes advantage of the variety of sexual entertainment available there. "But what do you get out of it?" she asked him.
"Well, the Thai women—they're so much gentler!"

In Chiang Mai, along the banks of the Nam Ping river, sits a statue of the Buddha that is quite famous throughout northern Thailand. For generations, travelers have left offerings of food, money, incense, or lotus flowers in the hope that this Buddha will protect them on their journeys. A few years back some tourists posed with the statue for souvenir snapshots of their visit to this exotic land. One photo showed a merrymaker sitting on the Buddha's head. In a nation where people are not allowed to point their feet at a statue of the Buddha, this fellow had placed his butt on the most sacred part of the Enlightened One!

Tourists to Thailand can purchase almost anything; the country is infamous for this. The only thing denied them are icons of the Buddha, amulets that devout Thai Buddhists collect and wear. Because foreigners do not know how to treat these icons, the government has imposed a ban on their sale. So the vagaries of tourist privilege have taken their toll even on the Buddha. The commodification of culture necessary for tourism is based on certain assumptions and results in particular beliefs on the part of tourists. The rhetoric of tourism leads to the belief that the natives don't have a "real" culture, or "real" religion, certainly not in the sense that we know them. This is why we can photograph the natives at worship and drag video recorders into the midst of their most sacred communal rites.

Tourist privilege turns daily life into a spectacle. Therefore, the Buddha that has protected so many travelers now needs protecting himself from international tourists. He sits in a cage, and offerings to him must fit through the holes in the wire mesh.

The guys who took me to Bangkok's red-light district the first time were all foreigners working in the city: an Englishman, an Irishman, and two Americans. Conversation over a lavish dinner beforehand revealed that four of us were parents, three of us at the moment halfway around the world from our kids, and three of us (not all the same ones) with children who had been born in foreign parts. As the meal went on, we started telling stories—funny, ironic, frightening, sentimental—about the birth of our children. I'd never had a conversation like that in a mixed group before, much less one where I was the only woman, and I found it strangely moving.

Later, I realized that we'd been preparing ourselves for what we knew we'd be seeing across the road, putting on a kind of armor by reminding ourselves of the single most unalienated experience of our sexuality that we'd ever had. I don't think any of us believed that the only good sex is heterosexual and reproductive, but childbirth was something we could talk about. A woman and four men, barely acquainted, could hardly launch into comparisons of our most lyrical and meaningful orgasms, but we could and did talk about how our babies came into the world. And then we hit the go-go bars.

In the Penile Colony

Touring Thailand's Sex Industry

> The stories you've heard about the sex shows are all true.... It is not a place for the squeamish or those with feminist leanings.
>
> —*Insight Guide to Thailand*

"You have to do it," Ryan tells me. "You have to go there the way you have to visit Dachau." It's my first evening in Thailand, and I met my dinner partner, an American resident in Bangkok, just half an hour ago. After some general conversation involving our whole party, he addresses me privately for the first time, saying, "I want to take you to the sex shows."

"You what?" That's when he adds the remark about Dachau—a line calculated to provoke—and declares that as a feminist I must not leave without exploring international sex tourism as practiced in the nightspots of Bangkok. When I accept the invitation, I become, in essence, a sex tourist's tourist.

> Bangkok, the sexual Disneyland of the world, a place where everything is offered to anyone at all times—at little or no cost.
>
> —Linda Ellerbee, *"And So It Goes": Adventures in Television*

Sex isn't sold everywhere in Bangkok, but it's available in enough places and enough *kinds* of places at a low enough price to confirm the First World view that the whole city is an erotic theme park. In addition to classic brothels—many of them camouflaged as teahouses, barber shops, or beauty salons—there are massage parlors and all sorts of bars: plain pickup spots, dance clubs, go-go bars, and "skuller" (public blow-job) joints. Some of them feature boys rather than girls. A freelance tourist with a taste for variety might, in theory, sample all these venues. But that's only in theory; in practice, the clientele is segregated along national or racial lines. So there are different sites for the Japanese, Arab, Malaysian, Indian, Chinese, Thai, and *farang* (white foreign) customers. Within these limits, the customers—almost always men—seem to make their choices about the kind of site to patronize for cultural reasons, seeking the familiar even in an environment where "exotic" and "erotic" are sold as synonymous.

It's the go-go bars that seem to be the primary American way of sex, presumably because the setup permits the illusion of a relationship and mutual choice, though there is no doubt about the inevitable sexual outcome of the encounter the man chooses. The three blocks of Patpong, the single one of Soi Cowboy, and the upstart Nana Entertainment Plaza are lined with these establishments. Each bar on these streets has several small stages decorated with firehouse-style poles, a long bar, tiny tables crowded together, flashing colored lights, and loud rock music. The sound is so intense, in fact, that John Fogerty and the rest of Creedence Clearwater Revival seem to be leading me through the scene, running me personally through the jungle.

On stage, the women dance. (I say women out of respect for their work experience. The ones I see are teenagers, and in the gay bars they're boys.) Each dancer stands beside a pole that she caresses as she makes some rudimentary dance movements. They are dressed in beachwear, the youngest in one-piece numbers, while the most seasoned wear bikinis. When actually at the beach, Thai women are almost pathologically modest, undressing furtively for a swim and covering up as soon as they come out of the water. For a teenager fresh from a country village in the Northeast and now awkwardly on stage in a bathing suit, fiddling with the crotch to make it cover more than it does or can, this public exposure is the first shame—after which, perhaps, all the others seem inevitable.

The girls are not skilled dancers, and through a long night they put minimal energy into it. Their gestures are suggestive but not sensuous, understood as sexy only if the observer too has learned the erotic code in language foreign to the body. Like the girls in the massage parlors, who are displayed in glass cages for the customers to choose, the dancers have numbers pinned to their costumes. Waitresses move among the tables and along the bar, ready to take drink orders and girl orders. When her number is selected, the girl stops dancing and joins the customer, donning—in at least one bar—a bright silk robe, like a prize-fighter's, except that its hem stops at the top of the thigh. If she can get the man to buy her a drink, the fact is noted. At the very least, this contributes to her job security and may even earn her a percentage of the take.

At the tables there is not much talk—what with the volume of the music and the lack of a common language—but a lot of casual horseplay. This mostly takes the form of teasing and shoving, the occasional arm around a shoulder or waist, sometimes a girl sitting briefly on a customer's lap. The giggles and pushes take me back to the tentative interactions of junior high. And why not? That's the age a lot of these girls look to me; the customers, meanwhile, are old enough to be their uncles, fathers, grandfathers. In the brothels serving local men, where there's a premium on extreme youth and virginity, a girl who has not yet menstruated brings a price more than sixty times the usual. The locals say deflowering a virgin increases virility, and fresh prepubescent crops are brought into the city for good luck at the Chinese New Year. They also believe that very young girls, even if no longer virgins, are likelier to be free of disease. One study, however, estimates that fifty percent of the child prostitutes in Thailand are HIV positive.

A 1992 survey by the Thai Health Ministry indicated that 76,863 prostitutes were working nationwide at 5,622 establishments (20,366 in Bangkok alone). The numbers suggest precision, but the figures are generally considered absurdly low. Political scientist Linda Richter (1989) reports estimates of a million prostitutes, which she translates into 4 percent of the female population and a considerably higher proportion of those in the prime years of fifteen to thirty-four. Resistance efforts are on a considerably smaller scale. EMPOWER (Education Means Protection Of Women Engaged in Re-Creation), an organization serving prostitutes, enrolls only about one hundred women in English classes intended to help them avoid being cheated by foreign customers or eventually qualify for other employment. And the bar girls' *Patpong Newsletter*, sponsored by EMPOWER, has not yet had much impact.

> A whorehouse is always a good investment.
> —Jack Flowers, in Peter Bogdanovich's
> *Saint Jack*

In 1967, Thailand contracted with the U.S. government to provide "Rest and Recreation" (R&R) services to the troops during the Vietnam War. Today's customers at the go-go bars spawned by those contracts are not only white American but also European and Australian—all *farang*s to the Thais. In addition to tourists, they include permanent residents—what *New Statesman* writer Jeremy Seabrook (1991) calls "sexpatriates"—and workers rotated in from isolated, all-male environments such as oil rigs, corporate entertainment contracts having effectively replaced the military ones. The men look pink and flabby, and in the tropical heat (90 degrees every day in the "cool" season) I've become very sensitive to the strong *farang* body odor, wondering if I smell like that, too.

After playing around for a drink or two, a pair may come to an agreement to go off to an on-site room, or a "short-time" venue, or elsewhere, or to spend the rest of the night together. The possibility of the all-night, one-customer arrangement combines with the prestige of describing one's job as "working with foreigners" (and thus participating in modernization) and the fantasy of marrying a *farang* to make this a relatively privileged form of sex work. The customer pays the bar management a "fine" for taking away a dancer. (There are so many dancers that it is impossible to imagine what rush of clientele beyond the current full house would create a dearth of entertainers. Well, what if the fleet comes in? The fleet is *always* in, and the sexual message is always about abundance.) The sex worker may also receive a tip, but the basic transaction is between the bar owner and the customer.

The current official crackdown on child prostitution (there's always a crackdown on something, Thai friends explain, and this one has come and gone several times in recent years) has focused the glare of publicity on the money earned, which is at once very high and very low. In her 1982 study for the International Labor Organisation (ILO) Thai sociologist Pasuk Phongpaichit estimates the income of sex workers at twenty-five times that available in other occupations. Entire families in the countryside are supported on the earnings of one daughter in Bangkok, and entire rural villages are made up of such families. Indeed, the *Bangkok Post*'s two-page feature on the subject in January 1993 centered on one peasant family "hoping for a miracle" for their collective survival, now that their daughter had been summarily returned home. Yet the same article placed the girl's monthly salary as a dancer in the resort town of Phuket as 1,000 baht—about $40. The estimates I heard in Bangkok ran several times as high, bringing monthly wages in the big city to an amount roughly equal to the cost of two nights at an international class hotel. Meanwhile, the hideous fire at a doll factory outside Bangkok in May 1993 dramatized the conditions of employment available to young Thai women working outside the sex industry.

Vietnam-born feminist writer Thanh Dam-Truong (1990) insists that the relationship between tourism and prostitution should be understood not "only as an issue of employment alternatives available to women," but also in relation "to the internal structure of the tourism industry and to vested interests of a financial nature." But it's impossible to avoid seeing these as organically linked. It was in 1971, while the war in Southeast Asia still raged, that World Bank President Robert McNamara, who had been U.S. Secretary of Defense when the R&R contracts with Thailand were signed, went to Bangkok to arrange for the bank's experts to produce a study of Thailand's postwar tourism prospects. The economic initiatives consequent on the bank's 1975 report led to what is routinely described today as a $4-billion-a-year business involving fraternal relationships among airlines, tour operators, and the masters of the sex industry. In this sense, sex tourism is like any other multinational industry, extracting enormous profits from grotesquely underpaid local labor and situating the immediate experience of the individual worker—what happens to the body of a fifteen-year-old girl from a village in northeastern Thailand—in the context of global economic policy. Like all such industries, it fosters a myth of worker and client reciprocity meeting each other's needs in an economic universe where capitalist relations are constructed as a part of nature. From the perspective of First World customers, the international inequities translate into a great bargain, while their personal experiences of cut-rate ecstasy combine to make up those totals in the billions.

Traditional discussions of imperialism turn on the exploitation of labor and of natural resources in the colonized territory. The neocolonialist leisure industry tends to identify the two. In a public speech in 1980, Booncha Rajanasthian, Thailand's vice-premier (no pun intended in his title) asked all provincial governors "to consider the natural scenery in your provinces, together with . . . forms of entertainment that some of you might consider disgusting and shameful, because we have to consider the jobs that will be created." Thailand's landscape, sexual entertainment, and labor thus converge in a single economic meaning.

> Yeah, that's the first thing you learn
> after fellatio is how to listen.
> —Jane Wagner, *The Search for Signs of*
> *Intelligent Life in the Universe*

In the West, too, travel to Thailand is promoted through a double association of the available female body with usable nature and with the benevolent creation of employment. A Swiss tour operator describes Thai women as "slim, sunburnt and sweet . . . masters of the art of making love by nature." (Less lyrically, the GI acronym for prostitutes in the Philippines is LBFMs, Little Brown Fucking Machines.) Meanwhile, a Dutch agency's brochures explain that in the depressed rural and urban regions of Thailand, "It has become a habit that one of the nice-looking daughters goes into the business in order to earn money for the poor family. . . . You . . . get the feeling that taking a girl here is as easy as buying a package of cigarettes." Customers, lured by an appealing conflation of natural, social, and cultural forces, are themselves represented as inherently desirable: Thai girls "love the white man in a erotic and devoted way," which is why sexual services cost no more effort and only a bit more money than that pack of smokes.

In the imperial rhetoric of the Dutch agency, the sex workers are described as "little slaves who give real Thai warmth," thus naturalizing servitude. In fact, economically speaking, the women are not slaves—although 1993 I.L.O. findings include disquieting evidence of Thai "child catchers," who buy or steal children for sale to "private households, restaurants, factories and brothels." Pasuk (Phongpaichit 1982) prefers the term "indenture" to describe the economic relationship that the tourist literature characterizes in cultural terms. Sex workers are typically recruited from rural families, the sum given to the parents representing several months' advance salary, with the rest to be remitted after a ten-month or one-year term. The lump-sum payments provide subsistence for a family with few other resources and may even finance a new house, cultivation of the family's land, or schooling for younger siblings. This form of contract, stipulating interest that can be as high as 100 percent, binds the sex worker to her job, her sense of family obligation overwhelming negative feelings about the work itself.

First World feminists are frequently criticized for culturebound insensitivity to differences in the values, needs, and desires of women in other parts of the world. Warnings against cultural blindness—not to say arrogance—are never misplaced. But it is worth noting how neatly the enlightened relativist position dovetails with the language of the sex tourism industry, which also hypes cultural difference. Thanh-Dam Truong argues that the past two decades have witnessed a change in rural attitudes toward the value of female children. As a result of new opportunities to sell a daughter into prostitution, female sexual capacity is perceived as having a market value taking "predominance over male labour. . . . Families actually celebrate the birth of a daughter, because she now has potentially more access to social mobility" (1990, 74). So, in this case, "Thai values" amount not only to what I might unsympathetically call traditional sexism, but also to something considerably more familiar, the commodification of sexuality. It all adds up to another example of the ability of capitalist markets to reinforce traditional structures of privilege.

Even given our vast differences, in the latitude allowed to our sexual subjectivity, there is something in the bar girls' experience that is recognizable to a heterosexual First World woman like me. We are linked by men's ability to turn their own desire into a thing, as well as by an international system of labor and consumption—a system of international sexual alienation—in which all of us are actors. And we are linked in another way, too. The sickness of head and heart that I see in these transactions in Bangkok is not the only disease they foster. Nor is that sickness entirely eclipsed by the concrete bodily realities of AIDS. Each is the deadly mirror of the other.

The Public Health Ministry, which has instituted an extensive testing program, estimates that between 200,000 and 400,000 Thais are infected with the AIDS virus. Australian professor John Dwyer, president of the AIDS Society for Asia and the Pacific, calls Thailand and Burma, the nexus of the Asian sex and drug traffic, the "epicenter of the epidemic" on the continent. Thailand's projected population growth has already been affected by the epidemic, and Dr. Werasit Sittitrai of the Thai Red Cross estimates that by the year 2000 one-third of all deaths in the country may be caused by AIDS. Meanwhile, the *Bangkok Post*'s nightlife columnist, Bernard Trink, assures visitors that there is no AIDS or HIV among the bar girls of Soi Cowboy, Nana, and Patpong.

In one of the most explicit official acknowledgments of the connection between the AIDS crisis and international economic relations, Dr. Michael Merson, director of the World Health Organization's Global Program on AIDS, stated recently, "It's extremely important that developed nations understand that the focus of this epidemic is going to end up being in Asia and the Pacific. We are all dependent for survival on having this region of the world become prosperous." But, so far, the only route to prosperity recommended and sponsored by international experts is mass tourism firmly allied to the sex industry.

> As a rule, literary treatment of the orgasm
> in Thai literature is implicit and genteel. It
> is considered a kind of miracle.
> —Prapart Brudhiprabha, "A Socio-
> linguistic Analysis of the 'Marvel
> Act' of Love in Thai Literature"

"We have Japanese men here but we have never had a Japanese woman be-fore!" exclaimed the madam of a Bangkok teahouse to journalist Yayori Matsui. Matsui was researching the sex industry for her 1989 book *Women's Asia*, but even once they let her in, she could not experience the brothel *as* a brothel. Similarly, covering bars where my countrymen buy women, I could see only the externals of the transaction. It's as if the whole scene takes place inside a trans-parent bubble and I'm on the outside looking in. I'm told that the sex itself is strictly "vanilla." What the customer is buying, in addition to the unimaginative but unproblematic experience, is the woman's undivided attention. His over-night companion will also bargain with the cabdriver, work the unfamiliar pay phone, and order food. I have no way of verifying how this social submission translates into an erotic vocabulary. But nights that start with sexual exhibitions, where women demonstrate remarkable control of the vaginal sphincter—"smoking" cigarettes and catching Ping-Pong balls with the genitals or extract-ing strings of razor blades from them—must be conducted in a different dialect.

What's missing from all this talk of sex bars, sex tours, sex workers is, of course, sex—at least, sex as women might imagine it. Classic Thai love poetry, with the orgasm as a gift of divine grace, articulates a male fantasy. Elsewhere on the erotic register, established Thai institutions such as concubinage and prosti-tution put arguably less delicate male fantasies into action. On the *farang* side, the travel agencies hawk their wares in a commercial poetry that also stimulates fantasy. This one is about the male orgasm not as a breathtaking miracle, but simply as the material goal of the herds of pleasure seekers avid for exotic tech-niques. Bangkok's sexual entertainment is the concrete expression of that fan-tasy. Desire and fulfillment seem to have no female voice in either the traditional or the contemporary culture of Thailand. For women, Eros took a holiday, and it wasn't a trip to Bangkok.

"In the Penile Colony" was published in the *Nation* (New York) for 1 November 1993. The version included here has been slightly modified to reflect recent developments and to adumbrate issues addressed in the rest of this book. It's because of the article's reception that there is a book. By the cover date of the issue in which it appeared, we had learned that photocopies were already required reading in two university courses: "Feminist Theories of the Body" at the University of Pittsburgh, and "Biosocial Issues" at Tufts, where Professor Saul Slapikoff, whose private name for the course was "Ideology of Biology," paired it with statistics-studded accounts lauding the "Thai Economic Miracle." It was hard to imagine many other overlaps between the reading list for "Feminist Theories of the Body" and the one for "Biosocial Issues," and we realized that, for the Thai sex industry, no material existed that combined the preoccupations of the two courses. So we decided to write a book that would do so—collaborating, as we had on our initial visit to the red-light districts.

But it's one thing to say "We're going to expand this article" and quite another to devise a method for doing so. Precisely because we'd be bringing together concerns, approaches, and perspectives that are usually kept in isolation from one another, if they're considered at all, it was hard to envisage a structure through which to carry it out. Because our method is simultaneously economic and cultural, narrative and theoretical, descriptive and analytic—all of it centering on a subject that is simultaneously about girlie bars and international banks—there is a sense in which each of the principal topics should come first in any discussion. But everything *can't* come first. The method we came up with, therefore, was to have the narratives in this chapter and the revised version of "In the Penile Colony" lay out a number of themes that recur in the book and then proceed through them, returning to the base at intervals and picking up another theme to be woven into the evolving text. In our planning discussions, we used a musical metaphor ("antiphonal") and an architectural one ("spiral") to describe this process, which also embodies Jaques Derrida's notion of the problematic as a series of knots to be elaborated and teased out.

The text has emerged, spirally, from attempts to address issues broached in the *Nation* article, and others as well. At the same time, of course, the book can't adequately address all the issues surrounding so complex a phenomenon as international sex tourism. What it does try to do is to trace the historical, cultural, material, and textual traditions that have combined in complex ways to establish tourism—with the sex industry as its mainstay—as the basis of the developing Thai economy. Much academic research has concentrated on how tourism affects local tradition, and our inquiry considers this impact. But we also want to examine how local traditions and conditions play a role in their own exploitation—no noble savages or romanticized idyllic pasts here. Similarly, tourism research has often isolated the tourist industry from larger trajectories of development and modernization. We seek to place a particular aspect of the industry squarely within these trajectories to examine how women's bodies get cast as a natural resource in international development strategies and the national policies generated to implement these strategies. The viewpoint of tourists is also largely absent from tourism studies, but we focus on tourists and the cultures they come from, for as Roland Barthes pointedly observed, travel guidebooks are not really about other cultures at all; they are about the cultures that produce them.

Tourists continue a long line of explorers, invading armies, missionaries, colonial administrators, scholars, scientists, and international lenders who have shaped globalization processes—for better or worse—for centuries. Our focus is on that narrow part of the massive Thai sex industry that caters to our country-men: the bars and sex workers that service them. Although in the sheer number of bodies serviced and servicing, this sector represents a small portion of the industry, it brings in the bulk of the money that makes tourism Thailand's largest source of the foreign currency needed to pay for imported oil and imported debts. The book is, thus, about the role of tourism in modernization strategies, the role of sex in tourism, and the go-go bars that serve as sex venues, as well about the forces that drive men to act out sexual fantasies abroad and the related forces that bring women to the same site to make those fantasies a reality and a commodity.

Our working subtitle for the book was "Thailand in Postcolonial Sexual Cartographies," and the components of this polysyllabic mouthful help to de-fine both what we are trying and what we are not trying to do in the text. Although it is the only nation in Southeast Asia never directly colonized, Thai-land certainly has a place in the postcolonial global order. The maps that chart trajectories of power, desire, and consumption of the world's resources in the postcolonial world bear a striking resemblance to the earlier maps of the colonial world, whether drawn in Europe, the United States, or Japan. The relations between postindustrial nations and other cultures reinscribe multiple terrains of desire operating in an international market economy. We have tried to explore how constructions of sexuality in a postcolonial—but decidedly not postimper-ial—situation emerge in the realization of these terrains through global and local development policies; how international creations of "exotic" sex in a neocolo-nial environment relate to historical constructions of the native Other and result in a sexual subjectivity alienated enough to travel around the world to purchase its realization; and how such constructions become the lived experience of—not to mention the easiest means of survival for—a substantial portion of the Thai female population. Although Thai voices, traditions, practices, and policies occa-sionally punctuate our text, we have taken Aldous Huxley's advice that "anthro-pology, like charity, should begin at home," and so we concentrate on the home front at play abroad.

For this reason, we claim only to speak about, not for, the parties involved in this facet of the Thai sex industry. But what we say and how we say it varies with our different subject positions and with which voice—Ryan Bishop's, Lillian Robinson's, or our unified one—is speaking. The most obvious difference between us is that of gender, which necessarily shaped our interactions in the bar scene. Bishop, unlike Robinson, was able to move freely within this site in the guise of a potential client. As such, Bishop's body and sexuality marked him as "a marked man," whereas Robinson's body and sexuality marked her as an absence, even when present in the site. Whereas Robinson first became inter-ested in the relations between tourism, prostitution, and colonialism while serv-ing on the faculty of the University of Hawai'i and initially visited Thailand to participate in an American Studies conference, Bishop, who is married to a Thai citizen, has traveled to Thailand a number of times in the last decade, and taught at universities there for two years.

Although both of us would identify our "real" field as Cultural Studies, Bishop is by training a cultural anthropologist, with a strong literary background; Robinson holds degrees in the humanities and has been involved from the beginning in the efforts to establish Women's Studies as a field of intellectual inquiry. Her work is rooted in Marxist and multicultural as well as feminist approaches; Bishop's in postmodern, poststructural, and postcolonial theory. The fact that it is the male social scientist who makes use of contemporary critical theory while the female humanist relies on socially based categories also resonates in our collaborative work. Our conversation across theoretical and empiricist divides, gender and generational gaps, and disciplinary boundaries is responsible for the bumps, jagged edges, and not-quite-right fits of this text. Yet all these perspectives and experiences, conflicting and complementary, contribute to the stories we have chosen to tell about a phenomenon at once exotic and close to home, both apart from us and a part of us.

$$2$$

NAMING THE PROBLEM

The stereotype of Thailand as the playground of the Western world dominates the public imagination outside the country and is continually reiterated in the popular media. Audiences in tourist-generating countries have been bombarded with images and representations about the Kingdom and its international sex industry that reinscribe and perpetuate a stereotype of Thailand, calling forth sly winks, nudges, and charges of being a naughty boy. Only recently have some of the more malignant aspects of Thailand as prurient paradise appeared. The academy too has addressed the economics of tourism and considered some of its negative effects, including the international dimension of the sex trade. Each article, news feature, documentary, survey, or study tends to represent the particular problem it addresses as *the* story, arguing that all other matters can be boiled down to one essential element and that every vagary stems from this particular one. Since many of these pieces are rather brief, such condensation is to be expected. In the academy, disciplinary specialization virtually demands delimiting the focus. Whatever its origin, such telescoping results in an oversimplification of a complex situation, leaving important gaps in the narrative unaddressed.

In order to position this book conceptually and methodologically, we begin with a survey of the versions of Thailand, its tourist industry, and sex tourism that have been provided by Western scholarship and mass media. These versions serve to define the problem by naming its constituent questions and framing the discourse about them in ways that tend to elide or ignore the stories, issues, and perspectives that we consider most important. This happens in large part because the stories are presented in isolation from one another, obscuring

16

the connections and complexities needed in order to see the situation in different and possibly productive ways.

The media representation of the Thai sex industry as "a problem" has emerged primarily as a case study either of the AIDS pandemic or of child prostitution. Both are obviously serious problems, but the media imply that there is no story without *the* story, no problem without this problem. From their point of view, a problem occurs with international sex tourism only when the client or a child is threatened. Missing from the picture are issues such as environmental destruction, international planning, the creation of an unskilled labor force for international use, and those aspects of the sex industry—as either erotic institution or labor process—not related to AIDS or child prostitution.

If the media tend to say "the thing is," academics generally say, "the things are." The difference between the singular and the plural is significant and begins to redress "problem" myopia, yet it still only hints at the interrelated nature of the problems plaguing Thailand. The rhetoric of academic inquiry acknowledges the larger context but demands a concentrated focus. The academy just barely avoids the media's problems—highlighting sensational symptoms of systemic problems while shoving the various complementary causes of the disease out of the picture—but in the process often neglects issues we consider necessary to get an accurate view of the industry. Although we certainly do not claim to rectify this situation fully, this book does attempt to demarcate and fill in some of the gaps left by others' accounts of the scene, gaps that emerge in the definitions of problems generated by the popular media and in academic studies relating to the international sex industry in Thailand. Because the academic writings are less directly problematic but more complexly so, we address them first.

Academic Economics

The economic roots of sex tourism—and, underlying it, of the entire Thai sex trade—are acknowledged by the industry's apologists as well as its critics. If an Austin, Texas, cabdriver can state with confidence that Thailand's "whole economy" depends on prostitution, it is reasonable to expect academic studies of that economy to direct their attention to a rather more complex and nuanced analysis of this dependency, confirming or challenging the cabby's assertion, and studies focused on prostitution in Thailand to take account of the economic as well as the sexual aspects of the industry. But the former expectation is doomed to disappointment, and the latter is carried out with a tunnel-vision attachment to economics that almost entirely ignores the sexual aspect of the essential sex industry transaction.

With one exception, economists and historians focusing on political-economic trajectories tend either to ignore prostitution altogether or to conflate it with tourism in general—which, even in its strictly economic dimension, gets short shrift in the overall analysis, perhaps precisely because of this embarrass-

ing identification. In the 1960s, 1970s, and even the early 1980s, as commercial
sex with foreigners—military personnel, business travelers, and tourists—
became an increasingly significant part of the Thai economy, the standard academic studies and reference works remained silent about both phenomena.
Tourism figured in the national and international planning processes but not in
the analytic accounts of those processes. In 1963 it was possible for a study with
the sober title *Thailand: A Political, Social, and Economic Analysis* (published by
Praeger, a company with reputed CIA ties), to include its comment on sex only
in its chapter about the smiling Thai character. In addition to gambling, this
book informs us, "there are other recreations, notably drink and women
(*Mekhong* advertises a beautiful girl bending over a glass of their whiskey) which
are well [*sic*] provided" (Insor 1963, 176).

   Valentin Chu's *Thailand Today* (1968), Norman Jacobs's *Modernization without
Development* (1971), John Henderson and others' *Area Handbook for Thailand*
(1972), Frank J. Moore's *Thailand: Its People, Its Society, Its Culture* (1974), Lee
Baldwin and David Maxwell's collection *The Role of Foreign Financial Assistance to
Thailand in the 1980s* (1975), and John L. Girling's *Thailand: Society and Politics*
(1981) all avoid Insor's "wink-wink, nudge-nudge" tone by also avoiding any
mention of tourism or the sex industry—whether separately or conjoined. In its
chapter on the economy, the 1981 *Thailand: A Country Study* praises tourism for
its positive impact on many kinds of businesses, according light mention to the
sex and drug trades as "associated" with the influx of foreign visitors and then
referring the reader to the section on criminal activity (Burge 1981, 113).
Although configured very differently, all these books address economic issues—
including rural development and its absence, income inequalities, the labor supply, and foreign involvement—that are connected to the concentration on
tourism and the concomitant growth of the sexual services market. Yet all of
them stop well short of engaging these issues, clinging instead to familiar topics
within familiar terrain.

   By the time, not far into the 1980s, that tourism had ceased to be an emerging
industry (or complex of industries) and had become Thailand's principal source
of foreign exchange, the standard historical and economic studies no longer
ignored it. Even so, in these general works it did not receive attention commen-
surate with its role in the economy, and prostitution typically received even less.
In *Thailand: A Short History*, David Wyatt (1982, 293) makes a stab at placing
tourism within traditional economic categories, concluding that it "cannot be
classified as an export in the same way commodities and manufactured goods are,
but it is the equivalent of an export, because of its contribution to the Kingdom's
balance of payments." He touches on prostitution somewhat earlier, in a discussion of the impact of the American presence during the Vietnam War and its role
in encouraging poor rural youth to move to the city, "learn English and work as
waiters and waitresses, bartenders and hotel desk clerks, prostitutes and
masseuses, tour guides and souvenir shop clerks" (288). Although prostitution is
included as one of the many occupations that serve foreign visitors, no more con-

crete material link is suggested, much less examined, and these passages constitute everything this influential book has to say about the two subjects.

Five years later, in *Thailand: Buddhist Kingdom as Modern Nation-State,* Charles
Keyes (1987) discussed prostitution in relation to the U.S. wartime presence, the
migrants' labor market options, and the tourist industry. Because of the
American troops stationed in Thailand and the Kingdom's status as an R&R site,
Keyes explains, the war "helped create a new wealthy class in Thailand from
among those people who held contracts for construction or service to the United
States or the Thai military. It also contributed markedly to corruption in the military and police, as well as to a dramatic rise in prostitution, alcoholism, and drug
use" (113). Although he insists that "the high rate of prostitution in Thailand
must be understood as a consequence at least in part of the growing disparity
between the rural and urban economies," since many "rural women are drawn
into prostitution because of the poverty of their families and because they have
few qualifications for equivalently paid jobs in the urban sector," he argues that
the sex trade was not the principal destination for women migrants to the urban
centers (157). Some migrant women, he admits, did become prostitutes, but, in
addition to those whose education qualified them for white-collar or professional
jobs, "many have found work in factories and commercial establishments, and
some have established businesses in the cities or back in their home villages"
(124). (In other words, rural women may be a majority of the prostitutes in the
cities, but this does not mean that the majority of female workers migrating to
the cities become prostitutes.)

Keyes also connects the expansion of the service sector to Thailand's growing
involvement in the global economy, especially under the stimulus of tourism,
adding, "Recently, however, tourism has come under strong criticism because it
has been closely linked with the growth of prostitution, a 'service' much in
demand by many middle-class Thai males as well as by foreign visitors" (157).
As with his treatment of the proportion of prostitutes among the migrants from
rural areas, Keyes makes use of the attributed objectivity of "plainstyle" to cover
statements that elsewhere are highly contentious. And the passages cited are his
only references to these issues.

In contrast to the 1981 edition, the *Country Study* on Thailand issued in 1989
does include the by-then standard information about tourism as the largest
earner of foreign exchange, as well as a very rough estimate (100,000–1,000,000)
of the number of prostitutes in the country (LePoer 1989, 134, 93). A volume of
this sort, however, is meant to be a compendium of generally accepted facts and
figures (or, as in the case of the number of sex workers, estimates), not an analysis of causes and relationships. Such an analysis, however, is precisely the
province of a collection like *Culture and Environment in Thailand,* a weighty volume reporting the proceedings of a Siam Society conference—yet were it not for
the intervention of Pasuk Phongpaichit, an economist whose research we detail
further in this chapter and in Chapter 4, the whole lengthy discussion of environmental and social issues would contain no mention at all of either tourism or

prostitution. Pasuk's contribution is a critique of development—more precisely, of the Thai model of development as a fetishized category—for its negative effects on the environment. In what amounts to an aside, she assails the "cultural pollution" fomented by tourists, along with the more obvious material destruction accomplished by what she calls an "economic development culture" (Phongpaichit 1989, 341).

Another study in which tourism might have been expected to occupy the foreground, rather than the few remarks devoted to it, focuses on Thai-U.S. relations. But Robert Muscat's *Thailand and the United States: Development, Security, and Foreign Aid* (1990) is a classic example of Pasuk's "development culture," uncritically cheering on each step that Thailand has taken toward citizenship in the transnational capitalist family, particularly those taken under U.S. military or economic tutelage. In this context, references to tourism are very light and their tenor invariably upbeat. In more than one place, for instance, Muscat praises the Kingdom's approach to NIC (newly industrializing country) status through the growth of the manufacturing sector to equal agriculture, as well as the generation of domestic energy sources to decrease dependency on imported oil. The next item on his congratulatory list is the "remarkable expansion of tourist earnings" (47, 2). The only other indexed reference to tourism, a historical one discussing modernization of Bangkok's Don Muang Airport, states that at the time U.S. aid to this project phased out in 1974, tourism was already the fifth largest earner of foreign exchange, with 80 percent of visitors to Thailand arriving by air (105). What motivated foreigners to enplane—and continues to motivate them in increasing numbers—and what they choose to do when they alight does not fall within Muscat's demarcation of the issues, even when a portion of the foreigners are Americans.

Still, by the 1990s there was general agreement among pro-development academic specialists that tourism was important to Thailand's growth. Some qualified their enthusiasm in the light of the connection between tourism and prostitution, but even these did not acknowledge the centrality of sex in the marketing and implementation of the travel industry. And all figuratively threw up their hands in the face of the grim plight of Thailand's rural poor, for whom no survival solution other than migration to the urban labor market—including the sex market—could be envisaged. In all the works cited, moreover, tourism received remarkably little attention, proportional to its share of the gross domestic product (GDP), and it was still possible to elide the question of prostitution entirely, and, in so doing, ignore the contribution of the sex industry to the strategy of economic development through tourism.

What was no longer possible in the 1990s was a study with claims to intellectual credibility on political-economic matters that echoed the mentality of sex-industry customers when it came to questions of gender and prostitution. Insor's uncritical assertion that liquor and women are among "the Thais'" chief recreations and his delight in finding them united (just like home on Madison Avenue!) in the Mekhong whiskey ad would no longer go unchallenged on a scholarly scene where the consensus was that international prostitution is a "problem" of some sort. This is not to suggest that what we have characterized as the sex customers' mentality is absent from books about Thailand that are meant to be taken seriously as commentary, but simply that such books are journalistic rather than scholarly in tone, are meant for the general reader, not the academician, and do not have authoritative status in the field.

A good example of this genre is *Thailand's Turn: Profile of a New Dragon*, by Elliott Kulick and Dick Wilson (1992). When these two authors quote a woman who has made a fortune from the bars and massage parlors and who explains her success by stating categorically that "everyone likes sex" (78), they are accepting her assumption (which is not unlike Insor's three decades earlier) that the only people who count as "everyone" are male customers (unless they are making the even more naive assumption that all prostitutes are oversexed women who enjoy their jobs). When they celebrate the "healthy, natural attitude to sex in Thailand, quite free from the puritanism of Europe" (78), they distance themselves from critical scholarship and sign on to the long tradition of Western representations of the sexually exotic Other that we outline in our Chapter 5. And when they add approvingly that Thais treat sexual transactions unsentimentally, "as a matter of business, not in the least personal" (78), they are unconsciously echoing the assumption, built into that Western tradition for the last several centuries, that nothing is more "natural" than doing business.

Yet even Kulick and Wilson report that sex tourism is problematic for many Thai and foreign observers. They cite Kirrkiart Pipatseritharn, the rector of Thammasat University, arguing in the *Guardian* (12 May 1987), "There are prostitutes in every country but not to this degree. Not to the extent that men come from all over the world looking for women. Do we want to be a world power in this respect?" Their own appended comment, more provocative than they may have intended, is that "Thailand has not become a world sex power but it has certainly become a world sex magnet" (1992, 79).[1]

Political economists writing about Thailand in the 1990s are beginning to raise more questions about tourism, sex, and sex tourism, but they tend to leave those questions suspended and unanswered. Peter Warr's collection *The Thai Economy in Transition* attempts to "bridge the gulf between Thai and non-Thai audiences" (1993, xvii) by presenting the work of Thai economists—whose approach to their country's problems he finds less ideological, more subtle, and more pragmatic than that of foreign commentators in English, in a text published by the prestigious Cambridge University Press.[2] In terms of the issues with which we are concerned, his effort is only partially successful. His own 80-page introductory essay, "The Thai Economy," says nothing whatsoever about tourism, much less prostitution; all indexed references to either subject send the reader to the chapter on "Services," entrusted to Pasuk Phongpaichit, author of the important 1982 study of sex work as labor-market option, *From Peasant Girls to Bangkok Masseuses*. But in *this* context, tourism and prostitution take something of a back seat to the concept of service work itself and its new economic role. There is no place here for the economic data to emerge, and they are not addressed in the collection's chapters on, say, "Labour Markets" or "Poverty and Income Distribution," where they might well have something to add to the analysis.

From this point of view, the most recent and comprehensive history available in English, Pasuk Phongpaichit's own *Thailand: Economy and Politics*, written in collaboration with Chris Baker (1995), represents a startling innovation. The book departs from disciplinary tradition not only in its inclusion of tourism and the foreign exchange it attracts as an economic phenomenon worthy of serious scrutiny and of prostitution as a factor in the rise of tourism to its present importance in the economy, but also in the means the authors have devised to allow them to approach such a sensitive topic at all. Unfortunately, the study's limitations, particularly its failure to come to terms with prostitution as an economic and not simply a cultural fact, also reside in this methodological innovation.

Throughout most of their text, Pasuk and Baker follow the standard format of political and economic history, tracing economic policies through successive governmental regimes and drawing connections between the political and economic developments that define traditional periodization. For the post–World War II period they discuss foreign influences, the consequent balance-of-payments problem, import substitution, the economic role of the military and the state, the adoption of agricultural policies favorable to consolidation, and the creation of an urban services sector staffed by populations displaced from rural areas by those policies. Their general method entails a top-down account of developments, bolstered by statistical data. Although the narrative they delineate is focused on events and policies within Thailand, the role of international lending agencies and strong-currency powers is not entirely neglected. The advent of mass tourism as an economic force is situated first and foremost within the evolution of Thai policy and then connected to international planning.

The volume's prologue and epilogue, however, along with one discrete section from the second chapter, tell a different story, literally as well as figuratively. The prologue takes for its central metaphor the folk picaro Khun Phaen (the "Schemer" or "Planner"), here understood as the avatar of the Thai masses, hero and victim at once, the eternal adversary of Khun Chang ("elephant," hence "Mr. Big"), the "king's man." But Pasuk, whose feminism is reflected in her landmark study of Bangkok prostitutes, emphasizes that Khun Phaen possesses a gender as well as a class identity and that both contribute to his story. She does this through the contrasting fate of the heroine, Wantong, who lacks even the limited options that define Khun Phaen's parlous lot. So the prologue to this "straight" study of economic and administrative history ends with the description of a woman's fate as the archetypal folk story defines it:

> She is shunted between the two men, forced to put up with Khun Phaen's persistent philandering, abducted, gagged and raped, and dragged off to the woods. All young women in the story are portrayed first as the property of their parents and

then as the property of their men. They are valued for their youth, their role as mother and lover, their skill at embroidery. They have no means of escape into monkhood, forest, or robber band. They even get tossed into jail for the sins of their men. Nang Wantong has difficulty making up her mind which of the two men—Khun Phaen, handsome but fickle, Khun Chang, faithful but ugly and smelly—she can best tolerate as her husband. Eventually the king executes her for this indecision (Phongpaichit and Baker 1995, xvii).

It is from here that the authors launch their account of modern Thailand's economic evolution, starting with the description of landholding and labor relations on the mid-nineteenth-century Rice Frontier that led to the dominance of "King Paddy." They clearly believe that the best place for the reader to enter and engage this narrative is in the wake of a reminder about the sorry destiny of the Thai woman under whatever conditions prevail.

A detailed description of economic activity, emphasizing the moments of transition, occupies the next 76 pages. Then, after a discussion of the decline of agriculture, its origins and consequences, particularly in the creation of a mobile population of rural youth to provide labor power for the urban production and service sectors, the authors insert a section that is itself a shift as profound as the social developments they chronicle. This passage is devoted to the *culture* of the displaced young peasants, as expressed through the *phleng luk thung*, a country music form that arises from and validates the common experience of the migrants, packaging it and selling it back to them in song. Pasuk and Baker quote the works of major singer-songwriters in this Country-and-Eastern genre, stressing the presence of economics even in songs about the condition of the heart, as well as the way these songs explore the full range of the urban-migration experience as lived—differently—by both sexes. Women's songs speak quite openly about restricted job possibilities, the terrible pay and working conditions outside the sex industry, and the lives of those who become prostitutes. Indeed, almost all the book's references to prostitution, whether as economic phenomenon or personal experience, are contained in the discussion of the *phleng luk thung*. The peasant girl who now works as a waitress in a back street shop laments:

> Being poor, I had to leave home
> Hauling my virginity along.
> (Qtd. 78)

Her maidenhead is not only a burden but a commodity, and in a genre where as many as one-fifth of the songs deal with prostitution, themes include "life inside the brothel, being a 'hired wife' for a U.S. soldier, and working as a masseuse in Germany" (78). The economics and the affect are characteristically blended in lines such as these:

They call me the angel with a number
Have you ever come to my address
So many customers come, and leave with a lighter heart
The room's just a den for the lust of men
Who want only my beautiful body
The angel can stand it
Just by thinking of the hungry family back home
Every banknote has the same value
Even when stained with tears.
(Qtd. 79)

Without commenting in any way on this departure—analysis of a pop culture medium in the midst of a study of economic developments—the book returns to its more conventional narrative. More than 300 pages on, however, it closes with an epilogue that echoes both the prologue's concern with women's life histories in the Thai political economy and the focus on the *phleng luk thung* in the one short section of chapter 2. As the prologue was entitled "The Life of Khun Phaen," this epilogue is "The Death of Phumphuang Duangjan." Here, the archetypal Thai figure is a singer known in her lifetime as the queen of *phleng luk thung*, whose life, memorialized in her songs, mirrored that of the other migrant country girls and whose death at age thirty-one was a distraction from the aftermath of the political disturbances of May 1992. Again, songs of a country girl's poverty and struggle are cited, and this otherwise sober study of political economy ends with the statement that "political leaders turned aside from their mutual recriminations over the May events, and fought for the privilege of sponsoring Phumphuang's funeral" (415). So the country singer takes over the economic narrative, at the end, just as, in death, she assumed the symbolic center of political discourse—without her own words, describing her own experience, being overtly acknowledged *as* political discourse.

In short, *Thailand: Economy and Politics* employs the strategy of presenting the issues through folk tale and popular music, in order to discuss women's status, the female experience of migration, and the relation of both to the sex industry. No other political-economic question is represented in this way in the text; indeed, the book contains no other references to expressive culture. By cathecting the issues surrounding gender, sex, and sex work into the realm of culture, the authors are able to situate these matters within the political-economic discussion in a way that other economic commentators have not done. At the same time, once they have been defined as "culture," the issues around prostitution become immune from political-economic *analysis*, so, as we point out in Chapter 4, this study adds nothing concrete to an analysis of the economics of the sex trade.

The scholarship that focuses specifically on prostitution and sex tourism naturally presents quite a different case. The principal studies recognize that these issues must be understood within an economic framework; they concentrate on different economic aspects, each author insisting that, although the other perspective certainly has to be taken in consideration, her approach is the one that identifies the main issue. Beyond this polemic, these scholars see the problem so thoroughly in economic terms that they neglect to address the special nature of the sex industry's product as sex.

Pasuk Phongpaichit, whose contributions to our understanding of the broader economic issues we have been citing throughout, is also the author of the first serious study of Thailand's prostitutes, *From Peasant Girls to Bangkok Masseuses* (1982). As both this volume's title and its publication under International Labour Organisation auspices suggest, the focus is squarely on the sex workers as workers. The economic aspects most important for this approach are the disparity between urban and rural Thailand, young women's options in a region- and gender-stratified labor market, and the origins of the sex industry in its present form. This background is filled in further as the book foregrounds the results of interviews with fifty massage-parlor workers in Bangkok and a number of their families in upcountry villages. Text and tables provide details and a range of figures outlining the jobs the women held before entering the sex industry, their educational levels, ages at first sex-trade employment and at present, regions of origin, present income per month and per encounter, amounts of money sent home, and plans for the future. So the story, as Pasuk apprehends and presents it, is about the labor market experiences of these fifty young women—and, inferentially, of several hundred thousand like them. The way to change the story would be through a national policy—particularly in the areas of agriculture and education—that would provide other possibilities for rural families and their daughters (Phongpaichit 1982, 61). The customers, whether local or tourist, are marginal to the narrative, as is the process that has brought so many foreign clients; elsewhere, as we have indicated, Pasuk raises critical questions about the economics of tourism, but that is not part of the story she tells here.

Less than a decade later Thanh-Dam Truong, a Vietnamese-born scholar now a Dutch citizen, published *Sex, Money, and Morality: Prostitution and Tourism in Southeast Asia* (1990), which maintains that the issues Pasuk elides are the most important aspects of the story, if not the story itself. Truong is clearly aware of Pasuk's work, which she cites abundantly,[3] as she argues that the real issue is not young women's job choices but the economic planning mechanisms, national and especially international, that created the sex industry's local conditions and continue to provide the clientele.[4] Thus, although she discusses the ideological aspects of prostitution—in general and under the particular conditions that prevail in contemporary Thailand—she focuses on the economic infrastructures of tourism, from the postwar conversion of aircraft manufacturing for civilian uses through the networks of transnational corporations and lending agencies that set up, market, and profit from the sex industry as it serves foreign visitors. Truong does consider the condition of the Thai prostitute's job as a job, just as Pasuk considers the structural aspects of the economy, but it is clear in each case which issues are primary. Although the two studies are not precisely complementary halves of the story, both contribute to a richer understanding of the whole.

They both leave the same gap, as well. In describing different aspects of the prostitute's job—pay differentials for different services, the different types and levels of establishments in which the services are provided, the language employed to sell them to the overseas consumer—both Pasuk and Truong explicitly acknowledge the sexual nature of the services, but neither has much to say about whether and how the sexual dimension of the transaction is connected to its economic aspect. Pasuk's interviewees recall their initiation to sex work as a series of narratives about abuse, and they talk about how much they now get paid for various sexual acts that sound like little more than extensions of those first nights on the job. She does not raise questions about the sexuality of either prostitute or customer or the sexual culture(s) that produced them and that they produce. For her part, Truong quotes the seductive discourse of European travel agencies peddling sex tours. She also analyzes the growth of tourism in terms of the increasing role of leisure as a consumer item in Western capitalism. But *pleasure* as a product or commodity and its meanings in the commercial transaction have no place in her economic analysis. And fantasy has even less.[5]

Academic Tourism

If much of the academic material on economic development in Thailand ignores or slights tourism, the work on tourism largely avoids the sex industry. Because only a few academic works directly address sex tourism in Thailand, our survey of the tourist literature has to begin with the much larger frame of tourism in general. The scholarship tends to cast tourism as either the panacea for all economic ills that development strategists claim it to be—"manna from heaven," as one report called it (qtd. in Crick 1989, 314)—or interpret it as a contemporary manifestation of colonialism. Although studies of tourism have become increasingly nuanced and sophisticated, this oversimplified dichotomy still holds sway, as epitomized in titles such as *Tourism: Blessing or Blight?* (Young 1973) and *Tourism—Passport to Development?* (deKadt 1979). All accounts agree, however, that because people, information, and images are circulating the globe at unprecedented rates and tourism has become the largest industry in the world, employing more people than any other economic sector, it deserves more intellectual scrutiny than it has been allocated in the past (Greenwood 1989, 171). Yet the disdain in which most people hold tourists has also been the lot of tourism studies in the academy.

For the most part, issues of economics, culture, history, politics, gender, and sexuality in relation to tourism have been addressed individually, with only occasional studies bringing two of the categories together. By isolating these topics, scholars can more easily pass judgment on the positive or negative effects of tourism on a given site, although interpretations of the same data will vary widely. For example, does commodifying a culture preserve or prostitute it? Considering the topic—i.e., culture—in isolation leads too easily to polarized, either/or distinctions. As Hitchcock, King, and Parnwell point out (1993, 8–12), this view of culture emerges from assuming it to be a static entity—whole, enduring, homogeneous, and bounded: a *thing*, therefore, capable of being packaged and sold. This assumption ignores cultural process—in this instance, the complex, dynamic ways local people adapt and incorporate tourism and modify it to meet local needs as best they can; it also ignores how tourism in fact *creates* a kind of tradition. If we change these assumptions, we can examine how local traditions both adapt and are adapted by tourism. This more complex view means that "the definition of what is traditional culture, the specification of links between an invented present and an imagined past, is constantly being symbolically recreated and contested" (Wood 1992, 58).

Many of the studies about the economic effects of tourism have essentially been propaganda explaining that the "soft" development of tourism allows a country to package resources it already possesses—such as scenery, crafts, climate, and friendly people—and thereby leapfrog the damaging "industrial phase" of development experienced by the West. Alternatively, the studies critique strategies proposed by the World Bank and International Monetary Fund (IMF), arguing that the economic costs of tourism far outweigh the gains. These reports discuss economic "leakage" or repatriation of foreign currency, inflation in the cost of local goods, land speculation, and the reinforcement of extant social inequalities by differential access to tourism profits. From this perspective, the "friendliness" of the people actually reflects their subservience and capitulation to First World demands. Numerous studies illustrate both sides of the issue.[6] Some, like deKadt (1979), provide the facade of critique while actually being an apologia for the tourist industry and offering "policy recommendations" to address impediments to the industry's growth.

Perhaps a more productive approach to the economic effects of tourism may rest in avoiding the thumbs-up/thumbs-down assessment and, instead, relating economics to other factors such as globalization processes affecting national developments, cultural values, and cultural policies. Crick (1989, 335) and Wood (1993, 68) complain that many studies do not do a good job of separating tourism from other forces of social and cultural change in the contemporary moment, whereas we would argue that perhaps they should not. By placing tourism in a frame that explicitly links economic effects with historical processes and issues of representation, analysts can combine synchronic and diachronic concerns that provide a more complex picture of global-local interaction. An indirect example of such an approach can be found in the construction of tradition as theorized by Eric Hobsbawm and Terence Ranger in *The Invention of Tradition* (1983).

This text explores the social and political processes that construct the "traditions" that many people believe have been in place for centuries but that Hobsbawm and Ranger argue are actually recent inventions. Issues of whose "traditions" count as such and whose do not emerge in the cultural, political processes that manifest themselves as collective memory. In *The Predicament of Culture* (1988), James Clifford's theories about the ramifications of cultural identity as a process of contestation within global-historical forces likewise offer an example. Both works provide heuristic models for integrating previously isolated areas of inquiry in tourism studies. More directly relevant is Dean MacCannell's work on the creation of leisure in industrial societies, which is connected to the expansion to all parts of the planet of the ideology of modern society. In essence, MacCannell argues that we are witnessing a middle-class imperialism: the "effort of the international middle class to coordinate the differentiations of the world into a single ideology is intimately linked to its capacity to subordinate other peoples to its values, industry, and future design. . . . Tourism is an essential component of that consciousness" (1989, 13). This position is significantly more productive in its analyses than the usual claims about neocolonization, because it incorporates the empirical and symbolic effects of tourism as it restructures the world view of both hosts and guests. In effect, to rephrase George Marcus and Michael Fischer (1986), MacCannell's approach offers the promise of tourism studies as cultural critique.[7] To complement this position, Valene Smith argues that the post–World War II generation in the United States values money for play, not security. As the Protestant work ethic yields to the hedonistic play ethic, members of this generation use their incomes for travel (1989, 2).

Another area in need of attention and refinement which we address in this book is tourist motivation (Crick 1989, 316). For most tourists, the naive position that tourism promotes cross-cultural understanding, propagated by John F. Kennedy and others, plays a minimal role at best. What do tourists hope to achieve with their leisure time? What motivates them to travel halfway around the world to "experience another culture"? Do they in fact want to experience another culture, or some fantasy culture of their own and the tourist industry's devising? What are the global forces that place tourists in a site to be serviced and locals in the same site to service them? How do these forces play themselves out in the participants' psyches? These questions about tourist motivations and meanings invoke the issues and perspectives discussed above. These issues suggest that tourism studies can and should be about power/powerlessness and knowledge/ignorance, the construction of Others and Otherness, and "the consumption of images" necessary for tourism, thus bringing critical theory and cultural studies to bear on this topic (Crick 1989, 330). Wood (1993, 57–68) argues that "the positioned nature of cultural judgments" and the ways "tourism both engenders and becomes implicated in a broad range of cultural politics" should also reposition tourism studies.

Sexuality and the promise of sexual fulfillment has always played a part in tourist promotion. The triad "sun, sand, and sex," standard fare for resort tourism, signifies the conspicuous consumerism and hedonistic release offered to those who wish to pack the most into their leisure time. Sun, sand, and sex as goals of travel correspond to those of colonial travelers, and many have argued that the resort enclaves of the present produce sites of foreign privilege and pleasure from the colonial past.[8] Glimpsing the early stages of the postcolonial process looming on the historical horizon, Frantz Fanon (1974, 123) warned of this reinscription that operates under the guise of development, thus anticipating MacCannell's middle-class imperialism, in its creation of "centres for rest and relaxation" and "pleasure resorts to meet the wishes of the Western bourgeoisie" under "the name of tourism . . . built up as a national industry"— processes already begun under colonial rule. Hauntingly close in language and experience to the military's "rest and recreation" sites, these pleasure spots on the world map of desire raise the specter of sexual exploitation strategies to benefit the First World hordes. The nation that pursues such alignments, Fanon claims, "will in practice set up its country as the brothel of Europe" (123). By asserting that tourism, like colonialism, equals sexual exploitation, Fanon names a major problem of the Thai tourist industry. Both the causes of tourist-based sexual exploitation and its effects, however, are more complex and far-reaching than his analysis suggests.

Reading the academic literature that directly addresses the sex tourism industry in Thailand, one would be hard pressed to find these complexities addressed in any single work. Erik Cohen's insightful articles (1982; 1984; 1986; 1988; 1993A) primarily explore cultural assumptions about prostitution and their psychological results for both workers and guests, hinting at the wide range of tourist motivations and meanings. Cohen tries to schematize patterns of prostitute-client interaction and discern the psychological motivations driving each of them. In attempting a simultaneous Thai and Western emic analysis of these motivations, he provides a continuum of remuneration and interpersonal commitment that ranges from "mercenary" to "emotional": one pole is strictly financial for both parties; at the other, "romantic love" describes the participants' interpretation of the relationship (1993A). Although provocative, Cohen's work often remains locked in dualistic analyses: Thai and Western stand as largely monolithic antipodes, the two perspectives occasionally overlapping on matters that Thailand has "imported" from the West.

Psychological projection and its effects likewise figure in Lenore Manderson's interesting analysis (1992) of public sex performances for tourists. In these performances, Manderson argues, women sex performers rebel against strictly delimited notions of females in rural Thai society, at the same time parodically insulting their foreign male customers. If this analysis is correct, then the customers get what they want but don't know what they're getting. As with Cohen, Manderson discusses the sexual subjectivity projected by male tourists into the commercial site and the impact this projection has on the psyches of the workers fulfilling these fantasies. But in contrast with his approach, she concedes the difficulty of ascertaining exactly what customers and performers think, leaving her own interpretation of the events explicitly as interpretation.

Cleo Odzer's dubious book-length ethnography of sex workers in Patpong (1994) becomes a stage for her to explore her own sexuality as a First World subject: in effect, she transfers her perceived autonomy to the lives of the sex workers who, she claims, are better off than most Thai women. For Odzer, then, naming a problem related to the sex industry becomes a moot point, because no substantial problems in fact exist (Bishop and Robinson 1995, 69). At the other extreme, Catherine Hill (1993) claims that the entire industry is a problem. The two works thus encapsulate the binarism of tourism studies. Hill's brief article adds some gender concerns and thin cultural and religious analysis to recapitulate an argument centered on economic determinism. Interesting, informative, and provocative though these works may be, because they isolate the economic from the symbolic, the psychological from the discursive, and the historical from the experiential, none provides the complexity suggested by MacCannell and others.[9]

Three studies, however, do reframe the discourse through the productive combination of issues often isolated. Elizabeth Bounds (1991, 132) argues for using a "complex and nuanced theoretical model" to look at Asian prostitution, one that places sex workers in a "social context where structures of sex, class, economy, race, and imperialism all intersect." Her short, ambitious article attempts to construct such a theoretical model and apply it in many sites. She focuses primarily on the role of military bases in the development of prostitution throughout Asia—a major part of the story, to be sure. What most interests us, however, is Bounds's attempt to bring together often disparate elements of inquiry that need to be addressed in relation to one another. Likewise, David Leheny's 1995 article on Japanese sex tours asserts that sex tourism research should pay attention to gender roles produced by the industry and to the economic effects on individual and national actions. His examination of sex tourism as dependent on a "peculiar and unstable combination of sexuality, nationalism, and economic power" (369) links political economy, national policy, gender and sexuality construction, and local-global influences on individuals. Although Leheny is critical of it, Linda Richter's *The Politics of Tourism in Asia* (1989) includes much of what we find productive in his work. By arguing that tourism policies rarely receive the scrutiny of political issues—"who gets what, when, and how"—and attempting to provide that scrutiny, Richter's case study of Thailand offers productive modes of inquiry that complicate the move to simple economic or social explanations; her examination of the explicit connections linking tourism, politics, development policies, and daily life make it difficult to separate these factors. The work by Bounds, Leheny, and Richter helps us address the complicated nexus of problems related to the sex tourism industry in Thailand and frame our discourse about it in ways only hinted at in other analyses.

Thailand in Mass Media: The Prequel

> Well, you fall in love with the image of
> Thailand, don't you? You hear about it,
> and you come here, and the reality is
> nothing like the image. Nothing. But
> somehow, even after years of living
> here, you still love the image.
> —British expat in Thailand

In the mass media, the enormous surge in attention to Thailand coincides—ironically though not, perhaps, unexpectedly—with the insistence on a single focused narrative. The Western media can be said to have "discovered" Thailand as big news only *after* the conclusion of 1987's "Visit Thailand Year," and it was then that sex tourism became the background for a story focused on AIDS or child prostitution or on the (even more sensational) link between them. But this does not mean that before 1987 the media had nothing to say about the Kingdom or the sexual delights awaiting Westerners who happened upon them or journeyed to meet them.

In the late 1940s, as the map of the world acquired its Cold War configuration, Thailand, still called by its former name, Siam, acquired the double identity it was to retain in Western representations until the advent of mass tourism. On the shifting sands of Asian politics it was the Sole Reliable Bastion of peace and prosperity, and thus permanently committed to the "democratic" (which is to say, anti-Communist) camp, despite the equally permanent presence of successive dictators; at the same time, its strategic location (and perhaps the absence of democratic practices) made it a prime candidate for "next domino" status. What justified American confidence, bolstered by military and economic aid, was the people—the delightful, fun-loving Thais themselves, a recurrent representation of the Thai character that still dominates both "hard" and "soft" news stories about Thailand. An astute observer could probably chart with some precision the close juxtaposition of a "hard" news event in Thailand—another coup, another strong man—with a wave of feel-good pieces in travel and lifestyle publications.

Thus, starting in the 1950s the *New Yorker* began running a "Letter from Bangkok" every few years. Although not as central a place as Paris or London, from which permanent correspondents filed regular reports, Bangkok had made it to at least the periphery of the archetypal New Yorker's mental map. It was a place where someone might go, and the first "Letter" describes an already well-established tourist route, such that "if the party from Little Neck or Kansas City that you saw at breakfast doesn't cross your path at the temples, you are bound to pick it up again at the snake farm ... at the Royal Boathouse ... or at the floating markets in the *klongs*" (Moorehead 1952, 72).

Even earlier, however, an unsigned 1945 article titled "Our Own Baedeker" in the magazine's Talk of the Town section set the tone for much of the postwar combination of politics and cultural journalism. Beginning with the revisionist history that Siam had really been a secret ally in World War II, this piece covers recent history, flora and fauna, local ethnicities and cultures, religion, and royal family, constantly returning to the theme of lightheartedness (contagious, it seems, since the Japanese are described as having "lightheartedly presented" their apparent friends with a great deal of neighboring territory). "Of all the Orientals," this article tells us, "the Siamese are certainly the jolliest. They like to think of themselves as *snuk*—jolly, carefree, gay. In fact, the Siamese are so *snuk* that in 1932 they rebelled against the traditional absolute monarchies on the revolutionary leaders' promise that the new regime would be more fun than the old "(*New Yorker* 1945, 7).

As the political situation solidified, so did the rhetoric, bolstering its defense of dictatorship with its praise of the laid-back Thais. In 1949 even the liberal *Nation* (New York) told its readers that in "rice-rich Siam" . . . still "the most prosperous country in Asia," the "prevailing mood is still an easygoing relaxation" (Roth 1949, 317). The *New Republic*—which at that time still shared the *Nation*'s politics—emphasized the high standard of living, wherein "(t)he people share the fruits of a flourishing national economy" and where, since "(y)ou do not need to work very long or very hard to earn the cost of a bowl of rice and a sarong . . . everyone has plenty of time to spend at the convivial country fairs" (Briggs 1949, 15).

No less a commentator than Adlai Stevenson, touring Southeast Asia for a series in *Look* magazine, favorably characterized the Thai government as "an easy-going police state," pointing out that given Thailand's rice surplus, "even the plentiful poor have enough to eat. So there has never been much cause for unrest—either political or economic" (1953, 58). Popular novelist James Michener, whom *Reader's Digest* describes as "a renowned authority on Asia," weighed in with a call to respond generously when "the people of Thailand pray that the United States will support them" against a Communist takeover (1954, 66). The "free" Thai government, Michener explained, was run by the "Coup Party," whose four hundred or so members took turns in power and of which the "wealth of certain leaders is rumored to be incalculable." Michener realized that "American observers are apt to grow apoplectic when they see such wholesale manipulation. But by and large the government of Thailand is a good one. It has been called 'a dictatorship with 400 dictators.' More appropriate would be an analogy to a rich and prosperous corporation run by a board of self-perpetuating and tough-minded directors who vote themselves the first dividends "(63).

Alan Moorehead's first Bangkok "Letter" balanced the apparent disequilibrium between national character and political style by opining that "Bangkok is all so crowded, so vivacious, and so intent upon itself that one feels there may be something to Dr. Johnson's remark that men's happiness is not much affected by the sort of government they are obliged to live under" (1954, 74). From this point of view, as article after article in this period was subsequently to explain, in

"Bangkok there is a phrase that has been constantly on people's lips during the most critical moments of the recent months. '*Mai pen rai* . . . which is roughly equivalent to the Spanish '*Es igual,*' the Italian '*Non importa,* ' the French '*tant pis ,*' the German '*Wurst,*' and the American 'so what?'" (Moorehead 71). (You say these are not equivalent to one another? Well, *mai pen rai,* which really, by the way, means "never mind.") As the next "Letter" continued nearly two years later, "Siam is enjoying a period of tranquillity remarkable even for a nation whose inhabitants have always been noted for their ability to make the best of a lot that is not at all an unhappy one to begin with. . . . The celebrated Buddhist serenity of spirit is an important element in the Siamese character" (Busch 1955, 196).

The heading for an article on Bangkok in the *New York Times Magazine* put it all together: "The character of this city, headquarters for the Manila Pact powers, stems from its friendly, relaxed people, who don't take even their own problems seriously" (Durdin 1955, 9). The Thais' own problems, including "extreme government corruption, rising prices for the little man, dissatisfaction among intellectuals, and Communist infiltration," did make it into the opening paragraph, but foregrounded throughout was "the relaxed attitude toward life that gives to Bangkok its special charm. Tomorrow will do, the Thais seem to say; relax, nothing is *that* serious, life is amusing, why not enjoy it?" (11). After homage to the established motifs of charming, friendly people and their delightful dictatorship, this article introduces a third theme the media were to focus on, that of encountering all this personal and political friendliness firsthand by becoming a tourist to Thailand. The "amiable Thais" create the feeling of euphoria experienced by the visitor as soon as "he" hits town, being, as they are, "friendly, cheerful, relaxed, modern without being uprooted" (7). The sights of what had already become Southeast Asia's "chief tourist city" merited several paragraphs of breathless description: temples, palaces, the Floating Market, kick-boxing, exotic shopping—with the only hint of what was to come provided in the exuberant judgment that "undoubtedly the Thais of Bangkok are the greatest party-givers in Asia" (10; see also Nimantheminda 1956, 106).

Far more influential than any magazine article—or, for that matter, all of them put together—were the Broadway and Hollywood versions of *The King and I,* also produced in the 1950s. This avatar of Anna Leonowens's narrative impressed an apparently permanent image of Siamese life and values into the popular imaginary, particularly in the United States.[10] Although no one could call Yul Brynner's taut, energetic King a relaxed or easygoing figure, he and the court over which he presided nonetheless served to reinforce key elements of the Siam myth: absolute but ultimately acceptable despotism, abundant sexuality, and a strong connection between the two.

Once *The King and I* assumed canonical status in mass culture, it became almost impossible to write an article, whether focused on politics or tourism, without at least glancing reference to what the reader already "knew" about Thailand from this single colorful source. And though it is Anna Leonowens—

the "I" of the title (who is properly and similarly shocked at both sexual excess and political abuse) with whom the audience identifies—so that, in a very real sense, the narrative involves "the King and *us*"—a certain slippage may also occur. If you, the audience member as subject, were transported to "Siam" in reality and not just in fantasy, you would continue to share Anna's sense of superiority to the indigenous barbarians, of course, but you might also imagine yourself partaking of the economic and sexual privileges of the play's far more interesting character, the King.

The *New Yorker's* Bangkok "Letters" from the 1950s and the contemporary articles in travel and leisure publications (discussed in Chapter 3) make it clear that some Americans had already begun to place Thailand on their touristic agendas. That these seekers of the exotic—if not yet the erotic—Thai holiday may well have been inspired by *The King and I* is an irony lost on the Thai government, which rapidly banned all representations of the play and film within the country—a ban that remains in effect. In the 1960s, as the number of American visitors was swelled by both increasingly available jet-travel package tours and a growing U.S. military presence in the region, media representations of Thailand and the kinds of "rest and recreation" available there were slow to reflect any change.

So, as the Sarit regime ended, the *New Republic* (1963, 11) praised the dictator for having given Thailand "stability and the best government it has had since the end of the Second World War, 'offering' authoritarian but not unpopular leadership." The Sarit era is now referred to by many Thai intellectuals as "the Dark Ages," a period during which any expression of dissent from enforced optimism was punishable by imprisonment. For as E. J. Kahn more approvingly put it in another *New Yorker* "Letter from Bangkok," Sarit was a "benevolent dictator whose benevolence and dictatorship were both outsized" (1964, 165). Kahn even managed to find a certain stereotypically Thai laid-backness in the form repression was taking. His Thailand was one where students who wanted to demonstrate had to be gently reminded that demonstrations have been illegal for the six years that the country has been under martial law: "The students had apparently forgotten all about the martial law business, and no wonder, for Bangkok is by and large an easygoing, carefree metropolis where everybody laughs and chuckles and makes jokes, makes them, in testimony to the city's delightful inconsistency, about polygamy, at the same time that the papers have been running chilling accounts of a vengeful woman's blinding her husband with acid because he had taken a . . . minor wife" (163).

It is revealing that sex and gender enter into the "delightful inconsistency" argument only as a metaphor for "real" politics. The same "Letter" contains one of the few early references to economic inequality: Kahn asserted complacently that in Thailand, "labor is plentiful and, as elsewhere in Asia, cheap" (165). The reader was apparently expected to identify with the potential employer or consumer of labor and, making no connection between this cheap, abundant labor supply and the establishment of martial law, enjoy the ensuing anecdote about a newspaper run more cheaply with handset type than by automation. But the particular outlet for excess labor that concerns us here, the sex industry rated, as yet, no mention in the *New Yorker.*

As Thailand, without shifting its actual location, began to be described not as perilously close to China but as next door to Indochina, U.S. media continued to accept the imperative of heaping admiration and aid on any pro-Western government there. After all, as *Time* (1965a, 37) authoritatively proclaimed, whatever the outcome of the Vietnam conflict, "the next target of Communist aggression in Southeast Asia will doubtless be Thailand." And the *Nation* ran what might be characterized as a political "mood piece" about a train journey marked by the vestiges of colonial culture and the suicide of a young Thai guerrilla who had just been apprehended. The tone is that of world-weary fiction from exotic, intriguing battle zones:

> The Indian porter, in his bright costume, looked down at three yellow-labeled bottles of Schweppes quinine water he had salvaged from the sudden emergency stop (to retrieve the boy's body).
> "Yes, already dead."
> And he looked us straight in the eye, then away vacantly at the three Buddhist monks and, still thinking inwardly, still thoughtful, said, "Yes, that is a pity, isn't it?" And then he said, "Now that the train is stopped, do you think I should nip out and get some more ice?" (Eastlake 1966, 204)

Thai women made occasional appearances in postwar popular prose, though not yet as sex workers. *Coronet* magazine featured Thailand's "Women of Enchantment" as early as 1951. The beauty of the young Queen Sirikit was often cited as a national asset, although it had also been "used" by Sarit to "restore the popular appeal of monarchy" (*New Republic* 1963, 11). Successful local businesswomen, making "ever deeper inroads into Thailand's commerce," were nonetheless forced to "exercise great tact and diplomacy in dealing with their men" (*Time* 1965b, 92). On the eve of the American incursion, Thai women were thus known to be "enchantingly" beautiful, and that beauty informed their political role. They were entrepreneurial stars in the growing market economy, yet their competence as capitalists in no way detracted from their traditional subservience. Looking back, we can see the stage being set for the entrance of that enchantingly beautiful and quintessentially subservient little businesswoman, the Thai prostitute.

Although no Thai women are explicitly mentioned, the *New Yorker*'s 1967 Bangkok "Letter" is one of the few journalistic documents of the period to spell out the meaning of R&R: "Bangkok has become the liveliest, the loudest, and probably the most licentious city in Southeast Asia. New restaurants, bars, night clubs, and so-called 'massage parlors' are opening every week" (Shaplen 1967, 127). The historical value of the observation is undermined, however, by the breathtaking lack of prescience in this usually astute correspondent's confidence that "much, if not most of the conspicuous and inconspicuous consumption here would vanish at once if the American servicemen left" (140). More insightful to the hindsight-sharpened eye is the chillingly political metaphor, cutting two ways at once, that Shaplen extracted from a Thai military chief in reply to a query about the uses the Americans were making of their bases in Thailand: "I'm just a hotelkeeper who rents out rooms. I don't care what my guests do in the rooms or whom they invite up there" (137).

Smiling, laid-back Thailand was so well established as a media trope by the 1970s that it could serve as a counterweight, an absence noted, when the news contradicted the image. *Time* (1970) headlined one article about Thailand's shaky economy and the Kingdom's failure to shore up the teetering domino of Cambodia, "Gloom in the Land of Smiles"; in another it claimed that under the "spell" of *mai pen rai*, the traditional "never mind" attitude, Thailand had neglected economic diversification and was fast becoming a "Paradise Lost" (*Time* 1971). Thailand as the foreigners' *sexual* paradise began to enter these Miltonic laments for what had been lost—or at least mislaid—with the "steep decline" in the number of GIs coming to Bangkok for R&R: "Desperately searching for any business at all, many of the city's R and R hotels have shifted from daily to hourly rates. At some, curtained-off parking stalls hide the license plates of their embarrassed clientele" (*Time* 1971, 60). This article makes it clear that the scene had become markedly sleazier, while evading any direct mention of what it was like in the heyday of R&R arrivals.

Another lost paradise was that of Japanese businessman Toshio Tamamoto, who was forcibly ejected from the Edenic harem constituted by his thirteen schoolgirl wives, purportedly because of his outlander status and excessive generosity. According to *Newsweek* (1973), which headed the story with the "Paradise Lost" tag, he bought his girls, "aged between 13 and 17, from poor families at prices ranging from $350 to $500, sent them to school, paid them allowances of $25 a month and built houses for their parents." *Newsweek* noted that polygamy, even on this scale, was apparently not illegal in Thailand. No mention was made of whether trafficking in human flesh—as either buyer or seller—or child concubinage is condoned by law, or whether room and board and $25 constituted an appropriate monthly wage for a concubine of whatever age. The problem was apparently that "local procurers ... could not outbid Tamamoto." This Nipponese incarnation of Anna's King of Siam played what would become a familiar chord in foreigners' writing about the sex industry: the beneficent nature of his relation to what the reporter calls Tamamoto's "female acquisitions." That Thailand is home to about two million celibate Buddhist priests, Tamamoto explained, "means there are more women than men in this country. I think that what I did helped these single women." This self-serving explanation echoes that of short-term foreign visitors who represent their role as a beneficent one. He struck another familiar note in the foreign discourse about sex in Thailand when he said that if a jail term awaited him at home, he could cope with it "as long as I can look forward to returning someday to Chiang Mai, where I want to live quietly with my wives and children. I was happy in Chiang Mai. I enjoyed more than another man would experience in a thousand years" (52).

Intentionally or not, *Newsweek* thus supplied the American mass audience with further information about Thailand: that teenage girls could be purchased from their families at bargain rates by a sex industry with enough political clout to arrange for the arrest (ironically, on charges of raping a 13-year-old girl) of an intruder who interfered with trade by paying too much for the merchandise. It even gave the pathetically low dollar amounts that constituted unfair competition for the brothel owners. There is no particular reason to believe that these brothel keepers served the GI or tourist market, as contrasted with the larger indigenous one, but the story's inclusion—presumably on "human interest" grounds—and what it takes for granted offered a momentary window into something that tended to be euphemized or elided in U.S. news media. At a time when Pattaya, already a seaside red-light district, could still be referred to as "Thailand's Acapulco" (Focker 1977, 39), such information had to be seized wherever it could be found.

The euphemisms were not confined to leisure-oriented publications. *Newsweek*, reporting on Thailand's emergence as a newly industrializing "tiger," touches the familiar bases in order to show how the Kingdom is moving beyond them. Those bases are Yul Brynner's King of Siam, the hordes of Indochinese refugees, and "GIs resting up from the Vietnam War" (Moreau 1988, 52). Brynner's King is accurately recalled as "prancing," the refugees as "swarming." But GIs "resting" hardly conjures up the image or the experience that attracted them to Bangkok. Indeed, Robert Shaplen's *New Yorker* "Letter" had long since pointed out the irony in the bureaucratic formula: "In addition to the thousands [of American servicemen] stationed here, several hundred at a time come here from Vietnam for what is officially described as rest and recreation but seems to involve very little of the former" (1967, 137).

As the international clientele of Thailand's sex industry expanded and touring civilians replaced "resting" military personnel, Western media continued to ignore Bangkok's sex-based nightlife. An early exception was NBC's *Weekend*, a magazine-style television program of the mid-1970s. One episode showed a film about the sexual exhibitions in Bangkok's second-floor bars, that promised lurid revelations, with the athletic feats of female sex organs much to the fore. Unlike the sandwich boards worn by Patpong touts, they couldn't say "Pussy Pick Up Coin" and expect to get on the air, much less—contrary to the hype—*show* this version of a "collection box," even at the late-night time slot the program then occupied.[11] Instead, the camera was set up so far from the stage and the performance area was so poorly lit that viewers had to take virtually on faith everything we were told we were "seeing"—which, of course, had the quality been better, we wouldn't have been permitted to see. The noncommittal voice-over presented the show as a form of sensation, giving no indication of how the exhibitions fit into the overall Bangkok sex scene, much less of the scene's wide scale and international customer base. That media people were very much aware of the special treats Thailand's capital had in store for the male visitor is reflected in an anecdote told by Linda Ellerbee—who served as coanchor of *Weekend* sometime after the Patpong non-exposé—about the wedding of a woman colleague:

> When Suzy married a veteran ABC newsman, a world traveler who'd seen everything twice, she let him know his rooster days were over. . . . But during their wedding ceremony, at the part where they talk about "forsaking all others," she leaned over to her groom.
> "Bangkok," whispered Suzy, "doesn't count." (Ellerbee 1986, 245)

Weekend's segment on the sex shows was a way of having one's media cake and eating it too, "showing" the audience what it was literally incapable of seeing and providing no context that would illuminate what was actually on the screen—all this in a spirit of self-congratulation for the daring indoor shots and the equally daring investigative journalism they purportedly represent. This telecast was roughly contemporary with the World Bank's report recommending mass tourism as a key to Thailand's growth in the post-Vietnam period. In this context, if *Weekend*'s sophomoric effort sent any message, it was that something raunchy was happening over in Bangkok, and the only way to see it for yourself was to see it for yourself.

Another strain of this siren song of the late 1970s was constituted by the softcore pornography of the films in the *Emmanuelle* series, including the one in which the Asian-American heroine takes her erotic sideshow to Bangkok. Much as *The King and I* became the media touchstone for Thailand in the Cold War discourses of the late 1950s and the 1960s, *Emmanuelle in Bangkok* served the same media function for the jet-hopping 1970s and early 1980s. The film focuses on the fulfillment of erotic fantasy in a dreamlike setting that is explicitly identified with the possibility of such fulfillment, an exotic culture whose values support rather than repress the erotic. In the first half of the film, set in Bangkok, Emmanuelle provides the catalyst for sexual experimentation at the individual level, and the city and Thai culture provide the perfect context.

Emmanuelle in Bangkok serves as an extended advertisement for Thailand as a sexual smorgasbord for First World globetrotters. Emmanuelle herself spends her minimal time outdoors as the wide-eyed, mouth-agape tourist who takes in all the sights in between sexual bouts involving different genders, races, and numbers of participants. Every tourist venue provides not only a great snapshot possibility—Emmanuelle is a "famous photojournalist"—but also another excuse for sexual interaction. The audience constantly witnesses the collapse of tourist sight and sexual activity with a local. Whether a bellboy at the hotel, a masseuse at a massage parlor, or a royal prince who shows her the town, all the natives are remarkably friendly and willing to service visitors in any manner possible. Likewise, all aspects of the culture, from classical Thai dance to Thai cuisine, offer sexual adventure. In fact, the history of the Thai royal family given to Emmanuelle by the prince argues that its mandate to rule is predicated on sexual potency, which in turn becomes the excuse for massive promiscuity. All of Thai history and culture offer such promiscuity and fulfillment, all available to the tourist in the jumbo-jet age. One need no longer be royalty to be treated royally. The film characterizes the nation as at the service of these tourists who believe themselves to be overeducated and undersexed when they are actually undereducated and oversexed. The locals' raison d'être, likewise, is service. After finding Emmanuelle with the bellboy, her "boyfriend," shaking his head at her incorrigible behavior, says, "And I thought that stuff about Thai hospitality was made up by the guidebooks!"

Emmanuelle in Bangkok put Thailand on the map of the Western imagination somewhat as *The King and I* did in the 1950s, not by replacing the earlier icon—which was and is going strong—but adding another dimension to it. The line of cute progeny found in the musical has grown up to be an army of service industry workers. The tourist map the film delineates is a terrain of desire accessible through your friendly local travel agent.

In the last years before AIDS became central to the story of commercial sex in Thailand, this identification of the Kingdom with the erotic allowed the media to admit retroactively the real significance of "rest and recreation" and to connect it with the burgeoning sex tours. In 1983 poet and novelist Jay Parini, writing in the *New Republic,* found that for him as an American "the ghost of the Vietnam War hovers in the streets" of Thailand: "One remembers the barely post-adolescent boys from Cedar Rapids on their brief R&Rs. The Pat Pong Road still glitters with 'massage parlors,' go-go bars and sex shows. In the windows of the Mona Lisa, a landmark massage parlor, over one hundred girls sit scantily clad behind TV sets, numbers around their necks, for sale" (43). In his brief report, Parini devotes less space to the R&R sex spots than to Lucy's Tiger Den, "a famous watering-hole for soldiers during the war," now filled with vets reminiscing about what, to his astonishment, they call "the good old days" of 1967 and feeding their Rambo fantasies. So he does not explicitly connect the still-thriving sexual venues with the "redneck" bar and its peace-weary clientele.

By contrast, Mike Sager's 1984 piece for *Rolling Stone* focuses on the expatriate Americans in a way that makes the sex industry, wartime and postwar, central to a narrative entitled "Thailand's Home for Wayward Vets." The article opens tersely: "These men put down stakes in a place they thought was better than home. They came looking for a life, but found only an existence" (27). Despite this gloomy prelude, the focus is on successful acclimatizations to Thailand, many of them achieved through the sex industry. Indeed, L. T. "Cowboy"

Edwards, the U.S. Air Force retiree and bar owner for whom red-light Soi Cowboy is named, is featured—no less typical an "expat," in Sager's view, than the vets bored with their lives whom, in any event, he represents as being no worse off than they would be back in the States, even if "something is missing" from their expatriate existence.

Although there are vets involved in everything from a Catholic seminary to a rice farm to a soul food restaurant, the sex trade provides the chief link between past and present. Speaking of the principal U.S. air base in Thailand, Sager recalls that "Udon in 1974 was bustling. Thirty thousand Americans, cheap out-door restaurants on every sidewalk. There must have been 200 bars and clubs catering to GIs, and scores of hotels like the 69 and the Coconut, with bucking beds and fountains and mirrored ceilings in the rooms. An American could have anything he wanted in Udon, from a ten-year-old virgin to a hamburger pizza" (35–36). Postwar Udon may be quieter, but back in Bangkok, Patpong is boom-ing. If it is not as certain as it used to be that "a man could get a blow job while taking a dump in any bar in Bangkok," things are still hopping:

> The night streets of Patpong are elbow to elbow with Westerners, with *farangs*, maybe 99% of them men, all of them strolling and gaping. There are girls on high chairs outside doors of musky bars, and wooden racks of American cigarettes, and food vendors in bamboo hats with carts full of bubbling pots full of God-knows-what. . . . Tinsel streamers on the lampposts, chili peppers and disco and noncha-lant lust in the air. . . . Sin central of Bangkok, where any man, no matter how old or fat or pock-marked, can be Richard Gere for a night, as long as he has a purple one [500 baht note, $20] in his pocket. There may be loneliness in Patpong, but no one is ever alone (28).

The captions on Michael Nichols's photographs summarize Sager's story by focusing on four men settled into the postwar economy. One is Josh Gains of J's Soul Food, who "made his fortune curing homesick expatriates with barbecued ribs" (28). Another caption states rhetorically, "So what if no one in Bangkok is hiring chopper pilots like John Murdock. There's a hotel looking for tennis pros. Put on the Nikes, get out the old racket. Find a student. Now you're a tennis pro. Let the suckers roll" (28). Elsewhere, the reader is advised to "see Rick Menand if you want a girl for the evening. At his bar, the Grand Prix, macho is available on tap. Revel in the past with the Patpong Commandos, or revel in the ladies for a reasonable price" (29). And, of course, there's the top of this particular line: "Nine divorces and not a penny in alimony. A stable of thirty girls, half of them living in a dormitory one flight up from his bedroom. And plenty of booze. Where else but in Thailand? asks L. T. 'Cowboy' Edwards" (28). (In short, how're you gonna keep 'em down on the farm after they've seen Patpong?) Less than a decade later, *Rolling Stone* was to headline its feature on AIDS in Thailand "Death in the Candy Store." Even with the priest in his confessional and the rice farmer's aching back and water buffalo he's convinced are xenophobic, Sager's article is one of the sources for the popular image of the candy store that was.

In the 1980s musicals once again provided a way of conceptualizing Thailand in the global market. The representations had been updated to reflect what the audiences already knew about the country and highlighted the nightlife for sale there. *Chess*, a commercial flop, spawned one infectious hit song, "One Night in Bangkok," which continues to thump its way into the early morning hours in Thai bars. The song is the musical product of the male half of the smash disco group ABBA, but it is Tim Rice's lyrics that writers have latched on to. At once the anthem for many a sex tourist and a source of cliché-packed copy for journalists needing popular culture allusions more recent than Rodgers and Hammerstein, the lyrics juxtapose the ascetic, cerebral life-world of chess grandmasters and the thickly Orientalized sexotica of stereotyped Thailand. The mnemonic rhythms Rice's ABBA pals provided make it difficult for even the first-time listener to forget the chorus: "One night in Bangkok and the world's your oyster / The bars are temples but the pearls ain't free / You'll find a god in every golden cloister / And if you're lucky then the god's a she / I can feel an angel sliding up to me." Or its expanded version, with the added lines: "One night in Bangkok makes a hard man humble / not much between despair and ecstasy / One night in Bangkok and the tough guys tumble / can't be too careful with our company / I can feel the devil walking next to me." With amazing frequency for a song from a failed production, these lines recur in the popular media and in the testimonies of sex tourists on the Internet, which we discuss in our chapters on imagining sexual others and on the bar scene. No doubt the web-writers encountered the tune on their nocturnal rounds in the city itself, where it is a standard in the bars that cater to them. Watching the women who can purportedly humble a hard man grinding to the banal binarisms of heaven and hell, despair and ecstasy, and bars and temples makes for a surreal experience.

The other musical that visually and narratively plots the Thai sex industry is *Miss Saigon* (discussed at length in Chapter 5). Although an infinitely more successful venture than *Chess*, this play did not produce a catchy tune about the Bangkok bar scene; it merely uses the site for setting and spectacle. If theatergoers did not get enough Oriental female flesh in the opening scene set in a Saigon bar, they get another chance to see the flesh trade on a grander scale when the action shifts to Bangkok. The show's creators expect savvy North American and European audiences to identify Bangkok with the sex trade, but they do not assume any causal relationships between the play's two acts, except for that proffered by the thin, romanticized plot of lost love and maternal devotion. Although the media often mention the play in relation to Vietnam, virtually no one makes the connection between the U.S. presence depicted in the first act and the sex tourism presence depicted in the second. Evidently, the intermission includes a historic journey across the river Lethe, and the media wipe the slate clean accordingly.

The mass media of the 1980s sounded only rare notes of disapproval. One did come, however, by way of that subgenre of travel writing (described in more detail in the next chapter) devoted to the wonders of Bangkok's Oriental Hotel. In *Gentleman's Quarterly*, T. O. Allman tells of an occasion when, having returned to graduate school, he was no longer able to afford the Oriental's rates but stopped by for a drink. A reservations manager who had known him of old asked where he was staying. "'The Surinong Hotel,' I answered. The Surinong, one of Bangkok's more aristocratic short-time hotels, at that time, was favored by American GIs on R and R and the better class of Thai masseuses from Patpong Road. . . . I think of the frequent turnover in the other rooms as a kind of subsidy. Of course . . . the walls are lined with purple velvet and there is a gold-framed full-length mirror over the bed, and strangers do knock at the door once or twice a night" (1989, 163, 165). Allman's interlocutor got him a room at the Oriental for only eighty cents a night more than he was paying at the sleaze palace. This is one of the very few narratives in the popular tradition that acknowledges the existence of the sex trade and its supporting establishments while taking it for granted that the reader will share the narrator's attitude of amused contempt for commercial sex and its participants.

Christopher Hitchens, filing his *Nation* column one week from the Noel Coward Suite of the Oriental, calls Thailand "the Honduras of Southeast Asia." Citing a libertarian argument against further military aid to Thailand and in favor of allowing free market forces to do the same job, Hitchens characterizes the sex industry as the epitome of what "free market" means in Thailand. Of the Kingdom's population of 32 million, he explains,

> 1 million females at the lower end of the childbearing age are directly involved in the commercial sex trade. The impact of this on the whole of Thai social relations is impossible to gauge, but the impact on the young women is not. . . . Of course there is disease, as well as unexpected occupational injury. Women go deaf because of the incessant loud music in the bars and suffer intestinal disorders because they are forced to throw up so as to keep ordering expensive drinks.
>
> This is how a large portion of the capital for the Thai "boom" is raised. The tourist charters from Japan and the West are not catering to people interested in Buddhist traditions. They are no more attracted by those things than the American soldiers, who first got the hooker industry into high gear. . . .
>
> [The] idea of Thailand as a vast bazaar of and for American commodities and gadgets obscures the fact that human beings are reduced to commodities too. In . . . [a] laissez-faire utopia, who needs unions? In the actual world of the Patpong flesh market, everybody needs one. (Hitchens 1986, 598)

We cite this report at length because it is the only one, in the period before AIDS provoked the dramatic increase in American media attention to Thailand, that recognized the sex industry as a political issue embracing not only gender politics, but labor and international relations, as well.

"The" Story: AIDS or Child Prostitution

On a 1996 episode of NBC's popular comedy *News Radio,* comedian Phil Hartman explained a new electric massage chair to his co-workers. With each successively vigorous setting, the sexual innuendo and humor builds. The first setting is Shiatsu (titters); the second, Swedish massage (giggles); and the third "A weekend in Thailand!" (roars).

A "Campus Comedy" entry in the February 1995 *Reader's Digest* told of male college students' disappointment at a film club offering: they'd expected the movie to be "Babes in *Thailand.*"

In our internal shorthand as we planned this chapter, the preceding section was labeled "Media Prehistory." Representations of the Thai character and culture—especially as regards sexuality—and, eventually, of the sex industry are all "prehistory" in that they predate the enormous increase in American media coverage of Thailand and its commercial sex world. This later and continuing wave of material is determined to tell *the* story of prostitution in Thailand, the definite article signaling as definitely as it can that one single important issue makes Thailand a story. In some cases it is the AIDS epidemic; in others the exploitation of children is the sine qua non of the contemporary narrative.

The media prehistory created a set of themes and variations that constituted the cumulative meaning of "Thailand" in the Western imagination for more than forty years. In addition to stage and film representations, we culled it from some twenty-one articles: the earliest, the *New Yorker'*s "Baedeker," dates from 1945; the most recent, *GQ'*s paean to the Oriental and its readiness to rescue the writer from the jaws of a "short-time" hotel, was published in 1989. The file of print material on Thailand's sex industry in the light of the AIDS crisis, beginning in the same year, 1989, contains more than twice as many items although it covers only a seven-year span.

These articles, which appeared either in American periodicals or in sources widely circulated in the United States, often stress the centrality of commercial heterosexual prostitution to the spread of the disease. According to a subhead in the *Far Eastern Economic Review,* "The sex trade is so entrenched that neither AIDS nor embarrassment threatens it." The same observation might be made about journalistic clichés, for the article continues, "Like spicy hot food, elephants, Thai smiles and gleaming temple roofs, Patpong and sex are an indelible fact of the country's exotic image. . . . Visitors think that the [sex] business is somehow integral to the local culture. . . . It all seems so wholesome, so acceptable, like a walk in the park" (Handley 1989, 44). To be sure, the stereotypes, cultural and sexual, are often evoked to show how the advent of AIDS has challenged and destroyed them, but it is often hard for the reporter to let go. Thus an article about "100% safe-sex" brothels begins, "Even the happy-go-lucky Thais should now be worried about AIDS" (*Economist* 1991, 34).

As it became clear to the media that "the hundreds of thousands of prostitutes in Thailand's uncounted bars and massage parlours . . . [might] eventually push the amount of heterosexually-transmitted AIDS up to African levels" (*Economist* 1989a, 37), the exceptionally porous boundary between hetero- and homosexual commerce became the focus of what John Nguyet Erni (1997) characterizes as First World shudders at the horrors of the situation. Because the male prostitutes who service foreigners "tend to be heterosexual by preference" and pass the virus on to wives and girl friends who may, themselves, be prostitutes (*Economist* 1989, 37), homosexuals could not be targeted "as the cause of HIV's spread into the general population, despite a thriving and open male prostitution industry" (Handley 1990, 25). This flexibility in sexual behavior made it impossible to continue celebrating the charm of commercial heterosexuality and points up what Erni decries as the "Orientalist imagination" that shapes Western discourse about AIDS in South and Southeast Asia.

As Erni points out, the media have made every effort to represent "Asian AIDS" as an inherently "Third World" phenomenon, a disease spread by heterosexual Asian-to-Asian contact (65). So there is much emphasis on the "Thai male's penchant for visiting brothels" (Handley 1992, 29), with attendant pop sociology about indigenous constructions of masculinity. Even the belief of some prostitutes and brothel keepers that AIDS was a foreign import which could be contained by refusing sex with *farangs* could be twisted to fit the paradigm of Asian ignorance, superstition, and weakness that Erni identifies in this coverage. "'Don't worry about AIDS' said . . . (a) prostitute . . . 'Most of our clients are Asians and AIDS is a disease of you foreigners. We Asians do not have to worry'" (Shenon 1992a, 12).

Erni does not give enough weight to the countervailing Western tendency to recognize a story and perceive it as important only when it includes a Western subject. This tendency, combined with the fact that AIDS, although most prevalent among the cheapest prostitutes but not confined to them (thus the foreigner's money offers him only limited protection), means that prostitution and AIDS stories frequently focus on the international dimension of the sex trade. And if, with this shift, Thailand is relegated to the status of polluted "candy store" for the horny *farang*, the new emphasis also forces media attention, at last, onto the economics of prostitution and sex tourism.

One strand of this public recognition that sex is an economic category entails scrutiny of the overall economic picture; the other considers the situation of young women who enter the sex industry. For instance, in discussing the Thai government's long reticence about the presence of AIDS in the Kingdom, the Western media have to foreground the centrality of tourism to the economy. "Many in the bureaucracy still want to minimize the problem," runs a typical report, "from fear of hurting Thailand's expanding tourist industry, already the country's largest source of foreign exchange" (Erlanger 1991, 26). And not only officialdom but "the moguls of Thailand's flourishing tourist industry do not want bad news to interfere with good times, especially among all those single men who crowd Bangkok airport" (*Economist* 1990a, 36).

Remarks like this one also acknowledge the centrality of sex to tourism: "There is too much at stake, too many vested interests determined to see the sex business continue and the image of Thailand as a sex paradise preserved. . . . [And even though the Tourist Authority of Thailand officially denies that many tourists visit Thailand for or even avail themselves of sexual services,] TAT, whose advertising features the beauty of Thai women, cannot ignore the tour buses which regularly drop off male and female tourists at Patpong and at the Japanese version Thaniya a few blocks away" (Handley 1989, 44). As *Rolling Stone's* informant on the red-light districts concludes, "Shutting down the Thai sex industry would be like shutting down the U.S. automobile industry" (Rhodes 1992, 113). By 1992 the *Economist* could speak slightingly of those "businessmen who fear . . . honesty about AIDS is damaging Thailand's tourist trade," while pointing out the irony in current laws that penalize neither clients, pimps, nor brothel owners but only prostitutes, the ones placed under arrest for "preying on foreign tourists" (*Economist* 1992, 33). Although the media were not yet admitting that it is the prostitute rather than the customer who is the chief object of exploitation, covering the AIDS epidemic at least made it possible for them to identify the exploiters.

Another aspect of the macroeconomic picture entailed calculating the epidemic's economic costs *beyond* potential losses to the tourist industry. Making these estimates forced the various authorities cited and hence the media themselves to speak openly, for the first time, about the total number of prostitutes, the kinds of establishments that employ them, and the experience of freelance sex work. The figures are presented with so little documentation that they are too wild to be considered even in the portion of Chapter 4 where we highlight the widely divergent figures and the difficulty of making economic pronouncements on the basis of them.

Dollar estimates for the damages are equally wild. Early in 1992 the *Far Eastern Economic Review* put at $8 billion the probable cost to Thailand of the untamed spread of AIDS between that date and the year 2000 (Handley 1992b, 30). Taking into account the loss of work time, training investment, and hospitalization costs to employers or health insurance plans, another estimate stated that AIDS could cost $8.7 billion in lost income, as well as $2 billion in foreign funds, and spike an increase in health costs by a factor of 65. This article, leading off the "Business" section of *U. S. News and World Report* (1992, 52) and illustrated by a photograph of scantily clad masseuses at the Mona Lisa waiting for customers, points out that "no aspect of the Thai economy has more to fear than the $5 billion tourist industry. . . . Sex tourism is believed to be shrinking." (If so, the routine estimate of tourist revenues had suddenly gone *up* by a billion dollars.) Under the same rubric of competing but enormous numbers, Dr. David Bloom is cited as estimating that the half-million AIDS victims projected by the year 2000 "will cost the Thai economy *$18 billion*, a figure equal to 23% of GDP in 1990" (*Economist* 1993, 42; emphasis added).

The goal of this bottom-line passion becomes clear when a more recent article—citing a UN study of eight Asian countries—includes Thailand, indicating that "rates of GDP have not so far been affected and are unlikely to be affected in the future" but expresses "alarm . . . that this view will make politicians complacent" and ready to ignore the social costs of the epidemic (*Economist* 1995, 26). In a similar vein, recent economic reports target AIDS as a "disaster" for Asia because it is not merely a sex worker's but, as Tokyo has belatedly become aware, a "businessman's disease, contracted on 'sex tours' around the region" (Barnathan 1993, 52).

Following the other strand of economic inquiry, the one centered on the sex workers' material conditions, led the Western media to issues of income inequality, increasing poverty in agricultural regions, and the opportunities—real and apparent—offered to the rural young by the urban labor market as a whole and the sex industry in particular. It was an Indian delegate to the 1991 international AIDS conference in Florence who was widely quoted in the press as stating pointedly, "This is a disease closely linked to poverty and prostitution." Implicitly, at least, these two problems were also being "closely linked" to each other; the *New Scientist* concluded, correctly if impractically, that reducing the spread of the disease in Asia "depends on improving women's education and status and providing other basic health care" (Brown and Concar 1991, 18).

According to the *Economist* (1989b, 30), certain critics, including Thai women's organizations, argue that "it is the duty of the government to shut down the [sex] business and find its employees respectable jobs." This article, whose headline refers to prostitutes as "tarts," adds superciliously that "such demands, although sincere, assume that this is what the young ladies want"; it goes on to cite the "challenge" to this view represented by Pasuk Phongpaichit's *From Peasant Girls to Bangkok Masseuses*, which stresses how high wages in the sex industry are even at the lower levels, in comparison with those paid for production, domestic, or other unskilled service work. The article does not indicate that the ILO study (which, cited this way, not simply as Pasuk's book, assumes the authority of an international agency and, behind it, the entire United Nations) was commissioned and carried out in the early 1980s and that therefore no one asked the sex workers where they stood on the matter of higher earnings versus shorter life expectancy. (And no one considers whether improving the status of women, as *New Scientist* advises, might mean offering a respectable wage for those "respectable jobs.")

A reporter for the *New York Times Magazine* actually posed the very question that the *Economist* evaded. His interlocutor, a Chiang Mai cosmetics saleswoman now earning one-quarter of her previous income as a prostitute, says she herself would never return to sex work. But some of her former colleagues, she adds, ask rhetorically, "Why work in a factory for 2,000 or 3,000 baht a month [\$80 to \$120] when one man for one night is maybe 1,000 baht?" "Maybe it means dying, too," the journalist points out. "Yes," she says, "maybe" (Erlanger 1991, 26). The ambiguity of this reply loses some of its purely literary quality in the light of the passage that precedes the exchange. There, the ex-prostitute explains how a shy country girl can bring herself to dance naked or sleep with strangers: "You make yourself empty inside." Her terse "maybe" resonates with that emptiness.

For the American reader, the earnings cited in such interviews expose a dimension of the sex industry that most media ignored prior to the AIDS crisis. The contrast is nowhere more dramatic than in *Rolling Stone*'s "Death in the Candy Store" (Rhodes 1992). Eight years earlier the sweet merchandise had only a collective identity—as part of the decor at that "Home for Wayward Vets," where half of Cowboy's string of thirty "girls" lived right upstairs and Rick Menand at the Grand Prix could get you whatever you wanted in the way of sexual services. Possessing no individual identity, the prostitutes had no stories, no voices, no connection to an economic history that had made them so available. With the wayward vets as the focus, there was no call even to remember E. J. Kahn's 1964 celebration of Thailand's abundant cheap labor. In 1992, when *Rolling Stone* explored the same bars, and interviewed the same Rick Menand, even though the story was about the epidemic, and not about prostitution, the sex workers and the poverty that drives them had become a necessary part of the narrative.

"Why is Thailand the whorehouse of the world?" *Rolling Stone* asks (Rhodes 1992, 105), and it is a far from rhetorical question. After some generalizations about the national character (compliant) and the economy (straitened), the article goes on to explain that "bar girls are the daughters of the poor" (70), and lest there be any doubt as to what that means, a "pull-quote" states unequivocally in bold type, "Most bar girls come from villages where the per capita income can be less than \$250 a year" (69). In this situation, the attraction of Bangkok for the girls and their families is palpable, and with the aid of more quotes from Pasuk—who, once again, is represented as having the whole UN speaking through her research—is spelled out. *Rolling Stone*, erstwhile admirer of a system where "Cowboy" could pose as a "self-made man," now tells us that in addition to those whom poverty lures to Bangkok, there are "darker scenarios, girls sold into bondage" (113). Without AIDS as an issue, we would not be privy to these "scenarios"; they enter the narrative only as adjuncts to the central story of AIDS.

Still, certain prejudices die hard, even when another version of the same reality is available. *Newsweek*'s take on the lure of the city and its (red) lights is that "many provincial women want a taste of big city life, and they are often tempted by the fancy clothes, gifts and gadgets they see other women bringing back from

jobs in the city" (Moreau 1992, 51). Immediately following this translation
of stringent material need into shallow consumerism is a quotation from an
American volunteer with Bangkok's Population and Community Development
Association, who laments, "It's difficult to create viable income-producing alternatives that can compete with the earning power of prostitution." This more
serious evaluation may not be taken into account by the journalist who cites it,
but it is given some space, space that would not have been available were it not
for the "Sex and Death" foregrounded in the article's title.

It is also the epidemic that provided a platform for a Thai to proclaim, first in
the English-language *Nation* of Bangkok and thence in the *World Press Review*,
"Long-term measures to eliminate poverty and create well-paying alternative
employment would help to make women less dependent on selling sex" and to
opine that in the short run, "allowing sex workers to form trade unions would
increase their bargaining power to demand condom use" (Ungpakorn 1994, 54).
For an article that routinely confuses "free sex" with commercial sex, its lexical
and conceptual opposite, this one nonetheless acknowledges the sex worker *as* a
worker in a way that few mass media reports do.

Other vantage points on the sex industry are provided by articles oriented
toward the anti-AIDS movement in Thailand, the medical aspects of the epidemic, or the combination, especially as embodied in the articles devoted to the
educational campaigns of Mechai Viravaidya, the Kingdom's "Mr. Condom."
One of the earliest public demonstrations about AIDS issues explicitly told
8,400 American sailors arriving for shore leave at Pattaya—now characterized as
"Thailand's most notorious sun-and-sand resort"— to "fire your torpedoes elsewhere" (*Economist* 1989a, 37). The same activists also made an attempt to confront a Danish sex-tour group at the Bangkok airport (Handley 1989, 45). In
both cases, police and government officials were clearly shown as protecting
visitors from demonstrators in order to protect the sex industry and the tourist
dollar—shielding the foreigners from annoyance, in short, so as to be able to
continue exposing them to a deadly virus.

As the government was forced into greater openness about the AIDS threat,
American media continued to represent the Thai prostitute as a pawn in the
agon between activists and officials. Since AIDS prevention and education campaigns and proposed legislation were informed by the same repressive spirit as
the earlier denials, activists were critical of the prevailing gender bias in the
exclusive focus on prostitutes (Handley 1992a, 29–30). It was a focus, however,
that obscured the *actual* prostitute from view, as, for example, did the account of
the brothels in Khon Kaen that increased their profit margins by adopting a con-
doms-only policy (*Economist* 1991a, 34). A program that attempted a "100% condom" policy in all establishments did address brothel owners by entailing
increasingly long periods of closure for successive offenses of noncompliance;
proof that condoms were not being used would be provided by employees'
requesting medical care for any sexually transmitted disease (Handley 1992a,
29–30). The deadly dilemma this might cause for the employee in need of med-

ical treatment and also in need of keeping her job is not part of the narrative, nor is the fact that all this policy-making about condoms in brothels addresses conditions in an illegal industry.

Prostitutes were also visible in the AIDS story as statistics. The figures reported for Chiang Mai indicate that the higher the price of the prostitute, the lower the infection rate. In media reports of these findings, the sex worker suddenly came into view as the one who sets the price: "72% of the prostitutes tested . . . *who charge* Baht 30–50 are infected, compared with 30% of those *who charge* Baht 50–100. Only 10% of those *who charge* more than Baht 100 are HIV-positive" (Lintner and Noung 1992, 31, emphasis added). This particular version of the story also asserts that the "most disturbing finding was that among prostitutes who had been in the trade for more than a year—regardless of how much they charge—70% of those tested were positive." It is not clear from text or context on whose behalf the disturbance manifested itself: longer-term prostitutes or the poor, unsuspecting foreigners likely to hire the more expensive merchandise and thus get doubly cheated.

Newsweek's "Sex and Death in Thailand" summarizes the case squarely: "Asia is the newest battleground in the war against AIDS. The reason: prostitution" (Moreau 1992, 50). This article emphasizes the difference between "good" and "bad" Thai women in their approach to safe sex. Whereas prostitutes "are often too shy or too frightened to ask clients to wear" condoms, married women have taken to demanding them, "confronting their husbands and talking openly about sex in way that would have shocked their mothers" (50–51). Information about the sources of prostitutes' "shyness" and "fear," and hence about working conditions in the industry that employs them, is not explicitly provided, but through the praise of married women's greater assertiveness it is there for the reader to discover.

Science magazine's discussion of plans to test an AIDS vaccine also provides inadvertent information about the sex industry. Pointing to a bar whose doorway is framed by Christmas lights far out of season, a Johns Hopkins AIDS researcher is quoted as observing that "Christmas lights are pathognomic for indirect bars . . . a distinctive signal that, in addition to drinks, sex is for sale" (J. Cohen 1995, 905). Learning to "read" social symbolism as if it were a set of medical symptoms is an occupational disease of researchers that is apparently not worth commenting on, even when, as here, the "diagnosis" is inaccurate: In Thailand, what Westerners identify as Christmas lights are always in season; they provide a way to identify restaurants, particularly in the countryside. The actual point of the researcher's observation, though, is that he and his team "have found that 'direct' commercial sex workers (CSWs)—the ones who work in brothels—would not make good efficacy-trial participants [in the vaccine test], largely because they are hard to keep track of. But indirect CSWs, such as the ones at this bar and the many women who work in massage parlors, are less transient and may work out fine" (905). This discourse, chilling in both its inhumanity and its complete lack of self-consciousness, does offer a way into an interesting story. For reasons not specified or even inquired into by the journalist, prostitutes in the most confined work environment are transient, "harder to keep track of" than those in less formal situations. Thereby hangs a tale that, to put the matter in the most favorable light, one may pursue now that it has been indicated.

In defense of both the reporter and his interviewee, it might be argued that the apparent callousness functions in the service of a good cause. If they are going to test a vaccine—whose successful development is something that would benefit all humanity, after all—they need human subjects who can be responsibly followed through the trials. One category of at-risk subjects can be readily followed up; the other is harder to track. Whether the particular work site is related to the stability or transience of the group and what characteristics make it so are irrelevant to the researcher who has, in any event, identified a means of distinguishing "reliable" from "unreliable" subjects. But this line of reasoning carries conviction only to those who share the assumption that the only real story of the Thai sex industry is the story about AIDS. For anyone else, it raises far more questions than it answers.

The otherwise impersonal struggle against AIDS acquires a human face in the articles—numerous enough for us to call them a sub-genre, rather like the travel pieces about the Oriental Hotel—that focused on Mechai Viravaidya. In *People* magazine the piece describing the antics of "Thailand's P. T. Barnum of family planning and safe sex" (Grogan 92) is compartmentalized under "Medics." Its accompanying photographs respectively show Mechai in three poses: in their Bangkok garden with his wife and daughter, distributing fliers to uniformed schoolgirls paddling up a canal to class, and handing pamphlets to go-go dancers at a club called Goldfinger. ("Always insist your customer uses a condom," this literature advises.) Mechai's own colorful story is inflated until, like a prophylactic in one of his own condom-blowing contests, it covers up the whole issue of commercial sex, with the exception of that photo op at Goldfinger.

Although extending the cult of personality, other publications allow a bit more of Mechai's message to slip in. They all stress publicity moves like the "cops and rubbers" campaign in which traffic police handed out condoms—but whose punning name was clearly intended for an international and not a Thai audience—and Mechai's public appearances dressed from head to toe in a condom. But the *Economist* also encouraged the activist to speak about the roots of the problem in rural poverty: "Many of the girls who work in massage parlours have more or less been sold to them by their impoverished parents.... Mr. Mechai compares the relationship between the average Thai peasant and the country's economy to 'a dog watching an aeroplane'" (*Economist* 1990b, 40). It is unclear, of course, whether the message about the growing income disparity between the "haves" and the "have-nots" survives this metaphor.

For the *New York Times*, Mechai, perhaps disingenuously, distinguishes the tourist industry as such (which he claims he is trying to save by controlling the spread of AIDS) from *sex* tourism, which he openly attacks. Although agreeing that it is "hopeless" to try to eliminate commercial sex in Thailand, Mechai states unequivocally, "I find it disturbing that men who are products of highly developed economies come to a developing nation solely to exploit their women and children" (Shenon 1992b, 11). A more direct statement to hurl in the face of the Western reader is hard to imagine. Yet once again, it is AIDS, not commercial sex, that provides the motive force of the article, as it does of Mechai's mission.

It is instructive to contrast these articles with Christopher Hitchens's 1986 *Nation* column, cited earlier, where the pre-AIDS emphasis is on the (other) occupational illnesses of Thai prostitutes and their exploitation as workers who are forbidden to organize. Exactly seven years later, the *Nation* published Lillian Robinson's "In the Penile Colony" (Robinson 1993, see 6–12 above), the only American magazine article to connect the culture of the go-go bars with both development planning and the labor market for desperately poor young women. Ironically, the only line that the editors chose to highlight in a piece that tried not to treat the prostitutes as either passive carriers of a disease or passive children, was a statement hastily added in response to an editorial query: "One study estimates that 50 percent of the child prostitutes are HIV positive" (494). Even the *Nation* apparently felt it had to pay that much homage to the received wisdom that the story in the bars is about AIDS or child prostitution or, of course, child prostitutes with AIDS.

Because the convention is so pervasive, a survey of media treatment of the exploitation of children in Thailand's sex trade is as provocative as the one focused on AIDS. In a move that is suggestive in both senses of the word, the cover of *Time* magazine's issue for 21 June 1993 blared "Sex for Sale." Red letters made bolder by the black and white photo of a "Bangkok bar girl" being fondled by an anonymous Everyman client spell out the remainder of the tag: "An alarming boom in prostitution debases the women and children of the world." The article titled "The Skin Trade" features Thailand prominently in anecdotal examples and statistical information, drawing heavily on the stereotype of Thailand as *the* sex tourist destination. Early in the piece the general lack of government concern about prostitution enters the discussion in this way: "If 100,000 German men choose to visit Thailand on package sex tours, who is to object? Only recently has anyone begun to ask how many of Thailand's 2 million prostitutes are minors; how many have been sold by parents or husbands as indentured servants to brothel owners" (Hornblower 1993, 46). The passage neatly summarizes one of our major points. That a hundred thousand Germans take sex tours to a particular country becomes an issue—or a problem—only if children are involved and possibly even sold into bonded labor.

Before trotting out most of the sensational numbers and examples of abuse found in international prostitution, however, the *Time* piece takes an interesting direction, similar to that of Nicholas D. Kristof's *New York Times* article "Asian Children Sacrificed to Prosperity's Lust" (1996). Both invoke the role of global economic forces and the development of "free" markets in countries new to them. *Time*'s article makes an indirect argument about a continuum of exploitation of one nation's women by an economically more powerful nation: the Czech

Republic by Germany, Yugoslavia and Hungary by Italy, and Russia by Israel. Kristof is more explicit in his analysis. He claims that three factors help create the problem of child prostitution in Southeast Asia: first, "rising economic development," which increases the demand for child prostitution while outstripping supply; second, the "rise of capitalism," which creates markets "not just for rice and pork but also for virgin girls"; and third, "the fear of AIDS" (1, 6).

Although both articles invoke global economic conditions as factors in the sexual exploitation of both adults and children, neither does much with this information, focusing instead on sensational items geared to hook and appall readers. Kristof, for example, includes a posting from the Internet claiming that in Cambodia "a six year-old is available for US $3." This precedes the subhead, "Family: Mother and Sister Pimp for the Kids." Another subhead reads, "Betrayal: Selling a Daughter for a Karaoke System." But the text hedges this supposition in favor of conjecture about how a destitute Filipina mother funded this luxury item: "Where did the family get the money for such a purchase? *Apparently in part* from Mrs. Olyares' oldest daughters, aged 10 and 12" (6, emphasis added), who were taken by a Japanese man claiming to want to photograph the girls. With such a rhetorical construction, the grotesque, sordid details overwhelm any possible broader economic, cultural, social, historical analysis. Likewise, the demand side of the market equation is completely overshadowed by parental greed. A British documentary aired by the U.S. cable show *Investigative Reports* in the fall of 1993 also highlights parental guilt, showing the father of a young girl rescued from a Bangkok brothel as a gambler and drug addict who sold his daughter to feed his habits. The two reports reduce the ostensible causes to the dysfunctional family level.

The same cannot be said about the second part of the *Time* cover story with regard to demand. "Defiling the Children" concludes with the role that customers play; it quotes a French priest and long-time opponent of child prostitution who says, "We live in a world of contradictions, lies and cowardice. This problem is not just Bangkok's, Colombo's, Manila's. It's Paris's, Brussels's, Rome's. It's the nice respectable white man who goes down there to molest these kids" (Serrill 1993, 55). Yet even though the priest makes an important point about the hypocrisy of developed nations, First World culpability is reduced to deviant individual behavior, effectively eliding broader social analysis.

The focus on individual culpability is reinscribed and placed on the shoulders of German tourists in the article's closing example which returns readers full circle with an explanation of the Lauda Airlines controversy. The charter flight company advertised its services and destinations with a mock postcard featuring a bare-breasted little girl with a heart-shaped framed inscription "From Thailand with Love." The greeting side of the fake missive from abroad told its recipient, "Got to close now. The tarts in the Bangkok Baby Club are waiting for us," and was signed "Werner, Gunther, Fritzl, Morsel, and Joe." The shocking forthrightness of the advertisement is all that *Time* points out to its readers, reinforcing the earlier suggestion that only the bizarre and perverted behavior of certain individuals gives rise to the problem. By implication, then, other types of sex tourism aren't really a problem, because the sex workers involved are adults—people over the age of eighteen or twelve, as the case may be—who have made "free choices" in the "free market" global economy. This conclusion is given further credence by the tag line following the article's title: "In the basest effect of the burgeoning sex trade, the search for newer thrills has chained increasing numbers of girls and boys to prostitution." The child prostitution industry, evidently, results solely from decadent First World citizens searching for "newer thrills" and has nothing to do with global processes perpetuated by governments and multinational companies working on inherited notions of Otherness that include damaging assumptions about race and sex.

One of the most salient attacks on the child prostitution industry in Thailand came recently from longtime children's rights activist, lawyer, and author Andrew Vachss. Offered a deal he couldn't refuse, Vachss was "lent" the character of Batman and the weight of Time/Warner Communications to wage his war against child abuse on a larger stage, address an audience he doesn't often reach, and launch a boycott of Thai products in the hope of effecting change within the Kingdom. He produced a novel about the caped crusader titled *Batman: The Ultimate Evil* (1995b), which also provided the narrative for two full-color DC comics and an audio novel. But, as Vachss told us in an interview (1995a), he "couldn't care less about Batman"; his main agenda was the establishment of the organization spearheading the boycott: Don't! Buy! Thai! "Batman is a story and Thailand is not enough of a story," he explained, "not enough to cause change." Whatever the effect of D!B!T! Vachss is an intelligent and committed advocate. David Hechler's article about child sex tourism (1995), which Vachss commissioned at his own expense, appears at the end of the novel and the second comic book. Accessible and factual, Hechler's article avoids much of the sensationalism found in the popular media, leaving that to Batman's exploits. Thailand is the focus of Hechler's article, although Vachss himself says that it "is not by any means the only offender in this situation" and that it is "not enough of a story."

Perhaps the matter is one not of quantity but of focus. Thailand is, in fact, conspicuous by its presence in the popular media. So Thailand *is* a story, but audiences always receive the same story. The photos for *Time*'s "Defiling the Children" and the bulk of its text center on a man who pimps young boys in Moscow, yet Thailand figures prominently in statistics and examples, as it did in "The Skin Trade." Both Hechler's article and "Defiling the Children" explain that entire villages in northern Thailand are virtually bereft of young girls because they have been sold into the sex industry, and that estimates of HIV infection for child sex workers run as high as 50 percent. Found in virtually every story in the popular media about the sex industry in Thailand, the specter of AIDS lurking in the specter of child prostitution becomes the *real* story audiences receive.

"Defiling the Children" neatly illustrates this point. Most of the Thai portion of the article tells the story of Armine, a twelve-year-old who puts a face on the thousands of young girls "sold into prostitution, often by their parents willing to sacrifice a daughter for payments that range as high as $8,000" (Serrill 1993, 54). But this amount of money is presented in a vacuum. Why is $8,000—or $8—too small a sum for one's daughter? Would $8,000,000 be more acceptable? Why would people accept any amount of money for a child? What are the factors that make this move an option? Like the *Investigative Reports* documentary, the article gives us nothing but parental ignorance or dissembling. The parents tell the reporter they knew the girl was going to work in a beach resort, but not as a prostitute. The particular example ends with the police finding the girl. "But they arrived too late: Armine is HIV positive and will die of AIDS" (54). The simplistic causal relationship in which HIV always leads to death by AIDS and the assertion that the police are "too late" because she is already infected—and for no other reason—reflect the other oversimplifications operative here, the ones that result from decontexualizing human lives and willfully ignoring the many factors that shape human choices. This leads to telling the same story over and over again.

If Thailand provides a synecdoche for the international sex industry, then the ubiquitous case study that constitutes "the human element" in journalism functions as a synecdoche for the industry in Thailand. Virtually every article deploys this same standard format: the opening narrates one child's horrific condition in the present tense, the journalistic "now," to draw readers in. Once hooked and disgusted, readers are told the main point of the story—governmental reforms, government neglect, worse AIDS statistics, new survey statistics, or whatever. Then the child of the introduction is reinvoked. When we meet her in the conclusion we are told how little the story's topic has affected her destiny; she dwells in the squalor, disease, and degradation of the journalistic present. This device, deployed by *Time*, the *New York Times*, *Far Eastern Economic Review*, and others, most recently by CBS's *60 Minutes* in October 1996, is not the problem; how it is deployed often is. As with the conclusions one is led to reach about the demand side—that the industry is the result of perverse Western individuals—the victim case study focuses on individual misery, often the result of alleged greed on the part of unscrupulous parents or other relatives. Almost never is the individual placed in a local, national, and international context that explains why the people there have the choices they have, and why they make certain choices and not others.

One might think that media sources closer to the scene would avoid some of the problems of decontextualization that foreign outlets perpetrate and perpetuate. But the most respected English-language newspaper in Thailand, the *Bangkok Post*, also falls prey to this journalistic trap. Covering the Chuan administration's crackdown on child prostitution, the Sunday edition on 17 January 1993 devoted its weekly feature "A Post Inquiry" to the fate of sex workers rounded up in the government actions. The ever present case study article discussed the situation of sixteen-year-old Noinar, who was arrested and sent home. Like the *Time* and *New York Times* articles, this one simply states that the lack of local jobs and greedy parents were joint culprits in the girl's entering the sex industry. Noinar's mother says, "The money meant so much to us. We had a feeling it wasn't a good thing to do. It felt like we were selling our own daughter. But we didn't have a choice" (Charasdamrong and Khuenkaew 1993, 19). The unexplained absence of employment possibilities takes a back seat to the family's economic plight, occulting any possible connection between the two. The main article, "Ex-Child Prostitutes Facing Many Hardships after Crackdown," likewise invokes the mysterious dearth of work. It cites a multitude of officials in the northeastern region of the country who echo the words of one public welfare chief: "Returning home after the crackdown means loss of jobs and incomes. They're now unemployed and there are only a few jobs here" (18).

That these women have little education, few qualifications, and even fewer job prospects reveal some of the local, national, and international reasons for the existence of the sex industry, yet both officials and the media refuse to see these facts as causes, and instead invoke the hardships the crackdown is imposing on individuals and families. They ignore the further fact that hardships also exist when the industry operates, and invariably avoid the conclusion that the lack of local jobs helps meet the labor supply for sweatshops as well as the sex industry. Such articles thus point toward a context that could help readers make some sense of the situation but rely instead on sensational statistics and horrible stories, while remaining silent about possible causal relations. The government, in fact, is perceived not as rectifying hardship but as creating it, and this not by failing to provide or show the way to alternatives for victims of the crackdown but by cracking down in the first place. Local media thus perpetuate the folly of the international media: the feature's title implies that if the government stayed out of the way, hardships for child prostitutes and their families would not exist.

An article in *Spin* magazine (Vollmann 1993) takes this media myopia, sensationalism, and decontextualization to jaw-dropping depths. Its tag lines give readers a sense of the adventure and horrors that await them: "IN THAILAND, pimps buy young girls from poor families, then rent them as concubines. William T. Vollmann travels through jungles and dungeons to purchase a prisoner and set her free" (74). The journalist-as-hero/savior lives on in this author, who has written fiction and travel accounts about the sex industry in different parts of the world. To apprehend Vollmann's world view and subject position, consider his introductory typology of prostitutes:

At the top of the list are the prostitutes who really love you, the ones who marry you for life or even just one night but always with sincerity; the ones who sing after making love. Next come those who love the money, the vacations, and the new clothes. They are honest about what they do, at least sometimes. Well-paid, professional though they are, they may become fond of you. If not, they will pretend that they are and have a good laugh later.

Then there are the professionals who may not be quite as well-paid, the ones you order at the bar by number who say: "I smoke you!" and rush to gobble the penis down. They're the ones who say: "Me no money. Papa Mama very poor!" and if you ask them if they like this job they say softly: "Me no like."—But many will come to feel affection for you just the same; they can be made happy; and some are sex addicts who in any case would need to give what they're lucky enough to be able to sell.

Below them come the Kong Toi girls laughing and singing: "*I fuck you why, I doan know why. . . .*" You pick them out from behind glass in dirty brothels that are lit up like Christmas trees; they don't bother to say much; they don't let you touch them; they spread their legs and then hurry away. These are all voluntary prostitutes, although they may not like their profession for its own sake; the same is true of most janitors, garbagemen, and clerk typists. A little below them are the drug-addicted ladies of the American streets who must trick and claw and extort; most have sad lives; many were started on their career by rape or incest; and yet they bear responsibility for what they do tonight and tomorrow; no one is "exploiting" them; perhaps they exploit themselves. For me they comprise the baseline of the tolerable.

Below *them* begins the inferno of actual slavery. . . . For me perhaps the saddest phenomenon of all is forced child prostitution. Most of the time children don't have to be chained, only commanded (Vollmann 1993, 74–76).

Without being given the explicit criteria that Vollmann uses to create his hierarchy of female sex workers, we can only assume that income, pleasure, and choice figure into it in some way. Yet near the top of the list are the penis gobblers who softly say they don't like the work and that their parents are poor; evidently no correlation exists between filial responsibility and fellatio for cash. In fact, some are fortunate because, as "sex addicts," they are able to sell what they would otherwise give away, which is what clients have always suspected. Still in the realm of "voluntary" sex workers are those who are chosen by number from behind glass walls. None of these women, so Vollmann assures us, is "exploited." Only those who dwell in an "inferno of actual slavery," those who are "imprisoned" and "chained to the wall," count as exploited, especially when they are children.

Since the audience of *Spin* overlaps somewhat with Vachss's Batman audience—teenage males—we imagine a Bart Simpsonish "Coooool!" escaping their lips as they visualize Vollmann's empirically gathering this vast store of prostitute knowledge, and perhaps even as they think about Vollmann himself. His pity for the sex slaves, then, may be a little too late. All other categories of sex worker are voluntary and therefore cool—print confirmation of all his readers' wet dreams. (That *Spin*'s publisher is the son of *Penthouse*'s publisher may further aid this audience response.) But Vollmann's definitions of exploitation and individual volition echo those offered by sex tourists, which Vollmann also is. After telling readers that he plans to purchase one of these pitiable slaves and deposit her at a Bangkok shelter for abused women, he and his photographer head to the southern border town of Ranong, where they establish themselves as sex tourists looking for young flesh. To establish a reputation with "any whoremasters seeking credit references" (78), they quickly procure several "voluntary" prostitutes who, he claims, often like their jobs (76). Each time, they take women in their late teens or early twenties and tell the pimps that they yearn for younger ones. The two men work long, hard hours establishing their cover.

The would-be rescuers get advice about the major, dangerous players in the business from a clergyman familiar with the local sexploitation industry. They also draft a Burmese prostitute named "Miss Yohne Yhan" to provide translation, undercover work, and sexual services; Vollmann tells us that she "was proud that prostitutes can be happy and enjoy what they do" (81). Moving the narrative along at a Hemingwayesque syntactic clip, Vollmann finds a brothel of imprisoned sex workers, which he and the photographer visit in order to identify potential candidates for rescue. They find one. Pretending that the photographer has fallen in love with her, they return with Yohne Yhan to tell the brothel owner that they wish to purchase the young lady. The asking price is 50,000 baht (US $2,000), which Vollmann rejects as too high. They bargain and get the price down to 7,000 baht (US $280) which "sounded more reasonable" because "if it costs ten dollars to sleep with a woman once, then why should it cost more than $300 to marry her and sleep with her for life?" (82). Ever the sex tourist, Vollmann essentializes all human relationships as economic ones. Sounding like any Patpong client who claims that women cost you one way or another and that buying sex is simply a more honest way of working male-female relationships, he allows his empathy for enslaved girls to give way to economic pragmatism.

When the tactic of buying the girl from the brothel falls through, the backup plan results in having a young girl delivered to their hotel. Named Sukanja, she gives her age variously as sixteen, fifteen, and fourteen, but she "looks 12" (142). Readers are privy to Vollmann's self-reflective ruminations meant to confirm he's really a decent sort deep down: "I had wondered whether I would feel any desire for such a young girl. As I gazed upon her in the skimpy pajama-dress that showed her dirty brown knees, I found that I had in me only pity and determination to protect her" (143). Given his recent exploits, we are relieved to read even this self-serving announcement. Vollmann's indignation appears again when he asks the girl about her background and work. Through Miss Yohne Yhan as interpreter, we hear, "She say father no house. They sell her to buy house. This job she no like" (143). The author responds, "Her father sold her?" Confirming the article's tag line, the question addresses parental greed only.

After fleeing the scene, Vollmann and the photographer place Sukanja at the Saskawa Women's Education and Training Center in Bangkok. During the long trip the girl shows no joy, no trust, no understanding of what is happening to her; she just can't comprehend exactly how much these brave lads are doing for her. Once at the center, she withdraws further and further from Vollmann and the photographer. Instead of the massive outpouring of gratitude he expects, Vollmann receives sullen hostility, a response he cannot fathom. Sukanja eventually refuses to see them when they come to visit her. Converting his disappointment to anger and confirming greedy parents as the villains in these tales, Vollmann says he would like to find Sukanja's father: "We want to meet him. I want to give him some money and then I want to tell him I will kill him if he sells his daughter again" (147).

The anger dissipates, though, when he actually meets the father, a frail, thin man living in an equally fragile shack in the northeastern part of the country. It also turns out that it was not he but his son-in-law who arranged Sukanja's contract. Yet, the father says, "Prostitute no problem. Any job that gets money is no problem" (148). The causes of the family's economic plight are ignored and only the perceived immediate solution, short-term cash, is mentioned. Vollmann's sympathy, withheld from prostitutes chosen by number or even those who explicitly say of their jobs, "Me no like," now extends to the father: "I looked over at this man who had nothing and was nothing. He did not seem to be a bad person. Hardly anybody ever is. I give him another hundred [baht—US $4]" (148). His pity stems from equating material wealth with individual worth and determining that this guy was a cipher. Likewise, Vollmann can justify his pity by explaining that bad conditions make good people do bad things. This nugget of wisdom, though, appears with no context whatsoever, no explanation of the conditions or their possible causes, and no thought that he himself may have some part in perpetuating these conditions when he assumes the role of sex tourist.

In the narrative's closing anecdote the author, photographer, and interpreter go to another town and hire some more young prostitutes. The three attempt to persuade these workers to leave their jobs, but they refuse. The translator says for the girls, "No way. Never. They very very happy this job. She is like Sukanja father, no brain thinking. In her village so much come to this job because it's so poor. Many many normally come here." Asked if they want to stay the night at the hotel, the translator speaks for the women in the article's final line: "They prefer to go back to work" (148).

The end of the article echoes the sentiments found in the introductory list of prostitute categories. What, given their destitute situation, are these women to do? We read no questions about why the poverty is so extreme and pervasive; no theory that might explain why so many poor families sell their daughters into the sex industry or why this industry is so lucrative; no consideration of the demand side of the equation. All we get is the same journalistic sleight of hand highlighting human misery, a trick that fools the eye and makes it unable to see the machinery of the act. Vollmann's relationship with the sex industry reinforces the idea that only children and sex slaves are exploited, for to be exploited one has to be under the age of consent or literally chained to a bed in a room with no windows. All others are "voluntary" workers who might even be counted among the fortunate, given the size of their paychecks relative to their education and skill levels. (Why they have such low levels, apparently, is not relevant.) The "free" market means "free" choices for those who participate in it. The rationale of the international sex tourism industry that occurs either explicitly or implicitly in the popular media is the same one that sex tourists themselves advance.

It is fair to say that without AIDS and child prostitution, the sex industry in Thailand would continue to receive as little notice in the popular press as it did in the earlier decades. It would not be cast as "a problem." Only when the client or a child is threatened by the industry is it interpreted as a problem. Even *with* the focus on AIDS and child prostitution, the fact that perhaps 4 percent of the country's total female population is employed as sex workers still does not count, evidently, as "a problem" because so little is heard about it in international discourse. If one listens to the laudatory accounts of development in Southeast Asia that grace business magazines and newspapers, these women are, in fact, part of the solution, bringing home paychecks in amounts undreamed of for uneducated, unskilled rural workers. Their situation is an assumed good insofar as their work furthers tourism and the narrowly defined goals of national economic development.

In a sense, the silence surrounding the foundations of the sex industry and the assumptions regarding its role in the overall economic picture constitute the Othering of the problem. The attention of the outside world concentrates elsewhere, not on the "adult" sex workers and the external influences that make this industry an important component in tourism development. From this shortsighted perspective, the "clean industry" of tourism remains pure, so tourism is surely not a problem. Although the constitution of "a problem" in various international discursive practices has been the subtext if not the pretext for this chapter, it is beyond the purview of this book to address this issue in explicitly theoretical terms. Instead, using a series of inductive moves to point toward theoretical possibilities and parameters, we have revealed some of the assumptions underpinning the construction of "a problem" and how they help establish and maintain a site where such an industry can flourish.

3

LANGUAGES OF TOURISM

The discourse of tourism is a form of
extreme language.
—J. Febas Borra, "Semiología
del lenguaje turistica"

Tourism in many Third World countries
is little more than whorism.
—Harry G. Matthews, *International
Tourism: A Political and
Social Analysis*

One of the ironies attendant on the recent construction of sex tourism—or,
indeed, any tourism—as a "problem" is that for so long it was posited as a "solution." For almost half a century the rhetoric of tourism as a panacea for Third
World ills has been wedded to the discourse of development, in a context where
the euphemism for the "ailment" we call poverty is under- (or "less") development (whence the complementary notion that more development means less
poverty). Tourism-as-solution has been widely embraced at the international
and national levels, and with each "success" story the languages of tourism have
multiplied and diversified to trumpet the success far and wide. The discourse
that makes possible accounts retailing the triumph of tourism is complemented
by discursive practices that narrowly limit the definition of "problems" caused

by the same industry and the economic assumptions that construct it. They are the sinister twins of one another.

The movement of people from metropolitan center to underdeveloped rural or urban site for the purpose of exploiting local resources can, of course, be found in both colonial and tourist projects. Thus, in the postcolonial, postmodern moment, cartographies (that is, economic and social representations or mappings) of desire are being drawn by market economies, international investment and development and global tourism. With all tourist sites, commerce depends on the construction of a desirable Other—often one that titillates as well as appeals— capable of attracting outsiders. This construction can create inequitable interactions between local and traveler that actually serve to reinforce disparity while being represented as mutually beneficial. In these international interactions, including the sexual ones, the flow from center to periphery, from here to there, is virtually unidirectional; the trickle in the opposite direction largely provides education for an elite academic and political class. The disparity of interactions can be charted in this flow: when "they" come "here," we educate them; when "we" go "there," they service us.

Although some academic writing about tourism broaches these concerns, they are largely missing from the other languages of tourism, which discuss universal understanding, cross-cultural empathy, and mutually profitable global-local relations. John F. Kennedy's famous statement that each tourist is a cultural ambassador reveals the optimism projected at the dawn of mass jet travel. Echoing Kennedy's sentiment, the 1963 United Nations Conference on International Travel and Tourism proclaimed that tourism would destroy stereotypes about the world's peoples while perpetuating peace and prosperity. Such rhetoric nicely fit First World policymaking in the transition from earlier Cold War strategies to those that invoked "hearts and minds." That 1967 witnessed both UNESCO's Year of the Tourist and the U.S. contract with Thailand to provide R&R sites further illustrates the intimate connection between tourism promotion and global policy formation. The optimism surrounding the beneficent uniting of tourist travel and policy implementation spread rapidly through the UN, UNESCO, the WTO (World Tourism Organization), the World Bank, and the IMF; each created bureaucratic structures to perpetuate tourism. Who in the world's developing nations dared doubt the wisdom of these respect-worthy institutions that so controlled the world's capital and politics? Tourism as a central development strategy for the Third World—with international agencies and foreign governments lending funds, providing credits, and proffering expertise—became an easy sale.

But the mystified rhetoric of peace and understanding was belied by the pragmatics at work. Despite their both emerging from the same pro-tourism camp, the 1977 Pacific Area Travel Association slogan, "The consumer—the only person who matters," counters the Hilton hotel chain's encapsulation of pro-travel propaganda: "World peace through world travel." The tensions reflected in the two mottoes highlight the issues that we address in this chapter, which examines the languages of tourism operative at the international and national levels, and in the external and internal representations of the nation and culture *qua* commodity from official government brochures to travel agency come-ons. We read these representations against the grain to grasp the implications and effects of the rhetoric deployed in support of this largest of world industries. With Thailand as our focus, the vast sex industry becomes the ever present absence haunting many of these discourses. This integral component of Thailand's tourism success, present in the statistical information but missing from the lush tropical scenery and images of gold-roofed temples, shows us problem-solving's other side. When every year becomes, in essence, "Visit Thailand Year," how does a nation continually repackage itself for consumption abroad? And how does this packaging play out as national policy at home? The cartographies of desire shimmer with alluring lands and peoples, as do the many languages of tourism that the cartographers and imagemakers seek to represent.

International Representations: Tourism in Worldspeak

More than six hundred delegates from eighty-four countries around the globe descended on Rome—arguably the destination with the longest continuous history of mass tourism—in August and September 1963 for the United Nations Conference on International Travel and Tourism (McIntosh 1977, 3). This event, which confirmed U.S. and World Bank activities of the 1950s in support of tourism and gave the impetus for a number of initiatives within and outside the UN's own structure, from UNESCO's involvement with the creation of model tourism projects in developing nations (including Thailand's historic site at Sukothai, the first "national" capital) to the establishment of the World Tourism Organization and its regional avatars. Perhaps equally important, the UN conference was also the fundamental source of the discourse that is now codified as the rationale for international tourism.

Along with two other UN documents, the Universal Declaration on Human Rights (1948) and the International Covenant on Economic, Social, and Cultural Rights (1966)—both of which assert "everyone's" right to rest and leisure, including paid holidays—the Rome conference established what may be called the "high style" (and certainly the high road) of tourism discourse. This approach links international travel with cultural enrichment and exchange, greater understanding among individuals and nations, and the simultaneous and purportedly harmonious goals of preserving the local within greater internationalization of "everyone's" experience.

Subsequent commentators have challenged the uncritically optimistic empiricism underlying the notion that greater knowledge leads to greater harmony or that such harmony, even if achieved through "understanding," has much to do with averting international conflict. But the assertion that it does, which became routine after the 1963 conference, has in fact played a strategic role in peace and human rights negotiations over the past three decades. In the formulation and implementation of the International Covenant on Civil and Political Rights (1966) and the Helsinki Accords (1976), the appeals that all nations permit freedom of travel in both directions led to the establishment and in some cases the enforcement of human rights even more fundamental than the right to travel and leisure: continued survival and freedom of movement within and across national borders.

Nonetheless, the UN conference was not conducted solely or even principally on the level of altruistic abstraction. Rather, it consistently linked the objectives of improved international relations to those of economic development, highlighting the role of tourism in both areas, and concluding in its final document "that it is incumbent on governments to stimulate and coordinate national tourism activities (UN 1963, 17). The Statutes of the World Tourism Organization, as recognized by the UN General Assembly, state that organization's goals as contributing "to economic development, international understanding, peace, prosperity, and universal respect for, and observation of, human rights and fundamental freedoms for all, without distinction as to race, sex, language or religion (WTO Statutes, qtd. in Hague 1989 preamble).

The UN's bland assumption that peace and profitability are congruous and even comfortable companions is anticipated in a document produced under contract to the U.S. Department of Commerce and published by the department in 1961. Essentially a feasibility study of Asian and Pacific tourism development commissioned from experts in the economics of tourism in that region, this document includes a foreword by Luther Hodges, secretary of commerce in the Kennedy administration, that typifies contemporary Cold War/Cold Peace rhetoric in support of tourism-as-development. Every sentence is informed by the tendency of American government monologues to identify world peace, capitalist profits, and political freedom as a single ideological package:

> The development of tourism in many countries of the world has been a major factor in building international understanding and, at the same time, in providing a significant source of income for those nations which have encouraged and fostered it. . . .
>
> Tourists bring wealth into a country—wealth in the form of good will and understanding; wealth in the form of foreign exchange, vitally needed for international trade; wealth in the form of financing for further tourist and other economic development.
>
> It is the policy of the United States Government to assist free nations in making the fullest possible use of their own resources in order that they remain economically viable and politically free. . . .
>
> This . . . [book] was prompted by a desire to assist the countries in the Pacific and Far East region—which of course includes some nations already highly self-

sustained—in building up the basis of a prosperous tourist business as an element in their economic development. (Hodges 1961, np).

It is from this perspective that the book's assessment of Thailand's possibilities as a destination for tourism has to be understood. The Kingdom was deemed to possess "enormous tourism potentials," since it has the right "raw materials to development tourism. Its people are friendly and their way of life is colorful. Bangkok, the tourist center of the country, is packed with attractions" (127). It is almost redundant to conclude as the authors of the study do, "Our enthusiasm for the potential of Thai tourism is considerable" (127) and worth recalling that this bottom line is prefaced by an official statement in which metaphoric and material "wealth" serve equivalent, if not indeed identical, discursive functions.

International documents about tourism subsequent to 1963 almost invariably pay homage to the conference at Rome, as well as acknowledging the contributions and frequently incorporating the language of the applicable UN declarations and a growing list of other international gatherings, especially those at Manila, Acapulco, Honolulu, and New Delhi. Thus, the Tourism Bill of Rights and Tourist Code, adopted at the WTO's Sixth General Assembly in Sofia, extends the rights to both work and leisure enunciated in the Universal Declaration of Human Rights to include the right "to travel freely for education and pleasure and to enjoy the advantages of tourism, both within . . . [one's] country of residence and abroad" (Sofia preamble). And it takes from the Manila Declaration on World Tourism (1980), "which emphasizes the true, human dimension of tourism," its inspiration to use tourism to protect and enhance "the tourism resources which are part of mankind's heritage, with a view to contributing to the establishment of a new international economic order" (Sofia preamble). Nowhere in the document is there any indication of what kind of "new international economic order" is envisaged.

The *Hague Declaration on Tourism* (1989), produced by an international colloquium under the joint sponsorship of the Inter-Parliamentary Union (a worldwide organization to which 112 national parliaments and the European Parliament all belong), and the World Tourism Organization, begins with the standard references to predecessor documents and their high-minded appeals. A series of numbered "Principles" follows, collectively covering everything from the threat to tourism represented by terrorism to the proper training of travel industry personnel. The heart of the document is a series of "Conclusions" and "Recommendations" (many of which are, in fact, problem statements and proposed solutions) that place the pragmatics of running the business under the rubric—albeit at some distance—of world peace and human rights.

Recent documents appeal to the principles enunciated in earlier ones to address some of the abuses that have accompanied tourism in general and, in particular, mass tourism to less developed countries. Environmental destruction, exacerbation of economic inequality, direct exploitation, and health-related problems (including discrimination against HIV-positive travelers) are among the issues implicitly or explicitly mentioned in statements attempting to make concrete the promise that tourism promotes understanding. In this spirit, tourism professionals and suppliers of travel services are enjoined *"in particular"* to "refrain from encouraging the use of tourism for all forms of exploitation of others" (*Hague* 1989, Art. 8, emphasis added), while tourists, who are of course, extremely unlikely to be reading this lofty statement, are told that they "must also ... refrain from exploiting others for prostitution purposes" (article 9). Similarly, if less specifically, "World Peace through Tourism," the so-called Columbia Charter, which resulted from the 1988 global conference in Vancouver, British Columbia, on the theme "Tourism—a Vital Force for Peace," echoes, from its title on out, the WTO's motto "Tourism: Passport to Peace," and connects tourism to the widest-ranging network of peace initiatives.

Even when they call for entirely new assumptions about the social contract or the consequent nature of civil society and economic life, and even when they refer specifically to the elimination of exploitation, including the form inherent in prostitution, these documents have no place for acknowledging and recognizing contradiction. With their eyes firmly and admirably fixed on peace and justice, they say nothing about how to make possible an increase in tourism —which, as one document asserts, has "potential as an influencing force for global peace through respect for human dignity, cultural diversity and the natural environment which supports all life"—while discouraging the sex industry that brings so many travelers to such destinations as Thailand.

Internal Representations: The Government Speaks Tourism

> In a world that is drifting toward greater political pluralism, opening up more business opportunities and markets worldwide, it is in corporate interests to discourage policy vacillations and fend off events that can disrupt markets.
> —Imtiaz Muqbil, *The Thai Tourism Industry*

Excerpted from a study of the tourist industry sponsored by the Thai government, the quotation above couples the language of tourism with that of international business strategies to assure readers that the future will be peaceful and profitable. Following the drift of this argument, we are told that on the high seas of global marketing, little can affect the juggernaut of capital that sets policy. Not even "a major catastrophe" can knock tourism off course. Nothing will go wrong, because it simply wouldn't be good business. The hand on the tiller will keep the ship of state steady as she goes. All this is meant to be good news to readers, but it is a point of view that obviously ignores the plight of anyone who is not currently benefiting from tourism's economic boom and who, in fact, may be suffering because of this particular interaction of global business concerns and government policy. For such people, the status quo means more of the same dire situation. But the "success" of the Thai economy is a given in the eyes of international development agencies, and the national government, of course, echoes these stories of economic success.

The economy has "ranked high among developing countries, for more than twenty years" says a 1991 report from the Prime Minister's Office (114). This government report, *Thailand in the 90s*, admits that "some basic problems such as income disparity, the need to conserve natural resources, the uncertainty of export markets, and the need for improving administrative efficiency, remain to be solved but judging by past performance as well as from the present economic outlook, it is clear that Thailand has the potential to expand its economy and thereby improve the welfare of all its citizens (114). Tourism has played an increasingly important role in this economic success and, as of 1988, could be called by the Thai Farmers Bank "the core support of the economy" (qtd. in Muqbil 1989, 5). A tourist-industry study commissioned by the national air carrier THAI International includes a chapter titled, "The Economy: Records Fall as Tourism Leads the Way," which claims that the industry provides "a major [source of] income to spur on the domestic economy" (21): the influx of global travelers creates local prosperity. The study also elaborates the government's interpretation of tourism as primarily an economic enterprise: "Tourism policy is guided by the Sixth National Economic and Social Development Plan which places special emphases on international tourism promotion to boost the national economy and balance the trade and current account deficit" (114); it concludes, "virtually everyone agrees that tourism, while not a panacea for poverty, is important for national economic development" (124). The peace, understanding, and prosperity of international pro-tourism rhetoric has telescoped to exclude everything outside the industry's strictly economic function.

The Thai government started taking an interest in tourism as an economic force in the glow of the Cold War. After a 1959 visit to the United States, where he was impressed by the success of the American tourist industry, Field Marshal Srisdi Dhanarajata established an autonomous "Tourist Organization of Thailand," a government bureaucracy primarily charged with promoting the industry through publicity campaigns at home and abroad. Reconfigured in 1979 as the Tourist Authority of Thailand (TAT), the better to cope with the age of widebody jets and mass international travel, the agency "supports tourism resources conservation in local areas, and supports Thai culture and tradition to attract tourists" (TAT Homepage). Regarding this cause-effect relationship, the TAT's delivery of increased arrivals is an undeniable success: it claims that tourist arrivals increased at a rate of 10.53 percent per year from 1980 to 1987, growing from 1.85 million to 3.48 million visitors (TAT Homepage).

Nowhere was this "success" more apparent than during the "Visit Thailand Year" of 1987. The global response to this all-out blitz promoting tourism in Thailand caught everyone by surprise. King Bhumipol's sixtieth birthday provided the catalyst and justification for putting the tourist industry into high gear. Public and private organizations cooperated in the venture that resulted in "Southeast Asia's highest surge in tourist arrivals" (Muqbil 1989, 122). The "satisfactory figure" of tourist arrivals, according to the TAT, topped 3.48 million, marking an enormous increase and netting more than 50 billion baht from tourism alone (TAT Homepage). The next year, 1988, saw 4.23 million tourist arrivals; 1989, 4.8 million. From the government's perspective this wildly successful promotion showed that tourism's promise could be realized. National prosperity and economic success were hailed as the logical results of tourism.

The 1987 Visit Thailand Year spawned numerous similar "years" in countries throughout Southeast Asia. The income Thailand had generated gave tourism new "respectability" and economic clout. Because of this success, the various members of the Association of Southeast Asian Nations (ASEAN) each took a turn promoting tourism in their respective countries, culminating in a cooperative 1992 "Visit ASEAN Year." Each nation was rewarded with increased arrivals and income (Hitchcock, King, and Parnwell 1993, 3–4). Although the results of the 1987 campaign were greater than anyone had imagined, the event did not manifest itself in a tourism vacuum. A prelude to the event, the 1980 Year of the Tourist, had provided much of the infrastructure needed for the success experienced seven years later. (The proximity of the Year of the Tourist to the end of the Vietnam War and of U.S. military presence in Thailand shows the swords-into-ploughshares conversion of R&R sites into tourist destinations, which, in this case, meant the conversion of whorehouses into—whorehouses.) Prime Minister Prem Tinsulanond built Chiang Mai International Airport, eased visa restrictions, and supported hotel expansion to aid this trial run for Visit Thailand Year. All branches of the government cooperated, the Minister of the Interior Police notably announcing that his department would "respond to the Cabinet's resolution to promote tourism by lengthening service hours of entertainment places in Bangkok to welcome visitors" (*Documentation* 1983, 40).

The TAT, THAI International, and the Office of the Prime Minister all cite different reasons for the "success" of tourism in Thailand, ranging from "its many attractions located in various parts of the country" to "the uniqueness of the Thai people"—"their friendliness and hospitality." But the gesture by the Minister of the Interior Police allowing "entertainment places" in Bangkok to stay open later and thus better welcome tourists, may have provided the real key to success. THAI International's tourism industry report contains a chapter titled "The Success Story in Statistics and Trends," and the numbers reveal why this gesture has borne such fruit (Muqbil 1989, 23). The visitor profile shows that from 1986 to 1988, an average of 66 percent of the tourists to the nation were male; 70 percent of those were between the ages of twenty-five and fifty-four (Muqbil, 26). Three years after the gracious offer by the minister, the TAT figures indicated that 89 percent of the visitors to Bangkok—a city with half a million more women than men—were male (ctd. in Richter 1989, 86). Likewise, 86 percent of the tourists to the famous R&R resort of Pattaya were men (ctd. in

Hill 1993, 138). This increased international male interest in the Thai people's "friendliness" substantially boosted foreign currency earnings.

Also, according to government sources, the growth in tourist arrivals and tourism earnings has translated into general social and economic improvement in the nation. The section headed "Contributions of Tourism" in a report published by the prime minister's office claims that tourism has preserved many traditional customs, handicrafts, and occupations "which otherwise would have died out," and "the end result of all this activity," the report continues, "is that the public is more aware of the nation's long history; seeing tourists coming to admire their country and what it has to offer has made Thais even prouder of their cultural heritage" (*Thailand in the 90s* 1991, 209). A photograph just below this statement shows a float in the Chiang Mai Winter Festival Parade; flowers have been arranged to evoke a beach scene, and two bathing beauties lounging in seaside chairs complete the picture. The anomaly of an American bowl game-style parade, replete with beauty queens, as an example of Thai "cultural heritage" perfectly illustrates the distance between the representation of tourism's success and the industry's various manifestations, for this is a definition of success as surreal cultural incorporation.

The same report also claims that, in Reaganomic terms, the wealth generated by tourism "trickles down" to all sectors of the economy (210). With these results and in this spirit, "government policies and guidelines have been drawn up for the systematic development of tourism, designed to sustain growth and at the same time raise the quality of tourism services" (213). Readers are told that "Thailand's tourism industry has been set on the right course of growth and is expected to remain the top income earner for many years to come, providing jobs for thousands of people and contributing to the equitable spread of income" (213). Interestingly, the THAI International report from just two years before had claimed that tourism exacerbates, more than it alleviates, existing economic disparity (Muqbil 1989, 10). But that statement focused on the flow of male laborers from farms to hotel lobbies and the sociopolitical impact on the nation of this shift of laborers and labor performed. Missing from the analysis, again, was the rural-to-urban flow that female laborers have experienced for decades, a flow integral to swelling tourist arrival numbers.

As may be discerned from these publications, tourism is generally held in high esteem by the government. Some lip service is paid to "the social, cultural, and environmental impact of tourism" in the prime minister's report (*Thailand in the 90s* 1991, 213), while the THAI study devotes an entire chapter (Muqbil 1989, 122–27) to the issue of the environmental strain the industry exerts. The former report is somewhat glib about governmental response, but the latter argues that there are real threats to the industry (not to the nation or its people): AIDS and environmental destruction "are reaching dangerously close to plague proportions," it states. "Indeed, it is here that the true danger lies, where the true impact of money, power and political connections merge to extract [*sic*] the most severe impact on the Thai tourism scene" (11–12). As with the media representations of the tourism industry examined in Chapter 2, the only way sex tourism enters the scenario outlined in government reports is through the threat presented by AIDS. In the media, AIDS is a problem because tourists could be infected; in this report, AIDS is a problem because tourism could be infected. Readers are assured that Thai policymakers "want to tackle the problem in a frank and forthright manner yet do not want to trigger public panic, *especially not such that it deters tourism*" (139; emphasis added). The problem will be addressed so long as such addressing does not impede the flow of tourists and their foreign currency. The implication is that if the flow is impeded, then the forthright problem-tackling will cease forthwith.

The study states that the way to address such problems is to target a different class and kind of tourist—an implicit admission that sex tourism has been an explicit component of previous tourism planning—yet mentions sex tourism only once in its 145 pages: "Though Thailand is downplaying its sex attractions, a legend borne [*sic*] out of neglect will not die easily. Hard though it is to accept, Thailand's sex-life does attract a certain class of traveller" (135). The language of the text turns planning into "neglect," neatly relegating responsibility to the diffuse realm of ignorance. The answer to industry problems rests in new clientele, a different group for whom *this* year can become Visit Thailand Year. But how different are the new tourists?

In 1992 came Women's Visit Thailand Year, which David Leheny calls "a symbolic and perhaps only partial effort to eradicate Thailand's image as a sex market" (1995, 380). In fact, there were two discrete and incongruous strains at work in that project. Although AIDS activist Mechai Viravaidya and the chairman of the TAT cooperated in naming and planning the year, their intentions can never have coincided. Mechai's position was unambiguous:

> We want women to come particularly from countries where some of their men have come here on sex tours. . . . We want them to see what their men get up to and how they have exploited uneducated women and children. We want them now to come and see the good Thai women and encourage Thai women to stand up to the brutality and disrespect they have suffered. More action must come from Thai women themselves, otherwise the country will still be seen as the brothel of the world (Kelly 1991, 44).

The antithetical position posited by the TAT may be found in its press release for Women's Visit Thailand Year, which claims that "Thailand's image as a desirable tourist destination was significantly damaged by a series of publicity [*sic*], especially the image of Thailand as a country with many long-standing unique selling points." The final phrase is meant to indicate that Thailand still has many unique selling points, despite reports to the contrary. Addressing Thailand's image abroad as "a center for sexual activities," the document goes on to say that this "image greatly affected the reputation of Thai women in the international community with sex-related business inflicting serious damage. This situation must be immediately rectified through several measures concerning controls, prevention and public relations in order to salvage the tourism identity of the country." The final sentence reveals the basic difference between Mechai and the TAT. The latter seems concerned only with the country's image and the reputation of its women. The relation between the image or reputation and the lived experience of Thai women seems irrelevant.

Leheny (1995), who interprets Thailand's efforts to attract Japanese women visitors as a genuine attempt by the TAT to expand the nation's tourist base, provides a kinder reading of the situation than we do. The obvious parallel to 1987 in the planning of Women's Visit Thailand Year highlights the fact that the unmarked case for tourism to Thailand—and most places, for that matter—is the male traveling alone for business, pleasure, or both. In his study for THAI International, Muqbil optimistically argues, "travel agents point out that every business man who comes on a working visit will at some stage bring his family back for a holiday. Businessmen visiting Thailand are increasing by leaps and bounds and sooner or later will return as tourists" (1989, 135). He therefore recommends that the government do more to promote business travel that can be converted later into tourist travel. In essence, this sounds like the status quo, only wrapped in the assumption that these men will return in the future with their families. Given the length and expense of such a family trip for *farangs*, we can legitimately ask how likely this is. Nonetheless, there has been a concerted effort to promote tourism to CEOs and other white-collar business travelers, an effort apparently conceived by the government as entailing an increase in female tourist arrivals.

This "new" group of potential tourists falls into an area known as "incentive travel," which is used by businesses as rewards and bonuses. A company called Incentive Asia Destination Services promises to "turn fantasy into reality and reality into fantasy" for "deserving high achievers" (qtd. in Selwyn 1993, 133). Richter argues that because of the success of sex tourism in Thailand, the official literature "is not obliged to mention women explicitly in its promotional narratives" (1989, 86). But the indirect and often not so implicit evocation of women and the sex industry permeates much of the tourism promotion generated by the government.

A magazine-format brochure by THAI International pitching "incentive travel" belies Richter's point and reveals that the new target clientele is being sold essentially the same goods and in much the same way as the old. Titled *Thai Values: Incentive Travel to the Land of Smiles* (1995), it is aimed specifically at the company executive in a position to make decisions about which employees receive a splendid, luxurious vacation as part of a corporate incentive package. The brochure plays up THAI International's—and, by extension, the nation's—desire to serve this person. The CEO, in essence, plays the role of the colonial home officer pulling in profits from around the globe and rewarding his troops for their good performance by sending them on corporate R&R. The ways in which the colonized periphery services the cosmopolitan center are reinscribed in the "values" this brochure touts, a wedding of international corporate business and full-service tourism.

The ambiguous title *Thai Values* suggests many different "values": for example, the values of Thai culture and people, what and whom THAI International values, and the values ("good buys") one gets from the Thai nation, airline, and people. Some of these are articulated in the brochure's headings. Each two-page spread states a different theme or topic in boldface print: *Thai values make Thailand the ultimate incentive; So much for so little; Beauty and the beach; Antiques, Thai arts and crafts—all at bargain prices; Living values; The most affordable luxury in Asia;* and *All the pageantry of Thailand—at your command.*

The cover photograph represents a stereotypical fantasy/fear: the fantasy of the businessman abroad, the fear of the wife left at home. A *farang* couple faces the camera while a Thai woman stands with her back to the reader, which marks her as faceless servant in the form of airline employee. As she places a jasmine garland around the man's neck, the white female looks on with a nervous smile. The Thai woman seems to be pulling the man toward her with the garland, and he leans forward smiling broadly. The white male white-collar traveler receives the hands-on attention of the Thai female servant. She represents the airline, which as national carrier serves as a synecdoche for the nation, the culture, and the people. All of these are waiting, so the photograph suggests, to service corporate executives, the "higher-quality" tourist the government wishes to attract.

The photograph reminds us that when reading these self-representations against the grain of intention, it is necessary to consider explicitly *who* get photographed and *what* they are doing in the pictures.[1] Just as useful is who does *not* get shown. Hitchcock, King, and Parnwell (1993, 15) argue that the predominance of the "classical dancer" and the "craftsman" in the Visit ASEAN Year promotional material has its roots in colonial imagery. These two tropes figure heavily in the THAI International promotional brochure, as well. After assuring the CEO who wishes to "reward [his] hard workers" that "THAI believes the passenger is special—to be spoiled with superb service," the section explaining "so much for so little" breathlessly details the wonders of this exotic realm: "The huge and ancient Buddhist temples are breathtaking. The traditional Thai dancers are captivating. And the night life enticing. Whatever takes their fancy, visitors are bound to find it in Thailand. And for a country that offers so much, it all costs surprisingly little." The text moves from the sacred to the profane in three sentences. The two accompanying photos feature a large temple and a small inset of Thai dancers; the nightlife is left to the reader's imagination, the female dancers serving as a conduit for the transition. We are told that everything our imagination might fancy, from the devout to the debauched can be had here, and on the cheap, to boot. Now *that's* value.

Turn the page and we find ourselves at "Beauty and the Beach." After the initial paragraph describes tropical isles, a single-line paragraph states, "This is Thailand." For the reader not yet familiar with columnist Bernard Trink's recurrent "TIT—This Is Thailand"—catchword, a photo just to the right of the declarative statement shows a Thai woman wading in crystal blue water up to her buttocks. Back to the camera and again faceless, her shapely tan torso is barely clad in a very un-Thai string-bikini. Faceless and seminude, this woman embodies the nation that will service deserving corporate functionaries. Combining the photograph with the sentence defining the nation—"This is Thailand"—readers easily move from the copula of definition to an intimation of copulation. Throughout the brochure, images of Thai women outnumber those of men by four to one. We see women working, serving, smiling, or gazing seductively. In the section devoted to the direct selling of the incentive packages, all but two of the THAI International employees represented are female, and each of these is helping white, predominantly male customers. Potential travelers, therefore, are assured of female servitude every step of the way.

The brochure highlights the unique combination of "the ancient" and "the modern" that tourists encounter in the country, with the former cast as "exotic" and the latter as familiar. This highlighting suggests that Thailand is exotic enough to pique one's interest while familiar enough not to be frightening: different but not too different. Readers are told, however, that modernization does not threaten tradition, and that "[t]he ancient Siamese culture is still very much a living heritage." Travelers, the brochure assures, will still see "the real thing," *and* their visit will not endanger "the real thing." Instead, much as the Prime Minister's report claims, such visits preserve ways of life that would otherwise fall prey to entropy.

More Thai values await in the section explaining why Thailand is "the most affordable luxury in Asia." Beneath a photo of a disco we read, "Bangkok's lively nightlife offers a wide range of attractions to suit every taste." In this, "Asia's most exotic destination," travelers-to-be are offered an "unlimited scope for shopping, sports, nightlife—in fact, just about everything you look for in an incentive destination." Plenitude and good prices combine in the incentive reward. But there is still more. The three activities an incentive traveler supposedly values most function in a cumulative way. The tourist's triad of "shopping, sports, and nightlife" becomes a mathematical formula of sorts. Shopping equals procuring; sports equals pleasurable physical exertion; nightlife equals the addition of the two: the procurement of pleasurable physical exertion. Just in case the nightlife spills over into the workday, we are told that this destination offers a range of meeting venues. "For more discreet and intimate gatherings, there are any number of delightful hotels with fully equipped meeting facilities located in idyllic rural or oceanside settings." Who knows when inspiration might strike these gung-ho employees? The nation is prepared for any eventuality.

The vestiges of colonialism haunt not only the photograph's tropes but also the text's. The heading "all the pageantry of Thailand—at your command" spells this out. The first line asks CEOs to "imagine traveling back in time," invoking the power and control of the colonial past. The text conjures up the imperial hegemonic position of having a nation's entire resources at one's disposal:

"Everything is laid on specially for you to enjoy, and to share in the richness of Thailand's cultural heritage." The riches of exotic Asia can be dangled before the eyes of one's employees, to encourage them to perform at their best. For the individual who does so, *everything* the nation has to offer will be *laid* on for his enjoyment. No riches, no pleasure, no desire will be denied this special employee.

The *Thai Values* brochure is by no means unique in the commodification of culture necessary to promote tourism—brochures pitching virtually every Third World destination engage in this practice—but it is unique in targeting a specific class of traveler, one that the government perceives as a "higher quality" tourist who can be readily converted into a family tourist. Nor is the brochure unique in veiling of the sex industry as a possible lure for tourists—but its implicit invocation of this industry undermines any effort to transform the incentive traveler into a family tourist, for the pleasure partaken of abroad would not be appreciated on the home front, nor, probably, would it be shared in travel tales told by the family hearth.

The TAT publication *Tourist Attractions in the North* (1995), which targets couples and families as well as single travelers, similarly works in contradictory ways. It too invokes the lure of the sex industry, though perhaps more covertly than *Thai Values*. Of the 1995 series of magazine-format brochures that slickly tout the various regions of Thailand, only the one devoted to the North hints at this aspect of tourism. Following a brief paragraph naming the provinces in the region, the second paragraph reads: "The north is the home of Thailand's earliest civilization and is famous for its beautiful women, and hospitable and courteous people, as well as many sites of archaeological and cultural interest." The beautiful (youthful) women of the text, wedged between an aged civilization and archaeological sites, are pictured on the cover and inside. These women have been placed on the same level of tourist interest, that of a commodity for tourist consumption, as the cultural sites of an ancient civilization. The north may have had civilization in the past, but now it has crushing poverty. The north and northeast, therefore, supply the vast majority of the women recruited to work in the segment of the sex industry that caters to *farang* customers.

The portion of the brochure devoted to Lampang, an area infamous for selling its young women into this industry, includes a photo bearing the title "Lampang's ladies in local dresses." The ages of the females in the photo run from about seven to twenty-five. They kneel and smile alluringly, wearing tops that bare their shoulders—unusual, given traditional female modesty. Local dress, too, evidently features carefully salon-coiffed hair and cosmetics that turn lips ruby red (*Tourist Attractions* 1995, 16). The village of Lamphun, featured in the *Bangkok Post* series on the child prostitution crackdown discussed in Chapter 2, is represented in the brochure by a photo of a beauty contest winner and the runners-up (19). But the industry behind the industry is missing from the text, as is the fact that beauty contest winners often fetch high prices in this industry or as minor wives. We are told, instead, that the horse-carriage transportation and the training school for baby elephants "account for the bulk of Lampang's Thai and foreign visitors" (16). Some might opine that it is the content of the photo reproduced on that page, the "lovely ladies" of Lampang, that create much of the tourist traffic.

The TAT itself, in fact, has said as much in the past. When constructing the hugely successful Visit Thailand Year in 1987, the agency fully understood the power of the written word to create representations of a site that might translate into tourist revenue. The press packet for this massive tourism promotion provides, as the initial page, a sheet headed "The Writer's Thailand." Wading through a long list of "delicious" images that the proper noun "Thailand" supposedly "evokes," writers-as-readers encounter references to "Bangkok's vibrant, almost legendary nightlife" and "classical Siamese dancing's absorbing sensuality." The introductory page claims that from a writer's point of view Thailand is a "literally inexhaustible source of material, so varied are her charms, traditions, sights and sounds" (this is the first and only time the third-person female pronoun is used, here to personify the nation), but readers in their role as writers are told not to worry if the "literally inexhaustible source of material" should manifest itself as their own literary exhaustion, because they are free to quote liberally from the press packet's prose.

Journalists who accepted that 1987 offer, especially when writing about Bangkok, would have had infinitely more explicit material than that provided in the 1995 TAT brochures. The pullout sheet called "Bangkok, City of Angels" touts the town's citizens as being like "other Thais"—that is, fun-loving people— and the city's "boxing stadiums . . . opulent nightclubs . . . concert halls, teahouses, cocktail lounges . . . bars, museums, theaters, art galleries, massage parlors . . . and cinemas lure pleasure seekers throughout the year." To go native, then, means to become a "pleasure seeker" lured by the plethora of pleasure providers found in the list. But the city's charms fully manifest themselves after the museums, theaters, and art galleries close. "With darkness," we pleasure seekers read, "Bangkok assumes another mantle, and the atmosphere becomes soft, magical, sensual." This statement introduces a long list of snapshot descriptions of the many folks who service voracious tourists, all caught in their preparations so to service: "Classical Siamese dancers make up and prepare to don brocaded costumes and exotic masks and headgear." "In nightclubs, lights and microphones are tested, dance bands assemble and cabaret *artistes* make final prop checks; lissom [*sic*] go-go dancers limber up in bars and make final adjustments to scanty bikinis." The present tense deployed throughout implies that these people and their wonderful services are always available to the tourist. Not only is this service ever present; it is also cast as "natural": we are told that between nine and midnight "nightlife undergoes the natural progression from lively to livelier to liveliest, tapering off in the small hours." The nightlife's progression starts with heady fare and builds to the climax presented in the superlative: the "liveliest" nightlife anywhere. One need not exercise much imagination to understand how the scantily clad dancers figure in that superlative.

After the climax, the tourist can "taper off" in the glow of dawn and watch the workaday world of the city come to life, a world the pleasure seeker can eschew for the nonce, for "already there is a tangible, keen anticipation of a new day in which to discover something new to see, to do, to touch, to taste, to feel, to buy, to enjoy." The language of discovery and novelty merges with that of sensory fulfillment extolled in the list of infinitives assuring us that such fulfillment is readily attainable. All that we need do to feel, to touch, and to enjoy these sensual wonders is "to buy"; in fact, the list suggests that "to buy" *is* "to enjoy." It is inevitable that all this will be ours, if we have the cash: "It couldn't be otherwise in the Orient's most exotic capital—Bangkok, City of Angels." The proximity of causal relations and unambiguous results neatly links services, sensual fulfillment for the serviced, and the purchase of all of this pleasure in one unique site.

In short, what the 1995 brochures approach indirectly was articulated quite explicitly when the government spoke the language of tourism in 1987.

External Representations: The Languages of Tourism from the Outside

> What I don't understand about the campaign against sex tourism in the Realm is what's the point? ... (E)ven if they didn't come for it, the availability of play-for-pay is made clear throughout their stay. Whether they take up on it depends on the individual tourist.
>
> —Bernard Trink, "The Nite Owl" column, *The Bangkok Post*, June 1996

Thai social critic Siriporn Skrobanek claims that "The ruling class values the bodies of poor women as a means to attract tourists to earn foreign exchange. This strategy made Thailand a country where 'all people who go there, like it and long to return. It is beautiful and there is something for everybody'" (qtd. in *Documentation* 1983,13). Skrobanek's critique of national policy scathingly deploys the governmental language of tourism against itself, and we leave it to indigenous scholars like her to challenge government policy directly. We would, however, emphasize the demand side of the equation: without a large set of clients the international sex industry could not flourish. It is not only the national but, more important, the international ruling class that values the bodies of poor women and makes these corporeal commodities a primary impetus for mass tourist travel.

If the self-representations of tourism mostly hint at the sex industry operating within the country, descriptions produced by external sources are far less modest or discreet. Some, in fact, leave nothing to the imagination. Representations by unscrupulous tourist agencies explicitly hawking sex as the main tourist attraction could and should provoke the ire of anyone who cares about the nation's image, not to mention its people. In order for the global clientele to learn about this particular allure that Thailand holds for them—and incidentally, to fill airliners, hotels, and other tourist providers—a specific set of representations drawing on a long history of eroticizing the exotic Other and catering to an alienated sexual subjectivity has been generated. A significant part of this set can be found in the abundant travel journalism that accrues around any popular destination. Such journalism may or may not inspire travel to a given site, but its intent is not necessarily to do so; it seeks chiefly to inform. Guidebooks and travel brochures, on the other hand, actively prompt their readers to visit and tour the destination they tout. In combination, these three genres constitute the languages of tourism from the outside.[2]

Travel Journalism: Good News and Bad News

> The places in the glossy brochures of the travel industry do not exist: the destinations are not real places, and the people pictured are false.... One cannot sell poverty, but one can sell paradise.
>
> —Malcolm Crick, "Representation of Tourism in the Social Sciences: Sun, Sex, Sights, Savings, and Servility"

Magazine articles, addressed to both the armchair traveler and the likely prospect, speak in a less explicit register than some other genres. But if, as indicated in Chapter 2, even "hard news" articles on Thailand have relied on and thereby perpetuated a fixed series of tropes about the Kingdom and its people—land of smiles and *mai pen rai;* Anna's colorful, polygamous King—features and travel reporting have been even more assiduous in the construction of Siam-as-Shangri-la, a sexy Shangri-la. The report of each critical news event from 1945 on was followed by a wave of such articles, like a bevy of court attendants dancing attendance on (say) the King of Siam. Sometimes the two were combined.

Thus, *Time*'s cover story on King Bhumipol's return to take up his duties is headed "Garden of Smiles." The king's homecoming occasioned the smiles, to be sure, but *Time* goes out of its way to let us know that they reflect an innate national spirit, as "Siam's 18 million cheerful, childlike citizens prepared to make the most of it." Indeed, when a crowded landing-stage and its occupants—Thais hoping for a glimpse of the royal barge—fell into the Chao Phraya River, "since all Siamese seem to be born swimmers, no one was drowned. Since all Siamese are born cheerful, all came up grinning" (28). This news story is illustrated with a stylized map of the country and photos of kick boxers, an astrologer at work, a scantily clad female temple figure, and the (girlishly attired) Queen Sirikit—all serving to turn the article from a narrative of grim events and forebodings into a compendium of precisely the sort of exotica that appeal to tourists. And local sexual customs are part of the formula. A long note about the royal "harems" of the past concludes with the information that although present Thai law "allows each man only one wife at a time . . . many a Siamese goes ahead and takes another wife anyway" (29).

A *Reader's Digest* feature spells it out: "a man may register only one wife, but he may, with no stigma, live with as many women as he chooses" (Clark 1950,129). Bringing this state of bliss a bit closer to home is the mention of an American businessman's employee, nationality unspecified, who "lives happily with a legitimate wife, eight unrecorded companions and their 20 children" (129). Throughout, the article is more travelogue than analysis. Bangkok, a "city of the sun," is "colorful, clean, and splendid . . . it scintillates" (125). The "happy-go-lucky Siamese" (129), who are so exotic as to have created an art and architecture that "no Western mind could have conceived" (125), "have the latch out for us" (130)—no telling how many "unrecorded companions" waiting for us behind the door.

Long before "One Night in Bangkok" became a song cue—and, in its turn, another in the congeries of commonplaces about Thailand—a former official of a U.S. aid mission described such a stopover. After a paragraph in which Somerset Maugham, Joseph Conrad, and "small brown women" jostle for space on the river and the page, he tells us how to spend a night on the town: "In the hotel lobby, a mimeographed notice describes the challenger in the night's Siamese boxing match as 'he of the lightning knee and ruthless elbow.' You either verify this understatement, or go to the classical dancing show. . . . You ride in *samlors* . . . and the *samlor* boys . . . take you to Chez Eve . . . for filet mignon. . . . Afterwards . . . they . . . make some dubious propositions about which there can be no doubt whatsoever, since they employ gestures and photographs. . . . The Shadow Book, a guide to the many sin houses of Bangkok, is on sale at all newsstands" (Robertson 1953, 66).

This degree of straightforwardness is unusual for *Vogue*, where it appeared, since that magazine's reportage from Thailand tended for several decades to take the high road in its ethic of consumption. Thus, the "wondrous, golden" Kingdom was represented chiefly by photographs of its Royal Family and their surroundings and a couple of paragraphs of gushing, adjective-laden prose (Clarke 1965, 89). Another *Vogue* article alliteratively singing the praises of the "lure of living lavishly" at the Oriental Hotel, ends with sunset—no nightlife chronicled here—but the day's lavish living does begin at breakfast, served "with style and smiles by young Thai women in sarongs" (Alleman 1983, 135, 136). A traveler weary of the "whirl of shopping, eating, and sight-seeing halfway around the world" is slated for, of all things, "R&R" in the "new glamour in the Far East . . . the next place to go": the resort island of Phuket (Kaye 1986, 221). Although the emphasis is on wallowing in relaxation, we are also informed that Patong Beach (whose name and nature must make many *farangs* think it is a branch of Patpong) "is known for nightlife and bars" (234). This article ends by invoking the Michelin tag "worth a detour."

Two years later a new resort on Phuket, itself "no longer news," is rumored to be "worth" a similar detour. Although Phuket has been "cleansed" of its hippie image, the true Gauguin version of "getting away from it all" is to be found, for the moment, on the smaller island of Ko Samui; it may shortly have to be pursued even farther afield, on Ko Phangnga and the even more unspoiled island beyond called Ko Kao, billed as the only place on earth where three beaches come together. "I'm not sure exactly what that means," the reporter comments, "but it certainly sounds seductive" (*Vogue* 1989,124). By contrast, the "boom beach" of Patong, site of more mundane comings together, is now "crowded with cottage colonies and mid-rise hotels, New Zealand steak houses and Aussie pubs with names like 69, Love Bar and My Way, where Thai girls and boys sell sex" (123). What is objectionable about this, apparently, is that, with "cranes and construction crews everywhere, Patong is a frightening vision of development run rampant" (123).

Vogue may seek luxury in exclusiveness, a staged simplicity to complement Dean MacCannell's (1989) "staged authenticity," rejecting the more visible manifestations of the sex industry as tacky. But the resolutely middle-brow and middle-class *Saturday Review*, following the Thai royals to their vacation home at Hua Hin (Simms 1969), also celebrated the "standard of comfort" of the overnight express train between Bangkok and Chiang Mai, from whose windows at twilight the traveler could observe "sarong-clad Thai girls emerge, ethereally modest, for their baths in the canals." Meanwhile in the diner, which doubles as a club car, "a boisterous all-male crowd was cheerfully working its way through a second case of Mekong whiskey" (G. Smith 1979, 49).

Vogue was and remains dedicated to the marketing of "elegance," with travel and other life-style features the handmaidens of women's fashion, whereas the now defunct *Holiday*'s subtitle frankly announced it as "The Magazine of Leisure for Richer Living." The languages of tourism were exercised in several new directions in *Holiday*, *Travel*, and the combined *Travel-Holiday* into which they merged in the 1970s. The upscale readership of these publications for the travel-oriented consumer is wooed in a language of sensuality in which below-the-belt pleasures—or at least those situated below the belly—go unmentioned. A two-article feature in 1985 concentrated, first, on Bangkok's canals as a watery road to exoticism: "Fragile-blossomed orchids hang in empty beer bottles from the roof and a pigeon, cheek twisted under a wing, perches on the railing. As the boat makes for the bridge where it will moor for the night, the sound of melodious laughter drifts across the water from the house" (Narula 1985, 61). After the "more flavorful do-it-yourself canal excursion," *Travel-Holiday* recommends that, for "travelers disappointed with the highly commercialized Floating Market Tour" (60), the next stop is the land-based "buyer's paradise" for luxury goods: "stunning silks and leathers, sparkling sapphires, rubies and emeralds, glistening lacquers, exotic arts and crafts" (Fowler 1985, 61). But, the article admits toward the end, "no tourist travels this far for bargains alone" (107), so the consumer is guided from the wares sparkling on the gem-cutters' shelves to the Temple of the Emerald Buddha, the Reclining Buddha at Wat Po, the charming stands outside that temple where it is customary to free a caged bird for a small sum of money, and at length to "another popular stop," the Weekend Market, for some additional exotic shopping.

A year earlier, *Travel-Holiday*'s focus was on the palate, in an article about the food of Bangkok, centering on classes at Bangkok's Thai Cooking School (Gordon 1984, 52–57). The language of luxury tourism is preeminently a language of the senses, in which Thailand's exotica inferentially exists to be consumed through sight, touch, and taste—all mediated, of course, by the action of the wallet. At this level, sex is mentioned only by its absence, as when, in an article about the sensual—but not sexual—delights of Chiang Mai, the journalist and a friend are assigned female university students as guides, "chaste Christian girls very much into round-necked blouses and fits of giggles" but also, needless to say, "pretty (as the girls of the north are reputed to be)" (Atcheson 1973, 37).

Travel-Holiday comes closer to classing female attractiveness with consumable goods in a paragraph that describes Chiang Mai's geography and climate, and then adds, "The women may be among the most beautiful in the world. Petite and light-complexioned, with long black hair and smiling eyes, they are a blend of the Chinese of the North and the pure Thai of the South, the most photogenic members of a very considerate and gracious people" (Aiken 1980, 46). By contrast, a professional travel photographer gets through his musings on "The Land of Smiles: A Nice Place to Visit—Over and Over," without a word about feminine pulchritude. Touring the country during and after a convention of the Society of American Travel Writers, he concludes, "Thailand gave me the sense of a country that is at peace with itself and in harmony with its tropical environment. Each few minutes unfolded new visual experiences. In two weeks I shot more than 80 rolls of 36-exposure film, and it was one of my finest 'takes' in years" (Purcell 1982, 152). Lacking the photographer's occupational preoccupation with the whole visual feast, the *Weekend Australian* makes women part of the scenery. Immediately after directing "jaded executives" to Phuket accommodations that "range from good hotels to simple Thai bungalows that are ridiculously cheap," the article states baldly, "In Chiang Mai . . . the women are recognized as the most beautiful in Thailand and the colorful hilltribes lend an exotic note" (Scriber 1981, 63).

Perhaps the most egregious blending of the lyrical language of tourism with description of the sexual landscape is Pico Iyer's 1980 account, "The Smiling Lures of Thailand," which *Time*'s editors crassly headed, "a hot holiday spot offers exoticism and bargains" (85). Thailand's "smiling gracious people," Iyer tells us, "make 'tourist industry' sound like a contradiction in terms," yet he distrusts the success of the "imported dreams" (86), the very attractions that lured him there: "So giddy is the world's romance with the smiling kingdom . . . that some people fear the country could lose itself in the lights, or turn into a synthetic version of itself" (85). Iyer feminizes the entire culture by establishing as a fact of nature that the "paradox of beauty" is that "it will not be left alone; it begs, almost, to be compromised, homogenized, packaged, roughed up" (86). Thailand is female and, like any lovely woman, is (almost) asking to be ravished.

The natural and the lyrical come together in Iyer's discourse when he describes Bangkok as "a lyrical place where it seems almost natural to spend a morning in a walled compound full of temples, an afternoon shopping for sapphires, silver and lacquers in an air-conditioned arcade, an evening dining in spicy splendor along the Chao Phya [sic] River, and a night on Patpong, the most free-wheeling bar strip in the world" (85–86). Iyer (whose later essay on the prostitutes of Bangkok we explore in Chapter 5, "Imagining Sexual Others,") worries, here, that Thailand may prostitute itself; he sees the actual sex trade as a metaphor for that already metaphoric transaction, citing the "embarrassing statistic" that perhaps as many as "250,000 women in Bangkok alone respond to the siren call of a business that goes hand-in-hand with tourism" (86). But commercial sex seems to him far from the worst symptom of what can go wrong, for "the get-rich-quick promise that tourists embody has also led to shadier [sic!] enterprises. Thailand is already famous for its pickpockets, smugglers, and heroin dealers" (86). The difference, of course, is that the sex bars, the "almost natural" conclusion of a lovely day of seeing and spending, offer the visitor further pleasure, whereas thieves and drug dealers might rip him off—that is, "exploit" him! Thailand itself as the ambiguous eternal feminine might also be in danger of exploitation—but not, apparently, the living, breathing females employed in the sex industry. After all, of them, it could be said, as it is—fulsomely—of their country, that their "charms are so real that it is hard to tell the extent to which they are being exploited; and . . . [the] magic is so supple that its source remains . . . known only to itself—and, perhaps, the gods who dreamed it up" (86).

Although the Latin word *luxuria* can mean "lust," rather than the elegant comfort suggested by the English "luxury," a portion of luxury-travel journalism devoted to Thailand has added another layer to the languages of tourism by explicitly steering its readers *away* from the sex industry. An anomaly even among these anomalous articles is the *Harper's* piece on hill-country treks where opium is among the exotica to be sampled. Although the writer doesn't go so far as to provide addresses of the best agencies in the poppy-tour business, he does point out that opium's "effect is pleasurable and it makes a great yarn back home" for those "tourists hungry for a touch of the uncommon" and whose hunger "can be satisfied at negligible cost," concluding that, all told, "the beauty of the place far exceeds the danger" (Kearney 1983, 27).

More typically for this no-lust genre, the "night on the town" recommended by the *South China Morning Post*'s "Exotic Bangkok" consists of dinner at a "superb restaurant," followed by "graceful traditional Thai dancing in full costume" (Reisender 1985, 62). In this lexicon, "exotic" and "erotic" are far from synonymous; the proof that in Bangkok "the incredible is commonplace and the East is still mysterious" is not the acrobatic vaginas of Patpong (pussy play Ping Pong, pussy smoke cigarette) but the department store where tiger cubs—*truly* wild pussies—are for sale (62). In a similar vein, though without the wildlife, the *Sydney Morning Herald* sends its readers to Patpong only for the outdoor market, and dwells at far greater length on the question of which of half a dozen recommended restaurants is really Bangkok's best (Powell 1989, 62).

Forbes directly addresses that business traveler so dear to the hearts—or at least the pocketbooks and the prose—of Thai tourism planners, advising him that the "prescription for a successful business trip to Bangkok calls for a well-situated [luxury] hotel, a [chauffeured] car with a phone, patience—and a few days at the [upscale] beach to unwind" (Gubernick 1989, 290). Although the reader is also given a list of classy restaurants and instructed to "get in some shopping" (rubies, silks, and couture designs are recommended, and counterfeit brand names are labeled both illegal and amusing), the man of affairs reading all this in *Forbes*'s "Personal Affairs" section is guided away from equating "personal" with "sexual": "As for the seamy side of Bangkok's nightlife, the bars that sprang up to service soldiers during the Vietnam War are still around. Most of them are on Patpong Roads I and II, privately owned streets that are a warren of strip joints and escort services that seem to be caught in a curious sort of time warp. Don't bother" (292).

The distaste evinced by this female journalist is elaborated by a male editor of the right-wing *National Review* writing in the equally conservative *American Spectator*: "Why it should be assumed that everyone who goes to Bangkok also goes . . . [to Patpong] is mysterious to me, for I would think that there are better reasons to cross the Pacific Ocean than to ogle prostitutes doing tricks with razor blades and fruit. . . . Thais are freer about sex, the line goes, so the scene isn't so grim. Well, the girls are teenagers from the north who have been sold into the business by their parents, and the disease timebomb atop which they are sitting must be immense, so it sounds pretty grim to me" (Brookhiser 1989, 46). Although the ready invocation of AIDS and parental greed recalls the "problem" articles discussed in Chapter 2, this conservative thinker at least recognizes that the results of greed are not fun for everyone, and that the explanation by way of cultural differences ("Thais are freer about sex") is no explanation but a "line"—one with a long, ignoble genealogy.

Considering *National Geographic*'s historical contribution to the othering of exotic places and peoples and, more particularly to objectification of the woman of color, its negative approach to the Thai sex industry is both ironic and note-worthy. Environmental depredations attributed to tourism are the focus of a 23-page article in which even the photo captions make devastating points about unregulated development. But the sex industry comes in for as much criticism as "runaway growth, pollution and deforestation" (Grove 1996, 82). The first reference is relatively neutral: foreigners "come to see the Emerald Buddha in old Bangkok and the golden stupa at Wat Phra That Doi Suthep near the north-ern city of Chiang Mai, where holy relics of the Buddha are laid to rest. Visitors bargain for silk and gems, ride elephants through forests, and relax on the beaches of Ko Phuket and Ko Samui. Foreign men come to see Thailand's beau-tiful women and to enjoy a thriving sex industry" (89). But after ringing the usual changes on the Bangkok traffic, the beloved royals, the rapid economic growth, the never-formally-colonized national history, the drug trade then and now, and the cultural role of Buddhism, the reporter returns to the sex scene. A Bangkok author who deplores the effects of modernization has just explained that in contemporary Thailand "the noble truths of Buddhism are being ignored, such as lack of greed and the importance of suffering and humility" (93–94). Whence the journalist segues into the condition of Thai sex workers: "Noble truths are often in short supply in the lives of Thai prostitutes, who enter the world's oldest profession because they can earn as much as five times the national per capita income of $2000 a year" (94). Interviews with prostitutes whom he has bought out for the evening and taken to dinner, accounts of devi-ous or brutal recruitment methods, an outline of the AIDS crisis, and a descrip-tion of various rural improvement projects follow. But this is still *National Geographic*, which means the article never crosses the (admittedly unstable) line between travel writing and investigative journalism. As a sample of the travel genre, it evokes a desire to see for oneself the temples and the threatened beaches and forests but does not provoke a complementary desire to go and despoil Thai women. If no overt judgment is passed on those who do visit Thailand to "enjoy" the "thriving sex industry," the reader is clearly positioned elsewhere—defined, if male, as not that kind of man.

Following the Guides

The language of guidebooks, like that of travel journalism, often addresses the reader directly. "You" should expect this result, try that experience, avoid the other option. The reader, especially at the high end of the market, is frequently constructed as an individual with the same interests and tastes as the magazine audience, to be directed toward similar objects of desire. But the guidebook audience is made up of those who, having read the "fine writing" addressed to the sedentary reader and the lyrical appeals to get out of that armchair and visit Phuket, the Floating Market, or Patpong—lyrics that may have appendages in the form of sidebars with useful addresses and toll-free numbers—have decided (or almost decided) to go. The guidebook is usually obtained in advance of the trip and so may serve to complete the "sale" of Thailand as destination, as well as help to plan the journey and accompany the traveler in country.

One consequence of the fact that this audience has reached the stage of serious intentions or actual presence is that although the guides may echo both news and travel journalism in their evaluations of a national character based on perpetual smiles and *mai pen rai*, at the same time they foreground enough common scams to suggest a kingdom of "easygoing" con artists. Whereas there are no rip-offs in *Vogue's* cosseted prose, the guidebooks alternate a similar style with a tone of pinched, eternal vigilance.

It is in this context of bargain hunting and theft avoidance that the specifics of the sex scene are introduced. The first two editions of the *Insight Guide* (Van Beek 1988; 1991) typify the genre pre-AIDS: explaining how to negotiate the transactions in a massage parlor and how to buy a bar dancer out for the night, advising against taking a prostitute to a first-class hotel (and obligingly mentioning that some Nana Plaza bars have their own guest houses attached), sending "you" to the Thermae to meet freelancers, and recommending Trink's column as appropriate reading matter. Photos (one of which is captioned "the real thing") relish the raunch and join the text in assuming that every red-blooded male reader will want to get into the swing of things, although some experiences are "not for the squeamish or those with feminist leanings." Even here, however, the same paragraph suggests that Patpong visitors sit at the bar for greater freedom of movement, and that they try to make the girls laugh: "dispensing laughs can often reduce the amount of cash you must dispense" (Van Beek 1988, 191). And, if "you" are going upstairs in Patpong, where "the real raunch" is kept behind locked doors, you should not "believe the touts on the street who say the upstairs shows are for free: after the show, a huge bill arrives" (1991, 117–18).

The third edition of the *Insight Guide*, published in 1993, takes a substantially different approach. Much of the practical information about where to find the sex industry and how to negotiate one's way through it has been relegated to the "Travel Tips" section printed on gray, matte-finish paper at the end of the book, along with lists of hotels and restaurants and instructions on airport transportation, snake bites, and shoe repair. The glossy pages that make up the body of the text still have two color photos of go-go dancers at work, one labeled "After sundown, Bangkok shows a different face" (although faces are not as easy to see as other flesh), and one captioned, "An all too obvious Patpong night scene" (Van Beek 1993, 132–33). It may still be the "real thing," but it gets less attention than a full-color shot of fully clad Thai "revellers at one of the many discos in Bangkok" (130–31). The nightlife copy still mentions the sex scene and refers once (131) to "delectable-looking" young ladies (who may turn out to be transvestites), and the "delectable lass" who will feed you your meal at the No-hands Restaurant (133). Moreover, we are told that the question of whether "the massage parlor originated in Bangkok . . . or whether they have merely reached their apotheosis here is a question best left to scholarly debate" (132).

What is new is a warning—"With AIDS rampant in Thailand, it would be foolish to assume anyone is safe; take appropriate precautions" (133)—and the emphasis on alternative forms of nightlife, characterized in class terms as "more up market" and appealing to *farang* couples as well as to the male traveler on his own (400). Thai women may still be described with gastronomic metaphors, but the classier tourists are "interested in sex shows more as dabblers than as gourmands." The advice about buying out bar girls for the evening is followed by the admonition, repeated from the earlier guides, that first-class hotels will not admit prostitutes. But further caveats now follow: "the hotel will normally demand that the girl leave her Identification Card at the desk until she leaves. Girls do occasionally walk away with watches and cash, so it is not a good idea to leave valuables lying on the night table. Similarly, with AIDS on the rise, do not be foolish; there is a drug store just down the street" (401).

In short, although the *Insight Guide* still maintains a relatively cheery tone about the reader's possible sexual escapades, it also reflects the new preoccupations typical of the 1990s guides: fear of AIDS contesting the center of anxiety with fear of theft, anxiety in general competing for center stage with desire, an emphasis on entertainment not linked to the sex industry, and class-based language used to describe older and newer styles of nightspot.

The anxiety level is even higher in the other mainstream guidebooks. Fodor's guides to Thailand, Bangkok, and Southeast Asia, for instance, repeat in identical words the judgment that in Thailand's capital tourism "has propagated the most lurid forms of nightlife," and they warn of false advertising for the sex shows: "Expect to be ripped off if you indulge" (Fodor 1991, 448). The text does proceed to direct the reader to Patpong, Soi Cowboy, and Nana Plaza, indicating both gay and straight venues, girlie shows, and transvestite entertainment, but it devotes the same amount of space to describing what happens if "you" protest higher prices than were touted downstairs and a cover charge where none was supposed to be levied.

Thomas Cook and Sons, a firm founded by a Victorian Baptist preacher who enforced missionary morality on his clients, has come a long way from its origins: its guidebook sternly advises that "missing out on Patpong would be like coming to Athens and not visiting the Parthenon," and includes the "world-renowned red light strip" in one of its self-guided walking tours (*Passports* 1992, 146). Bangkok nightlife, we are told, emphasizes "innocent fun, with the air more of a party than a brothel," (*Ibid.*), but "some upstairs bars are known as clip joints" so, if charged an "exorbitant price for a drink" you should pay up and then report the incident to the tourist police "conveniently situated at either end of the road," who will help "you" get your money back (146–47). Again, after warning about AIDS and other sexually transmitted diseases, Cook also makes sure you know about Soi Cowboy and "the cheaper, raunchier and more downmarket Nana Entertainment Complex" (147).

The consumer goods market on Patpong, Frommer's guide warns, "has undercut the impact of the once all-too-obvious market in flesh, so you may be disappointed." The sexual exhibitions are similarly disappointing when you do tear yourself away from the bargains: "The shows tend to be pretty routine in style, though if you've never seen one (and you probably haven't), this is the place" (Levy and McCarthy 1994, 126). Warnings follow about clip joints and AIDS—treated with precisely the same degree of gravity, though with more space devoted to your rights as a consumer than the threat to your health. Although the Bangkok sex trade is characterized as "abusive," all the information about how to order a "body-body" massage (or a "sandwich" with two masseuses) is also made available. The obligatory "word of warning" speaks of the dangers of being drugged and robbed by the prostitute whose role as the victim of abuse has just been alluded to and promptly forgotten (127).

Some 25 pages further, when the traveler has moved on to Pattaya, the "Adult Entertainment" section is worth quoting at some length:

> Examples of the go-go flesh trade abound in bars . . . where Thai beer and a look costs about 125B ($5), though the girls work off commission and encourage clients to buy rounds for everyone. A classier act and higher prices prevail at any of the new *karaoke sing-along hostess clubs.* . . .
>
> *Warning:* The police frequently clamp down on drug sellers and buyers in these venues; ignorance of the law is not an accepted defense in Thailand. . . .
>
> Typically, [in the massage parlors], dozens of girls with numbered signs wait to be selected by clients, who are then whisked away to private massage rooms.
>
> *Repeat warning:* Police frequently clamp down on drug sellers and buyers in these massage parlors.
>
> All-night companionship is easy to come by, though payments to club owners, security guards, etc., mount up. Beware of "companions" bearing drinks laced with "knock-out" drugs; watch your wallet; wear a condom (153; original emphasis).

This grim experience in repressive tolerance is followed by the section on shopping, which begins with indications of where to buy "sex-joke T shirts and postcards" and proceeds to the usual silk shops and jewelers.

Lonely Planet tells the Lonely Reader that "Bangkok is, of course, known as the Oriental sin city extraordinaire . . . and hordes of (male) package tourist descend upon the city simply to sample its free-wheeling delights" (Cummings 1994, 726). The Lonely Guy apparently is not as free-wheeling or delighted as all that, however: "In Thailand, a 'body massage' means the masseuse's not yours. Avoid Bangkok's large massage parlours . . . which cost as much as $US40 for a lukewarm bath and massage." Indeed, "many Bangkok visitors find that indulging in the pleasures of sin-city can easily lead to social diseases or worse ... so the use of condoms—or total abstinence—really is imperative" (726). The ritual proximity of warnings about AIDS and about price-gouging suggests a semiotic connection under some joint joyless rubric like "The Price You Pay."

Along with the hot addresses, some guides also offer a bit of potted sociology. A cruder version of the cultural relativist argument we discuss in Chapter 5 may be found in a French guidebook widely available in English translation: "Though the reputation of Patpong is mainly due to the development of mass sex tourism, one should keep in mind that traditionally in Thailand sex education for males starts with a visit to a brothel. Despite the natural shyness and puritanism of the Thais, prostitution remains an accepted part of life" (*Thailand: Knopf Guide* 1993, 180).

Filling in more of the social background, a later Passport guide explains that "beautiful girls, usually from poor northeast villages, are skilled in all sorts of [sexual] feats" (Osborne 1994, 34). Of course, it is not entirely clear from this way of putting it whether or not the skills in question are a craft native to "poor northeast villages." This explanation that fails to explain is sandwiched between comments about Bangkok: the statement that it is "world-famous for licentious nightlife ... [offering] red-hot, buffet-style entertainment. Appetisers range from family-type Thai classic dancing and boxing to 'the other,' which is what most tourists want to see," followed—on the other side of the "poor villages" line—by a description of bars, brothels, and massage parlors. It was this publisher, speaking in the persona of Thomas Cook and Sons, who compared Patpong as a tourist attraction to the Parthenon. Here, continuing the gustatory metaphor of the buffet, we are informed that "massage parlours and Bangkok go together like a gin and tonic" (35). On the same page, within an inch of each other, the reader encounters the observation that "you get what you pay for—and careless men pay dearly" and that "'body' massage means sex. There is a basic hourly rate and the amount to tip depends on any 'extra services'" (35). Getting what you pay for, metaphorically speaking, melts effortlessly (if schizophrenically) into the pragmatics of how to go about paying for what you get.

Schizophrenia is also the dominant note of Lonely Planet's City Guide to Bangkok. (Cummings 1995). Whereas the publisher's regional compendium, released a year earlier with a Thailand section written by the same author (Cummings 1994) combines distaste with directions, this one—although repeating a number of phrases verbatim, from references to the "real raunch" upstairs to a misdefinition of "high tea" in the restaurant section that immediately precedes "Entertainment"—strikes several new notes. The "naughty nightlife" is linked to the history of Vietnam-era R&R, with the "throwbacks" described as "seedy, expensive and cater[ing] to men only," as contrasted with the apparently more acceptable "new breed" of "classier and more modest S&S (sex and sin) bars" (1995, 235). Overpayment anxiety is allayed by supplying the names of the only two Patpong bars "that consistently eschew the practice of adding surprise charges to your bill" (236).

The gesture to sociology here is a densely printed pair of facing pages (244–45), in smaller type than the rest of the volume, containing a brief history of Thai sexual customs, including the origins of "true" prostitution and an overview of the present economic, medical, and legal situation. Thereafter, the body of the text (back in normal type and advice-giving mode) goes on: "The fact that many of the modern [i.e. not traditional or medical] massage parlours . . . also deal in prostitution is well known; less well known is the fact that many of the girls working in the parlours are bonded labour—they are not necessarily there by choice. All but the most insensitive males will be saddened by the sight of 50 girls/women behind a glass wall with numbers pinned to their dresses" (246).

Descriptions of the "superstar" and straight-massage sections of the establishments follow, and then more advice: "Before contemplating anything more than a massage at a modern massage parlour, be sure to read the Health section. . . . Condoms can lower the risk of AIDS considerably, but remember that an estimated 11% of commercial Thai condoms are barrier-defective" (246). The sensitive tourist may be "saddened" by the spectacle on display behind the glass, but only considerations of health (his own) would presumably deter him from picking out a hot number for himself.

Only the most "countercultural" volumes are consistent in their disapproval of the sex trade. Rough Guide's "Gay Thailand" section states categorically, "The most public aspect of Thailand's gay scene is the farang-oriented sex industry, which, with its tawdry floor shows and host services, bears a gruesome resemblance to the straight sex trade" (Gray and Redoit 1995, 50). For many of Bangkok's straight visitors, it acknowledges, "nightfall in the city is the signal to hit the sex bars" (122). The policy here, however, is to mention no commercial sex venues but instead highlight, on the gay side, "low-key meeting places for Thai and farang men" (50), while pointing out that for heterosexuals, "within spitting distance [sic] of the beer bellies flopped onto Patpong's bars lies . . . Bangkok's most happening after-dark bar, pulling in the cream of Thai youth and tempting an increasing number of travellers to stuff their party gear into their rucksacks" (122). This vocabulary, contrasting the cream of Thai youth with the beer bellies on Patpong's bars, is reminiscent of Lonely Planet's preference for the "more modest" and the "classy," but in this case it accompanies a rejection of commercial sex, rather than a mere preference for S&S over R&R style.

Finally, the *Let's Go* guide to Southeast Asia, one of a series for backpacking youth that originated with the Harvard Student Agencies, states unequivocally that "tourism and the [sex] industry are mutually reinforcing" (Grayman *et al.* 1996, 183). In addition to information about both the economics of prostitution (as a forced choice in a regionally inequitable labor market) and statistics about the AIDS epidemic, *Let's Go* has a section on "Bars and Pubs" which distinguishes two types:

> First and *most atrocious* are the infamous go-go bars, which are a mainstay of the Thai prostitution industry. Women and children (of both genders) from all over Thailand are sold into slavery by their impoverished rural families and sent to work in Bangkok go-go bars, which are fueled by the bucks funneled in by overseas visitors. *These are not listed.*
>
> The second type is the "hostess bar," where attractive women are hired by the management to serve you drinks and sit with you. Some of these bars are fronts for prostitution, some aren't. *These too are not listed* (326, emphasis added).

If the information is slightly inaccurate and the tone a tad self-righteous (and, one can't help thinking, very young), it is also sincere, unambiguous, and, at the very least, refreshing in a genre whose usual purpose is to provide the reader with a standard list, whatever ambivalence may creep in. And the authors have gone out of their way to identify "the few pubs where people can get together without participating in the skin trade in any way," and which, despite the "romping nightlife," are "amazingly difficult to encounter" (326).

Travel Brochures: The Real Come On

> American soldiers ... have unfortunately spoilt a great deal as far as sex is concerned. But someone who no longer gets on with his wife in bed and has to fly all the way to Thailand to have a good screw, will hardly be interested in the individual personality of the girl.
> —Anders Reisen, "Tips and Tricks for Tramps and Travellers"

Before any guidebook can be purchased, the potential tourist must make the mental purchase of a particular destination. To separate one site from the array of possible sites, the tourist brochure enters the lists of external representations. The cookie-cutter imagery and superlative-ridden hyperbole that so characterize this genre are the stuff of cliché, if not of kitsch. The brochures for Thailand, however, feature a cultural commodity that both is and is not advertised in pamphlets hyping other destinations. Thailand is by no means the only tourist spot featuring sex. The Philippines, Kenya, the Virgin Islands, and Hawaii can be included in this roster. In fact, any tropical resort implicitly includes sex in the list of s's it offers tourists from colder climes: sun, sand, surf, service, and subservience. While each destination exploits the stereotypes of package-tour exotica, it must also attempt to distinguish itself from the others selling virtually the same commodities. Consequently, the representations both resemble each other in specific ways and attempt to diverge for exactly the same reason. Advertising demands variations on the imagery and rhetoric of the tourist brochure genre, and apparently the only variation that truly exists is how explicitly sex is represented as part of the package.

One such brochure, for a British tour operator, draws on popular culture images to convey the sense of wonder and otherworldliness the male tourist supposedly has awaiting him in Thailand: "One of the very early episodes of Star Trek saw Captain Kirk and his crew on a distant planet peopled by a beautiful gentle race of people where life was given over totally to pleasure. Kirk and Spock had a hard time on the philosophy front, trying to convince the aliens that there ought to be more to life than the pursuit of pleasure. Well for 'distant world' [*sic*] read Thailand, the pleasure centre of the world" (qtd. in Selwyn 1993, 122). The irony of using a science fiction television show as an analogy for a "real" place where they "really" pursue pleasure is overwhelmed by the stunning ethnocentrism of the advertisement. In the analogy, Kirk and Spock represent tourists, yet the locals they visit are identified as "aliens." The pervasive I-as-center-of-the-universe is the a priori perspective of both text and tourist, and it is this same subjectivity that searches for a site where every desire can be instantly satiated, while simultaneously ignoring the locals who labor to make the pleasure possible.

Perhaps this is not a fair analysis. The indigenous people *are* addressed in most brochures, but their "character" or "nature" becomes part of the product being sold to potential tourists. Adopting a quintessential colonial stance, the British brochure explains how travelers should interpret the local folk. "To come to terms with the unique character of the Thai people," it tells us, "you must regard them all as Peter Pans. Eternal children who have never grown up. . . . The lights are on but nobody's at home" (qtd. in Selwyn 1993, 123). Even though the allusion foregrounds the element of fantasy, the text pretends to provide ethnographic information. Tourists are told that the host-guest relationship is analogous to that of a child and an adult. The locals, it seems, are innocently playful but slightly dim and should be treated as the colonial masters of the past treated those they ruled: with a kind but firm hand.

Such treatment extends to all who service the tourist abroad, as a brochure by Germany's Anders Reisen reveals: "Contact with ladies of pleasure, if one treats them well, can be an emotionally vigorating [sic] experience. . . . In Southeast Asia . . . one can experience venal sex as something friendly, pleasurable and really erotic" (qtd. in *Documentation* 1983, 52). Simultaneously childlike and erotic, the Thai people are represented by tropes that have been part of colonial discourse for centuries (an issue examined at length in Chapter 5). But the main point of these brochures is to assure would-be tourists that their satisfaction is never in doubt; it is, in fact, an inherent part of the cross-cultural interaction, much as European enrichment was a presumed element of colonial encounters.

Continuing its ethnographic information and attempting to distinguish Thailand from other tourist destinations, the British brochure claims that the Thai people "are the most sensual and overtly sexual on the earth" (qtd. in Selwyn 1993,123). That the natives are naturally, openly, and innocently more sensual and sexual than the tourist—indeed, more so than any other people "on the earth"—becomes a major selling point for the company. Certainly other sites have sensual people, readers are told, but Thailand has the *most* sensual. Why consider another destination if this one offers the sexual superlative? This language of tourism naturalizes a particular interpretation of another culture's sexuality, just as it naturalizes the market economy in which the sex industry operates. Sex tourists, then, are simply going native and partaking of the culture, which just happens to be "overtly sexual." But the ability to travel and go native, to partake of the sexual culture, derives from economic power, as the brochure makes clear: "The truly nice thing is that in spite of all the blatant sex . . . in [Bangkok] you can buy anything . . . one can walk in total safety" (123). One purchases both perpetual pleasure and peace of mind. No one shall interfere with the tourist's pursuit of happiness, not even the police or the thugs they arrest. You, the brochure assures, are safe to act in ways that back home might land you in a seedy part of town, if not actually in jail. The freedom that travel allows an individual evidently extends beyond the intellectual and the sensual to include the legal.

The commodification of culture that occurs in these external representations of tourist sites is further naturalized by focusing on the tourist body. The brochure genre elides the inequitable economic relations between bodies being serviced and those servicing. Only the satisfaction of the one matters, and economic power ensures that satisfaction. The tourist who has labored hard to earn the money for this vacation learns from these representations that an integral part of leisure travel is complete corporeal satiation, and what is more "natural" than physical appetites? Food, drink, warmth, recreation, and sex reward the tourist for his work and his travel. Resorts around the world make the slaking of bodily thirsts a priority in the advertisement of their services, and the abundance of physical luxury has become the stock in trade of such imagery. But the language of brochures, going beyond mere satisfaction to indulgence, insists on opulence. These representations entice travelers with Rabelaisian spreads of hedonistic wares. Tables groaning under the weight of their bounty fill the photographs, and visceral pleasures swelling to the point of bursting occupy the text. The British brochure says of Pattaya, Thailand's famous R&R site now become a tourist destination, "If you can suck it, use it, eat it, taste it, abuse it, or see it then it is available at this resort" (qtd. in Selwyn 1993, 123).

The concentration on basic bodily appetites virtually infantilizes the reader, making him an id-driven, somatic, polymorphously perverse being. In this sense, it is the tourists and not the locals who seem to be "eternal children," for the language of these brochures appeals to the arrested adolescence of potential tourists. Further, everything the nation has to offer any traveler has become a generalized thing, an "it" to be purchased, consumed, and used in any way the tourist desires. The conversion of an entire culture, history, and people into the impersonal, inanimate, pronoun "it" neatly expresses the assumptions that guide the fundamental relationships operative in this language of tourism. Needless to say, it is difficult to reconcile the perspectives these brochures articulate with those proffered by the pro-tourism propaganda of international and national agencies. The promise of every tourist as cultural ambassador loses out to the reality of every tourist as hedonistic consumer. But are the two really antipodal? Given the homogenization of values and the ascendancy of international capital in the latter part of this century, hedonistic consumers actually *are* universal cultural ambassadors, espousing as they do the values of the global marketplace and the globe-as-marketplace.

4

A VERY POLITICAL ECONOMY

> She became the victim of her own vulnerability, and was setting out now to victimize those more vulnerable than herself.
>
> —*From Peasant Girls to Bangkok Masseuses*

"Nightlife" is the Bangkok guidebooks' universal euphemism for the sex trade. Of course there are other after-dark activities in Thailand—the reader interested in theater, folk dance, ballet, or film can readily find all of them listed under "Culture," which is apparently defined as something quite distinct from nightlife—and, of course, commercial sex, like the homemade kind, is not restricted to the hours of darkness. Still, "nightlife," with its evocation of the world of bars, clubs, raucous music, and girlie shows, readily expands to encompass the massage parlors, go-go bars, and kinky exhibitions that are the sex trade's characteristic venues.

We chose the title *Night Market* for this study in order to bring together the suggestion of sexual entertainment implicit in "nightlife" and the explicit commerce involved in anything called a market. But there are actual night markets all over Thailand, open-air emporia whose stands do a brisk trade in Thai handicrafts, trademark knockoffs, and prepared foods. In the culture of mass tourism, where sightseeing and shopping are barely differentiated, the guidebooks delightedly direct you to the best wares and the most abundant bargains, with the

nighttime setting assuring the exotic and picturesque character of the experience. Our title is therefore meant to connect the two kinds of tourist-targeted
nocturnal commerce, a link that is underscored by the presence of a thriving
night market in the very midst of Patpong, the street famous the world over as
the center of Bangkok's sex industry.

It turns out that the street markets also provide metaphoric reflections of the
basic economic issues upon which the sex trade's complex superstructure is balanced. For instance, the Night Market (often called the Night Bazaar) in Chiang
Mai is probably the best known one in the country. (At the risk of several kinds
of confusion, you could call it the Patpong of street bazaars.) So it is only fitting
that it should also harbor the most salient collection of metaphors representing
the economics of the sex industry in relation to tourism and of both to the Thai
economy as a whole. The bazaar in Chiang Mai was originally set up to serve
comparatively privileged visitors from the Bangkok area. Here, craftspeople and
sellers of regional delicacies from outlying rural areas converged on a provincial
urban center to sell their wares. They came after dark because not only was it
cooler after sunset, but operating the market at night met the needs both of visitors from the big city (who found Chiang Mai a rather sleepy burg after dark and
relished the exotic character of nighttime shopping) and the needs of the sellers,
whose market sales supplemented their income from their day jobs. In this scenario, central Thailand was the home of the "true" Thais, the unmarked case,
while people from the North in general and the hill tribes in particular were constructed as the Other, the inferentially less evolved creators of exotic crafts and
specialty foods.

In recent years, as international tourism has become an increasingly influential factor in the Thai economy, the focus of commerce has shifted from local to
global: away from the Thai customer, for whom the provincial North is the
source of charming art objects and tasty dishes, to the foreigner who experiences
a fundamentally undifferentiated "Thailand" as the bargain paradise. Although
regional goods continue to predominate, all sorts of Thai paraphernalia are now
sold in the market, along with bootleg audio and video cassettes addressing an
international audience, and art objects and jewelry that are of no interest to most
Thais. To mark and reinforce this shift, the city authorities have underwritten a
cleanup of the market space, displacing toward the rear the sloppy food stands
and other unsightly stalls frequented only by locals and foregrounding attractive
new stands catering to the tastes of foreign tourists. Crowning the entrance to
several arteries of the new space is a neon sign emblazoning the words "Night
Bazaar"—in English.

Chiang Mai's Chang Klang Market thus models a structure of inequality and
dependency in which a national elite is catered to by (often ethnically distinct)
rural and provincial populations and is then superseded by an international customer to whom the entire nation offers its products, including its inhabitants, as
commodities for sale. (In fact, for at least some of the international customers,
the Chiang Mai Night Bazaar offers an infinite regress of otherness, in which

they get to experience the hill tribes as the ethnic Other of the exotic Other.) In the sex market as in the street stalls, the inequality and dependency between the metropolis and the less favored regions underlies both the thriving venues serving Thai men and more recent institutions such as the go-go bars, which were established for and appeal chiefly to the *farang*.

The declining importance of agriculture in the national economy and the consequent inability of many families to wrest a living from farming alone assure a steady—indeed, an increasing—supply of young workers for jobs in Bangkok's rapidly growing service sector. A substantial portion of these service positions are related to the tourism and hospitality industries, and a large number of the young women migrants end up in the sex trade. For anyone seeking to understand the economic underpinnings of the sex industry, the first requisite would be a description of the rural economy, the migration of village youth to swell the supply of cheap, unskilled urban labor, the development of mass international tourism, and the ways these intersect. One must also try to understand how much intentionality there is in the system, the extent to which national and international economic planning for the tourist industry took account of the conditions of immiseration in the rural areas and deliberately exacerbated them: weakening traditional patterns of land ownership, engaging in deforestation schemes, denying credits for investment in family farms, and manipulating crucial water and irrigation policies.

The night market on Patpong reflects some of the difficulties entailed in finding answers to even the most apparently straightforward questions about the economics of the sex industry in its relation to development strategies. One guidebook blandly and uncritically reassures its readers that "Patpong is quite safe, well patrolled by police, and even has a night market where Thai families shop" (*Fodor* 1991, 79). All the foreign sources that mention the Patpong market emphasize that the Thai shoppers there are middle-class family groups, who are determinedly—if apparently effortlessly—ignoring the bright lights, the sights and sounds of go-go bars, and the touts whose sandwich boards advertise (admittedly in English) precisely which feats are performed by the versatile "pussy" in which upstairs venues.

The coexistence in the same public space of the two kinds of nighttime trade impresses most commentators as either highly ironic or as further proof that the entire Thai populace shares a relaxed and permissive attitude toward sexuality and its public commercial manifestations. In reality, the individual families are acting out the kind of denial of the unspeakable that we discuss in Chapter 7. The juxtaposition of the two kinds of commerce is in fact an all too apt figure for the problems of fitting the economics of the sex industry into a larger analysis. Like the Thai shoppers on Patpong, economists know the sex industry is there. They often devote a paragraph or two to its origin in rural poverty and its connection to the big business of tourism. At the same time, sex workers, their customers, and their employers are hard to locate in economic statistics. Does the sex trade produce part of the $4 billion in foreign exchange provided by tourism as a whole, or is there a separate figure, and if so where and what is it? The figures for the proportions of women workers employed in different job categories add up to 100 percent, and those presenting them often acknowledge the existence of prostitution, so the prostitutes must be included—but how can they be if no one can tell with any certainty whether there are 100,000 or 1,000,000 of them? Thanh-Dam Truong (1990, 128) maintains, "Unlike their flesh, the contributions of prostitutes' labour to . . . [the] process of accumulation remains invisible." More precisely and even more frustratingly, it is simultaneously visible and invisible as an economic fact, at once acknowledged and ignored.

Another approach to the Patpong night market and its proximity to the flesh market is suggested by the *Insight Guide*, whose 1993 edition makes the claim that "drastic changes" have taken place in the Thai nightlife scene. Although, from the information provided, there appears to be no diminution in "traditional" sex trade activities, the guide tells us that some bars (and some customers) have changed their focus and that shopping has replaced sex as "the queen of nighttime activities." (So the prostitute, while still a lady of the evening, is no longer Queen of the Night.) The text justifies this bizarre observation by calling attention to the proliferation of night markets: "Even that wrinkled old harlot of a street, Patpong, has not been immune to the breezes of change," it points out. "Vendors' tables choke the street, drawing more patrons than the bars. A wealth of cheap goods, most of them counterfeit—fake Rolex watches, fake Benetton shirts, fake cassette tapes—vie with faked orgasms at seedier upstairs sex shows" (Van Beek 1993, 100). Other observers, whether writing travel guides or political economy, are so far from sharing this particular "insight" that it appears almost grotesquely exaggerated. Yet it too affords access to a range of material issues, these focused on the linkages between sex tourism and consumer society.

In this chapter we examine the issues that cluster around each of these approaches to the night-market-as-economic-metaphor: the relation of metropolis to dependent region, as played out on the scene of international tourism and in development planning; the curious simultaneous presence and absence of the sex trade in (and from) economic description and analysis; and the connections of tourism in general and sex tourism in particular to the consumer economy.

Base Notes: Economic Foundations

> A business which . . . [recruits] girls out of the poorer parts of the country-side and sells their services to the urban earner and to the foreign visitor is merely the mirror image of . . . [the] hierarchy of dependence.
> —*From Peasant Girls to Bangkok Masseuses*

There is a standard "objective" narrative about the Thai sex industry. It begins with a reference to "the decay of local communities leading to large-scale migration by rural girls (and later, also boys) to work in prostitution for the U.S. soldiers, for an increasingly prosperous urban market, later for the tourist trade, and finally as an export commodity" (Phongpaichit and Baker 1995, 75). By characterizing this version of the origins and progression of the sex trade as "standard," we do not mean to imply that it is a mechanical litany devoid of truth. In fact, it has become standard if not, indeed, conventional precisely because, as far as it goes, it is an accurate summary.

It is troubling chiefly because it is incomplete—and often unselfconsciously incomplete, at that. The book from which this particular formulation comes is an overview of Thai economic and political history with a strong emphasis on twentieth-century developments. So each of the elements in the story—the decline of agriculture, the migration to Bangkok, the U.S. presence, the rise of tourism, and the export of sexual and other labor—is discussed in detail, with its economic implications to the fore. The principal author, moreover, is also the author of the foundational study of Bangkok masseuses (Phongpaichit 1982), and her perspective here is not incompatible with her earlier focus on sex workers. But perhaps because the subject of the book is the evolution of the economy as seen from within, the authors have a tendency to represent particular policies, their success or failure, and the chain of causalities they entail, as a self-contained and almost natural process. (In the case of the progression of clientele from American troops to local urban men to tourists to the export market, the word "almost" could be dispensed with, since the authors make the "progression" sound like an inevitable evolution.) It is an approach that tends to downplay the importance of development planning, especially on the international scale, even as it concerns such unequivocally international phenomena as tourism and the export of labor.

A diametrically opposite approach emphasizes the roles of international lending agencies and transnational corporations; the "brotherly" relations between airlines, hotels, and tour packagers; and the connection of all of these to the delivery of sexual services. The sex tour with "entertainment" included in the package is the most obvious result of this collaboration. But it is also possible to foreground the role of the World Bank and the international tourism conglomerates while focusing, as we do, on the go-go bars, which are a legacy of the U.S. military presence and an extension or perpetuation of this imported (more accurately, translated) sexual institution for the benefit of foreign customers. The go-go bars, with their superficially open transaction format, simply reflect a customer demand based on a configuration of sexual fantasy different from the fantasy catered to by the sex-included package tours. This does not mean that the bars are any less implicated in the larger international conception of the industry.

A third approach is to downplay the importance of the international dimension, on the level not only of development planning but also of the relatively modest share of the sex industry involving foreign customers. Journalist Donald

Wilson of the expatriate Anglo-American Crescent Press group takes the position that emphasizing the tourism connection, when so many more sex workers service local men than foreign clientele, constitutes a tendentious scapegoating of the United States, "blaming Uncle Sam." He maintains that "US marines on R&R, together with sex tourists cannot really be held responsible for corrupting Thailand's morals and spreading prostitution in the country—only for making it uglier and more obvious. . . . [Rather,] the reasons for Thailand's development as a sex centre are older and deeper, lying buried, perhaps, in an easy-going, often commercial attitude towards sex" (Wilson 1994, 6).

No one on any side of the issue denies the existence and scale of the indigenous sex trade. Even Sapharit Koonpraphant, director of the Centre for the Protection of Children's Rights, which actively works against the practice of indenturing young daughters to the sex trade, admits that the practice "is deeply rooted in Thai culture" (qtd. in Tasker 1994, 23). Both the widespread prostitution and the pattern of family authority and loyalty that sustain it have deep roots in Thailand. Courtesans, concubines, and prostitutes all play a role in traditional Thai life, each reflecting "a particular class accommodation to extra-marital sex" (Richter 1989, 97). In the earlier part of this century a relationship with a concubine or secondary wife was the recognized privilege of elite males, providing social mobility for the favored women and fueling the dream of it for many others.[1] This history and the mythology to which it has given rise interface with the reality of an indigenous commercial sex world that is by no means limited to the upper-class male engaged in semiofficial polygamy. Some of the most luxurious massage parlors and brothels serve an exclusively or almost exclusively local clientele, as do some of the cheapest and grimmest ones. In fact, many of the customers at the low-class establishments are the male counterparts of the working girls, youthful migrants from Burma or the rural North and Northeast of Thailand who have come to Bangkok to look for jobs and who find themselves on their own in the big city without either the constraints or the supports of village life. These boys, still teenagers themselves, "look to brothels for comfort and fun" (Fairclough 1995, 28).

If sheer numbers were the principal criterion, the emphasis on the local trade would be compelling. Even as it is, the scale and ramifications of the sex market for Thai men must always be borne in mind by anyone attempting to understand the special scene catering to tourists. But even when the same sexual and financial transactions take place in both local and international markets, the one involving the foreign tourist is accessory to an industry that earns $4 billion a year in foreign exchange, giving the interaction and the industry that fosters it a different economic meaning. As long ago as the late 1960s, it was estimated that tourists to Thailand spent approximately 400 million baht (about $16 million) a year, a sum then comparable to the aggregate average income of a quarter of a million Thais (Richter 1989, 87). As the revenue from tourism has grown to 250 times that size, with real average income growing considerably more slowly, the disproportion becomes still more dramatic (Krongkaew 1993, 410–12). The disparity echoes another one, the relatively small item that sexual services represent in the individual customer's budget, as contrasted with the "simply astounding" earning power that the same payment represents for the prostitute from a poor rural family (Phongpaichit 1982, 74).

Ever since 1982, moreover, the year that it overtook rice exports, tourism has been the country's largest earner of foreign exchange;[2] the amount is high enough that in some years income from tourism alone more than covers the total trade deficit (Richter 1989, 84). In these circumstances, when the very definition of "tourism" in the Historical Dictionary of Thailand begins "The major source of foreign exchange in the present-day Thai economy" (Kayr-Win and Smith 1995, 181), public policy concerning prostitution is formulated and implemented with an eye to its effect on tourist arrivals, rather than on the larger segment of the sex industry catering to the domestic market. If the tourist dollar were not an issue, the attitude that Pasuk characterizes as a "positively malign" neglect of AIDS (Phongpaichit 1993, 168) would probably not have predominated for so long over public health considerations, and the various legislative initiatives to control the industry (increasing penalties for child molestation, banning the selling or indenturing of one's own children, criminalizing the customer) might have met a different fate. Whatever its congruencies with Thai sexual tradition, sex tourism assumes the importance it does precisely because of its international dimension.

This international dimension is present in the planning and the profit-taking, as well as the clientele. It was in 1971, at the height of the Vietnam conflict, that Robert McNamara, then head of the World Bank, visited Bangkok and arranged to send the bank's tourism experts to plan the development of Thailand's tourist industry. The rationale for this move was, in fact, the "unstable geo-political situation in Indochina" and the consequent unreliability of the R&R supply, though the report issued by the specialists from the bank's Tourism Projects Department in 1975, as the war ended, "assessed the growth potential of tourism . . . irrespective of R&R" (Truong 1990, 162–63).

This is not to say that the infrastructure established through the R&R contracts was irrelevant to the World Bank's assessment. Quite the contrary. Contemplating the elevated cost of airfare to Thailand at the time, even at package-tour rates, one would not have had to be a rocket scientist but merely a development banker with a knowledge of the travel industry to see that the prospects for mass family tourism or the honeymoon market were extremely limited. And if the single traveler with disposable income (which, in the first instance, means an unaccompanied male) was to be targeted, the R&R services already in place clearly represented what Thailand had to offer that traveler.[3] When, moreover, the World Bank's agreement was negotiated by the same executive who, as U.S. secretary of defense in 1967, oversaw the R&R contracts, the special kind of tourism envisaged was virtually a foregone conclusion.

Since it is almost universally acknowledged that the prevalence of prostitution in Thailand is to some degree a consequence of the increasing gap between the rural and urban economies, it is not just paranoia that prompts one to wonder whether that gap was created and maintained as a result of development planning centered on tourism (Keyes 1987, 157). In 1976 the head of the Tourist Authority of Thailand acknowledged with some qualifications the truth of the accusation that tourism encourages prostitution but added, "prostitution exists mainly because of the state of our economy because everyone needs to earn their income. If we can create jobs, we can provide per capita income and do away with prostitution" (qtd. in Truong 1990, 179). But it is hard to see how economic growth arising from prostitution-based tourism could do away with prostitution. On the contrary, since the market sets up a permanent demand for a sex- and age-specific labor force which, as it happens, ages very rapidly, the way to assure the constant availability of fresh supplies from the rural areas is precisely to pursue national planning policies that systematically deemphasize agriculture and displace fishing and to withhold resources from the regions where they historically constituted the economic base.[4]

Pasuk Phongpaichit also attempts to envisage the conditions that would eliminate the need for a young peasant girl to choose prostitution or have it chosen for her. She says of one of the Bangkok masseuses featured in her study that if "Lek" had had "alternative employment in her village, her parents might not have encouraged her to have [sic] such a fate." But she quickly adds a bitter rider: "It could also be argued that had Lek's parents had access to good credit or had the government provided a better irrigation scheme for the farmers, the family would not have to live in abject poverty and drive their daughter to prostitution" (Phongpaichit 1982, 61). She does not have to spell out that the absence of those alternatives has the predictable opposite effect and that this predictability may well have entered into a planning process that is nothing if not thoroughly rational. With Thailand the fifth largest borrower from the World Bank (Phongpaichit and Baker 1995, 148), it is also hard to avoid assigning responsibility for this cynical "rationality" and thereby, indeed, "blaming Uncle Sam"—if not Uncle Scrooge.

From the perspective of national and international policy, "Lek" and her thousands of sisters make it possible for Thailand to be an exemplary client of the World Bank. Although the country's rate of borrowing is very high—yielding a deficit in yen, as well as in dollars—Thailand has not been reduced to the debt peonage characteristic of so many other oil-importing nations that have no stable source of foreign exchange. Thailand has been able to meet the interest if not the principal on its deficit, so that economic growth has not been slowed, even as the proportion of foreign debt to GNP (Gross National Product) has more than trebled (Hill 1993, 138; LePoer 1989, 134). This enormous increase is precisely coeval with the accession of tourism to the status of top earner of foreign exchange, which means that Thailand's ability to maintain growth while meeting its responsibilities as a debtor nation has been achieved on the backs of its female service workers—a significant proportion of whom are working on *their* backs.

What this suggests is a dramatic change in the material and social meanings of prostitution in the postcolonial situation. The culture of colonialism traditionally entailed the prostitution of local women, along with practices such as individual and mass rape, in which territorial and economic conquest were enacted on women's bodies. Throughout the nineteenth century, for instance, the British made provision for prostitutes to serve the sexual needs of their troops in India, so as to avoid the (apparently equally threatening) pitfalls of homosexuality in the ranks and true intimacy with native women (Ballhatchet 1980). However fundamental these practices were to the project of domination, they could hardly be confused with the purpose of the conquest; despoiling native women was incidental to the economic mission of looting mineral and agricultural resources. (Indeed, as we make clear in Chapter 5, what we call the "despoiling" was typically represented as a positive engagement with a different —an exotic—sexual morality.)

In Thailand and in other locales where tourism plays a central role in development strategy, the presence of the foreigner means an invasion of currency, not an extraction of value. Tourism is a major factor in the economic structure, part of the base. To the extent that tourism is marketed by its vendors and understood, purchased, and experienced by its consumers as access to sexual services, prostitution also moves from the superstructure to the base—which means that sexuality itself not only constitutes part of culture but becomes part of political economy.

Just the Facts

> Prostitution is criminalized under the Penal Code. At the same time it is formalized under the law governing industries. Under the Penal Code it is defined as "a crime of promiscuity." It is defined as "personal services" under business law, and as "special services" by the Police Department. The law recognizes "personal services" as a business and ensures privileges to investors and at the same time criminalizes workers in the business.
> —*Sex, Money and Morality*

It is always hard to see the forest for the trees, and it is harder still if the trees all have signs nailed to them reading NO FOREST HEREABOUTS; WATCH OUT FOR LOW-HANGING BRANCHES. This is what it is like to read about the Thai economy, looking for answers to questions about the specific economy of the sex trade: How many women are engaged in prostitution? How much do they earn? How do indenture and other conditions of recruitment and employment function? How much money does the sex trade put into circulation and what happens to it? The contradictions become particularly intense when the answer has to be expressed as a number, since even the most clearly enunciated statistics seem neither to include nor to exclude prostitution from their purview—or sometimes to do both at once.

Part of the problem with the simultaneous presence and absence of information about prostitution in economic accounts has to do with the issue adumbrated in the epigraph above: the sex trade's ambiguous legal status. It is this ambiguity that makes it possible for an otherwise sensible, categorical work like the 1981 *Country Study* of Thailand to include no "Prostitution" entry in its index and to content itself, in the text, with the almost imbecilically uncritical observation that "Foreign commerce and a thriving tourist industry brought income to small businesses and service industries, but prostitution, associated to a considerable extent with the influx of foreign visitors . . . occupied the attention of police. (See Problems of Criminal Activity)" (Burge 1981, 113).[5]

Virtually all other commentators, in or out of Thailand, take a far more nuanced position on the "concern" evinced by law enforcement authorities, acknowledging the tension between traditional morality and economic considerations. Charles Keyes (1987, 157) uses the mild tone characteristic of foreign travel writers and scholars alike when he acknowledges that, although prostitution is illegal, little has been done to enforce the law (157). But Pasuk Phongpaichit, writing, not in her study of the Bangkok sex workers but in the chapter on "Services" in a general collection about the Thai economy, states unequivocally that "the blatant existence of a large-scale sex trade would have been impossible without the tacit blessing of the Ministry of the Interior," which is officially responsible for the prevention of prostitution (1993, 164).

Pasuk takes an even more cynical line in *From Peasant Girls to Bangkok Masseuses* maintaining that the rare police raids on massage parlors are motivated not by zeal for the law but by disagreements over the price of protection (Phongpaichit 1982, 11).[6] Even though her study is now some fifteen years old, it is worth noting that this aspect of her remarks is far from out of date. A news item published in December 1995 reports that the standard bribe an immigrant prostitute must pay to avoid deportation is 500 baht. (An indirect effect of this graft is to keep the sex worker working, since borrowing the sum needed for the bribe increases her debt to the brothel owner.) The same article tells of a prostitute in a combination massage parlor and karaoke lounge in Mae Sai who, when guests seemed startled by the appearance of a policeman on the premises, reassured them by explaining, "No problem. He works here!" (Fairclough 1995, 28). For that matter, Thermae, the sex industry's after-hours "headquarters" bar, is almost universally believed to be police-owned.

According to the *Bangkok Post* for 11 August 1990, police corruption and "deeply entrenched apathetic attitudes" on the part of the Thai public toward both the sex industry and administrative abuses are joined by the overriding fear that taking action to curb the sex industry could create adverse publicity that might "hurt" tourism. This fear is exemplified by a recent report that in Hat Yai, the prime site for visitors from Malaysia, it is not only those directly implicated in the sex trade but also "local hoteliers and retailers [who] have been complaining that a [still rare] police crack-down on prostitution is scaring off tourists and pinching profits across the board" (Fairclough 1994, 30).

The *Far Eastern Economic Review* article that focused on developments in Hat Yai is subtitled "Government Tries to Uproot Prostitution from Economy." Although it does not question the good faith of this effort, the article concentrates on the obstacles to its effectiveness. In common with nearly everyone else who writes about the subject, the author, Gordon Fairclough, takes for granted the centrality of prostitution to the national economy and illustrates his piece with a few pointed anecdotes and quotations demonstrating the broad social and economic impact of any attempt to intervene in the free operation of the sex trade. Again like other commentators, he provides a few figures to lend point to his anecdotes; we learn, for example, that the manager of a bar featuring sex shows told police he took in about 80,000 baht a night (Fairclough 1994, 30) As is all too typical of the genre, however, the article provides no context in which to place this figure and so allow it to illuminate the sex industry's role in the economy. Even piecing together such details from hundreds of articles still does not make for a complete and comprehensive picture.

One of the most basic questions is, of course, how many women are employed in the sex trade in general and how many in those branches catering principally to foreign tourists. The one thing we think one can say with certainty is that the more precise the figure, the less trustworthy it is likely to prove. In Chapter 1, we cite the Public Health Ministry's 1992 conclusion that there were 76,863 prostitutes working in Thailand (*Bangkok Post*, 17 January 1993, 18). This degree of precision is presumably meant to create the impression that the ministry has counted every last nose, but in fact it has the opposite effect; it is so ridiculously low that anyone who has ever gone out on the town in Bangkok is tempted to exaggerate in the other direction, asserting that you can see that many sex workers in a single night on Soi Cowboy!

According to the 1989 *Country Study* of Thailand, estimates for the number of women in Bangkok alone who are "engaged in prostitution or related activities" ranged from 100,000 to 1,000,000 (LePoer 1989, 93). What Paul Handley (1989, 44) calls "reasonable estimates . . . based on calculations from police lists" total half a million, which is to say, 1 percent of the total population at that time. But he adds without comment, "Some argue it is double that, with a substantial number being children."[7]

How do these 100,000, or 400,000, or 500,000 or a million women, as the case may be, figure in the overall picture of women's employment in Thailand? And how can they figure anywhere if we don't know which number is right? An article by Harry and Ormsin Gardiner about the status of women in Thailand reflects one way to dispose of the problem. This piece gives the occupational distribution of working women in Thailand as 76 percent in agriculture, 4 percent in white-collar positions (professional, administrative, or clerical), 3 percent in service, 10 percent in sales, and 7 percent in production. Expressed as the proportion of women among those engaged in various job categories, females were 39 percent of all professionals, 60 percent of salespeople, 44 percent of service workers, 49 percent of those in agriculture, and 30 percent of production workers (Gardiner and Gardiner 1991, 104). Since no mention is made of prostitution, it is safe to assume that although the distribution percentages add up to 100, one class of worker is omitted. Even the proportional category "other," 4 percent of which is female, apparently does not include *these* "others."

A more responsible—though hardly more conclusive—approach to the issue is provided by Thanh-Dam Truong, whose exposition of the options is worth quoting at some length. After mentioning the 1974 police figure of 400,000, she cites a 1981 estimate of 500,000 to 700,000 reported by the Thailand National Council of Women's Affairs. She then uses United Nations statistics to follow up several hypotheses, some of them mutually exclusive:

> The total number of women employed in the service sector is 1.11 million. It is not known how many of the estimated number of prostitutes are included as being employed in the service sector, but if they are, they could constitute more than half the total number of females employed in . . . that sector. If they are not counted in the service sector data, they represent an additional contingency [*sic*] of more than half the total. . . .
>
> Given the total female population of 22.27 million . . . it follows that some 2.3 to 3.2 per cent of the total female population are presently engaged in some form of prostitution. As the share of female population between 15 and 34 years of age . . . is 8,084,000, and assuming that prostitutes are within this age bracket, between 6.2 and 8.7 per cent of the female population of this age bracket work in prostitution.
>
> If the age bracket of prostitutes used by the Social Welfare Department is correct, then this percentage will be higher. The Social Welfare Department estimates that the majority of prostitutes are women in the 16–21 age group. . . . In addition to or included in this figure, there is an unknown quantity of indentured and slave labour . . . sold into prostitution by parents (Truong 1990, 181; emphasis added).

This admirably lucid summary of the possibilities can serve as a model for how to think about them. The trouble is that Truong can only indicate what would follow in one situation or the other, and there is no way of knowing which in fact is the case. The model protects us from making the most naive sorts of errors, but without these unknown answers it is ultimately of no more use than the Gardiners' percentages, which are apparently based on precisely those most naive mistakes. And even this limited model is called into question by the final, almost offhand mention of indentured or enslaved sex workers, the reference to whom begins with the maddeningly imprecise words, "In addition to or included in this figure."

Throughout her study, Truong makes what initially seems like excessive use of the verb "to disaggregate," almost invariably preceded by a negative; nobody counts what we want to know about, and the meaningful figure being sought cannot be separated out from the one provided. Given the difficulties involved in trying to establish how many prostitutes are working in Thailand, it is clear that there is at present no way to "disaggregate" from the highly flexible estimates a further figure about how many prostitutes work primarily or exclusively for a foreign clientele.

After this experience with the "how many?" questions, it comes as no surprise to learn that "how much?" yields a great many numbers and even more estimates but that these do not add up to the sum being sought: the sex trade's overall contribution to the economy. One problem is that the most detailed source of figures, especially about women's earnings, is Pasuk's *From Peasant Girls to Bangkok Masseuses* and although most of the generalizations made in her study are still timely, the money amounts are out of date. For instance, when Pasuk says that a prostitute in a massage parlor can earn about twenty-five times as much as "the median level to be expected in other occupations" (Phongpaichit 1982, 8), our knowledge that there has been little palpable improvement of wages or conditions in those other occupations lends continued credence to her statement (Krongkaew 1993, 404, 407–8). Similarly, when she indicates that the lowest-paid 4 percent of her informants report earnings five to fifteen times lower than those of the highest 4 percent and half to one-sixth of the median earnings, these proportions are probably still in effect, even though all the earnings may be higher (Phongpaichit 1982, 19).

The monthly income figures for the massage parlor employees Pasuk interviewed in 1980 ranged from 1,000 to 15,000 baht ($40 to $600, with the baht constant at 25 to the dollar), nearly a third of them falling in the 5,000- to 6,000-baht range (Phongpaichit 1982, 19). Thepanom Muangman's study, also dating to 1980, estimated an average monthly income for his subjects of 8500 baht (ctd. in Phongpaichit 1982, 19). The amount per transaction reported in *From Peasant Girls to Bangkok Masseuses* ranged from a low of 40 baht per hour, earned by a "not-so-pretty" girl in a "low-class" house where no actual massage was performed, to a high of 350 baht for a half-hour at an upmarket establishment, with two women performing "special services" (Phongpaichit 1982, 9, 11). Even Pasuk's survey, restricted to a small number of establishments, all of the same type, found a wide variation in real income, depending on the portion of her earnings from each sexual encounter that went to the sex worker and whether, out of that amount, she paid for board, lodging, and medical care.

For bar employees, the question of salary supplemented by tips further complicates the matter. A twenty-one year-old bar girl working on Patpong focused on the bottom line: "In the bar, one month, I get maybe 3,000 to 4,000 baht. If I work other job, shop, I get maybe 800 baht. . . . Farang say, 'Go for free.' I say, 'Fuck off! I don't want go for free'" (Walker and Ehrlich 1992, 72). Evidence from the novels of Christopher Moore and interviews with expatriate and tourist customers (see Chapter 6) suggest that a "purple" or 500-baht note, is widely regarded as the current standard payment for a freelance prostitute or bar employee in Bangkok. This would appear to be somewhere in the middle of the very wide range of prices on massage parlor menus, which still vary—as they did in 1980 and much as restaurant prices do—according to the class of the establishment and the particular services purchased.

Although the rhetorical phrase "selling one's daughter into prostitution" has wide currency among scholars, as well as journalists and activists, the actual arrangement is more often presented as either a loan to the family or an advance payment for the girl's (usually unspecified or misrepresented) services. The interest on these "loans" is often 100 percent and the principal may be increased by other debts—for living expenses, medical care, bribes to officials—accrued once the girl has begun work (Wilke 1983, 254). Pasuk's 1980 figures for the amounts initially paid out to families ranged from 1,500 baht to a reputed 100,000 baht. This latter sum was said to have been paid for an unusually beautiful girl whose family urgently had to raise money after her brother was arrested on drug charges, but Pasuk expresses her suspicion that the amount was inflated in the telling; 50,000 baht was otherwise the highest sum she encountered, and 5,000 to 10,000 baht was the average (Phongpaichit 1982, 65). The various personal narratives included in *Behind the Smile* (Ekachai 1990) mention figures from 2,000 to 20,000 baht ($80 to $800). Where actual outright sales can be documented, as with the abduction of 13- and 14-year-old Chinese virgins traded over the border, the amount quoted in 1992 was $4,000 and the subsequent profit taken would be much higher (Xin Ren 1993, 97). Other recent reports on the slave market in China cite figures as low as $600 (Gooi 1993, 36) or a range of "anything from $2,000 to $4,000" (Barbour 1993, B1).

Bangkok Post columnist Bernard Trink (interviewed for the chapter on the bars) is the only commentator we have encountered who doubts that many Bangkok sex workers contribute to their families' support. Since Pasuk consulted the records of money orders cashed at the post offices in her respondents' home villages, however, there is independent evidence of the existence and scale of such remittances. Elizabeth Bounds (1991, 138) concludes from her own interviews that "the prostitutes feel tremendous responsibility for the welfare of their families, which include parents, siblings, extended family, and children. . . . For almost all Asian prostitutes, the major reason for working is to send money home." As a twenty-three-year-old bar girl told Dave Walker and Richard Ehrlich, "Europe women are prostitutes only to take drugs. Thai women are prostitutes to take care their families" (56).

So the real question, once again, is how much they send, which would appear to be another highly fluid measure. Whatever arrangements were made with the parents at the time of recruitment, almost all of Pasuk's respondents said they sent money to the family—often including their own children, as well as parents and siblings.[8] A couple indicated that payments were "irregular and according to need"; others said that they "made fairly regular remittances" in amounts ranging from 500 to 10,000 baht a month and most falling between 1,000 and 2,000 baht (Phongpaichit 1982, 23). The Patpong bar girl quoted earlier explained, "My mother, father sell food, chicken, eggs and vegetable. . . . Now they not working. Every month, I give maybe 2,000 baht, maybe 1,000 baht" (Walker and Ehrlich, 74). Seeming at first to confirm Trink's cynical position, another interviewee admitted paying her gambling debts by telling customers that her mother was ill. But even she adds, "I send every month 2,000 or 1,500 baht to my mom. No more play cards" (118). An updated figure is provided by a seventeen-year-old male prostitute who reports monthly earnings of 10,000 baht, 5,000 of which go back to his unsuspecting parents in Burma, who believe he has found a good job as a waiter (Fairclough 1995, 28).[9]

As to how the remittances function in the rural economy, the Employment and Development Department of the International Labour Organisation, which sponsored Pasuk's study, stresses the point made in the text that monies sent home by sex workers "have contributed substantially to meeting the basic needs of their families for housing, water and education, but little to productive investment in rural areas" (Phongpaichit 1982, v, see also 24). Pasuk mentions that many of her subjects had built or were planning to build a new house for their families, an expenditure equal to two to four years' average earnings, but few had subsidized the cost of farm animals, seeds and fertilizers, or additional labor beyond their own replacement at harvest time. Foreign residents sometimes refer sneeringly to "Water Buffalo U," the "alma mater" where the peasant girl acquires the misinformation that going to work in the sex industry will enable her to buy the work animal that will save the family farm. What she learns in Bangkok's school of hard knocks is that buying the water buffalo will not make the needed difference. The system is designed so that, either way, the result is the family's continued dependence on sex-industry earnings and a guaranteed sex-trade labor supply in the next generation.

Not only do conditions in the economically depressed rural areas assure the flow of labor to the industrial and service sectors, including the sex and tourism industries, they are also one of the places where the economic effects of those industries are most marked. Since funds sent home to the villages tend to be used for subsistence rather than development, it is not the most active sort of return. But it is there and it is visible, in a way that other economic consequences of the industry are not, even though there are no official figures for the amount of money sent home, individually or in the aggregate.

Where it is structures and institutions that have to be described rather than specific figures, the coexistence of the parallel legal and illegal labor markets actually serves as an analytic model. Thus, in characterizing the labor conditions the sex industry entails, Thanh-Dam Truong (1990) is able to characterize the job as possessing at the same time both objective and subjective, structured and casual dimensions (186–87). She locates the objective aspect in the fact that the job qua job entails skill training, wage systems, and defined working hours; but subjective in that it involves "the ideology of patronage and protection" in the relation of the worker to the owner of the establishment. We would emphasize that this "subjective" ideological model of patron-client relationship is a hallmark of Thai society in all sectors: the military, the civil service, politics, private business, and even, in a sense, the family. Craig Reynolds (1987) argues persuasively that patron-client analyses prevent class-based ones. "The search for a non-Marxist social analysis led to the client-patron paradigm among anthropologists, who devised and popularized it, and historians, who welcomed it"; this paradigm results in a reciprocity that "obscures exploitation of the poor."

Truong argues that the prostitute's job is structured in that it makes a direct contribution to profits, but casual in that there is no (single) "fixed contract for remuneration or social benefits" (1990, 186–87). Thai sex workers are thus workers in more than just name. Yet even if one does not adopt Pasuk's almost admiring view of the "entrepreneurial move" that took so many young women out of the village and into the sex trade, it is clear that in many branches of the industry prostitutes are at once wage laborers and freelance operatives, carrying on a direct rather than a mediated economic relation with the customer, negotiating on their own behalf for prices and tips, and taking a percentage of the surplus their labor creates.

At the other extreme of the entrepreneurial continuum are sex workers who have no direct economic relation with either the client or the employer. In the post office at Dok Ka Tai, a village famous for its beautiful girls and (hence) a good recruiting ground for the sex industry, Pasuk found records showing a great many postal orders addressed to different families but signed by the same few senders in Bangkok. This suggests that the remittances were sent by agents whose contract was with the parents, not the workers, and who, after taking their own heavy cut, were "forwarding money which the girls had earned but perhaps never handled themselves" (Phongpaichit 1982, 70).

A final example of the doublethink around the sex trade concerns attempts on the part of feminist researchers and activists to help the prostitutes organize as working women. (This in a country that has a long history of suppressing labor activity and a consequent low rate of union membership, even in the industries and trades that have historically proved fertile sites for labor organizing in industrialized countries. It goes almost without saying that Thailand's uncongenial attitude toward trade unions is a major source of its appeal to foreign investors and runaway shops.) Those who joined or worked with the early prostitutes' organization, Thai 'N' Girls, encountered the expected political repression from the state and economic sanctions from employers. Less expected, at least from an outsider's perspective, was the authorities' assumption that it was the potentially militant self-organization of prostitutes, not the notoriety of the sex industry itself, that threatened Thailand's prestige abroad. To counter that threat, a joint order from the Office of the Prime Minister and the Tourist Authority of Thailand prohibited officials of all national agencies from discussing the problem of prostitution while participating in conferences and meetings abroad. This bizarre order was promulgated more than a decade ago (*Bangkok Post*, 12 August 1984). Recent developments, including the acknowledgment of AIDS as an issue for Thailand, have given rise to a different rhetoric of simultaneous admission and denial, which amounts to burying one's head in a different part of the sand.

Consumer Cultures

> In the larger massage parlors, the girls are on display behind a one-way glass show window and customers select the one they want by her number, rather as you would select a fish from the tank in a seafood restaurant.
> —*Insight Guide* to Thailand

The two kinds of night market on Patpong carry information about consumer society in both its economic and its cultural dimensions. Not only is shopping increasingly understood as the moral equivalent of sightseeing for the tourist, but the tourist locale—even the land itself—is represented as consumable goods. Involvement in consumption is also constructed as a positive route to modernization for the indigenous population, including the prostitutes, who themselves participate in the culture as both consumers and objects of consumption. Sex workers personify consumable goods, just as the landscape is feminized on analogy with the prostituted body, and as sun, sea, sand, sex can make a single semiotic unit.

On the global scale the economics of tourism embraces considerations like the industrialization of leisure, the interests of transnational airlines and hotel chains, and the provision of hard currency to developing areas. In the host (or target or object) country, one sector of the economy stimulated by tourism is engaged in the identification, production, and retailing of items for tourists to buy. The consumerist language adopted by tourist brochures to sell the sexual aspects of travel to Thailand parallels a more general tendency on the part of travel professionals to erase the distinction between the experience and the souvenir; shopping for things to take back, in fact, becomes part of the experience of being there. Dean MacCannell (1989, 76) draws a similar connection between the specialty trades in consumer goods and in sexual entertainment when he discusses the *articles de luxe* that have long been considered as much a part of the total tourist experience of Paris, "the West's most seductive city," as her "naughty stage reviews." Although the larger implications of all this are outside the scope of our study, the developments that are most pertinent to the economics of prostitution are the encouragement of a consumer mentality on the part of the Thai populace and the consumer approach to local natural and cultural resources including—semiotically and literally—the sexuality of local women on the part of the tourist.

The introduction into rural Thailand of modern means of transportation and communication—the (American-sponsored) highway system, the widespread availability of television, and the dissemination of popular music—supplemented educational, religious, and military initiatives to recruit the countryside to a national culture (Anderson 1985, 21, 24). The imposition of national culture had the effect of eroding local culture, leading to a decline in the prestige of village leadership, the weakening of community cooperation (including exchanges of labor) and a deemphasis on "the rituals emphasizing the importance of ancestry and place." Phongpaichit and Baker argue (1995, 75) that the decay of local communities on the cultural plane contributed to the large-scale migration of young women to the sex industry. In this sense the well-meaning school teacher who tries to do something to stem that exodus may actually be aggravating the situation, through his or her very function as a representative of the centralized national culture that is eroding local ties.

The villagers Sanitsuda Ekachai observed celebrating a joyous harvest festival are well aware of the changes, their political-economic origins, and their import: "Many of our young people have already left the village to find jobs outside. . . . Parents and children no longer live together. If our village's culture fades away in time, it is mainly because of our financial pressures, our debts. . . . Life has changed so rapidly, it probably won't be long now before our children stop practicing the things that we're doing this year" (Ekachai 1994, 21–23). The prostitutes' own "Patpong Musical," *This Is Us,* as presented at the Limelight Bar in November 1987, tells the same story from the point of view of the young migrants: "Usually you are called by the place where you were born. . . . But those in Patpong are definitely not Patpong people. And where do they come from? There, over there." These words introduce a multimedia number (slide show, song and dance) about the Northeast as the home they were forced to leave behind. The opening and closing lines of the song are the same:

> The land of Esan is harsh and dry
> With no one to turn to.
> Waiting for years, yet the rain and sky have not been kind.
> Neither are the powers-that-be.
> (EMPOWER, n.p.)

Another way of looking at the issue as manifested in the villages focuses away from what was destroyed or eroded and toward what was imported, the content of the new national culture. One element of that culture was the "good life" conceived in terms of possessions—some of these, like the television set, being themselves consumer goods that opened up broad vistas of further possibilities for consumption. Since these moves came at a time of decline for regions that had never been particularly prosperous, they incongruously but insistently brought the notion of consumption into a context where the real preoccupation was an increasingly difficult subsistence.

An official 1984 statement on "national identity" stresses (and, in fact, sentimentalizes) the antimaterialist character of traditional village life: "The village is a peaceful place, its slow pace reflecting the serene, unassuming nature of the villagers themselves. . . . Most farmers are content to earn enough to support their families. . . . Wealth is not something most villagers actually crave. . . . The natural affection Thai villagers feel for their land minimizes population migrations. Moreover, villagers have little ambition to change their lifestyle" (qtd. in Phongpaichit and Baker 1995, 319). Although the national identity statement was, by definition, a national initiative, other forces at the national level were working at the same time to erode the village way of life and the values underlying it. Vigorous promotion of agribusiness entailed providing no support or protection for poor peasants, who were being rapidly reduced to the status of agricultural laborers—or migrants to the urban labor pool.

Consumerism has been understood by some commentators as the "carrot" to the "stick" of hostile or negligent agricultural policy. Japanese development specialist Katsumi Mitani considers the successful implantation of a consumer mentality to be one of the keys to economic growth in Thailand. He argues that increased mass demand for consumer goods not only stimulates investment but raises the morale of the workers. What he actually says is that it will raise the working masses' "moral." This may be a Freudian typographical error, since consumer values help erode traditional morality—a process Mitani celebrates, declaring that "instead of 'merit making' for happiness after death, they [now] work to satisfy their worldly wants. The heightened morale of the workers raises their labor efficiency and encourages mobility."[10] Mitani is also convinced that "it is no exaggeration to say that a healthy expansion in . . . consumption by the masses of the people . . . has led to a rise in productivity, a greater capacity to supply goods and services, and a rapid growth in the national economy of Thailand" (1968, 193). Reading each item on his list from a perspective informed by what we know about the existence, scale, and experience of the sex industry makes for a grim counterpoint, as it underscores the overlapping trajectories of desire at play in the (spatially conjoined) Patpong markets.

Promotion of tourism means promotion of shopping as well as sex. One way these coalesce is in the representation of the land. Natural beauty, "scenery," becomes a commodity that can attract tourists, much like regional festivals, costumes, and cultural practices that acquire fresh status as "colorful" customs packaged into "staged authenticity" (MacCannell 1989, 91–96; on the packaging of Thailand's hill tribes, see Cohen 1989). Charles Keyes (1987, 203) remarks caustically that "peoples holding distinct ethnoregional identities are not necessarily eager . . . to see themselves presented as objects of tourist attention." But the landscape can't talk back, even in the limited ways available to newly charming tribespeople. So its integration into the longstanding discourse that feminizes and sexualizes the land encounters no direction opposition.

When land that has been employed and understood as a means of production is translated into the aesthetic realm, reconceptualized as "scenery," it is by definition valued for what it looks like rather than what it makes or does. Tourist advertising and the abundant literature of travel extol its beauty and associate the "natural" with the primitive, the exotic, the mysterious, and the erotic—not an undifferentiated eroticism but one that shares the characteristics of the Thai woman as represented in tourism discourse. It too is lying there in its exotic beauty, passively waiting to be done to, waiting for the foreign visitor to come.[11] If an analogy exists between the environmental effects of tourist development (erosion, air and water pollution, and outright destruction of natural sites) and the impact of sex tourism on the young women of Thailand, the semiotic sisters of the despoiled landscape, that too is the result of those overlapping trajectories of desire on the map of Patpong—and the world.

5

IMAGINING SEXUAL OTHERS

A story in our introduction draws an analogy between William Blake's London and late twentieth-century Bangkok, marking two points in the trajectory of global capitalism as manifested in urban sites. Blake's poem "London" was used in a class for graduate students as a vehicle for approaching current conditions resulting from development strategies. That anecdote serves to introduce numerous themes and issues addressed in this chapter, as well as to invoke some of our strategies for exploring them: namely, discursive and historical relationships between Western capitalism and fantasies of the Orient—proximities physical and cognitive—and examination of both synchronic and diachronic considerations. With regard to this latter strategy, we will bear in mind the broad structural parallels that made Blake's London similar to the students' Bangkok while also understanding that specific cultural and historical trajectories for each site yield both differences and similarities. That is, for any given discursive site, we look at specific diachronic issues that yield general synchronic similarities. For London, these diachronic issues include, for example, the Land Enclosure Movement, the Evangelical Revival, the constitution of gender roles and nature in the institution of marriage, the social, moral, intellectual impact of evolution theory; for Bangkok, the conversion of Vietnam R&R sites to foundations of international tourism, water-use policies that destroy subsistence farming practices, the pricing of unskilled labor wages in the international market, traditional familial gender and economic roles. The sexual cartographies traced in this chapter map Western moves to bring Thailand to a point in modernity where "orientalist sex" became both a fact and a fiction too costly for it to embrace and even more costly for it to give up.[1]

112

Paradoxical Others: Sexual and Otherwise

When I was in the boat, I took a beautiful Cannibal girl and the admiral gave
her to me. Having her in my room and
she being naked as is their custom, I
began to want to amuse myself with
her. Since I wanted to have my way
with her and she was not willing, she
worked me over so badly with her nails
that I wished I had never begun. To get
to the end of the story, seeing how
things were going, I got a rope and tied
her up so tightly that she made
unheard of cries which you wouldn't
have believed. At the end, we got along
so well that, let me tell you, it seemed
she had studied at a school for whores.
—Michele de Cuneo, letter from
Columbus's second voyage,
28 October 1495

The Oriental Woman is no more than a
machine: she makes no distinction
between one man and another.
—Gustave Flaubert, 1851

Chinese love is not European love....
The European woman is in a transport
of love for you—then all of a sudden
she forgets you on the edge of the bed,
musing over the serious side of life,
about herself, or nothing, or maybe she
has merely relapsed into "White anxiety." ... With the Chinese woman it is
not at all like that. The Chinese woman
is like the root of the banyan, which
turns up again everywhere, even
among the leaves. Thus she is, and
when you have admitted her to your
bed, you will not be rid of her for
days.... The Chinese woman takes
care of you. She considers you are
under her treatment. Not for a moment

does she turn over on her side. Always
intwined around you, like the ivy that
does not know how to live alone. . . .
And she is so affectionate. . . . Such is
the Chinese woman.
—Henri Michaux, from
A Barbarian in Asia, 1933

The English word "desire" comes from the Latin *desiderare*, literally, to be away from the stars, whence to cease to see, regret the absence of, to seek. The desire of cultures to seek out Others in order to fill perceived absences in themselves is manifest in the genealogy of representations examined in this chapter. Likewise, the etymology of the English word "desire" tells us much about many of the concerns and issues that drove these Western representations of desire found in the sites and cultures of Others. Within the cultural history of an idea as theorized by Nietzsche and Foucault, any genealogy necessarily entails a certain degree of abstraction and reduction. By highlighting specific tropes that recur in discursive representations of Others across centuries, ours also abstracts and reduces. Of primary interest here are related discursive attributes that help perpetuate an understanding of Other cultures as qualitatively and quantitatively different with regard to sexual practices and mores from those of the European-North American cultures whence the representations emerge. The perpetuation of these discursive practices maintains cross-cultural beliefs about sex and sexuality. The beliefs, appropriated in turn by international development strategies, national policies, and the international tourist industry, help cast activities surrounding the sex industry in Thailand as "naturally indigenous" to the culture, region, and populace. These tropes portray the activities as part of the "history" and "tradition" (even the religion) of a given site so important in the commodification of culture necessary for tourist consumption.

In a sense, these discursive trajectories—found in the writings of explorers, travelers, historians, natural historians, missionaries, colonial administrators, anthropologists, ethnographers, novelists, journalists, and orientalists—affect cross-cultural interaction today. We argue not that present-day international tourists, or even international development strategists, *know* these discursive traditions, but rather that these traditions form the very context and basis for their travels (or interventions), their assumptions about their ability to travel, and their interactions with others when traveling. Similarly, in the past these discourses yielded the possibility of identifying and naming these sites, and the peoples and cultures within them, as places of conquest, curiosity, wealth (to be taken away), and desire (to be satiated). Finally, the sites became a means by which Europe (and later North America) could produce ideas and conceptions of itself—no matter how various and contradictory—in relation to something labeled "the rest of the world" (Pratt 1992, 5).

A vast range of writers from Homer and Herodotus and Marco Polo to

Columbus and de Cuneo, to Denis Diderot and John Stedman, to Anna Leonowens and Carl Bock and Pico Iyer produced texts about "the rest of the world" that provide us the means of examining the processes by which Western cultures generate images of themselves (both laudatory and critical, and often both in the same text) through representations of Others. This centuries-old worldmaking and subject-formation through the act of worldmaking remain powerfully influential in late twentieth-century discourses of international development and international tourism. We examine some of the discursive tropes and patterns that play throughout this varied discourse to consider aspects of the continuities at play, leading us to a discussion of the constitution and representation of indigenous sexual cultures.[2]

Whether savage, barbarian, wild, primitive, cannibalistic, noble, natural, pure, wealthy, poverty-stricken, heathenish, fallen, indolent, or wise, whether in accounts from the ancient Greeks, fifteenth-century European explorers of the Americas, nineteenth-century colonial administrators, late nineteenth-century governesses to royal courts, twentieth-century travel writers, or late twentieth-century Internet messages on the Worldwide Web, the Others constructed in these discourses have been decidedly contradictory—even schizophrenic. People with the power to travel and encounter—not to mention conquer—other cultures have constructed and represented them in markedly paradoxical ways: savage but wise, uncivilized but attuned to nature, potent/fecund but uncontrolled, materially wealthy but only so *in potentia*, indolent but productive, immoral but happy, craven but carefree.[3] Obviously, many diverse purposes drove the representations of Others: ethnocentrism, justification for conquest, the need for funds for future exploration, the expansion of Christendom, the wish to make "disinterested and objective" contributions to the storehouse of knowledge, potential fame and glory, and the promise of large book sales. But whatever their motivations, these discourses about Others reveal more about those representing and the impulses behind representation than they do about the represented—a point that did not escape many of the scholars writing about "primitive" cultures. In reviewing Herbert Spencer's 1877 *Principles of Sociology,* the famous British anthropologist E. B. Tylor notes that it is the "besetting sin" of those who examine "primitives" to "treat the savage mind according to the needs of our argument, sometimes as extremely ignorant and inconsequent, at other times as extremely observant and logical" (qtd. in Stocking 1987,187).

The deeply conflicted discourse about Others has certain specific antecedents. Herodotus provides the authoritative precedent for a stream of negative accounts—including tropes of savagery, anthropophagy, monsters, and barbarism—especially in Latin and medieval writings; Marco Polo supplies the basis for positive descriptions, including tropes of intelligence, wisdom, gentility, and subservience (Hulme 1986, 21–22). Homer, of course, yields examples of both, but Herodotus and Polo offer the authoritative discursive sources that the explorers in the fifteenth and sixteenth centuries used in framing and representing their encounters with Others. A trope shared by both discursive streams, one that will become increasingly important in later writings and for our examination of contemporary international encounters, is wealth. Especially relevant is the relationship between wealth and the notion of reciprocity in all its various guises, which framed most cross-cultural interactions, and the larger rubric of capitalist relations as natural and universal.

Many of these texts also shared the trope of promiscuity as prevalent among distant peoples. As John Gillies (1994, 13–19) has observed, in the Greek and Latin writings so important to Renaissance sensibilities, an inverse correlation existed between proximity and promiscuity: the further one traveled from the *polis*, or the site performing the representation and creating knowledge about other sites, the more debauched the local inhabitants became. As Gillies puts it, "The ancient other is constructed in terms of an idiom which recapitulates geographical 'exorbitance' as moral transgressiveness" (18). As we will see, however, certain behavior—particularly sexual behavior—labeled as morally "beyond the pale" by Renaissance norms was recast by Enlightenment critiques as "natural." These critiques argued that perceptions of this behavior as morally corrupt came from backward and artificial beliefs imposed by Western, Christian culture and its institutions. Thus, the typologies of human behavior, and the labels they generate, become slippery indeed when applied to Others.

The Persistence of Schizoid Othering

To sample the tenacity with which the paradoxical constitution of Others clings to accounts of them, we need only look at a contemporary text that received critical praise for its intelligence and perceptiveness: Pico Iyer's *Video Night in Katmandu and Other Reports from the Not-so-Far East*. Witty, clever, and intermittently compassionate, Iyer's account of his travels through postmodern Asia opens with an insightful discussion about East-West relationships. He argues that these are too often cast in simplistic, romantic either/or categories that plague contemporary public discourse as much as they did academic and popular writings of the past. Iyer, a member of the privileged diaspora, spent his youth shuttling between California, England, and India, and he draws on his multiple rootedness and multinational experience to contextualize his travel accounts. In so doing, he warns against the myopia of humanist moralizers and proposes a more complex perspective about globalization processes.

Iyer provides especially sound observations with regard to the complex relationship between globalization processes and their local manifestations. Yet in his chapter on Bangkok, "Love in a Duty-Free Zone," he fails to heed his own warnings about "all too easy conclusions" (287–315). Having heard so much about the Mecca for sex tourists, he decides he must see the place himself and sets out armed with travel books and works of fiction (John le Carré, Graham Greene, and Alec Waugh among them) that have helped him imagine the scene before he arrives and memories of films that hint at the titillation awaiting entire culture, or constituting how one acts in Other cultures, has a long discursive tradition, as the Diderot text we examine below exemplifies.

If Iyer has difficulty reconciling the behavior of sinning monks and saintly whores, he makes it equally difficult for the bar girls with whom he speaks to convey "the truth" about their lives. Several pages summarize the narratives he elicits from these women without ever arriving at what he recognizes as "the truth" (304–10). Many of the women tell virtually the same tale of poverty, lack of opportunity, and familial responsibility, and since these stories are all the same, Iyer decides they cannot be true. Likewise, if a given woman provides slight variations of "facts" (such as her age) in different accounts of her own narrative, then she cannot be telling the truth, either. Thus, the narratives are false if consistent and false if inconsistent—the classic "double bind" of Others.

The point here is not to skewer Iyer or his writing, but to understand him as operating within a textual and discursive tradition that predisposes him to interpret cultures and human actions along certain axes and in the light of inherited tropes—even when he is cognizant of such oversimplifying moves and beseeches readers to avoid them. Genealogies are difficult to slough off.

In what follows, moving from eighteenth- to nineteenth- and then twentieth-century Western texts that engage in the eroticization of Other cultures, we chart a trajectory of accounts: Other sites constituted as sexual within the realms of "Nature" get transformed into the unnatural harem, which in turn becomes the brothel, and finally the bar-as-brothel.[4] As with all such trajectories or given genealogies, this one is not intended to be *the* way in which Other sexual cultures have been represented in the West, but rather *a* way of reading such representations and their reception—a way we argue that has resonance for and influence on the rise of international sex tourism in a specific local site.

Denis Diderot's Critique of French Morality

> Of all existing peoples, the Caribs have least departed from the state of nature, and it is they who are most peaceful in their sex lives and least subject to jealousy, even though they live in a hot climate, which always seems to make passions more active.
> —Jean-Jacques Rousseau, *Discours sur l'origine et les fondements de l'inégalité parmi les hommes* (1754)

In 1771, after returning to France from circumnavigating the world, Louis-Antoine de Bougainville published his hugely popular *Voyage*, which included among other fabulous tales a laudatory report of sexual mores and ethics in Tahiti.

travelers to Thailand (*Emmanuelle in Bangkok*). Iyer's cautionary advice to tourists goes missing once he is immersed in the site. His coolly detached observations of the sex market are swamped by an attraction to a particular bar woman with whom he has several conversations. Eventually, he feels he must do something to help this woman and strikes out in search of her. When nothing comes of his goodwill efforts, the crestfallen narrator, feeling that he has been duped by the woman he sought to aid, gives in to despair. His initial readings of the site have been undermined by his experiences, and the more complex hues that manifest themselves in Thai culture befuddle him and force reinterpretation.

Despite Iyer's insightful and thoughtful efforts, he lapses into a tried and true—not to mention tried and tired—discursive stream of manifest incommensurabilities, blatant contradictions that blur the sacred and the profane in this foreign site. Dubbing this "the Manichean setup of Bangkok," Iyer describes the effusive binarisms:

> The city's two most common and appealing sights, after all, were its holy men, in spotless saffron robes, and its scarlet women. By day, the monks evoked a vision of purity, of hallowed groves filled with golden novitiates; by night, the whole grimy city felt polished, renewed and transformed as sequined girls sang the body electric. At least, so I thought, this day-and-night division would ensure that good was good, and evil evil, and never the twain would meet.
>
> But no. For after a while, I began to notice that, as the whores were engagingly girlish, the monks seemed endearingly boyish (311).

Supposedly anomalous accounts follow of monks watching TV, listening to Walkmans, smoking cigarettes, and actually murdering some fellow monk—in short, being all too human. Likewise, the bar "girls" visit the temples to pray and make offerings to the Buddha and the monks, causing Iyer to begin viewing them "as something close to martyrs" (311); they too are human after all. For some reason, the tautologically inherent humanity of humans elsewhere, complete with foibles, failures, triumphs, and everydayness, perplexes even keen and clever observers, forcing them to fall back on discursive stereotypes several centuries old that repeat the extreme either/or categories Iyer addresses in his introduction.

Having earlier warned readers against leaping to "all too easy conclusions" that cast the West as completely evil and domineering and the East as wholly virtuous and pure, Iyer nevertheless succumbs to similarly simplistic interpretations of indigenous groups. Either the monks are as pure as they appear or they are unredeemably fallen and all the worse for presenting the illusion of holy piety. The "scarlet women" embody "evil" itself until he learns they may behave otherwise, at which point they become virtual "martyrs." Like people everywhere, they can rarely be categorized with such structural neatness. Yet the dichotomy monk-by-day and libertine-by-night becomes, in Iyer's text, a metaphor for Thailand as a whole. Such a binarism operating as an analogy for an

Following hot on the heels of an earlier text by Philibert Commerson, the naturalist on Bougainville's ship, which told of a blissful sexual utopia on the same
island, this account helped to generate a concept of South Pacific islands, especially Tahiti, as sites of sensual satiation undreamed of in European climes.
Although the reportage had more to do with European fantasies than lived native
reality, these documents and their effects on French popular imagination led
Denis Diderot to publish his fictional "Supplement to Bougainville's Voyage , or
Dialogue between A. and B. on the Inconvenience of Attaching Moral Ideas to
Certain Physical Actions Which Do Not Admit of Them" (*Correspondance lit-
téraire*, September–October 1773 and March–April 1774). From that moment on,
the text has had tremendous circulation and influence in European and North
American imaginative and intellectual thought—so much so that Jacques
Derrida, in his influential work *Of Grammatology*, situated Claude Lévi-Strauss's
monumental work *Tristes Tropiques* in the intellectual canon by calling it "a sort of
a supplement to the *Supplement au voyage de Bougainville*" (1974, 107).

As Tzvetan Todorov notes (1993, 277), Diderot's text plays fast and loose
with the Bougainville original, and the structure of his work helps readers understand his relation with the text it supposedly supplements. The characters A.
and B. engage in three separate dialogues; between them, Diderot provides
readers with passages allegedly excised from Bougainville but actually fictional
products of his own, which serve as content and context for A. and B.'s discussions. One of these passages contains an extended dialogue between the chaplain aboard Bougainville's ship and a Tahitian nobleman named Orou, the
chaplain's host.

Diderot's fictional supplement to Bougainville's "Tahiti dream" actually
serves several polemical purposes; primarily, it chastises European sexual morality while simultaneously maintaining European intellectual superiority over
other races (thus perpetuating and legitimating various eugenic enterprises that
were under way at the time). The text, therefore, amounts to an appeal to
Reason in all its Enlightenment senses: that is, the use of superior critical reasoning skills to throw off inferior, backward belief systems about human behavior, systems institutionally dictated by and inherited from the Church
authorities then under attack by humanist Enlightenment projects. As the title
of the work maintains—and as any "rational man" would admit—it is inconve-
nient, if not unreasonable and absurd, to connect moral ideas to certain physical
actions. Thus, the compartmentalization of the human body, so important to the
Enlightenment, is continued as Diderot casts "Nature" as being morally neutral
and moral interpretation of "natural acts" as largely arbitrary.

Such issues are succinctly articulated in the dialogue when A. and B. discuss
whether or not monogamy is a part of Nature; B.'s comment about fidelity
asserts that it is "among us, almost always a well-meaning obstinacy and slow
self-torture; in Tahiti, a chimera" (Diderot 1991, 105). That the text's focus
remains mostly European also is articulated in A. and B.'s commentary on the
Bougainville text. A. comments that the dialogue between the chaplain and

Orou is "European in its style" (102), and does so just prior to a passage that discursively exemplifies the schizophrenic relationship between Europe and its Others. In a paraphrase of the chaplain's text, the Tahitians are described as "a people wise enough to opt for mediocrity, favored enough by its climate to enjoy untroubled hours of ease, active enough to provide for all of its basic needs, and indolent enough for its innocence, its tranquillity, and its happiness to be in no danger from the great leap forward of mind. Nothing, there, was branded as evil by public opinion or the law save what was evil in its intrinsic nature" (102). This passage contains a number of common tropes about Others: mediocre, innocent, favored by nature (in all respects), unconsciously wise, indolent, happy, and unfettered by intelligence—a list of backhanded compliments, at best, often attributed to another European stereotype: the holy fool. Yet despite the self-reflexive cultural critique aimed at Europe that operates on one level of the text, Diderot perpetuates the inferiority of Others while ultimately maintaining European superiority. Likewise, by so representing Tahiti and its sexual culture vis-à-vis Europe's, Diderot also provides us with one of the more famous texts of Enlightenment (s)exotica.

Diderot's account of the chaplain includes a famous episode that draws further on stock European comic figures and situations. Signifying his hospitality, Orou offers his guest his three "naked" daughters, as well as his wife, for sexual pleasure. The chaplain's calling and its attendant vow of chastity are mightily tested by the offer, even more so when Orou acts insulted by the initial rebuff. By the time Orou and the chaplain engage in a philosophical discussion about the nature of Nature, religion, morality, fidelity, and sex, the youngest daughter (who earlier supplicated the man of the cloth to make her with child) has already shared his bed; the others follow in reverse chronological order. The philosophical dialogue—which of course comes off without any linguistic difficulties at all, as is often the case in such accounts, "fictional" or not—allows Diderot to rail against backward European morality, which is wholly out of step with Nature. At the same time Orou and his daughters, despite their being in "no danger of the great leap forward of the mind," recognize European intellectual superiority and wish to practice their own form of eugenics by improving the intellectual stock of their culture. Thus, Diderot's polemic essentially serves to affirm European prejudices and ascendancies even while seemingly undermining them.

Also at issue in the dialogue is the influence of the private and public spheres with regard to monogamy or polygamy, fidelity, and sexuality. The Tahitian describes a culture that offers, in accordance with the laws of nature so often perverted by European culture, a much more public sense of sexuality than the European models, which emphasize monogamy and private "ownership" of others through the institution of marriage. In perpetuating a discourse about the "naturalness" of multiple sexual partners (understood as "natural" and practiced the world over by "primitive" cultures untainted by European morality), Diderot supplements the sense of entitlement with which European males encounter female Others. Since these women have been cast as public property by the discourse, the male who so perceives them is merely acting according to the cultural norms (themselves aligned with natural law) practiced in these sexual utopias.

In a sense, Diderot extends and projects onto another site understandings of women that date from preindustrial European thought. Anthropologist Pieter Spierenburg argues that in Europe from about the thirteenth century to the end of the seventeenth century two distinct categories for women existed: "the virtuous and the public," the former made up of "virginal daughters, faithful wives, and chaste widows," the latter of "prostitutes . . . [and] promiscuous and adulterous women" (1991, 260). In such a division, Spierenburg maintains, any woman not under some form of patriarchal supervision was considered by the larger society as some sort of whore, and thus public property. By extension, women in other lands, especially "savage" ones, *never* live under patriarchal supervision of a kind recognized by European males—who assume the men there to be less-than-men—and are thus, by default, public. Although Diderot might not agree with this position, since his argument follows the lines of natural versus cultural acts more than public versus private entitlement, his discourse nevertheless seems to perpetuate such a division of women.

Orou explains the native "public morality" when he describes courtship procedures. Boys and girls keep strictly to themselves until the male's "virility [is] continuous and the frequency of his emissions and the quality of his seminal fluid give [the community] confidence," and until the female reaches "an age to conceive desires, to provoke them effectively, and to satisfy them effectively" (Diderot 1991, 86). The moment at which sexual partners choose one another is called "emancipation" (leaving no doubt about Diderot's opinions on the matter), and its representation of the girls displays a female sexual subjectivity virtually unheard of in European high culture and usually missing from accounts of Others and cross-cultural interaction—except when it is cast as rabid female desire for a European male, a favorite trope.

Shortly after the passage about courtship, the chaplain contrasts France and Tahiti, especially their viability as nations, by examining their different positions regarding female beauty (87). The European nation dismisses beauty as a "passing pleasure," whereas the island nation understands it as a "lasting utility." That is, the European male may find a woman a suitable candidate to be a wife, regardless of her appearance, if she possesses the physical attributes to bear a significant number of children; the Tahitian, on the other hand, recognizes that beautiful women will produce beautiful children capable of attracting partners, thereby making beauty integral to perpetuating the reproductive cycle. Despite these apparently different notions about beauty, then, the main criterion for determining aesthetic desirability is biological productivity. The chaplain writes, "The Venus of Athens . . . is the Venus of flirtation," while "the Venus of Tahiti . . . is the Venus of fecundity" (87). Despite the obvious dichotomy of unattainable promise versus attainable satisfaction, the passage reveals that the productivity of reproduction overdetermines the European discourse about females, Other or otherwise.[5]

In this island utopia, there is fecundity and plenitude also in the sheer number of willing and available women—a virtual cornucopia of sexual partners provided by bountiful Nature. Given the general availability of unfettered sexual interaction, free of moral guilt and in accord with "natural" law, as found in Diderot's and Bougainville's Tahiti, prostitution does not exist in this ideal space. The communal life represented there, of course, goes hand in glove with a complete lack of economic or material need or inequity. In fact, such considerations receive little attention at all in Diderot's account. Orou *does* claim, however, that he (and, by extension, his community) has "tax[ed]" the Chaplain by "taking his blood" (98–99): that is, the semen deposited in Orou's daughters, which will yield children capable of cultivating idle land—and, one infers, of cultivating the land more intelligently. Again, the productivity of the womb becomes essentialized, while the native discourse takes on terms, concepts, and motives that make it sound like that of a merchant banker or colonial bureaucrat. Diderot's critique of European culture exemplified through communal living, equity, and liberty yields to a promotion of capitalist values and gains lurking in the critique. In fact, the text reveals Diderot's assumption that humanity in "nature" possesses capitalist values, naturalizing those values and marking them as a universal norm.

Similarly, when the attack against European sexual morality expands, Diderot's argument retains multiple but not necessarily complementary applications. Orou explains why sex, "the strongest of all attractions" to be found in Nature, "has become for [Europeans] the greatest source of depravity and evil" (107). His reasons, in essence, articulate Diderot's belief that European mores, laws, and institutions systematically corrupt Nature. It can be argued, certainly, that this critique of European inequities concerning gender relations, sexuality, and marriage as an institution yielded some generally positive results. It can also be argued, however, that such lists of civilization's corruption of erotic impulses, complemented by a naturally sexual utopia found in Other cultures, help generate a desire on the part of European males to travel to such sites and seek a satiation there that is unattainable at home. This several-hundred-year-old discourse (complete with its massive economic inequities) gains an added dimension with the jet age, which makes international tourism possible for an ever growing number of individuals. When the discursive tradition is added to contemporary tourism, where international tourist advertising preys on such constructions, then the flowering of an international sex industry seems a plausible, "natural" result—even if spurred by the cultural critique and self-reflexivity operative on one level of Diderot's text.

The complex combination of discursive practices regarding sexual Other cultures, international tourism and international advertising reveals serious consequences when we consider how it manifests itself as prescribed behavior abroad. The psychological rift a First World male subject experiences when private desire that would be publicly censured at home confronts him abroad in apparently abundant availability is healed by understanding that acting upon his private desire is both attuned to nature and publicly sanctioned in the indigenous culture. Diderot seeks to guide actions at home and abroad accordingly, and his text lays the foundation for justifying what international tourists now do. B. states, "Let us imitate the worthy Chaplain and be a monk in France and a savage in Tahiti," to which A. adds, "Don the garb of other countries when one goes there, but dress like one's neighbors when at home" (112).

The most apparent polarity makes the subject celibate and godly at home, lascivious and lusty abroad. Cultural projection provides the perfect excuse for the desired interaction. Acting in accordance with "nature" and another's cultural customs *just happens* to satisfy one's deepest desires. Following Diderot's prescription for behavior at home and abroad proffers the best of both worlds, without relinquishing either, to those European males fortunate enough to travel between them: absolute satiation coupled with absolute salvation.

John Stedman and the Myth of Reciprocity

If Diderot's text helped establish the Nature versus Culture dichotomy as basic to the understanding of human behavior, then John Stedman's widely published *Narrative of a Five Years' Expedition against the Revolted Negroes of Surinam* (1790) aided the circulation and acceptance of the trope of economic reciprocity in cross-cultural human relations. This trope manifests itself in Stedman's work under the narrative guise of conjugal love, with the added taboo of interracial love. Just as the Nature versus Culture concept plays an integral role in justifying the international sex tourist industry, the notion of economic reciprocity— even within vastly unequal power relations between nations and individuals, and occasionally embraced by humanist proclamations of conjugal and interracial love—strongly informs the same contemporary industry.

The tremendous popular success that Stedman's book enjoyed in Europe stemmed in large part from the narrative about his relationship with an indigenous woman named Joanna, a theme that separated his travel accounts from the multitude of others rolling off European presses at the end of the eighteenth century. In the full flush of global colonization, Stedman's story about Joanna gave a human face and romantic cast to colonial encounters that more often rendered the Other as an anonymous member of the underdeveloped masses. Stedman furthered his individuation of the Other through a romantic interest whose publicly forbidden interracial aspect led the public to the book in droves. Yet as Mary Louise Pratt's perceptive reading argues (1992, 90–102), the seeming assault on colonial hierarchical relations posed by this romance eventually capitulates to a perpetuation of these hierarchies in a different form.

Stedman's account of his protective and sexually generated love for Joanna runs as follows. He meets the beautiful Joanna, a servant in the house where he is staying, shortly after his arrival in Surinam. The progeny of a relationship between a European male and a native slave woman, she has become the property of a European woman impoverished by her husband's mismanagement of his affairs and cruelty to his slaves. Though a family "favorite" and treated tenderly by her current owner, Joanna learns that she is primarily a financial asset and therefore to be sold so that her mistress can clear herself of the debts incurred by her husband. Joanna lapses into tears, and Stedman finds her weeping: "She gave me such a look—ah! such a look!—From that moment I determined to be her protector against every insult" (van Lier 1971, 59). Eventually, Joanna agrees to "marry" Stedman—after he has purchased her, of course—though she knows that fate may force them to part permanently at some time in the future. Dividing their time between idyllic moments together and periods of work-related separations (he to the jungles battling slaves in revolt and she to her plantation work), they have a child and live as man and wife. The ever imminent day of formal separation arrives when Stedman's regiment is reassigned to Europe. Joanna refuses to follow him on the grounds that she would prefer her status as first-rate "citizen" among her own people to that of third-class citizen in another country. For this insight regarding her preference, however, readers have only Stedman's word to rely on, for as is often the case in the textual representations of Others, the Other remains mute.

Stedman explains that although love played a role in his relationship with Joanna, both knew from the outset that theirs was essentially a union based on economics. Financial need had brought them together; each had profited from the relationship in his or her own way. Love and sentiment may tinge the story with tragic hues, but it is Stedman's bottom-line analysis that the parties involved enjoyed material advantage from each other. Yet despite such assertions, Stedman consciously highlights the romantic angles of the story while downplaying its commercial aspects, as the differences between his Surinam diaries and the text generated from them reveals. In their introduction to the 1988 reprint of the book, Price and Price (xxxii–xxxvi) show how Stedman's account of Joanna changes from the diaries' depiction of a woman who provides standard sexual services in exchange for cash to the published edition's idealized construction of "the Sable Venus."

Pratt (1992, 95–96) notes that Stedman's tale offers a "romantic transformation of a particular kind of colonial sexual exploitation," in which European males purchased native women to serve as their "temporary wives," sexual partners, and domestic servants for the length of their sojourn in the colonies. The women themselves or their families, received some sort of financial remuneration for services rendered. Colonial bureaucracies found these arrangements useful, for the native women could provide local knowledge regarding the food and medicine necessary for the survival of the administration's minions while simultaneously meeting these workers' natural urges. Such women later became standard figures as the selfless caretakers of European men in sentimental anti-conquest colonialist literature. The underlying rationale, however, whether or not wrapped in the sentimental garb of a love that transcends race and culture, was economic advantage for all involved (from the individual to the corporate to the national level).

Women of this type also played an integral role in the U.S. presence in Southeast Asia during the Vietnam war. Many of the thousands of soldiers based in Thailand procured "temporary wives" who were "rented" for the length of the men's tour of duty. As in the Pira Sudham short story discussed below, these women filled exactly the same roles that their colonial counterparts had served more than a century and a half earlier. And in mirroring the conversion of R&R sites into tourist-based service centers, the "temporary wife" lives on in some of the roles played by bar prostitutes today. Many male tourists establish a relationship with a particular prostitute that extends far beyond simply satisfying carnal demands. In such situations, the women aid the men in negotiating the vagaries of being in a different country and culture. They shop and bargain in the local markets for the men, help them make intracountry travel arrangements, accompany them on trips, cook for them, and take them to doctors and help them procure medicines if needed. Such an arrangement combines comforting nanny/nurse with naughty night partner and untroublesome travel companion, and it does so without any real commitment from either party. Under the false consciousness of economic reciprocity (crudely stated as "I get what I want; she gets what she wants; everybody is happy"), these temporary relationships provide a late twentieth-century postcolonial replication of eighteenth- and nineteenth-century colonial hierarchical relations, themselves likewise justified at the time under the ruse of reciprocity. The bar prostitute finds a distant relation in Joanna and the sentimental trope of the "nurturing native" (Pratt 1992, 96) of numerous popular narratives. Textuality and discursive practices provide, yet again, maps for navigating cross-cultural encounters with regard to economic and sexual praxis.

Both Pratt (1992, 96–102) and Hulme (1986, 249–63) discuss the mythos of reciprocity as it pertains to the complex interaction between romantic love and capitalist commerce—an interaction obviously operative in the tourist-based sex industry, which targets North American and European males. Both understand travel and literary narratives within a textual genealogy of expansionist literature stemming from the classical tradition, as exemplified in the works of Homer and Virgil. Each text manifests the same narrative sequence: foreign sojourner's need, rescue by the native meeting said need, resultant love, and eventual leave-taking. Although specific variations of this structure are evident in the texts, the sheer repetition of it prescribes the expectations of both the traveler who lives it and the audience who vicariously experiences it: the encounters have already been charted.

As a guiding principle for the subjectivities involved in these encounters past and present, though, the power of reciprocity cannot be underestimated. Hulme (1986, 147), reiterating Marx, argues that global capitalism destroys any true reciprocity operative in social relations while simultaneously perpetuating reciprocity as a legitimating tale of how capitalism functions in the world. Pratt devotes an entire chapter (1992, 69–85) to "the mystique of reciprocity" in representations of encounters with Others that has remarkable salience for postcolonial tourist interactions. Joanna and Stedman's relationship is replicated all over the globe today, the Stedman stand-ins invoking reciprocity to displace any hints of real tragedy emanating from the relationship.

What must remain absent from tales of reciprocal interaction, however, is the asymmetrical power relations involved, because reciprocity assumes equality. When equality is assumed and remains unsaid, then inequalities are either elided from accounts of interactions or dismissed as not having existed in the first place. Either way, the "mystique of reciprocity," integral to the international sex industry, perpetuates exploitative policies and enactments of them under a general misconception that if each person works for his or her own personal profit in all social and economic relations, the community as a whole will advance. The false consciousness that results from this misconception does a great deal to unburden the subjectivities of those who do profit and benefit from the assumptions upon which reciprocity functions. It is easier for sex tourists to play the role of Stedman if they believe that their contemporary Joannas profit at least as much as they do from their liaisons.

Jeremy Seabrook makes this same point regarding the perspectives of "sex-patriates,'" but he also seems to agree with the tourists: "Although at first sight it looks like another straightforward version of exploitation by the rich of the poor, the reality is perhaps less clearcut than moralists might imagine. For it is, generally, a doomed encounter between victims—the wounded (if privileged) of the West and the most impoverished of the South. It is an unsatisfactory symbiosis, based upon mutual desire for escape, from loneliness and poverty, and it thrives upon fantasy and illusion" (1991, 12). Seabrook is certainly right that the international sex industry can easily be oversimplified, especially by naive moralists. But oversimplification also occurs when those who suffer from lonely privilege are equated with those who suffer from crushing poverty. One is seeking sexual succor; the other is seeking mere subsistence. Both may be exploited by the same global systems built upon "fantasy and illusion," but that does not negate a continuum of exploitation or render all suffering the same.

As demonstrated by Diderot, Stedman, and many others, Enlightenment explorers interested in the "irrational practices" of non-Europeans catalogued events and actions intended to "prove" that sexual satisfaction was a human universal. They showed as culturally relative, however, the sanction or non-sanction of specific practices related to fulfilling this universal drive. Many of these explorers, especially those making early forays into ethnography, seemed interested in compiling accounts of sexual practices, forbidden in European culture, that went unchecked in Other, "primitive" ones. Continuing the genealogy that casts Others and their practices as simultaneously repulsive and enticing, these accounts of unabashed sex, general nakedness, and rampant promiscuity struck many European readers in decidedly paradoxical ways: morally offensive and secretly stimulating, primitive and natural, seemingly degrading and ultimately satisfying. The specter of the Enlightenment binary of Culture versus Nature found titillating form in these detailed accounts. Not limited to academic or scholarly consumption, these texts circulated widely among an ever expanding literate population.

In the eighteenth century, shamanism had already been established as an ethnographic category, and a confluence of shamanism and the unusual sexual practices associated with it often found its way into writings about Others (Flaherty 1988, 261–80). Accounts of shamanistic rituals provided detailed descriptions of "the sexual aspects of the preparations, the music, the chanting, the trance, the convulsions, the writhings and the ecstatic visions" (267). Ceremonies and rituals under shamanistic influence seemed imbued with a highly charged eroticism capable of transcendence and transportation. Beyond mere magic, a sexual prowess of superhuman capacity was also embodied in the powers of the shaman, as accounts from the Americas to Africa to the Middle East to South Pacific islands attest (266–271). This marked the shaman as a site of wonder and envy for the European reading public. Flaherty discusses the writings of Jerome Grub, an eighteenth-century physician, which express a desire to obtain shamanistic secrets for a drug-induced stupor that produced a "vision of having been transported after a long aerial journey into a distant place, where [shamans] intermingle, cohabit, and dance with others of their ilk" (266).

With sex tourism, this eighteenth-century desire has become a twentieth-century reality except that the shaman/tourists need not take drugs but merely a plane to arrive at their fantasy site, and they may imbibe the stimulants after arriving. Though they intermingle with those of their own kind, they cohabit not with them but rather with those others who inhabit the distant place of their sojourn. Here the shaman/tourists witness and partake of the erotically charged performances that Flaherty describes; all the qualities ascribed to shamanistic ritual can be applied to the sex bar scene of Bangkok and the ritualized ecstasies encountered there. These twentieth-century travelers believe that they wield the power and sexual prowess of shamans documented in the eighteenth century. The innumerable natives who willingly yield to this power attest, in their subjectivities, to this fact. Although tradition and delusion make for heady influences, the magic exercised in these new shamanisitic sites is one of sheer economics. To travel, encounter, and engage in activities under the auspices of reciprocity has been and remains a powerful lure.

Harems: Imagined Sitings

> [The sound we were looking for in *The King and I* was like] a series of Siamese paintings done by Grant Wood.
> —Richard Rodgers, composer

In the late eighteenth-century accounts of Other cultures we have examined, the abundance of sexuality, sexual opportunities, and available women conforms to the laws of Nature, in which fecundity rules and scarcity results from the artificial constraints set upon Nature by backward culture. With the harem, we witness a shift in the discourse. The very abundance previously constructed as natural now becomes an unnatural overabundance of sexuality (especially female sexuality and, as such, in need of constraint). As Malek Alloula writes, "What is remembered about the harem ... are the sexual excesses to which it gives rise and which it promotes." The seraglio as a discursively constructed site provides an "ideal locus," "a universe of *generalized perversion* and of the absolute *limitlessness of pleasure*" (1986, 95).

Textual stereotypes about the harem of the Middle East (or the Levant) were appropriated by various travel writers of the nineteenth century and transposed to Southeast Asia and Siam. Similar stereotypes and representations remain at play in the tourist literature and advertisements of the twentieth century. We should constantly bear in mind, however, the constructed and projected nature of the attributes operative in constituting the harem as an imagined site. Alloula's study concentrates on early twentieth-century French postcards depicting Algerian "harems" reconstructed in photographers' studios. About these, David Spurr writes: "Their staging of exotic ritual is a bogus repetition, a false repetition of Algerian traditions for the minor amusement created by commodity production ... [and] it corresponds to that aspect of colonial discourse in which an indigenous culture is reinterpreted under conditions determined by the observer, resulting in a presentation of indigenous life that merely reflects the framework of values imposed by the colonizing eye" (1993, 176). The inequitable power relations involved in contemporary international tourism replicate those of colonialism.

Two texts can help us examine the harem in nineteenth-century Siam. The first comes from the pen of Anna Leonowens, the producer of the most enduring images and understandings of Siam (or Thailand, for that matter) in twentieth-century popular imagination. In 1944 her writings and life were combined in a dubiously biographical work by Margaret Landon titled *Anna and the King of Siam*, which provided the basis for *The King and I*. The text we consider is Leonowens's second book about her life in the Siamese court: *The Romance of the Harem*, originally published in 1873. Our other text is *Temples and Elephants: Travels in Siam in 1881–1882*, by Carl Bock. A self-described "naturalist," Bock claims to have gained favor in the court of King Chulalongkorn, Leonowens's most famous pupil.

Anna Leonowens's *The Romance of the Harem* appeared in reprints under a variety of titles: *The Romance of Siamese Harem Life; Siamese Harem Life; Siam and the Siamese*. According to Susan Morgan's introduction to the 1991 edition (xxi–xxiv), the title changes reflect attempts to minimize the fictional elements of the text and play up the factual. Leonowens's preface to the 1872 edition clearly states, however, that despite her evocation of "romance" in the title, the stories she provides are true. For us, largely concerned with representations and reception, the difference between fact and fiction is moot. Leonowens herself attempted so wide a variety of self-fashionings that as, with her text, the lines between fiction and fact become difficult to distinguish.[6] Relating some verifiable incidents from her life to her accounts of the Royal Harem, however, will help us understand her interpretations of what she encountered. After the 1859 death of her husband in Penang, Leonowens lived in Singapore for a while but found it hard to earn a living. In 1862, she was hired by King Mongkut of Siam, as part of his gradual modernization and internationalization policies, to teach English language and culture to the women of the Royal Harem (in Thai, *Nang Harm*). Her more than five years in Bangkok gave her access to the court, the harem, and their inhabitants; thus she left the only account of that harem by a Westerner (Bock visited a prince's harem but not the king's). We argue, however, that certain events and experiences in Leonowens's life, as well as her familiarity with certain tropes about Others in English discursive practices, shaped the way she understood what she experienced from her unique vantage point.

First, whether born in Wales (as she told it) or India (as the documents seem to indicate), Leonowens spent much of her youth and young adulthood in India, where Mughal-Islamic memories and manifestations of harems existed and populated lived reality as well as popular imagination. Second, at the age of fifteen she traveled to the Middle East, unchaperoned, with a Reverend George Percy Badger (and his wife, claimed Leonowens, though Badger was apparently unmarried, and for an "educational tour," she further claimed). Whatever the relationship and however long the stay (anywhere from a few months to two years), the Middle East trip further exposed Leonowens to the Muslim harem, as well as the orientalist figurations of it, as part of her informal education. All this leads us to suggest that just as Indian and Hindu customs color and prefigure Leonowens's accounts of daily Thai life and religious custom—she even employed Hindi terminology to describe them—her experiences with Muslim harems (as both real phenomena and imagined fantasies) affected her understanding and representations of the "harem" in Thailand. The false cognates of *Harm* in the Thai name of the site and the English word "harem," borrowed from Arabic for use in English, may have added to the confusion. There are analogous relationships, too: India and Hinduism are related and similar to Thailand and Buddhism (which is not to suggest that these nations, religions, cultures are monolithic entities, but merely that they get used as such for various purposes). The differences, however, are vast.

The *Nang Harm* that Leonowens knew bore little structural or functional similarity to harems of the Muslim world. They had in common the fact that they were sites in which a large number of women under the "protection" of a powerful male ruler were isolated from the outside world, and that some of these women acted as wives or concubines for the ruler—substantial similarities, to be sure. But the Royal Harem in Thailand served as an integral social institution that unified the nation and its people. As Leonowens herself writes, the Royal Harem constituted an autonomous city-within-the-palace: physically a city complete with homes and parks and wide streets, and organizationally a city in which women filled all social roles (save that of ruler): from servants to cooks to soldiers to doctors and judges. (No Mughal harem we know of ever occupied such a space or had that internal structure.) The population of *Nang Harm*, between three and nine thousand in the 1860s, also dwarfs most if not all Muslim harems. This is because it functioned within the larger feudal society of Thailand in the mid-eighteenth century to supply the royal genealogy and connect the national elite in complex social and economic ways unique to Thailand.

As Morgan highlights (xxxiii–xxxvi), Leonowens's major textual preoccupation with the harem was the oppression of the women within it, as well as the complex systems of slavery—including loan bondage—that perpetuated the oppression. Interestingly, bonded-labor slavery—means of working off debts based on exponential interest growth—exists in a modified form in contemporary Thailand and plays a vital role in the sex industry there. As part of brothel recruitment strategies, procurers who prey upon impoverished rural people offer a sum of money up front to a young woman's family for services to be rendered later. The lump sum carries a very high interest rate, however. Women who work in brothels to pay off these debts incurred by their families participate in a unique blend of traditional bonded labor and contemporary capitalism. This is often the only means by which families forced off subsistence farms can acquire the money needed to survive in the cash-based developing economy. The underlying system of bonded labor presented by Leonowens as operative in the mid-eighteenth century provides useful historical context for the complex interaction between local values and traditions and the specific manifestation of international globalization development strategies today.

Returning to the polemical aspects of Leonowens's text, we find that she represents the Royal Harem as not only a city, but a city-as-prison. This trope, Malek Alloula argues (1986, 95–122) functions within Western colonial representations of the Muslim harem: the harem-as-prison provides justification for the "liberation" of the harem site by colonizing forces, while ignoring the fact that the liberated occupants have just been colonized. Further, Alloula asserts, the "liberation" converts the site from feudal harem/prison to colonial brothel, a conversion useful for our trajectory and one that is played out in the indirect colonization of global economics today. The dependence on such tropes exacts a toll on Leonowens's book by deflecting the reader's attention from activist causes; *The Romance of the Harem* wraps populist antislavery issues and protests against the crushing abuse of the women in the Royal Harem in popular melodramatic tales of oriental exotic excess. Despite operating, as Morgan argues (1992, xxxv–xxxvi), in the great Victorian "realist" tradition of novels concerned with social injustices, despite presenting humane and empathetic portraits of the women in the Royal Harem, and despite being a virulent antislavery tract (as the author's contemporary Harriet Beecher Stowe believed), the text was intended to sell. Hence, Leonowens flaunted the "romance" of the title, which translates into the orientalist tradition of popular writing, and trotted out the clichés and tropes found in the paradoxical representations of Others outlined earlier in this chapter; in a narrative intended to titillate as much as educate, she drew particularly on those associated with the Muslim harem as a site of sexual overabundance and intrigue. We cannot ignore, then, that Leonowens was working with—and within—the genealogical traditions charted in this chapter.

Morgan argues that we should not allow the "major icon of American culture" that sprang from the text to obscure our understanding of it now or at the time of its production (1992, xxvi). Such a tack is useful for a specific reading but ignores some important questions about reception. Why are some major issues of the nineteenth century that are "united in this populist book" (xxvii)—imperialism, slavery, and women's rights—overshadowed by the sensationalist and sensualized incidents that pepper the text? Morgan asserts—correctly, we believe—that the way it was received had to do with the book's emanating from a nonsanctioned source of authority (xxvii), that Leonowens's race (rumors of mixed blood), class, and gender undermined the authority that is usually accorded the presence of the eyewitness. We would add another possibility to the mix. Perhaps the elements that found their way into *Anna and the King of Siam* (and the films, musical, and TV show it spawned) were the ones with which audiences were most comfortable, elements that conformed to the schizophrenic representations of Others which hark back to Homer and Herodotus. The reception of Leonowens's text in the popular arena provides a valuable example of the strength of the genealogy of a given group of representations and tropes. Even when facing a text that provides a powerful critique of imperialism and slavery and ostensibly promotes women's rights (which this book does), audiences trained to find the countervailing messages of opulent sexuality and tyrannical cruelty (which the book also provides in abundance) will ignore what falls largely outside the textual tradition and cling steadfastly to what remains firmly within it.

Bock's *Temples and Elephants*, originally published in 1884, reveals the qualities of "anticonquest" narratives by naturalists so popular in the nineteenth century and discussed at length by Pratt, who defines this mode as "the strategies of representation whereby European bourgeois subjects seek to secure their innocence in the same moment that they assert European hegemony" (1992, 7). Authors of travel and exploration writings, especially those related to natural history, cartography, trade routes, and so on, develop a subjectivity wholly constituted by objectivity, the innocent bystander "merely" collects: "Here is to be found a utopian image of a European bourgeois subject simultaneously innocent and imperial, asserting a harmless hegemonic vision that installs no apparatus of domination" (Pratt 1992, 33–34).

Despite the passage of time since the original publication of Bock's book, the Oxford University Press reprint of 1986 claims on the back cover that "much of the life and culture of the countryside . . . will be familiar to the modern traveler in Thailand today . . . [though] some of [it] is gone forever." Like that of twentieth-century international tourists, Bock's understanding of his experiences in Siam has been largely determined for him by preconceptions formed through his reading: that is, the various representations offered by writers such as

Leonowens who have generated certain expectations regarding a given cross-cultural encounter. In the section of his fourth chapter subtitled "A visit to the harem," Bock invokes these stereotypes to stage a sequence that employs his desire to have the stereotypes realized as the basis for the self-deprecation that characterizes the sequence. (At the same time, he playfully undermines the authority of presence so necessary to travel writing and ethnography.)

> [The] unexpected invitation [to a prince's harem] conjured up strange visions of all the mysterious scenes of beauty and luxury of which I had heard and read so much. I had known sultans and rajahs who kept harems filled with damsels of all ages and nationalities, but had never had the privilege of setting my profane eyes on the jealously-guarded interior. Even the Sultan of Koetei, whose intimate friendship I had enjoyed, and with many of whose secrets I was acquainted, had never allowed me to invade the precincts of his sanctum sanctorum. But now the second most powerful prince in Siam had actually, of his own free will, offered me, a visitor and stranger, this privilege (1986, 36).

Bock thus initiates the episode by inviting his readers to call forth the images of "beauty and luxury" associated with harem life that he knew he could count on as shared knowledge, stereotypes long circulated in print culture. In so doing, he covers a spectrum of cultures—"sultans and rajahs" (Mughal and Hindu) and "damsels" (Northern European)—to trace the sacred-versus-profane dichotomy necessary for sustaining the clichés of the harem. The sanctum that is the harem would be viewed by Europeans as inherently profane, thus adding to the titillation. All this combines to heighten his—and his reader's—anticipation of the opulent treasures in store for the visitor, the reader's proxy, the better to set up the humor. The comic aspect emerges in Bock's and his reader's frustration when they find these well-worn images and representations largely empty of any referents in reality: "Behind the screen, who could tell, perhaps the ladies slept. . . . As we paced through this chamber, Mr. Newman whispered that we were approaching the central object of our visit. 'But,' he added irreverently, 'don't deceive yourself by thinking that [the prince] will let you see all his pretty girls. They ought to be there'—pointing in front of us—'but they will be invisible'"(37).

The veil worn by harem women is reproduced not only by a screen, but also by an even more impenetrable shield: the power of the prince to render his "pretty girls . . . invisible" to the eyes of others. Seemingly, the orientalist tropes of mystery and power take precedence over the travel writers' tropes of unveiling mystery and sharing a rare experience. Bock banks on his readers' desire to have Mr. Newman proved wrong and the rhetoric of discovery prevail. But "on the floor . . . reclined or sat a number of female figures—not with the beauteous faces my ardent imagination had pictured, but with wrinkled cheeks and grey heads. Mr. Newman was right. The ladies of the harem had been carefully secluded in anticipation of our visit, and replaced by others who a generation, or perhaps two generations ago, had been the concubines of the [prince's] father—if not his grandfather" (37–38).

Although the obvious "humor" of the episode rests on having elderly women greet his view as he invades a sacred/profane space rarely seen by Western eyes—and not the beauteous ones his "ardent imagination" had enticed him with—the effect requires that Bock's readers' share his "ardent imagination" and disappointment at having it undermined. The humor depends on deflating the stereotypical representations of harems while paradoxically maintaining them, for the "pretty girls" are presumed to exist, though they remain *harim* (Arabic for "forbidden") to Westerners. Humor also emerges from the revelation of the selectivity of the harem fantasy, one that elides older women and children (turn-offs, after all) from a site they obviously do occupy. The stereotypes have prescribed Bock's encounter to such an extent that any sight or phenomenon not fulfilling the clichés can be surprising, disappointing, and funny. That Bock could so depend on this textually generated shared knowledge of the representation of sexual Other cultures in the late nineteenth century, that he could construct a humorous episode by having the text of his experience clash with the context of his discursively driven expectation, speaks volumes for the power of such representations to prescribe and inscribe cross-cultural interactions.

From Harem to Brothel

As the site of Others moves from naturally sexual to unnaturally fecund (the harem), as the harem becomes brothel and the brothel-as-bar of the late twentieth-century tourist excursion emerges, the genealogy of these discursive practices is woven into the DNA of cross-cultural expectation and experience. Belief that Thais are "naturally" more sexual than any other people in the world naturally finds its way into manifold representations of the nation and culture, from novels to travel accounts to tourist brochures, and it lurks behind many development strategies that determine national policy. These discourses have a history, as do the tropes they rely on—a history in which large-scale domination, exploitation, and satiation are the natural results for one side of cross-cultural relations and transactions.

Jack Reynolds's 1956 novel, *A Woman of Bangkok*—once lauded by the *Asian Wall Street Journal* as "among the 10 finest novels written about Asia"—provides a highly literary and allusion-ridden account of the burgeoning prostitution business in post–World War II Thailand. In a stunning recapitulation and secularized update of Diderot's chaplain, Reynolds's first-person protagonist, Reggie Joyce, leaves the dreary, repressive West (here, England) for the warmer, more "open" climes of Bangkok. That his journey from England to Asia is also a journey from romantic/sexual frustration at home to the promise of romantic/sexual satisfaction elsewhere is exemplified by the plane trip taken in the first chapter.

Reggie's departure finds him face to face with Sheila, his love, who has forsaken him and married his brother. At the airport Sheila claims that Reggie failed to win her admiration because of his sexual timidity, which stems, she asserts, from romantic ideals found in the poetry he immerses himself in. In this instance, then, Reynolds not only acknowledges the power of textual representations to constitute expectations and influence behavior toward others (this becomes even more apparent in the Asian sections of the text), he also uses the conventions against themselves. That is, he subverts reader expectations to a certain extent by rendering the clichéd "good" woman in England as "bad" (that is, possessing a sexual subjectivity) in order to posit the clichéd "bad" prostitute in Bangkok as "good."

Reggie departs England in confusion but hardly with his world view, a textually based knowledge, undermined. This becomes apparent by the end of chapter 1: Reggie gains self-confidence and strength from the grandeur of his global journey, evidenced by his flirting successfully with a waitress during a stopover in India; the white Western male confidence is bolstered by his "successful" interactions with female, non-Western Others onto whom he can project his hopes of desirability. The Other female presents an opportunity not available from the women back home: "It seems almost like treason to the image of Sheila to feel happy *already*" he muses on the plane (29). The promise of self-fulfillment through sexual assertion, which lingers in the textual genealogy we have examined, blooms full-blown in Reynolds's account of Rangoon, the penultimate stop on Reggie's physical and psychic journey. The Orient as sexual satiation beckons alluringly in the protagonist's textually generated imagination, despite the reality that the site does not match his expectations: "Rangoon which we reach in the small hours is a drab place, not at all what you would expect the cradle of . . . a houri to be. There are no buxom cushions, no hanging brocades, no shapely brass pots, no exotic perfumes, no Negro slave-girls (and why in blazes should there be?) naked to the waist, idly waving huge fans. There are only sleepy, irritable waiters, unpleasant coffee, a plain hostess in a white suit, and lost frogs hopping disconsolately across the restaurant floor" (29).

Like Diderot's chaplain, Reynolds's Reggie wages a battle with himself regarding sexual morality and conduct, and like Diderot—not to mention much of the Western Enlightenment tradition—Reynolds constitutes the problem within the dichotomy of Culture versus Nature. When Reggie first confronts the brothel site—an encounter that emerges from a night of carousing with both foreign and Thai business associates—he experiences much psychological dissonance. The discomfort is both moral and ethical, and gendered and individual—the tension between "proper" behavior and embarrassment at his being a virgin (and therefore not a "real" man). Like his plane journey, the trip to the bordello becomes an integral aspect of Reggie's education about himself, the world, and his position within it. In the brothel his discomfiture attracts the attention of an American companion in the adventure, who instructs Reggie about "proper" behavior, expectations, and attitudes in *this* particular site of global-local gendered interaction. In response to Reggie's claim of "being bored," the American responds, "It isn't our sex that gets bored in a brothel" (63)—a bit of wisdom that seeks to dispel any culturally instilled qualms about ethics, morals, or subjectivity. Reggie learns that business is business and that satiating his sexual pleasure is not so much a privilege as a right in this place.

Still, the tension remains and is explained as the unnatural cultural limitations on natural desire that we read in Diderot. Moreover, the voice of Reggie's father, a clergyman, haunts his conscience. And it is to these thoughts—the articulation of Western morality and cultural restraint of nature—that Reggie attributes the depression he feels in the brothel (63). Eventually, he flees. As he does so, he imagines his cohorts feeling relief at his departure (his moral quandaries no longer infringing upon their fun) and condemning him: "Goddamned Puritan son of a bitch" (67). In essence, the protagonist's attempt to satisfy his natural urges through physical copulation are thwarted by his own cultural mental machinations—or so the discursive tradition of Diderot's dichotomy would have us believe.

Back in his hotel room, the dilemma is explicitly played out in his mind. He wonders about the women he encountered at the brothel, particularly one he has dubbed "Venus." But his curiosity about what motivates these women, or what leads them to their work, is overwhelmed quickly by the issue at hand: the subjectivity of the customer—one "not quite so inhibited, not quite so pre-occupied with morals, his own or other people's" and one who sees in the person of the prostitute "the possibility of a moment's satisfaction" (70). Like A. and B. in Diderot's dialogue, Reggie learns his lesson about the folly of cultural constraints and heads back out into the night to heed "the amplified voice of all Nature's fiercest obsession" (71). From this moment in the text, Reggie has become as his brothel brothers, regularly visiting prostitutes and eventually falling in love with one. To show the maturation of his self-knowledge, to fully expose the psychological machinations of Culture versus Nature and reciprocity, Reynolds has his protagonist—near the novel's end—upbraid an American for his own moralizing.

I'd said that he'd started off just as I'd started off years before, observing the tablets of an outmoded Law and damaging my brain and body and spirit, thereby imposing on myself abnegations which were advocated by all my mentors and strengthened by my own personal timidity, but false. "Such self-denial never gets a man anywhere unless he's got religion and can turn himself into a monk," I'd said. "Like Crashaw and his 'sweetly-killing dart.' . . . A few good nights out with something like that"—I'd jerked my head in the direction of our room [where the woman of the book's title lay]—"would have turned Crashaw into a master-poet, instead of a trunkful of conceits. But you're no poet; you're trying to sublimate your glandular urges in good works, which is even more futile than poetry. Good works won't unbind you, chum. You need a female chest with bubs on it" (270).

This section ruthlessly reveals the callow subjectivity of the men in the bar-as-brothel scene, who themselves operate in a discursive, textual tradition that feeds on fear, cynicism, and the false consciousness of reciprocity. Although Reynolds does not completely distance himself from the views his protagonist expresses here, he does reveal the ease with which people from certain places, operating within particular traditions, fall into such perspectives—as well as some of the consequences of doing so.

Reynolds's position on these issues, the seemingly contradictory nature of his protagonist's relation to those he encounters in Thailand, emanates from the same textual tradition that bestowed upon him the Culture versus Nature binary trope featured so much in the novel. The paradoxical representation of the site at hand operates strongly within the tradition of schizoid othering that we found Pico Iyer falling prey to. For a strong example, we need only refer to the passage in which Reggie first visits a brothel, a site where all these diametrically opposed responses seem to converge. As the men begin to act upon the idea of "going for a walk" (a Thai euphemism for brothel visiting), the music from a *ramwong*, a rural dance for young adults, can be heard in the distance. "There is terrific sexual excitement in such music—I sensed it the very day I landed in Bangkok—it is quite different from other music—fierce and impatient yet at the same time relaxed and happy—the music of a people who die young but without regrets, worn out by the unbearable pleasantness of life, its alternating delights of desire and satiation" (53). The least mimetic of all art forms, music here embodies and represents all that a sexual Other site could possibly offer, in all its blazing contradiction. Yet in this site the music, at least for this subjectivity, primarily conveys life as ultimately oscillating between desire and the satiation of it; the paradox collapses into the fulfillment of one's deepest desires as indigenous to the space and its population, just as it did for Diderot.

Reggie's mood shifts, though, as the gang makes its way through darkened streets toward the brothel. In his mind he associates the brothel with the bar where he has seen the prostitute for whom he eventually expresses his love. The bar and the brothel collapse into the bar-as-brothel now found on our fin-de-siècle maps, and in so doing, undermine his joviality regarding desire and satiation: "Suddenly I am sick of Thailand where Sex stalks naked and men and women hurt themselves and each other so much in worship of him. It is more decent to hurt yourself in solitude with yourself and the horror. . . . But I am with this gang now; nor do I altogether want to escape" (58).

When the journey to the brothel begins to nauseate more than titillate, Reggie reveals the position of hermetically sealed isolation from which many travelers experience encounters with Others. What they read as inherent in the site actually emerges largely from their own projection of desires and fears (as we have seen). As Reggie moves toward the satiation of his desires, the artifice that provides justification for acting upon them begins to show itself for what it is. When he slips into moral despair and eventually flees the site, he blames his "timidity" not on the inequitable power relations at play in the brothel but on the unnatural constraints that culture places on natural desires, and he allows his projections to regain their sway over his actions as he later heads back to the brothel to prove or attain his manhood. The passage quoted immediately above provides a wonderful articulation of the pulls and paradoxes at play in encounters with sexual Other cultures, especially as the encounters and the expectations and assumptions that drive them emerge from the textual genealogy under scrutiny in this chapter. The Culture versus Nature dichotomy may indeed exist, but it does so in the cultural representations of Others as naturally sexual, not where or how the texts say it does.

The eponymous woman is named Vilai, the notorious White Leopard. She works in the Bolero Dance Hall. We find in the 1950s dance hall a pre–Viet Nam version of the go-go bar that now serves international tourists: the prostitutes went from dancing *with* men prior to getting down to business to dancing *for* men. The change reflected in the prepositions removes any hint of autonomous female sexual subjectivity and choice. In the dance hall fronting for prostitution, some genuine contact had to be established: the woman and the customer must interact and talk. The go-go bars demand no such interaction. The deal in the dance hall necessitated at least a semidialogical exchange. In the contemporary go-go bar the male customer passively observes the dancers in their artificial environment before choosing one to his liking, much as a restaurant-goer selects a lobster from a tank. In both sites, though, the would-be client encounters numerous choices. Reynolds therefore presents Vilai's fundamental understanding of her body as a commodity. When readers first meet her she is immersed in the process of making herself up for the evening's work, and we are privy to her thoughts about the previous night's events at the dance hall. The intimate connection between her body-as-commodity and the site where she sells her wares is made explicit: The dance hall, as she understands it, clearly connotes the space in which her sexuality is sold.

This site from the past is a prototype of the current one, and Reynolds provides a succinct description of the self-loathing mixed with the promise of self-fulfillment and satiation that operates within the psyche of the customer: "Suckers dragged in by their testicles to be fleeced by brewers and harlots" (96)—an articulation of the bar clients' position still salient today. The customers indeed believe they are often the ones being taken advantage of. The fear of being "overcharged," part and parcel of the tourist mentality, runs the gamut from "clip joints" that gouge through drink prices and bar fines to the price of the sexual act itself. The legitimating trope of reciprocity cannot conceal the fear that in any given exchange of cash for material goods or labor one of the parties will be taken advantage of, thus rendering the falsity of the trope explicit.

The clients similarly believe that if a relationship passes beyond "mere" economics, then the woman's affection for the man should be expressed by her not charging him for sexual services. In the woman's interpretation, on the other hand, such affections should lead to more pay, reflecting the man's care and concern for her. If he values her, so the argument goes, she should be able to demand higher pay. Such cross-cultural miscommunication occurs at length between Reggie and Vilai, predicated on the differences between sex-for-money, sex-for-love, and money-for-love. Reynolds's novel, on the whole, deftly explores the complications that emerge out of the "simple," "basic" economic transaction that many a client claims it to be. *A Woman of Bangkok* presents an insightful reading of the bar-as-brothel in its nascent, post–World War II state and skillfully explores the subjectivity of the various actors in this site.

We have been considering a representation of the bar-as-brothel from the outside. A very different take on reciprocity and exploitation appears in Pira Sudham's "Siamese Drama." This short story by a Thai author who writes in English corresponds with the Stedman narrative of temporary wives as it answers the question posed by Reynolds's Reggie regarding how nice girls like the ones he encountered came to work in such a place. Many Thais dismiss Sudham's writing as "nothing new," as simply putting into English and into print what everyone in Thailand already knows. (That this material constitutes absolute shared knowledge in Thailand but remains "unspeakable" is addressed in Chapter 7.) The ordinariness of the topic and narrative, however, render it all the more important for our understanding of the forces at play in the development of the international sex industry and its manifestation in the daily lives of the women involved in it. The title itself, in fact, evokes the everyday quality of the material and indicates that such lives constitute the prototypical, if not stereotypical, plot of female *dramatis personae* in contemporary Thailand.

Sudham packs the short piece with all the clichéd events that were repeated over and over again for Iyer. Rather than having such repetition call the validity of the narrative into question as it does for Iyer, however, the fact that such events have become banal heightens the tragedy and irony for an international English-reading audience. In the particular cash-based market economy of international development that has become the global norm, the drama faced by a village woman with little education and few marketable skills becomes *the* Siamese drama, for such is the condition of a majority of the population. Sudham's flat prose, his disclosure that commercial sexual practices are so commonplace as to have entered everyday discourse, and his introduction of new lexical usage that illuminates the explicitly economic nature of human interactions all appear in the story's opening paragraph: "The first woman was Salee, known to the neighbourhood as a kept-woman. Some of the neighbours preferred to refer to her as 'that rented wife.' 'Rent' had recently been applied to women of Salee's profession since many Americans stationed in Thailand during the Vietnam War had rented many Thai women as temporary wives. The term stuck and had become a household word" (1983, 29).

The primary relationship in the piece is between Salee and Nipa, identified as "the second woman" (30). As much a type as Salee, Nipa represents the woman who has worked for a time as a prostitute but, because of advancing age and deteriorating looks, has graduated to manager and procurer of prostitutes—a common career shift and one generally considered an upwardly mobile move. In

Nipa, Salee glimpses her own possible future, and readers witness how the sex industry perpetuates itself through usury, cash-based economics, and exploitation within as well as across socioeconomic gender relations.

As the story opens, Nipa has written to Salee just as the latter has determined that her position as "minor wife" (or mistress) of a Thai man is not going to bring her the material rewards she had anticipated. Nipa seeks to bring Salee to Pattaya, where she can work the bars that foreigners frequent. The letter prompts Salee to reflect on how she arrived at her current position. Like thousands before her, she was tempted from her village by promises of an income. She remembers being removed from "the front line" in the brothel after one year and replaced with "teenage girls freshly procured from the country" (33). Eventually, the enterprising Nipa purchased Salee's freedom from the brothel and placed her as a mistress. Seeing that her investment has not paid off as well as planned, Nipa visits Salee to lure her to the resort town south of Bangkok famous for its prostitutes. As Nipa moves through Salee's home, chastising her for her lack of business acumen, "Salee saw not only Nipa but also a horde of women, pimps, murderers, thieves and uniform-wearing men who had lived off her flesh" (33).

Nipa's cajoling works, and Salee relocates to Pattaya. Sudham contextualizes the site for his English-reading audience, some of whom may be unaware of its history. In so doing, he articulates many of the global-local, cultural-economic relationships integral to this book.

> The sight of rich foreign tourists made Nipa look for ways to make a fortune out of this seaside resort. Because she was ugly and growing old, she had made little money from the Vietnam War when a lot of Americans on holidays swarmed the bars and brothels. That war was over. But now there was Pattaya. The mighty mark-carrying Germans had colonized the town. Pattaya seemed to have grown overnight. Every so often one heard people brag of striking gold, that dealing with the Germans was more lucrative than with the Americans. Besides, the Americans only *rented* their women while the Germans tended to take their women with them (37).

This paragraph shows war yielding to tourism as the direct, local, and military colonization processes operative from the end of the fifteenth to the mid-twentieth century give way to the indirect, oblique, global management of economics, politics, and culture of the present. Although prostitution operates under both rubrics, it flourishes under international tourism, and opportunity improves for women like Salee, but only because German tourists may provide her a chance, virtually absent from interactions with American soldiers, to flee her country—to escape her Siamese drama. The postcolonial map tells her that survival at home is difficult at best.

The two women, one with a keen business mind and the other with a bankable body, attract many clients. As is often the case in even brutal situations, the discourse of development and progress is taken up by those it exploits. Salee feels "proud" to be "one of those who were responsible for attracting so many foreigners to Pattaya" (40). (Sudham plays with the word "thai," which means "free" in the Thai language, by connecting "Thai" and "freedom" to the money these providers of pleasure receive from tourists. They are free because they are not "free"; that is, they charge, but their freedom derives from the largesse provided by tourists for sexual services.) Nevertheless, the women's partnership dissolves over a dispute about—what else?—money.

When Salee returns to her Issan village, Sudham neatly evokes the prevailing understanding of rural versus urban life in Thailand, a difference upon which development strategies depend and those in the sex industry prey. The elderly women in the village bemoan the fact that Salee had "lost [her] city life" by exchanging it for "one of drudgery in the village" (43). All in the village live in awe of Bangkok—in Thai, *Krung Thep*, meaning the "city of angels": "The mere mention of the name Krung Thep had a magical effect. It had always been the home of affluence, attracting adventurers and hopeless peasants alike, to seek fortunes and employment—their share of the nation's wealth within its limited radius" (45). Once again, Sudham makes clear that the postcolonial development maps chart very specific sites for the infusion of wealth. At the same time, the new modes of production and cash-based economy make village life virtually impossible. Thus Salee does not regret her past because it has translated into her ability to provide for her family, as tradition dictates: "The end result— the cash sent back home by money order—had meant survival" (45). Sudham evokes for an English-speaking audience what Gayatri Spivak has called "the aporias or ethico-historical dilemmas in women's decolonization," showing that "one of the bases for women's subalternity . . . is the internalized constraints seen as responsibility" (intro. to Devi 1995, xxvii). Although she is writing about Mahasweta Devi's fiction, Spivak's words are equally applicable to Sudham's story when she says that this writing "dramatizes that difficult truth: internalized gendering perceived as ethical choice [which] is the hardest roadblock for women the world over" (xxviii).

Despite Salee's apparent lack of regret for it, her past reappears in the corporeal form of Nipa, who arrives in the village ostensibly to lure Salee back into the business. When Salee refuses, Nipa takes solace in the laws of supply and demand: knowing that rural poverty outstrips even the sex industry's massive demands, she decides to recruit more young women from the village for Bangkok brothels. That she is perceived by the villagers as "exuding wealth and civilization" (43)—in conjunction with the mystique of Bangkok, the promise of material wealth, and the abject poverty in the village—makes Nipa's job an easy one. In fact, the two girls she selects are understood by the villagers as having exceptionally good luck, acquired from merit accumulated in past lives: "Their reward was the chance Nipa offered to take them away from the mire of peasant life" (46). Such an interpretation of events under international development pressures reveals the symbiotic relationship between the adaptive flexibility of capitalist exploitation and the perpetuation of traditional structures of privilege (Bardhan 1986, 5).

Salee, however, reads the situation differently. Banking on Nipa's greed, she lures her former manager to an isolated spot with the promise of showing her a particularly promising prospect—one who could attract a large price for the loss of her virginity. There, taking matters into her own hands, Salee slays Nipa. The villagers are left to console the girls who have lost their chance at fortune, or at least of avoiding the desperation of the status quo. Again, it is worth repeating that the drama of choices, or lack of them, operative in this tale is so commonplace that most Thais dismiss Sudham's writing as taking advantage of English speakers' ignorance. Additionally, it is worth repeating that this very everydayness lends the story whatever power it has for readers of English because, for many of them, the cliché is startling, and all the more so for the insight that it is a cliché.

Twentieth-Century Postcolonial Sexual Encounters

Our trajectory has taken us from a site constituted as sexual within the dictates of "nature" to the site of the unnatural harem, to the harem-become-brothel, to the contemporary bar-as-brothel. Keeping the focus on this last site, we shift from texts that represent themselves as fiction to a pair that represent themselves as factual accounts yet which also reinscribe, near the end of the twentieth century, the genealogy of discursive practices regarding sexual cultural Others for which Diderot has served as a kind of metonymy. In addition, they share attributes that we find particularly troubling. One comes from the World Sex Guide on the Internet, posted 23 August 1994, titled "Sex in Thailand Part I: The Basics." The other is a 1994 publication, *Patpong Sisters*, by a recent doctoral graduate of the New School for Social Research.

The Internet piece was posted by a longtime traveler to Asia, and the language, issues, and tropes he employs derive largely from those that many tourists have inherited from the sixteenth century on. The author uses his years of experience to establish his authority on the topic of the sex trade in Bangkok, but he does so in the chatty, informal manner common to the Internet, to which he adds the simultaneously kind and chiding tone of an older brother teaching a younger sibling the ways of the world. An additional move to build a credible persona appears at the very beginning of the text with his "disclaimer": readers, he says, will find minimal information regarding "gay sex" and none about "pedophilia" because he has "no personal interest" in the former and finds the latter "pathologically evil" (1). He thus establishes himself as a "normal" heterosexual male with an ethical foundation that can erupt as moral indignation. His assertion about pedophilia collapses the discourses of morality and mental health to form a discourse of medical morality in which "pathological" is an intensifier for "evil." And finally, the entire "how-to" manual appears gratis on the World Wide Web, revealing the author as a beneficent human making his contribution to the late twentieth-century version of the storehouse of knowledge—much as naturalists, natural historians, travelers, and anthropologists of the eighteenth and nineteenth centuries did, simply sharing their wealth of knowledge and experience with the rest of the world without personal gain (as did Diderot and the Encyclopedists). The discourse and rhetorical position of the text recalls that labeled by Pratt (1992) as "anti-conquest." Anti-conquest subjectivity and discursive practices often operate with both tourists and international development strategists, especially under the guise of that "reciprocity" which so determines accounts and understandings of capitalist-based interactions.

After first converting the metaphysics of presence into a legitimation of his authority to author the text, he then structures the piece in a question-and-answer format. The second answer yields the most relevant information for our purposes. To the question of how Thais regard prostitution and prostitutes, this expert—sounding as if he could be either A. or B. in Diderot's supplemental dialogue—responds: "Prostitution in Thailand has long been an accepted (if not universally loved) part of the social fabric. It does not carry the stigma, either for the women or their customers, that it does in the West. IMHO [In my humble opinion], this is primarily due to the fact that Thais adhere to a very different tradition from the guilt-laden and highly proscriptive Judeo-Christian one" (2–3). The evocation of a backward Western morality inherited from religious authority, which prevents one from acting upon one's natural impulses, seems straight out of Diderot, and we would argue that it is. Stating that Thais are not similarly bound by this perverse proscriptive behavior makes them the discursive, as well as racial and imaginative, cousins of the Tahitians. Thus, the tourist to Thailand, like the chaplain in Tahiti, should check his baggage of Western morality at the border if he wants "to fit in."

The author's next sentence, however, immediately undermines the validity of his assertion regarding a lack of stigma attached to prostitution: "In general society, prostitutes are not very discriminated against; but you wouldn't want to bring one to a party (where, no matter how conservatively-dressed and soft-spoken), she would, by a mysterious process, be instantly identified as what she was and cut out of the conversation" (3–4). On the one hand, prostitutes suffer no discrimination, but on the other, once identified, they become ostracized. (The "mysterious process" of identification comes from Thai stereotypes about prostitutes' skin color and language—their use of Lao terms and phrases, as well as a linguistic register that reveals both low educational and social levels.)

Following the discursive pattern of benign, if not beneficent, distributor of knowledge about a specific form of cross-cultural interaction and true to "anti-conquest" strategies, the author gives over a large part of his text to demystifying the process of procuring sex by addressing issues related to the women working in the industry. He attempts to "humanize" the women and to use his "how-to" manual to make life infinitely more pleasant for all parties involved, as exemplified in his charge to the customer/reader: "If [the bargirl] sits down (most likely on your lap), you have one job and one job only: to make her laugh. These girls take more BS than you can imagine; if you make her laugh (it isn't hard), you'll both have a lot of fun" (3). The awkwardness of the encounter, like that of a first date, is broken by humor, leading to a mutually pleasurable experience.

In answer to the very first question, "What should I know about Thai women?" he answers, sagely, "Thai women are like women anywhere: some nice, some not so; some pretty, some not so" (2). Of course, elided from this answer dripping with universal egalitarianism is the grossly inequitable economic foundation upon which the interaction is based, as well as any sense of willing subjectivity involved in the interaction. In an attempt to address the latter issue, the author provides the bar "girls" with an apparent sense of choice: "If you spot a girl on stage that you'd like to meet, ask one of the waiters to call her down. The girl will eye you, and if for any reason she doesn't like your looks, she'll shake her head" (5). This "choice" exercised with regard to the individual customer (something we have not witnessed) masks larger issues of choice regarding employment opportunities, control over one's body, and the like. The author comforts the spurned customer with the assurance "Let it go; there are many others" (5). Although partially hidden by reciprocity, fecundity, as in Diderot's Tahiti, plays a vital role here in the context of capitalist laws of supply and demand—which is why very few bar women would exercise this choice. For every customer there are more than fifteen potential providers of services—a virtual cornucopia of sexual partners, to repeat a phrase from the discussion of Diderot.

Once an agreement is struck and the woman accompanies the customer to a hotel room, the author anticipates the customer's question regarding what she will do. He answers, "Straight or oral sex. Period. Forget anal or anything exotic. These are simple working girls in a hurry. Nothing personal—it's economics" (5). We should note how rapidly the discourse of a sexually different culture—one free of moral stigma—has given way to the pragmatics of economic transaction, much as Orou's discourse of communal living—free of property—yielded to one replete with taxes, deposits, and capital storage/investment. Discourse based on "when in Rome . . ." cannot contain that of economic inequity and the power emergent from it.

In fact, the Internet author has recapitulated the common tourist desire not to be exploited while engaged in the act of exploitation. He does so again under the guise of explaining how to avoid a cultural/situational faux pas. He discusses when bargaining should occur, suggests a range of "fair" prices (reciprocity yet again), and warns against staking out "extremes" when bargaining. The range of prices provides customers with clues that would indicate when they are being taken advantage of. The author boils the financial dealings down to a succinct assessment of fairness—customer satisfaction: "After all, if you're happy, $100 is not bad; if you're not, $10 is too much" (11).

The piece's coda segues from a description of his favorite "massage parlor" and what the anxious customer might encounter there to the refrain of the women's humanity: "Almost without exception, in my experience, these girls are very, very good at what they do. That said, it would be well to remember that what these girls do, each for their [*sic*] own reasons, is not what they are. Often they are quite funny and bright. Even if not, if you never cease to remember that they are, before anything else, human beings with human feelings, chances are good you'll truly enjoy yourself, and you will have made her life, for a moment, at least, not as completely horrible as it might have been" (13). Cautioning reader-customers not to confuse actions with essence, the author feels compelled to reiterate the humanity of those providing the services. The necessity emerges from the encounter itself, which belies reciprocity and acknowledges the conversion of human being into commodity, first and foremost. Likewise, the language of mutual pleasure has been revised in explaining that the customer can "truly enjoy [him]self" while the provider experiences a moment "not as completely horrible as it might have been." Still, despite the slippage in the rhetoric, the author as worldly, humane adviser provides a scenario in which the customer (equipped with the author's wisdom) becomes the source of a brief respite in the prostitute's bleak existence. Completely missing from this scenario, of course, is the larger causal relationship that has created the encounter: the vastly unequal international economics of supply and demand in which customers demand that certain services be supplied by humans whose humanity must be consciously remembered by those demanding—even though it has slipped out of consideration in the mere moment of imagining the encounter.

As troubling and remarkable as the Internet text is, the one by Cleo Odzer (1994) is even more troubling and remarkable. Springing from the fieldwork Odzer conducted in Bangkok while working on her dissertation, it offers a combination of fieldnotes-as-text (much like Paul Rabinow's fieldnotes from Morocco, but without his brilliance, empathy, and erudition) and private journal (much like Branislaw Malinowski's Trobriander diary, without *his* brilliance and erudition but with his unbridled libido). As such, *Patpong Sisters* is not so much a revised, or meta-, version of the dissertation as it is a sub-dissertation—the story she wanted to tell but couldn't due to academic genre restraints. A more literary subgenre to which it also belongs is that of the confessional narrative, specifically the female confession as seduction, where what is told is meant to attract as well as inform; Odzer wants to turn us on as she relates the ways in which Thailand's sexual culture/industry turned *her* on.

The book's title, as a move to authority, recounts the metaphysics of presence invoked by the Internet author, as well as by those staking claims of knowledge about Others. The title suggests the archetypal anthropologist's narrative of initiation into the inner sanctum of the "tribe"—being made a member of the kinship system—which provides access to knowledge about the tribe known only to insiders. This narrative assumes a metaknowledge, or a level of self-reflexivity of the group's functioning *as* the group's functioning, on the part of the culture under anthropological investigation—a kind of awareness that rarely exists. Odzer merely mouths the discourse of anthropological anticonquest she has inherited from her discipline; however, she has also chosen to represent another and perhaps more pernicious aspect of this disciplinary discourse specializing in Others: that of the anthropologist-as-missionary. Early in the text she claims that after completing her course work she wanted to return to Asia, this time "in a manner that had meaning"; she "needed a mission" (9–10). Sounding indeed like a missionary heading to the heathen Orient, she writes: "Charged with dedication, I decided to do something magnificent for the prostitutes of Patpong. . . . My topic had become a cause I believed in. And I needed to do something worthwhile to make up for the years I frittered away in hippydom" (10). Thus, the cry "Save the prostitutes!" is actually "Save myself!"

What Odzer in fact argues is that the prostitutes do not need saving. (Thus she establishes her own missionary position.) This becomes most apparent in several of the conclusions she reaches, conclusions that represent Others in ways more beneficial to the argument that she wants to make (as Tylor warned of in the nineteenth century) than to presenting a wide array of possible interpretations, including those of the prostitutes themselves. In her penultimate chapter, Odzer puts forward some of these conclusions, asserting that "Patpong prostitutes had advantages over nonprostitute Thai women who didn't belong to the rich upper class. They had more independence and opportunities. They were more worldly. They met and maintained contact with people from all over the globe. They had experiences they'd otherwise never be exposed to, such as flying in planes and being taken abroad or going abroad to work (though these were few in number). People taught them to swim, bowl, play snooker, drive motorbikes. They learned English and other languages" (302).

That these women constitute a part of globalization processes that bring them into contact with "people from all over the globe" cannot be denied, but the desirability of that contact for the prostitute can be questioned, and the inherent value of cross-cultural interaction, in this case, may need reconsideration. Also, the amount of "independence" and kinds of "opportunities" experienced by women thoroughly dependent for their livelihood upon bar-owning pimps (who take a large percentage of their wages) and sex-purchasing foreigners may be more circumscribed than Odzer leads readers to believe. Finally, selling one's sexuality, often several times a day, seems a high price to pay for riding on a plane or motorbike, or learning to bowl or play billiards, or picking up a few phrases of English, most of which would probably have very limited application.

Most important, though, says Odzer, these women get money (302). That they do, and it is substantially more than they could ever make in a factory job; the government and international development schemes have seen to that. In a culture that has followed the values universally circulated in current globalization processes, money—almost completely regardless of how it is gained—carries influence and power. But Odzer confuses money with economic and existential independence; they are very different things. Although one can buy "the symbols of success" (302), one cannot buy acceptance from a community, nor does the stigma of prostitution disappear in Thailand under the weight of a bank statement. To a certain extent, Odzer fetishizes the supposed autonomy that comes with income and incorrectly equates purchasing power with social and cultural power.

To read a Thai sex worker as independent because of the income she earns is to create a false analogy with a wage-earning Western female. Such a reading emerges from an ethnocentric position, and a temporally limited one at that: to reach Odzer's interpretation of independence via income one must assume Western capitalist notions about what work means for women *at this moment*. Wage-earning, especially for women, has only recently come to be equated with autonomy in Western cultures. In making this pronouncement, Odzer is absolutely uncritical about the tradition of wages and the status of the individual in relation to independence. Similarly, she makes a false equation, or oversimplifies another relationship, by stating essentially that all sex is good sex—that women have been denied a sexual subjectivity for so long that *any* expression of it, and *any* employment of it, constitutes progress and autonomy. This oversimplification makes all other aspects involved in sexual relations less important than the expression of sexuality. To ignore power and economics in sexual relations, especially in an international sex industry, seems very shortsighted, indeed.

Odzer ignores both power and economics, or simply dismisses them, when she explains her own subject position in Thailand: "Suddenly I loved the Adam and Eve [a bar primarily for gay men in Pattaya]—luxurious and comfortable, with so many perfect men dancing in front of me. I felt right at home, even though I was female. Because I was a *farang* female, these places were open to me. With the history of the women's movement and the history of my rich country behind me, these delights were as much mine as any other tourist's. . . . I felt like a *farang* with the entire world as my inherited right" (289). Without the slightest hint of irony, she claims the world as her "inherited right," as have explorers, missionaries, colonial administrators, and international investment specialists. (We are reminded of art critic John Berger's remark about a sixteenth-century portrait of wealthy Dutch ambassadors: "They belong to a class who are convinced that the world was there to furnish their residence in it" [1972, 96]). Odzer also claims that her personal license can be explained by "the history of the women's movement." But what women's movement fails to recognize the connection between personal suffering and systemic forces? What women's movement does not believe that the personal is political, that individual situations are conditioned by power relations and in turn condition other power relations? What women's movement regards as a fact of nature the matter of which groups have power and which do not? What women's movement intentionally subordinates issues of race, class, and nation to greater gender equality among the oppressors?

Lest we seem too hard on Odzer, we close with a passage that terminates the last chapter set in Thailand. It contains a vast array of orientalist, (s)exotica-based clichés and tropes. Odzer deploys them in ways that Diderot would have easily understood, but she does so for mostly different reasons. Describing her last tryst in Thailand, with a tour guide on a trek in the mountains outside Chiang Mai, she writes, "We lowered our voices and drew closer together. When only the night creatures could be heard hooting and gnawing, the guide and I went to his personal hut made of bamboo and thatch by that mysterious tribe in that exotic jungle on a mountain somewhere near Burma." She concludes, "Thailand was a paradise for Western women, too" (305). To which we can only ask—as we would Diderot, Stedman, Bock, Reynolds, the Internet fellow, and the rest—was it as good for the natives as it was for you?

Genealogical Postscript: *Miss Saigon* as Corporeal Archive

Anna Leonowens was onto something big, in show business terms, and as we have argued, popular culture simultaneously reflects and shapes received notions. Her books spawned Margaret Landon's recasting of them, which gave birth to the Rogers and Hammerstein musical, two films, a TV series, and numerous revivals of the stage production—including one on Broadway as we write in 1996. A similar trajectory of desire and genealogical intertextuality, also ending up as a megamusical hit, can be traced from a from a French novel called *Madame Chrysanthemum* by Pierre Loti. This book inspired a play by the American author David Belasco, which became the inspiration for Puccini's *Madama Butterfly*. Besides recently being made into a French film (1996), the opera metamorphosed into the antipodal stage offerings of Henry David Hwang's *M. Butterfly* and Alain Boublil and Claude-Michel Schonberg's *Miss Saigon*. The two related trajectories of representations, also including *South Pacific* and *The World of Suzie Wong*, culminate in the stage spectacular of *Miss Saigon*. In all its hyperbolic grandiosity, this play exemplifies the staged, female oriental body as an expressive archive, a virtual enshrinement, of the genealogy of sexual Other cultures that we have delineated in this chapter.

The opening scene of the musical explicitly stages this body and places it on display as the half-French, half-Vietnamese huckster called Engineer presents a beauty contest in his bar; the winner will become the eponymous "Miss Saigon." In reference to this scene, Boublil says that he always wanted to include a beauty contest in a musical, but this one, he reveals, it is not "a real beauty contest" but a "vulgar imitation" of one (which is all a character like Engineer could stage).[7] Eleanor Ty maintains that the crowned Miss Saigon "represents all the qualities associated with the colonized city: the sensual, the dark, the mad, the primitive, the flesh, and the uncivilized" (1994, 20). In other words, she embodies the qualities outsiders have projected onto the city, but more than that, and true to schizoid othering, she also embodies the covalent qualities of the desirable Other. And as it turns out in the play, the winner this time is not a "whore" but an innocent woman named Kim. A victim of the war driven to the bars to eke out a meager existence, Kim meets on this, her first night in the bar, the American man who will father her child. As "the winner" of a grotesque parody of an event that many people already perceive as parodic in itself—"a real beauty contest"—Kim manifests the corporeal archive of inscribed, staged desire that is the result of centuries' worth of representations of the female oriental body: beautiful, sensual, seductive, exotic, kind, virginal, and smitten at first sight with a white male, all at the same time. That the whole contest is a charade to inflate the price of a bar hooker reveals the cynical economic realities underpinning the nature of these representations.

The construction of desire as a commodity emerges in the song that provides the context for the Miss Saigon beauty contest, "The Movie in My Mind." As the title would lead one to imagine, the song allows the women who work in the bar, appropriately named "Dreamland," to voice their dreams of escape. Cinema—inextricably linked to Hollywood, the "American Dream," and escapist fantasies—provides form, content, and motivation for these Third World women's "third rate" (Ty 1994, 16) dreams. They are the stuff not only that dreams are made of but that commercials, TV, blockbuster films, and stage smashes are made of. The women sing of an easy life filled with money, ice cream, big cities, and laughter all day. All it takes to get their psychological projectors going, so they tell us, are the arms of their military clients:

> They are not nice, they're mostly noise
> they swear like men, they screw like boys
> I know that there's nothing in their hearts
> but every time I take one in my arms
> it starts:
> the movie in my mind
> the dream they leave behind
> a scene I can't erase
> and in a strong G.I.'s embrace
> flee this life
> flee this place.

Thus the men, despite being vacuous and crude, remain the conduit for the women's dreams of escaping their degraded lives. Even though the women know these men to be false and interested only in sex, even though they know the men will never provide them the means to change their lives, they cling to the ideological dreams that the men represent and that they've been sold in the cinemas. While they have become the standard "comfort women" of war whom history ignores, in this staging they evidently do not begrudge their roles. Nor are they perturbed by the deception of the dream that is partially responsible for their current work situation, or by the men who dangle it before their easily duped eyes. Yet again, the male clients can have their consciences eased because this construction of the female oriental Other wants nothing more from them than the chance to escape her plight through a brief embrace by a white man and the flights of fancy this hug releases.

The action in the second half of the play takes place primarily in Bangkok, after the fall of Saigon, during the late 1970s. Bangkok has become a demilitarized and industrialized twin of Saigon, its R&R sites and war capital reconfigured as tourist entertainment centers and the freewheeling hedonism of the First World at play. (One of the tourists sings "I'm glad that my wife's not with me!") In much the same way that "Miss Saigon" symbolizes her colonized city, the relation of Saigon to Bangkok, as represented in the play, is that of Cio-Cio San to Kim: the city-as-prostitute to the military and to the world market respectively. The setting provides a specular view of the inner sanctum of the brothel, the whorehouse turned inside out. The streets of Patpong offer audiences a chance to view the bedrooms of brothels; the private is publicly and theatrically displayed.

Kim, now a mother, works the Bangkok bars that serve tourists. Engineer too has ended up in Patpong as a tout for a club called Le Moulin Rouge. A true citizen of the global market, Engineer feels he's wasting his talents and wants to go to the United States, where the dreams come from and capital accrues. He explains his situation in the song, "What a Waste":

> If you're looking for fun
> original sin
> if you want to put out
> then you gotta come in . . .
> [*to the tourists*] Gee, isn't Bangkok really neat?
> The things they're selling in the street
> fresh dog, if that's what you'd enjoy
> a girl, or if you want a boy . . .
> [*to himself*] I'm depressed
> for hustling amours
> to Japanese tours
> is not a treat in Bangkok
> I'm the best
> but where's a Marine
> with fistfuls of green
> I'd cheat him in Bangkok.

Vendors hawking knock-off products, drugs, and food play antiphon to Engineer's spiel:

> Hey, Joe, try taking a little excursion
> you'll all feel good from a little perversion

massage requiring total immersion
some strange positions they say are Persian.

The tourists respond, "Oh yeah! Wow! Oh no!" As jampacked with orientalist clichés as any text we've examined, this song provides a concentrated version of the eroticization of Other cultures (freely mixing and blending them all), the global economic forces that construct unequal relations in a given locale, and the cynical manipulation indulged in by virtually all involved in international capital's exploitation of labor. The site of all this action, the nexus upon which all vectors converge, is the staged, female oriental body. The metaphorical theatrum mundi of the imagination is conflated with the reality of the economic global stage.

The trajectory from *Madame Chrysanthemum* to *Miss Saigon* closes where we expect it would: again, the female, oriental body. Like her earlier incarnations, Kim makes "the ultimate sacrifice" by committing suicide to ensure that her child can go to live in the States with his father. "In the end, the many crucial and unresolvable issues raised by the musical—American blunders during the Vietnam War, Asian prostitutes, unequal power structures, abandoned Amerasian orphans—all become translated into and subsumed in the profound struggle of the family. Family love, here signified by the mother, is sentimentally constructed as the refuge from all political disorder, chaos, injustice, pain, and change. The mother becomes the overdetermined sign which no actual woman, whether American, European, or Asian, could live up to" (Ty 1994, 23). And Kim, like Cio-Cio San, doesn't live up to it. The only course of action left for this archival and staged body is suicide; such action preserves the purity of the representation. But although her idealized body cannot survive beyond the footlights of the male imagination, it lives on nonetheless in the bar scene of the international sex industry as manifested in Bangkok.

6

The Bar Scene

My best time was being with a squad
of deaf and dumb hookers who were
really nice because they never got on
your nerves with silly talk.
> —German tourist, in *Hello
> My Big Big Honey*

This space, transparent now, where
bodies are taken without any possibility
of refusal, where they abandon themselves ... is the *very space of orgy*:
the one that the soldier and the colo-
nizer obsessively dream of establishing
on the territory of the colony, transformed for the occasion into a bordello
where the hetaeras are the women of
the conquered.
> —Malek Alloula, *The Colonial Harem*

Yes, there is slavery in Bangkok. Some
girls work against their will. Most don't,
however, in the sense that they could
just as easily have chosen other

jobs.... The "kept" girls are usually
found in the short-time hotels—if this
is a problem for you, simply stay away
from the short-time hotels. Another
way of handling this is, of course, to be
gentle and gentlemanry [*sic*] and give
the girl a good time whether she is a
slave or not.

—Internet posting

Many lurid accounts of the Thai sex industry exist in print, electronic, and video
or film versions. The majority of these focus on the "upscale" portion of the
industry found in the go-go bars that are the focus of this chapter. (As we have
mentioned earlier, some argue that the attention is disproportionate to its actual
share of the industry in Thailand). Women bearing numbers for easy identification dancing on a stage, wrapping themselves around phallic metal poles, or
scores of bored women sitting behind one-way mirrors awaiting a client's selection figure prominently in these representations. The musical *Miss Saigon* features stylized, spectacular, full-stage scenes depicting the neon-lit streets and
bar interiors to be found in any one of the three major tourist zones for *farangs*—
Patpong, Soi Cowboy, Nana Entertainment Plaza—assuming that its cosmopolitan audiences will be able to identify the site. The popular and sensationalist
media swell with these images of degeneracy. When *Time* ran a cover story on
the burgeoning sex trade in developing countries, concentrating on the former
Eastern bloc, the cover photo showed not a European but a young sex worker in
Thailand being caressed by a faceless *farang*. So pervasive has the industry in
Thailand become that it stands as a synecdoche for its manifestation anywhere
on the globe. Likewise (see Chapter 2) images and stories of AIDS and child
prostitution abound, as do those stories of utter horror that erupt from the
indigenous sex industry every now and then, such as the Phuket brothel fire in
which scores of women died because they were chained to their beds and could
not flee the building.

   Little makes it into the popular media, however, about the extensive panoply
of venues available to the expatriate and sex tourist—or to the regular tourist
who also engages in sexual interaction. From the infamous massage parlors, tea
rooms, hotels, blow-job bars, and go-go bars to "short-time" possibilities with
waitresses, bank clerks, department store clerks, and beauty salon workers,
farangs can choose from a wide range of possibilities. Equally wide is the continuum of the "reality" of the relationships formed. The women who work outside
the sex industry but still make themselves available to *farangs* to pick up extra
cash are more likely to be interested in a long-term relationship—yet it is interesting to note that this possibility is most flaunted in the sites where it least
exists. Much of the sex industry for foreigners is predicated on the illusion of
relationships as part and parcel of the packaged product. The willed amnesia

and cultural schizophrenia carried in the clients' psychological baggage demands this be so in the marketplace. Like Disneyland, the go-go bars are a staged set upon which tourists enact their fantasies. Also like Disneyland, the go-go bar is a simulacrum: a copy of something for which no original exists. The entire scene is a projected fantasy. *Miss Saigon* redundantly stages something that is already staged: the "real" Patpong.

The longer one remains in the site, though, the more the illusion becomes apparent even to someone who has engaged in the multiple deceptions. This point is made by Rory O'Merry in a text that simultaneously recognizes the exploitative aspects of the industry and its impact on the daily lives of the workers, and instructs readers how to become proficient clients. As narrator, O'Merry lives with one sex worker, and remains a client of other workers, revealing the depth of the schizophrenia operative in this zone. "My original impression, in the bars downtown, was that everyone was having a great time. The longer I hung around and the more attention I paid, the more obvious it was that nobody was" (1990, 108–10).

Following arguments made in the previous chapters and using deKadt's assumption (1979, 130) that "tourist enclaves . . . have more to do with tourists' fantasies than the culture of the host country," we have taken MacCannell's suggestion (1989, 135) to generate "an ethnomethodology of sightseers." Such a pursuit "would explore the touristic consciousness of otherness, and the ways tourists negotiate the labyrinth of modernity." Because females have limited access to these bars and the interactions that can take place there, Robinson could not conduct the kinds of field research available to Bishop. The ethnographic sections of this chapter are, therefore, in Bishop's first-person voice.

Scenes from the Bar Scene

With Jeff, a friend of mine and long-time Thailand resident, I set out over the course of many nights to take in the go-go bar scene and speak to its patrons. Early on, we met up with a man Jeff knows. An American in his early forties, Peter had made many trips to Thailand as a sex tourist before inheriting a sum of money that allowed him to become an expat with the luxury of being gainfully unemployed. We asked him how to have a good time in Bangkok, how best to take advantage of what Patpong had to offer the sex tourist. These were issues Peter had spent much time thinking about and empirically experiencing. His account mimicked and elaborated many of those encountered on the World Wide Web and that can be echoed by hundreds of thousands of sex tourists who have visited the country.

Over his third beer, Peter launched into advice-giving mode. "First, check into a hotel near Nana and dump your load. I mean your bags AND your load. Call room service and ask them to send up some tart. Tell 'em you're horny and you've got a purply [500-baht note] for her if she's good. No muss, no fuss.

"OK. It's midafternoon. You've checked in and shot your pre-wad. Now go dive into a buffet in a nearby hotel and fuel up. One of the upscale ones that have *farang* food and no Thai customers. The Landmark's good and right across from *soi* 7, where you KNOW you'll be heading to next.

"Walk over to the GBG [German Beer Garden] when you're done eating. Hell, you can even eat there if you're horny enough and want to scope out the freelancers before it gets too late. Now, here you've got a couple of choices. You wanna look around, check out the goods, take your time, be cool. We're looking to take the edge off here, mind you, not to get fucking married. They've got a decent supply of purply freelancers wandering in and out of here ALL the time. They'll take one look at you and know. THEY KNOW!!

"OK. Pick one. Any one! We're talking short-time here, buddy. Who knows, maybe you get lucky and want to keep her on, but check her out first. There's plenty more where she came from, so don't sweat it. Take her back to the Crowne if your own place is too far away, or wherever, and do the deed. Take the edge off, bro, so you're not drooling later and do something foolish like spend too much or get shackled to a scuz. These girls aren't stupid either. Last thing they want is some horny buffalo crawling all over them.

"Dump her. Take a bath. Have a nap. Read the paper, watch the Bloody Boring Corporation on TV. Get a massage, a manicure, pedicure, haircut, and BJ [blow-job] somewhere. Suttisan's a good area for this. Just ask them if they 'sa-moke.' In Thai-English. 'Sa-moke di may?' [Smoke is ok, huh?] Another purple, big deal. You're being treated like royalty from top to bottom at twenty bucks a throw.

"Now you're moving into Big Mango mode. You're gettin' down and dirty and you're lovin' it! Admit it! You can't do this at home!! OK, now you're ready for the main course. You got a few options here, depending on what you want and how much you want to drop.

"The Japs got the best girls now, in Thaniya Plaza. Much better than what we've got. But if you want you can hang around outside and lap up their leavings. Sloppy seconds from Japs are basically virgins anyway, except for the S&Mers. Patpong: OK, some fine looking babes still there, but supermercenary. A few BJ shops but you've had that already. Getting expensive down there now and the girls have an attitude. Maybe check it out if you have the time some other trip. Me, I'd stay away from it myself. Cowboy: Fine but too tame. Some nice girls you can actually talk to, but if you're in town for a day or two, talk *is not what you're after*.

"Go to Nana. Yeah, Nana. Definitely. This is where it's at now—up and coming. Some good shows, some decent bars, middle-of-the-road—reasonable prices, and a few places to do short-timers right there so you don't have to break your stride. I've been VERY lucky there. Highly recommended. Take your time, though. Pick a winner and watch a show. Get a stiffy, give her your best smile, flash a few baht, buy her a couple of drinks and you're in.

"But listen up. You might not even score there. Might not find what you're after. If not, then there is always hope. THERE IS STILL HOPE IN THE WORLD AS LONG AS THE T-ROOM [the Thermae] IS OPEN, which it will be for fucking ever. I'm talking about the Chicken Farm . . . HQ . . . the T-Room . . . the meeting place . . . the best little whorehouse in the fucking world.

"And it swings into action when the other bars CLOSE!

"Go there. Sit down if you can. Order a set of Mekong. A couple of mamasans are always wandering around looking for buffaloes like you to buy them *khanom* [treats]. Tell them what you want. Big tits, little tits; Khmer dancer; *tua lek* [small body]; *tua yai* [big body]; BJ; twosome, threesome; WHATEVER! You've found your kingdom, revel in it. We only live once. Why do you think God made the Thermae?"

Soi Cowboy

A block-long stretch of bars sits just off Sukhumvit, *soi* 21. At the end of this same street is the main entrance to Srinakharinwirot University, the institution to which I was assigned during my Fulbright sojourn and the first Thai university to cater to promising students who did not come from elite families. I return some two years later to hit the bars. Some of the bars I used to go past are still there, but many have changed hands. The turnover rate in the bar biz is high, but each time one closes, another opens where the former establishment stood. In this one block, some fifty venues advertise their wares and compete for customers, of which there are many.

Jeff and I troll up and down the bustling, brightly lit block, soaking up the sights and fending off hawkers. The touts here are far less aggressive than they are in Patpong but persistent nonetheless. Many are women. A few Thai males lounge about outside, mostly motorcycle-taxidrivers waiting for fares. They smoke and talk and watch with bemused detachment the circulation of foreign males who gawk and gape at the lights and delights.

After a sweep of the block, we choose a smallish venue—Cowboy Two—and enter. The narrow pub stands perpendicular to the street, as does the dance platform that is parallel to the bar proper. In this shotgun configuration the patrons are squeezed into two small seating sections: one by the door and before the platform, and the other in the back and behind the bar. We choose the latter and order some beers. The waitress informs us that tonight is the bar owner's birthday, so we should stick around for the free food. (When Thais have a birthday, the celebrant treats friends and family to a meal, and the owner has adapted the local custom to include his patrons.) As my eyes adjust to the low light, I can see the place festooned with the appropriate celebratory paraphernalia.

This bar is like most on this strip and the others that cater to *farang* tourists: a translation of the 1960s go-go bar. On the stage, some five feet from where we sit, a half-dozen seminaked women gyrate to overly loud rock music. Creedence Clearwater Revival and the Doors (perhaps harking back to the Vietnam War era) predominate but are mixed with 1980s and 1990s dance music from the United States. In contrast to their earlier incarnation, these bars do not place the dancers high above the crowd in cages. The eye-level view of the stage yields instead a perfect crotch shot, and the narrow building makes this true "in your face" entertainment. It is impossible to make eye contact and impossible to avoid it. The only people who dance here are the workers, and although the dancers of go-go bars past may have been considered "loose" women, sex with customers was not part of their job description. Another difference between the 1960s dance bars and their 1990s imitators is perhaps the most obvious: no female patrons. The only women in these places work here.

Of the six dancers on stage, three stare off vacantly into space and sometimes jolt into a pelvic grind as if suddenly reminded of where they are and what they are doing. The glazed gaze could easily be drug induced, since many dancers now use amphetamines to help them maintain their heavy workload and heroin to dull the pain of their jobs. (A freelance hooker told me that lots of the women take "horse pills," a mixture of speed and heroin.) Their more alert colleagues seek out eye contact that might possibly lead to being bought out for the night. These try to capture our attention, and I avert my eyes to glance at other customers and dancers scattered about the small seating area.

The beers arrive. Jeff seems genuinely perturbed by the vacuity in the women's expression. "I haven't been here in over a year. The women used to be more playful, more fun. They are at other places," he assures me, and we quickly make an exit. The waitress reminds us to return for the festivities later. As we emerge into the crowded *soi*, a palpable sense of relief, like that of release from a densely claustrophobic space, comes over me.

At our next stop, a bar called Tilac, we encounter a large dancing stage capable of supporting sixty or more dancers at a time. The stage is also the bar, its three runways weaving in serpentine fashion throughout the establishment. Patrons sit and drink on the outer edge of the stage, resting their elbows on the black leather pad that runs the length of the bar. Bartenders serve from inside the loops, and the women dance on top. The ubiquitous metal poles run from bar top to ceiling. Some of the dancers merely hang on to these; others wrap their legs around them and pump their hips suggestively. Mirrors line the walls and columns, plunging dancers and patrons into an infinity of ever-shrinking copies of themselves. The entire scene invokes plenitude: of service, food, liquor, sex, and women.

We order a meal, brought to us from a nearby restaurant, and watch the dancers. They wear the standard-issue badge number used for identification and accounting (drink tabulation). At some places, when a customer wants to chat with one of the women, he merely orders her by number. The dancers generally wear swimsuits of different covering capability. Some wear lingerie. Whether in swim or boudoir wear, they all dance in high heels. For the most part, the women here are more animated than those at Cowboy Two, but a certain lethargy pulls at each movement. Before our food arrives, a dancer awaiting her turn asks if we will buy her a drink. We agree and tell her we want to ask her some questions. She accepts but leaps from her chair before we can do so.

Upon returning, she says to us, "This is my friend. She just arrived from the country." The friend, a small, shy, fully dressed woman sits down beside me. "Can I buy you a drink?" I ask her. She nods and says "Coke," which I order from a passing waitress. The dancer planted next to Jeff agrees to answer our questions. We have to shout to one another to be heard over the deafening rock music.

"How long have you worked here?" I ask her. "Five months," she says in Thai. "Before that I danced next door at the Crazy Cats, but I hated it there. The owner was very demanding; he had a narrow heart. He did not care about his dancers at all. He is Thai." Thai bar owners are reputed to be tight with money and demanding of their employees. *Farang* bar owners are commonly called *jai di*, or good-hearted, because they are more tolerant than their Thai counterparts, though exploitative nonetheless. This is the stereotype, and it is a common line the sex workers give *farang* clients. "Before I entered the bars," she continues, "I worked in Bangkok as a maid. The family was okay, sometimes nice, sometimes not. I earned 2,200 baht per month [$88], the same amount I usually earn in a week here."

Although foreign ownership of Thai businesses is illegal, the Tilac proprietor is a German, and she said there is little pressure from management to go with customers, though they do expect at least two buyouts per week. Her home situation, of course, had forced her to come to Bangkok to seek employment. Her father had taken a new wife—whether a second wife or a mistress is not clear—and needed a new house for her, so the daughter came to the city. "My father is not good to me. He abused me, my sisters and my mother. This is why I want a *farang* boyfriend. I hate Thai men," she says. "I did not want to leave home, but I had to," she continues. "My mother and grandmother cried for many days before I left. I have not been home since then."

Her friend, the petite newcomer, sits huddled closely and quietly next to me. Whenever I make eye contact with her, I smile, and though clearly nervous, she returns the smile. "Do you want anything to eat?" I ask her. She shakes her head no. "When did you get here? Where are you from?" I ask her in Thai. "I arrived in Bangkok five days ago from Issan. I was a rice farmer. But there is no water, and the rice prices change all the time. My family had a hard time, no food and no money. My friend," she points at the other dancer, "said come and work at Tilac. You can make lots of money there, so I came south." She claims not to have joined the dancers yet or gone with any customers, but only to be observing the operations of the bar and the workers. Very shyly, she looks at me, and asks, "Would you like to buy me out?" I say no, and Jeff and I decide to leave the bar. After I say good-bye to her, I remember that she too told me her mother, sisters, and grandmother had cried for many days before her departure.

This several-block-long stretch of bars, restaurants, offices, shops, and apartments is the equivalent for Thai customers of the areas—Patpong, Nana Plaza, Soi Cowboy—that cater to foreign tourists, even down to the ubiquitous beer garden. Here the clientele is almost strictly Thai, so when Jeff and I walk the blocks, the hawkers seem reluctant to approach us. Even more guarded is the response we receive when we enter a bar. All inside eye us suspiciously except for the dancers who seem rather interested in the prospect of *farang* clients.

The place is very dark and narrow. At the front and along the walls are tables with chairs. A handful of customers and many more dancers occupy them. The stage, built for one dancer only, hovers above the floor on the left. Farther back, behind the stage and barely visible from the doorway, is the bar; still farther back is a kitchen, the bathrooms, and living quarters. To the right, opposite the stage and close to the ceiling, perches a television set that silently flickers its blue-hued images into the darkness. While the clients look at the stage, almost all the dancers watch the TV.

We choose a table against the right wall near the TV. On the other side of the room a young Thai man holds forth with friends over plates of food and numerous glasses of whiskey and soda. Although, because of the blaring music, he is laughing and talking loudly to his friends, the dancer with him has fallen asleep on his arm. She does not move, much less awaken, the entire time we are there. Closer to the front of the bar sit the dancers awaiting their turn on stage. Among them is a young woman with pigtails dressed in a school uniform. It takes me a long time to ascertain that she isn't the daughter of one of the workers, sitting with her mum and doing her homework. My numerous glances in her direction as I try to determine her age make her think I have taken an interest in her—professional interest. Two other dancers join us as we order our drinks. Much is made over the size of my friend, who is quite tall and heavy. The usual play of touching and measuring ensues.

The woman sitting beside me notices my ring. "You have a wife?" she asks. "Yes, a Thai wife. She is in the States, but I am not a 'butterfly'" (Thai slang for someone who flits from one relationship or partner to another). "Your wife is lucky," she says. "It's hard to find a man with a good heart. I had a husband once. He was bad. He hit me, yelled at me, and took my money." We speak for about an hour, and I buy her drinks. She asks me lots of questions about my wife, and I answer them; however, she still wants me to buy her out for the night.

After the initial interest in our presence fades, the dancers not sitting with us turn back to the TV. They sit transfixed by it, especially a *lakhon* (soap opera) featuring, as usual, the activities of the rich and powerful. Surveying the room, I lean over and yell in Jeff's ear, "How many ways can one spell 'squalid?'" Just to the left of the TV, a woman energetically churns on the stage; numerous others waiting their turn lose themselves in the silent drama being played out on the television. I can't help thinking that a cause-effect relationship exists between the characters on the TV and those hypnotized by it. Virtually the same images had been broadcast to these women when they lived in dusty villages or in tin lean-tos without water, telling them that village and slum life were for fools. All the women sitting in the bar had left their homes, either upcountry or in the city, to work in this place because they desired to be like those they saw on TV, to be people with power, cars, maids, portable phones, gold chains, and endless supplies of food—not half-naked dancers with families back home to support. These same images of wealth and power have been intimately connected with national tales of progress, development, and internationalization. The bar women had bought the whole package, and here they sat in Suttisan.

Despite Suttisan's imitation of the go-go bars that cater to *farang* clients, much of the indigenous sex industry bears little resemblance to the one for international tourists. Most researchers agree that in sheer numbers, the part for Thai consumption far outstrips the higher-profile international portion. The money and prestige that comes from international sex tourism, however, provides impetus for the local industry. In much the same way that the Thai pop music scene models itself on Western pop music and would probably not even exist without it, the local sex industry might be less pervasive if the international one were not omnipresent. This is not to say, of course, as some xenophobic finger-pointers claim, that Thailand was a pure, innocent nation without any history of prostitution prior to the U.S. military presence in the 1960s and the advent of international tourism. Nor is it to perpetuate what many tourists want to believe: that sex in Thailand, especially with prostitutes, is less stigmatized than in repressive Western nations. That either/or casting is a gross oversimplification.

Reports about prostitution written by Dutch traders date from as far back as 1604. One Thai official was given a government license in the seventeenth century to establish a prostitution monopoly. He staffed the place with six hundred women whom he purchased for this purpose. Much of the early prostitution in the Kingdom, in fact, was an extension of concubinage or slavery (often debt-based, as it is in the present). In the patriarchal, feudal society of Siam the number of concubines a man possessed provided a measure of his power. Donald Wilson (1994, 4–6) of the Crescent Press Agency reminds us that in the 1850s, Sampung Lane in the Chinese section of Bangkok was infamous for its green-, not red-, light district. The Bowring Treaty of 1855, admitting foreign laborers into Thailand, attracted thousands of southern Chinese workers to the tin mines, and joining them on their trek were thousands of prostitutes. Wilson also reports that in the 1940s some eighty-five cabarets existed on Nares Road, with one block sporting about two thousand hostesses, and that Yaowarat Road reputedly housed in a nine-story building the largest brothel in the world. Bangkok also enjoyed the dubious reputation of being a major producer of pornographic movies during the 1940s. From 1902 until 1960, prostitution was legal in the Kingdom. Its being made illegal opened the door for the corruption and victimization that so characterizes the industry today. Obviously, then, the international presence did not *create* the sex industry in Thailand, but did take it to new and more visible levels that cohered with modernization strategies and generated staggering economic returns.

Because the amounts of money paid by clients and to workers in the local sex industry are much smaller than the sums that change hands with tourists, the venues and conditions of employment are much grimmer. The vast majority of the women employed to service Thai men are indentured laborers. More and more of these are illegally trafficked from Burma or South China, much as Thai women are taken to Japan and Europe, revealing an infinite regress in which one nation exploits the female bodies of another, "less developed" country.[1] Many are essentially imprisoned in the brothels where they work, some even chained to their beds in concrete-walled rooms without windows. Forced to accommodate five to fifteen clients a day, the women receive breaks only during menstruation. They are often denied any contact with their families and are threatened with prison or beaten if they refuse to meet every demand made of them by the brothel owner. Should they become pregnant or infected with the AIDS virus, they are tossed into the street with no money. These women live in constant fear of arrest because when the police raid a brothel, they are always the ones imprisoned; pimps, clients, and brothel owners usually go free.

The wretched brothels are not the only sex venue for the Thai market. There are also massage parlors and teahouses that offer somewhat better working conditions. And to bring pop music back into the picture, many hotels in rural towns offer a wide array of lounge singers whose entertainment of clients is not confined to the stage. The brothel prostitutes, however, who work in the worst parts of the industry, are perhaps the most numerous of all the sex workers in the nation. Male privilege in traditional Thai society means, according to the Public Health Ministry of Thailand, that 75 percent of all Thai males regularly visit prostitutes and 47 percent of teenage boys have their first sexual encounter with a prostitute.

Some scholars, including Truong (1990) and Hill (1993), claim that Buddhism plays a large role in perpetuating male dominance in Thai culture, making it easier for a sex industry to develop and to subjugate women. But virtually all the world's major religions include patriarchal power structures that do not necessarily lead to the establishment of prostitution as a major industry, and few other Buddhist societies have developed this industry to the extent Thailand has. Further, despite rumors to the contrary, Buddhism explicitly prohibits the practice of prostitution; and Thai culture, operating within institutionalized Therevada Buddhism, most certainly stigmatizes sex workers. Ironically, though, the high premium that male privilege places on female virginity prior to marriage can be used to force a woman's entry into the sex industry, in two ways. On the one hand, the much prized virginity brings a higher price for a girl sold into the industry, making the offer even more lucrative and attractive; on the other hand, recruiters often rape young girls, rendering them "damaged goods" on the marriage market and therefore likelier candidates for sex work. In both these ways, traditional values can be manipulated to serve modern interests.

Although not directly responsible for the local activity, the visibility of international sex tourism and the huge influx of foreign currency it creates help legitimate participation in all sectors of the industry. As Linda Richter succinctly summarizes the situation, "Perhaps because Thailand was never colonized, and also because the nation has a history of concubinage and prostitutes in its traditional culture, opposition was slow to recognize the difference in scale, violence, and social decay implied by sex tourism" (1989, 84).

A Home for Alienated Sexual Subjectivity

> People look down on bar lady. Some people go work first time, get lucky, meet man, take care this girl. But maybe you don't find man take care you. You have to sleep around. Sometimes the man looks like shit, have to fuck him.
> —A twenty-three-year-old bar woman, in *Hello My Big Big Honey*

> In Bangkok many *farangs*—the lifers— had a gross, nightmarish fear that they would be forced at gunpoint to jump the bones of a woman their own age. They had structured their lives to insulate themselves from the experience of two sets of old bones and flabby flesh struggling under the sheets to copulate.
> —Christopher G. Moore, *A Haunting Smile*

The bars that cater to the male *farang* tourist serve as both a physical and a rhetorical *topos* for this chapter, a virtual time capsule of late 1960s to early 1970s U.S. dance clubs, minus the female customers and their troublesome subjectivities. In a multitude of these "upscale" bars the tourist-cum-sex consumer can fulfill many of his desires. Lenore Manderson says of this site that: "sex remains a commodity; the bar a supermarket of desire, a commercial venue for the exploration of the edge of fantasy; the women workers are objects for sale. . . . While sex for sale is about power, the political economy, the domination of men and the subordination of women, it is also about desire and the corners of the imagination: that is the key to its success, if you like" (1992, 463).

Scantily clad, often half-naked women, any one of whom can be had for a pit-
tance, offer no doubt that sex will be the culmination of the encounter, without
placing any substantial emotional or psychological demands on the male. Yet all
this is wrapped in the illusion of a "real" relationship beneficial to all parties
involved, a scenario that complements the myth of economic reciprocity and
ignores the fact that the "real" relationship is itself part of the product provided
the consumer. The sexual subjectivity of the consumer materializes in this environment, contextualized by global development strategies that transform individual lives in rapidly changing economies and relations to production, and thus
provides insights not only about the customers but into the assumptions operative in national and international development strategies. What we find here are
many of the ways that "people's actions and desires are mediated through institutions of power: the family, the media, the law, armies, nationalist movements"
(McClintock 1995, 15) and textual genealogies.

It is very easy to oversimplify this site and overdetermine the continuum of
positions within it. Such a site is one of those that Pratt refers to as "contact
zones," or "social spaces where disparate cultures meet, clash, and grapple with
each other, often in highly asymmetrical relations of domination and subordination—like colonialism, slavery, or their aftermaths as they are lived out across
the globe today" (1992, 4). Here "emergence" occurs: "Emergence designates a
place of confrontation, but not as a closed field offering the spectacle of struggle
among equals. Rather, as Nietzsche demonstrates in his analysis of good and
evil, it is a 'non-place,' a pure distance, which indicates that the adversaries do
not belong to a common space" (Foucault 1984, 84–5). The international bar
scene in this sense is an uncommon site where dreams (both ecstatic and horri-
fying) come true, where the allure of travel brochures and genealogies of desire
emerge from the two-dimensional plane of the text into the three-dimensional
realm of flesh and depth.[2]

The appearance of free choice, the myth of economic reciprocity, and the
role-playing of the sex workers in Thailand provide the bar scene with the illusion of the "romance" or mutual attraction found in North American bars. Some
scholars writing about the Thai bar scene have noted this kind of confusion on
the part of male clients. Erik Cohen observes that many newly arrived *farangs*
refuse to label the women working in the bars as "prostitutes," and he claims
that their rigid categories about sex-for-money, as opposed to sex-for-love, do
not align with Thai categories regarding such behavior (Cohen 1987, 223).
Similarly, Brock and Thistlethwaite interviewed a general in the Royal Thai
Army who spoke very frankly about prostitution, but responded "with negative
vehemence" when the researchers used the common term "sex industry." His
argument was that "the words made a good thing sound loathsome, cold, and
mechanical, *like a business transaction.* He felt that the term took the romance out
of prostitution" (1996, 1, emphasis added).

Thai professor Yos Santasombut, in his useful introduction to *Hello My Big Big
Honey,* sets the stage for the misreading: when the typical *farang* tourist—often

an overweight, unattractive male—hits Patpong, he meets lovely, lively young women who express much interest in him (and say little, if anything, about themselves). Although he purchases drinks, and the woman may take a turn or two dancing on stage, there is no discussion of remuneration in the encounter until the client must pay the bar to take the sex worker out for a "short-time" or for the night. And even here, talk of money is usually confined to bar fines, not what the worker herself will receive for her labors. (The situation differs significantly with freelancers.) Santasombut argues that this lack of direct communication about exchanging a certain amount of money for a specific act baffles the first-time visitor: "The *farang*'s sense of the world, his cognitive map, is thrown into chaos because he cannot make sense of what is going on in the deal. He cannot apply his concept of prostitution to the Thai situation" (Walker and Ehrlich 1995, 16–17). In his mind the tourist has made the bar at home "the norm" and not only transplanted it overseas but improved on it. He has accepted all the good stuff (drink, conversation, women, and sex) while eliminating all the bothersome parts (qualms, scoring, and female subjectivity).

Although both Cohen and Santasombut may be correct in detecting *farang* befuddlement about the situation, and perhaps the tendency to mistake staged attention for real interest, this must be a willed blindness, akin to a theater audience's suspension of disbelief. The vast majority of male *farang* tourists do not accidentally stumble into Patpong or Soi Cowboy; rather, these places are the specific goal of their trips, sites they have read about in tourist brochures and heard of from friends. Thailand is largely defined in international discourse by the entertainment plazas, which emerge on global maps because of, *not* in spite of, the "cognitive maps" these travelers possess. Further, these tourists must surely wonder why a bunch of women (nearly a twenty-to-one ratio) just happen to be hanging about the numerous bars, with loads of free time between their brief stints on the dancing stage, and why they constantly suggest spending the evening together. It would seem that the usual phrasing "Do you want to *buy me out?*" should leave little confusion regarding remuneration.

Although Cohen (1987, 224–25) argues that the fuzzy area of tourist-prostitute interaction provides a useful synecdoche for the way newly arrived *farangs* cope with the "dichotomies" and "ambiguities" of Thailand, the fact that he chooses this particular "gray area" of cross-culture interaction as indicative of *farang* cultural confusion reveals the salience of the site. That is, the sex industry provides a substantial proportion of the tourist interaction with the Thai population and culture. Little is written about gray areas of payment for hotels or museums or tour buses. Cohen's and Santasombut's arguments can be considered legitimate only if we allow the tourists a willed ignorance about sites they have invested substantial sums in and traveled long distances to experience.

Yet hard as it is to imagine, confusion wrought by market forces and cultural assumptions does occur, and it does so in much the way that Jack Reynolds depicts it in his 1956 novel, *A Woman of Bangkok* (See Chapter 5). The male believes that a "real" relationship has been established and that he therefore should not pay for sex. The woman has learned the "real" relationship of her body to the international marketplace: it is a commodity; therefore, she believes the male should pay more once they have established a bond, thus showing her his true affection. We can observe this scenario in the following account posted on the Internet, where numerous sex tourists to Thailand feel compelled to recount their exploits for general consumption. After relating many experiences with sex workers, often multiple partners in one day, the author tells of meeting a woman named Malay who seems, he says, to be "a genuine, honest, nice person." He buys her out several times at 500 baht ($20) for the whole night. But after a visit to her apartment, he has an altercation with her.

> With our understanding being 500 baht for all night, I certainly don't expect to pay Malay that much for this short time visit. But as I head for the door I'm blocked and that much is demanded of me, her roommate saying she is paid 1000 baht by farangs. I refuse and Malay accepts 250. An ugly situation that quickly destroys a lot of good will. I leave thinking that's it and feel sad having thought she was different.... Apparently, her roommate convinced her I was taking advantage of her, getting her too cheap, though I'd been completely honest all along (Paranoia.com/faq/prostitution 3/27/95).

The fear that he is being taken advantage of emerges as the client's central concern and reveals the deep schizophrenia operative in this site. The customer simultaneously negates the commercial nature of the relationship and essentializes this aspect of the interaction as the only one ultimately worthy of consideration ("It's simply business"). His belief that "good will" had been established before it could be "destroyed" is a form of self-delusion that emerges from the dynamics of how the site meets market demands; so is his self-proclaimed honesty. His subjectivity allows him to elide the commercial basis of the relationship until it impinges upon his willed ignorance in the form of Malay's desire to get paid for her work—*not* her pleasure—and paid according to her sense of the market as well as her need. Thus, the illusion is shattered. This same author consistently manifests the *irrealis* of his interpretation of the sex scene and of the international market that drives and exploits it when he visits another sex worker's home. Of her apartment, which explicitly bespeaks the squalor and impoverishment that causes these women to enter the industry, he says "A rather depressing state of poverty, though they seem happy." Who needs money when the indigenous carefree nature of the natives allows them to live happily in destitution?

Several-day encounters are the exception rather than the norm for the bar customer, who usually opts for multiple partners in one day—not to mention one visit. But the cultural "confusion" regarding the nature of the relationship between sex tourist and sex worker is exacerbated by what Cohen calls "openended prostitution" (1987; 1993), in which the interaction not only extends beyond the usual one night but begins to include elements of interaction beyond the merely sexual: eating out, shopping, obtaining medical attention, and so on, provide the attributes of a relationship not based solely on money for sexual favors. (As noted in the previous chapter, this is the role indigenous women have performed, for pay, for colonial forces from at least eighteenth-century Surinam to the Vietnam War.)

"Open-ended" prostitution, however, reveals another important reason—one not to be underestimated—why these men travel long distances to partake of this tourist-based service industry: loneliness. Not only do the customers in general possess a sexual subjectivity so alienated as to naturalize the purchase of sex on a regular basis and an entire international industry to support it, but some also have an equally alienated individual subjectivity created by massive disaffection for the cultures and economies in which they live and work. For the most part, the bar customers feel their lives to be empty of any true meaning or relationships. Generally in their late forties to mid-fifties, they are often divorced and stuck in jobs from which they derive no satisfaction except that of the paycheck, which suggests some similarity of the systemic forces that lead both worker and client to seek each other out in this industry and the "non-place" in which it emerges. For these men, the bottom line of life and relationships is the bottom line. In the "contact zone," then, they look for companionship as well as sexual satisfaction. This partially explains why they repress many aspects of the sex industry transaction *as* a transaction. When the delusion of the relationship as "real" yields to disillusion at the economic realities underpinning it, then the confusion that Cohen and Santansombut discuss can materialize, resulting in increased cynicism and alienation for the *farang* traveler.

To get a better sense of the sexual subjectivity with which these men operate, as well as a sense of the discursive practices surrounding the "contact zone" of Thai bars and the clients who frequent them, we can examine the recent novels by expatriate Canadian Christopher G. Moore (1991; 1993; 1995), virtually all set in Bangkok. Given his frequent use of "insider" references and the authorial assumption of "shared knowledge" that allows him to make many kinds of allusions and employ specific terms without feeling compelled to explain them, his audience seems to be the English-reading expat community in Thailand, as well as those tourists who have made multiple visits to the Kingdom and participated in the commercial sex world. For example, like some *farang* residents, Moore refers to the infamous Bangkok bar the Thermae as "HQ" and the sex workers there as "Termites," labels the banknote most often exchanged for sex as "a purple" (a 500-baht bill—$20—is that color), describes the missionary position for a sex worker as "sunny-side up," calls a sex customer who does not use a condom a "bareback rider," and uses some Thai expressions as well. Moore's work provides a valuable sense of the expat and sex tourist subject positioning. Or rather, we get a good sense of how this community *wishes* to think about itself. In these novels, which often sound like Sam Spade and Rambo meeting at the Thermae to discuss sex in existentialist terms, the male characters are portrayed as having all the toys a boy could want: espionage, weapons, danger, life-lived-on-the-edge, intrigue, drink, sex, and of course women (referred to as "girls" and always included in any list of a man's possible wealth and possessions). Also, these ever present, bountiful women enter the scene only when the men want them, never asserting a subjectivity that demands attention or response; they simply acquiesce to male will.

According to Moore, some of the men who come to Thailand on business regularly and who constitute a substantial portion of the sex workers' clientele carry a "bird book," a listing of women available for the sexual services necessary to help seal a business deal. These men are the backbone of international business development strategies, and Moore provides a profile of a prototypical *farang* business drone—the type of person for whom such motivation might work. He was "university educated (redbrick university), over 40, divorced from two white women, an ugly baby boomer who was looking for that last chance for romance with a stunningly beautiful, exotic, erotic Asian lady. The Bird Book contained two hundred pages of snapshots. Asian girls along with their basic, barebone details, including age, breast, waist, and hip measurements, hobbies, interests, languages, horoscope, address and P.O. box number" (Moore 1993, 63). The catalogue in the "bird book" replicates the catalogue of development strategies: quantification, measurement, and objectification. All aspects of the Other culture become classifiable and remain potentially exploitable. Missing from the scenario and the description, though, is *why* these business types have a "last chance" at romance with a stunning "exotic" and "erotic" (here equivalents) Asian woman, *why* a forty-something divorced male might find romance with a woman half his age.

The answer can be found in the economic inequity of the global development strategies that place both man and woman in the bar. In an Internet posting on the World Sex Guide (WSG), the author writes about the plenitude and elides the subjectivity of the workers. The text is (un)remarkable for its travel brochure discourse of enthusiasm intended to inspire awe and envy in its readers:

> Invariably they are all beautiful to our eyes. Picking out the cream of the crop usually boils down to picky little things like hair style. When's the last time you choose [*sic*] your evening companion by picking the one with the best teeth? Going around the bars puts a new meaning in the phrase "Like a kid in a candy store. . . ." You often find yourself buying [drinks] for a bevy of beauties who are all vying for your attention simultaneously! Damn hard way to go. . . . Here you are trying to scope out the possibilities that interest you from 40 or so gals, 2 or 3 are hanging on to you passionately, and your heart is beating so fast you can't swallow. What makes this scene so very, very incredible, is that this bar is only the first of about 20 ON THAT BLOCK!!!! . . . With your choice of 1000 wonderful bodies within 100 yards, your choice is a hard one! It's a horrible job. . . . Someone has got to do it. AND WE HAVEN'T EVEN GOTTEN TO PATPONG 2 YET!!!!! (WSG 15 January 1995).

Men—both in and out of Moore's novels—who primarily tell about the site and what drives them to it explain that "feminism" has corrupted and ruined Western women. One character asserts that "fucking a white woman is a step away from homosexuality" (Moore 1993, 107). Another, who tried to return to the States was driven back to Bangkok by a "high-miler" (a white woman of his own age) who ignored him during a meal because she was angry with him. "In Bangkok no one would talk to her, he told himself. *Farangs* would scatter when she entered the room because she would demand attention, conversation and an exchange of views" (1993, 109). In other words, she would demand human interaction—a demand whose absence in the sex workers is an essential part of the purchased product and that "no one" would talk to her means that no male *farang* would talk to her. Only these men count as people; what Thai women might do is completely discounted because they are discounted as humans. Odzer (1994, 83) recounts a conversation between two *farang* males who lived in her apartment complex, about the "drawback" of the relationship between older men and younger women. The topic is summed up concisely by an Australian, who reveals the essence of what clients want from women: "Bloody hell, there's a drawback . . . but it's worth it for a sweet young thing who doesn't talk back."

One Moore character complains about the notion of "date rape" that he'd encountered back home: "You ever hear of such a thing? Any of the termites hear of date rape? Not a chance. And they ain't dumb. Most of them graduated to Bangkok whoring from Water Buffalo University. And they ain't never heard of dating. They don't know what a goddamn date is" (Moore 1991, 144). Yet another character tells a story of going to bed drunk with a prostitute. During the night he dreams of standing at the toilet urinating. "I ended up pissing on her clothes. Next morning, she was very nice about it. Never mind, she said. . . . These girls tended not to get overly stressed. Not like your American women who have been known to maul a man for leaving the toilet seat up" (1991, 73–74).

The sex workers' malleability and apparent subservience, emerging from unequal economic relations, are recast in the clients' psyche as womanhood untainted by "Western feminism," which they routinely conflate with individual subjectivity and (even minimal) assertiveness. Observers of the sex industry in Thailand note that once the men return home to their daily lives, this recasting is transformed into a nostalgia for what seems like the perfect woman in the perfect place. In a sense, though, the customers are right. Having purchased a commodity that they created, they find it fills the bill perfectly, although the commercial aspect of the interaction tends to be elided in nostalgic retrospect. The women capitalize on this scenario as best they can by hiring people to maintain correspondence with the men and to request money from them on occasion. As a further investment in future earnings, many of the bar women keep a photo album of former clients. A kind of underground twin of the "bird book," the album helps the woman recognize one of her correspondents at the airport should he return and wish her to meet him there. (It also reinforces his delusion that she recognizes him because he was so special to her.) The letter-writing situation is documented by Cohen (1987), Walker and Ehrlich (1995), and numerous others. Rory O'Merry (1990, 139) offers a viable explanation of it:

> The men send money to the girl of their dreams in Thailand. These were the women they had the time of their life with, and were easy to love. They don't feel as if they're sending money to a prostitute, but to a friend who was [*sic*] poor and living in a developing country, to help her and her family financially. She doesn't bitch and moan about his drinking or tell him her problems about the kids or the daily problems of running the house. To keep her happy, all he has to do is send her money. She'll write back and love him forever. . . . When he is in town he can have all the sex he can handle—No "I have a headache." The exchange rate makes him a millionaire. Paradise.

Once again the fundamentally commercial nature of the interaction on the personal level is ignored. As a result, the "pure womanhood" purchased on the open market essentially boils down to an elimination of female subjectivity: no problems of her own that cannot be solved with cash (and small amounts of that), sex on command without fear of refusal, and professions of love and devotion. Paradise can be bought because favorable exchange rates and inequities in global development make a working stiff a millionaire, and all qualms are mediated by the belief that one is simply helping an unfortunate, impoverished soul (and certainly not exploiting her).

Back home, the customers' dreams are haunted by memories of paradise and the perfect women who populate it. The same character befuddled by date rape in Moore's novel explains that he has been forced back to Thailand by the aberrations of male-female relationships in Western culture. Of primary concern is the nightmare detailed in the epigraph from Moore that opens this section. The male goes home to the United States, sells some property and is flush with cash, but he's lonely. So some of his buddies try to set him up with a woman named Sue. Conveying primarily an expat rather than a tourist point of view, the character tells his pals back at the bar the horror story:

> I say to this guy. "Yeah, I see Sue. But I ain't sure you see what I'm seeing. She's old meat. You gotta be kiddin'. In Thailand, they'd toe-tag her. Take her to the morgue. . . ."
>
> I told him straight, man. No bullshit facts of life. "You want to avoid screwing any woman over sixteen. . . ." Then he starts going into this creepy moral shit. "Man, how can you fuck a kid young enough to be your daughter?"
>
> This is coming from guys who think nothing of climbin' on one of these sweathogs and pumping something with an ass the size of a first-class plane seat. They're judging me. So I give them my standard answer.
>
> "These girls gotta eat, don't they? I'm putting bread on their plate. I'm making

a contribution. They'd starve to death unless they whored. Not something you can say about an old sweathog like Sue. . . ."

I couldn't stand it. . . . I was going nuts in California. Man, it was fucking awful. I was phoning the airlines two weeks in. Get me the fuck back to Bangkok. Can you believe they were fully booked? I was fucking stranded with sweathogs. . . . I didn't get laid once (Moore 1991, 144–45).

Full flights to paradise dovetail with the myth of reciprocity in justifying the character's behavior in Thailand: he is doing these women a favor (and so are many others if the flight loads are any indication). The law of supply and demand rules. To this extent, despite apparent differences, Thai and Western women share one attribute: they both cost the male. "Miss Stanford Law Review has her cost. And she has you paying one way or another. Emotional funds or dollars, whatever currency works on your psychological balance sheet" (Moore 1991, 44–45). Another piece of sage advice runs, "As a rule of thumb, it should never cost more to get divorced than to get laid" (1991, 27). Thus, the assumptions of the marketplace as the natural prime mover in all human relations perpetuate the myth of reciprocity that justifies the interactions taking place in the bar scene.

Likewise, the self-contradictory understanding of the relationship as simultaneously "real" and "only business" yields for the moment to the pecuniary side of the equation. Indeed, one of Moore's characters argues that the bar site constitutes a kind of taxation: "You gotta think of HQ as a tax system. It's pay as you go. Each night you know the bill" (Moore 1991, 114). The same character discusses a male who, like Reggie in *A Woman of Bangkok*, grew "confused" in his relationship with a sex worker and assumed that since they were in love, he no longer had to pay for sex: "He's fucking doomed. It comes from all those years in the 60's living on food stamps in California. It turned him into a human sponge. Sucking up shelter, food, clothes, and there never seems to be a bill. Paradise, you think. Man, the whole world must be organized like California. Big fucking mistake" (1991, 114).

According to this explanation, delusion results from believing in a communal alternative, whereas reality is the "free" market. As in Diderot, socialist/communal living as an ideal yields to a naturalized capitalism that is truth. And for Moore's regulars the myth of reciprocity reigns, absolving all moral qualms or inequitable power relations. "At HQ, you're paying for a female body to fuck. A young, beautiful, horny, well-dressed, big-breasted, long-legged whore, who is clean and loves oral sex. You pay to fuck her. You pay COD. This is her job. She goes with you on an employer-employee relationship. In that collective agreement, which every regular knows by heart, there are terms and conditions that apply" (1991, 115–16). That a "collective agreement" sets the terms of the interaction assumes equality in the negotiations—an equality that does not exist. That the women are horny and love oral sex (particularly with flabby white men twice their age) further levels the playing field. Going outside the agreement means addressing such issues as love, compassion, and care, which have nothing to do with the business at hand, which is, after all, business. The cynicism of the bottom line ultimately takes precedence over the advertised allure of love, and the men who buy into the confusion that they, as customers, demand have forgotten the basic tenets under which the market operates.

Moore labels his characters who are regulars at the Thermae "hardcores," and he spends many pages ascertaining the characteristics that define them. One way of knowing a "hardcore" is by his language, including the trope of the hunt. The Thermae is the *farang* male's "common hunting ground. The old hands knew the good places to spot fresh game. They talked like hunters, stalked like hunters, bragged and lied and drank like hunters. . . . The key was learning how to track, how to patiently wait out prey. . . . With unlimited game and open season, it didn't take much talent to have success" (1991, 71–72). The fight for survival at the watering hole—the primal struggle over limited resources—disappears with the excellent odds.

Another semantic realm that dominates Moore's novels is the Wild West. This discursive terrain, of course, conjures up associations with Vietnam and the final throes of U.S. imperialism in Asia as the true closing of the western frontier for the American psyche. It may also have associations with Soi Cowboy, so named for the Vietnam vet, L. T. "Cowboy" Edwards, who started the first bar on that particular strip. And an Internet posting noted a bar with "nuke Hanoi Jane posters" on the walls which was owned by "a group of ex Nam vets" (WSG 15 January 1995). Finally, this terminology evokes the romantic notion of the Clint Eastwood lone gunslinger as existential outlaw: solitary, capable, and hard-bitten. "Harry Purcell—a hardcore HQ cowboy of a time before bareback riding became a game of Russian roulette—believed the HQ species of male was hot-wired for danger and high-risk bucking horses. They sat around the table listening to the jukebox and exchanged cigarettes, ideas, beers, theories, whores and concepts such as whether the short-time Hotel Playgirl on Soi 11 had better towel services and mirrors than the Happy Day which was hidden away on a lane off Soi 31" (Moore 1993, 36). In a world in which cigarettes and whores are equivalents (and after all, the difference between horses and whores is merely the addition of a sibilant), competing services at sex-industry hotels can pass as "concepts." But such a world takes its toll on the hardcores.

> Tuttle was unshaven, his nerves all jingling and jangling like an HQ regular who's gone riding bareback, rolling back afterwards as if he had ducked out of a cowboy gathering around a campfire; all worried about whether he had climbed onto an HIV-positive pony. Tuttle's face matched the grayish mask—the kind worn by cowboys who didn't saddle up the HQ termites before climbing on and going hell bent into the night. . . . Sex had become an angry, nightmarish last round-up and HQ the last corral. The old-timers let their booze talk about how they wanted to die with their boots on and their gun blazing (Moore 1993, 27).

Aging, alienation, and intimations of mortality are among the main attributes of a hardcore. He sniffs the hint of his own demise that tinges the minor death—impotence—with traces of the major one. Fear of "the last roundup" shapes his interactions with sex workers and makes them "nightmarish" acts fraught with anger. Moore foregrounds all these elements in a second-person passage (again identifying the intended audience) about a male taking home a dancer who looks vaguely familiar; perhaps he has even been with her before, but he just can't place her. In the morning, when she says she is from Issan and shows the client a picture of her mother, it all becomes clear:

> Twenty-one years ago you had taken her mother. . . . You tear out of the bathroom and into the locked chest with the photograph albums you've kept of the girls. You take out the '68 volume, squatting on the floor, and her mother's picture is there. . . . And when you glance up, the girl is looking down at the nude picture of her own mother, not recognizing her. Thinking she's a ringer from HQ. And she calls you a butterfly. But the truth is always more difficult to explain in Thai. You've passed that magnetic field where few have ever trod: you're second generation *hardcore*, at best you have one generation left ahead of you before your knees buckle, the food won't stay down in your stomach, and you can't get it up. . . . Second generation you repeat to yourself, and give the girl back the picture of her mother. You had been inside her mother when this girl was still an unfertilized egg, and you thought one generation lasted forever (Moore 1991, 33–35).

That he could have fertilized the egg that became the girl in his room does not yet enter the client's mind. Both the woman and her mother, in fact, become part of the endless cycle of nature in which there will always be young women servicing men, regardless of *their* age. Solipsistic as a hardcore can be, he feels that only his aging can have any existential consequence. And the fear of aging is measured by the number of generations a hardcore gets through.

In Moore's novels, hardcores operate in a site in which the American dream of riches, development, and upward mobility as cast in Thailand's "American era" generates scores of connections between the Vietnam war and U.S. military decline on the one hand, U.S. economic growth and influence on values on the other: the military empire giving way to imperial capitalism. For one such hardcore in *A Killing Smile*, the "perfect revenge" (Moore 1991, 193) manifests itself as a frigid, miscegenated female who has completely captured the lust of the hardcore but whose frigidity denies him satiation. As might be expected, the young woman of his wet dreams turns out to be not only young enough to be his daughter but his actual daughter. Willfully blinding oneself to the consequences of one's actions (individual, national, international) leads to this near-incest scenario. The revenge, at first blush, appears to be the unrequited lust for the young beauty, but "the perfect revenge" occurs only when the hardcore (individual, or nation) must confront the corporeal consequences of capricious, greedy, unthinking acts—must come face-to-face with the effects of deeds past.

For all the shortcomings of Moore's novels, the intimate connections between empire (military and economic), shifting indigenous values, power, inequity, and globalization processes do make occasional appearances. Even the hardcores get a glimmer of causal relations.

A scene late in *A Killing Smile* nicely encapsulates the media's circulation of the images of desire central to international development strategies and displays the causal relations between consumer culture and prostitution. Among HQ hardcores passing time in their hangout, the expat Snow uses an issue of *Vogue* magazine to attract a crowd of prostitutes, and he narrates the scenario aloud, in English, to his amazed and somewhat amused comrades.

"This is better than drugs, man. The one item that gives them a real buzz. Has them jumping up and down, sitting on my knee, eyes bright. Never fails as a wake-up call." Girls swarmed around the booth, sliding onto everyone's lap. Snow had a girl bouncing on each knee. . . . Snow casually flipped the pages, their eyes grew large and bright and intense; a dozen small fingers touched the photographs, sliding down the images of high-fashion dresses, furs, shoes, bags, and jewelry. . . .

"This is about as deep as the girls ever get. . . . Selling their sweet ass for a lovely mink stole. Just the garment you need in Bangkok.

"*Soo-ay* [beautiful], yes, beautiful,'" said Snow, shifting the weight of one of the girls. "Everything in *Vogue* is *soo-ay*."

The girls had reverted to a two-word Thai vocabulary. "*Soo-ay*—beautiful. And *chawp!*—like."

Snow had opened the book of dreams; of happiness; of what they should desire so much that they would be willing to sell themselves to acquire these objects. . . .

"Open that beautiful Rolex foldout this way. . . . Uncle Snow's got you dreaming in color. . . . You want to change lives with the model in the picture. . . . Uncle Tuttle talks about rebirth, man. But this is what you want to come back as . . . A rich bitch in a Greenwich house. . . . I pulled out the dream book, and their brains kicked into overdrive, thinking, here, at last, is a *farang* who understands what is important in life. . . . You offer your sweet little body . . . so you can get your share of what's on these pages. . . . You really don't want Uncle Snow to fuck you. But he has that five-hundred baht note somewhere on his person. And that purple's gonna get you closer to what's on that page. . . .

"Pearls. *Soo-ay*. That strand will set you on your backside for about 250,000 baht. . . . Let's break it down in terms of the HQ formula. The pearl necklace is five-hundred purples. Five hundred nights of getting your ticket punched at HQ. Hordes of horny Gunters crammed in a couple of 747s. . . . You will have to fuck yourself into the next lifetime, darling, to get enough purples" (Moore 1991, 246–48).

In this passage, Moore evocatively connects the macroeconomic forces of development strategies and global sex tourism with their manifestation at the micro level, the women bouncing on Snow's knees as they yearn for goods displayed in a fashion magazine. The connection simultaneously dismantles the myth of reciprocity and the inherent desire of the sex workers for their clients. The "HQ formula" of acquiring what the sex worker "should" desire materially proves the impossibility of acquisition, an impossibility that keeps the market humming and the supply of sex workers endless.

Similarly, in *A Haunting Smile*, Moore recapitulates aspects of the trajectory regarding sexual Other cultures outlined in Chapter 5. In so doing, he provides a meditation on sex, armies, and conquest that ultimately links colonialism with tourism. The shift from one form of foreign occupation to another little changes the conditions of indigenous women or how their bodies are represented by and acted upon by global forces. Although Moore acknowledges these connections and relations, his prose also seems to naturalize them, as if suggesting not only that this is the way things are but also that they could hardly be otherwise. The lengthy meditation on these topics begins by addressing the role of "comfort women" in the conversion from wartime to peace. In focusing on the males, of course, and not the women, Moore perhaps unwittingly conflates the fear of imminent mortality experienced by soldiers with that felt by their contemporary counterparts, the hardcore tourists, as exemplified in passages cited earlier. "Comfort girls—a strangely accurate description of their function. Comforting a man facing the fear of a violent death, . . . comforting a man so he will follow the commands of his officers. . . . The comfort women were more than sexual objects—they were a lesson in fear. . . . These women had an ability to withstand the pain. . . . The women were sent into sexual battle, sending a powerful message to the men—are you less able to serve your commanders than these throw-away women—these worthless beings whose only function is sex and to comfort the soldiers guarding the Co-prosperity Zone?" (Moore 1993, 162–63).

Kazuko Watanabe sees "a clear parallel in a historical, political, economical, and cultural context between wartime comfort women and the Asian sex workers today. . . . Soldiers acted just like Japanese businessmen called 'economic animals' during the postcolonial era" (1995, 506–507). In the "contact zone" of war, the colonizers assume mutual gain—or at least they argue for it. In the same contact zone of the past, men marched to their demise for a purportedly higher cause, in pursuit of which they were provided with "comforts" so that they would not question orders or the validity of the higher purpose. In the contact zone of the present, which also assumes benefit for both sides, the soldiers have become business pawns; the higher cause is international development; and the men, for their sacrifices to the cause, are given the opiates their forerunners were also given: drink and women. In the past, Moore claims, not one man ever questioned the system or felt compelled to "rescue" a comfort woman. Likewise, the current absence of questioning the status quo—the apriority of development and progress that manifests itself as the international sex industry—is rarely addressed by anyone involved in the systemic forces that so circumscribe their lives.

Difficult as it is to fathom, however, Moore seems to ignore his hardcore tourists' complicity in these scenarios, leaving the bulk of empire-building past and present to forces other than North American and European: "With a few modifications, the Japanese adapted the comfort-girl . . . to peace time and discovered that it worked even better than in the war. The new Zone emerged in the post-war period. The Japanese Imperial Army had been privatized as business enterprises, and the new soldiers—the business executives—found themselves in private, Japanese-only salons and clubs. The comfort girls never vanished from the scene; their numbers increased, they were numbers" (Moore 1993, 165–66). Anticipating the objection that the women today are "well paid" and have "free choice" whereas comfort women received no pay and were forced labor, Moore's character, Purcell, claims, "Free will versus determinism. Where in the history of war and sex has such a false division ever been more wrongly placed? And what difference does 'peace' bring to women without hope and chance among those who occupy their land?" (1993, 166).

The claims and objections directed at the Japanese are well founded and nicely articulated, yet Moore almost perversely refuses to place the same responsibility on his own *farang* characters. After all, the postwar period in Thailand has been labeled by many commentators "the American era," not the Japanese era. Purcell neglects to mention that the commercial bars of Patpong, Soi Cowboy, and Nana Plaza replicate U.S. go-go bars of the 1960s and 1970s in much the same way that Japanese "comfort women" today share attributes of those in the past: another current commercial enterprise servicing a new economic army that invokes a nostalgia for a previous occupying military presence. Cynthia Enloe poignantly asks, "Without a sexualized 'rest and recreation' (R&R) period, would the U.S. military command be able to send young men off on long, often tedious sea voyages and ground maneuvers? Without myths of Asian women's compliant sexuality would many American men be able to sustain their own identities of themselves as manly enough to act as soldiers?" (1992, 23). The answers can be found not only in the venues that serve the military bases in the Pacific but also in Patpong, Pattaya, Nana Entertainment Plaza, and Soi Cowboy.

Moore also has his characters express a theory about the relationship between empire-building and sex which later in the text provides the basis for comparing colonizers and tourists. An American character chastises a British one for the priorities of his nation's imperial projects:

You guys had a great empire. A great empire. The sun never set on the British Empire. But you guys never got seriously interested in getting laid. The English never missed fucking because they never knew what they were missing. All that time in places like Eton and Harrow. Boys buggering boys. If you had gone to co-ed schools like normal people you would have made Thailand a colony two hundred years ago. Only someone who had gone to an all-boys school would have taken Malaysia and left Thailand. Even the French had the good sense to take

Vietnam. They knew the country was full of women. Malaysia. Why? Because you wanted rubber plantations instead of getting laid. You wanted to make money and to hell with fun (Moore 1993, 103).

Despite his false assumptions regarding the class status of British colonizing forces and his confusion of current Thailand with the Siam of 150 years ago, the character echoes Diderot in this passage: colonization should provide, *first and foremost*, opportunities to get laid. Malaysia, evidently, bereft of available women, received England's imperial attention because the empire builders had failed to listen to Diderot and allowed the enterprise to be driven by their wallet and not their libido. As Vietnam and Thailand attest, these mistakes were apparently not made by the French and the Americans. It is worth noting that "fun" and "money" seem to be the sole prerogatives of the colonizers, despite the constant invocations of "co-prosperity" and mutual benefit in imperial enterprises past and present.

In *A Haunting Smile*, Moore introduces the ghosts of Montezuma and Cortez as characters who provide historical commentary, specifically on the actions of the May 1992 crackdown in Bangkok and generally on the colonial relations of the past that haunt the present. In a sense, they serve as reminders of synchronic structures that contextualize diachronic events. Montezuma comments, "Look around. These people don't know how lucky they are. They don't have live Spaniards invading their temples. They have tourists paying for sex" (1993, 178–79). Apparently, invasion of religious sites is worse than the invasion of a country's female population, especially when the latter includes cash to lessen the impact. The connections, though, exist: "The Spaniards were among the first Europeans to feel, for a few hours, what it was like to be tourists" (309).

Moore invokes the hypocrisy at play in international development strategies of tourism—a will-to-ignorance at the national, macro level analogous to that operative at the individual, micro level. Cortez, in response to Montezuma's assertion that tourists travel to be entertained, says, "Obviously. They travel to countries which have not violated their gods of democracy and human rights. When they witness on their screens these images of Bangkok [May 1992], right on the avenue behind us ... they will feel horror, dread, anger, and danger" (245–46). His lines echo those in newspapers and government reports following the May crackdown, which expressed concern about what impact the violence flashed on worldwide TV would have on the tourist trade (which, we should remember, is the largest source of foreign currency for the nation). The concern was that the perception of human rights violations under the heel of the jackboot would render obsolete the site where such violations routinely occur at the individual level under the auspices of the tourist trade. This worry proved baseless, because delusion and amnesia operate so successfully in both spheres that the events of May 1992 barely dented the sex biz.

However concerned the world's citizens may be for people beaten in the streets by their own military, or even for the invisible women who provide services in the massive international sex industry, the real victims in the trade—if we are to believe many of the authors who recount their exploits on the Internet or in various books—are the clients. In Moore's recent novel, *The Comfort Zone*, Calvino, the protagonist, is a hardcore who works as a private investigator in Bangkok. He has lived the (s)expat life and has grown weary of it. He yearns to break from the power of "the Zone" and believes that only a "non-Zone woman" can help him evade its dreaded grasp on his life.

> Calvino lived for the rest of the year in the Zone. Old haunts, new bars. Places filled with a fresh crop of beautiful women, an endless supply. Nothing survived in the Zone but the moment of pleasure. Ninety percent of the *farang* took their women, short or long term, from some Zone establishment. The ice never left her, the sub-zero temperature of her past froze all possibility of a future. Ice cut off feelings. But the Zone was so much more: there was the surface ice, stages with naked girls swinging around silver poles . . . these places were on the maps, deep in the psyche. Cowboy, Nana, Patpong . . . here no one but the hardest of the hardcore *farang* had ever gone, and there were no maps, guidebooks, only word of mouth passed among a small group of Zone warriors. . . .
>
> Neon ice, dark ice. . . . In the end, the same thing happened, a man got himself lost, snowblinded by the towering ice domes; there were men inside who would die rather than leave the ice. Abandon the Zone. . . . [Calvino] had started to think that Vietnam might be a way out, a tunnel away from the ice fields and ice goddesses. . . .
>
> In the Zone, the ice walls and ice fields, thick, high, centuries old, translucent, and forever cold, contained unlimited sexual pleasure. . . . The women, the women, the women. Ice domes built from the bodies of women (1995, 26–27).

Poor icebound Calvino has fallen victim to the postcolonial sexual cartographies that created the site of his deepest desires. The map of his psyche, which charted his international alienated sexual subjectivity, has led him to confront his existential alienation. As frightening and sad as this is, Moore ignores Calvino's role and that of others like him in the construction of the Zone. Were it not for them, the bar scene would not exist, yet Moore makes it sound as if the multitudes of women and the establishments that offer them as commodities are acts of nature causing Calvino's despair. The machinations and manipulations of logic that lead to naming clients as victims is stunning, but no less so than those that lead to regardging the site as one of mutual benefit, as free of inequitable relations, and as an inevitable result of a naturalized "free" market maximizing natural resources in the processes of international development and global progress. What, after all, is more natural than ice domes in the tropics made out of women's bodies? Moore may seem ludicrous in this passage, but is he any more absurd than those who bandy about the rhetoric of development and point to Thailand as a paradigm of the success of international economic intervention?

Bernard Trink

Prices at massage parlors are shooting up. Under the double-tier system, farangs are charged twice as much as locals. Be warned! ... As for HIV-positives—where are they, pray tell? It is well known or it stands to reason that they must be there isn't good enough. 'Nuff said.... BCT (Bangkok Community Theater) will present *The Adventures of Robinson Crusoe* as an action packed musical.... Part of the proceeds from the shows will be donated to Thai charities for children.
—"Nite Owl," The *Bangkok Post* 18 November 1995

The characters in Moore's novels read and cite the weekly column of Bernard Trink, an institution in his own right in Bangkok, and they typify the men who constitute Trink's ideal as well as actual audience. Exploring Trink's columns provides further information about the subjectivity of the clientele.

To many an expat in and foreign visitor to Bangkok, Bernard Trink is a hero, mentor, and resource. His columns about the nightlife and the bar scene have been part of the English-language press for thirty years, covering almost the entire duration of what Benedict Anderson (1985a, 4–41) has termed "the American era" in Thailand. The "Nite Owl" page that Trink pens for the Saturday edition of the *Bangkok Post* is regularly read by expats and tourists alike. The paper is often provided free of charge by upscale hotels that cater to tourists, and the column is carried in the weekly international edition mailed all over the world and posted on the Internet by fans and the newspaper itself. A compilation of Trink's musings on any subject he likes, the column offers jokes, observations about life in Thailand, video reviews, and local gossip, but mostly lots of "insider" information about the bar business that serves the heterosexual *farang* male community. One can learn why, for example, each January the "selection" of bar girls thins considerably: many of them have regular European boyfriends who annually buy them out for a month's holiday at the beach, but readers are told "not to worry, they will be back." Trink sprinkles the column with his trademark explananda of perceived cultural confusions or irritating situations: "any comment would be superfluous," "'nuff said," "BUT, I DON'T GIVE A HOOT," "cases of 'MANURE' (huMAN natURE)," and "cases of 'TIT' (This Is Thailand)."

To perhaps as many expats in Bangkok, Bernard Trink is a joke and an embarrassment, a clueless anachronism who parasitically lives off the international sex industry and fancies himself an intellectual of sorts but whose every pronouncement only makes him seem more ridiculous. (In response to having his full page column reduced to half its usual length, Trink stated in August 1996, "I have no delusions of grandeur, but it's rather like Moses being told to reduce his 10 commandments to five because he's being given one tablet instead of two.") Regardless of one's opinion of him, it is inarguable that he has witnessed a great deal of the sex industry and that he occupies a unique position within the Thailand bar business so important to international tourism.

Though often spotted while making his nocturnal rounds, Trink is not an easily accessible individual. Not necessarily unfriendly but certainly guarded, he maintains a careful distance between himself and the larger *farang* community, which has taken more than a few shots at him. So I was greatly surprised when Jeff Petry told me that he had arranged for us to interview Trink at his office at the *Post*, especially since the renowned columnist had been uncertain about meeting us after the research project had been outlined over the phone. Whenever issues of national policy or international processes crept into Jeff's description of the project, Trink would lose interest and say he "did prostitution only." During our conversation, similarly, whenever I veered from straightforward, open-ended questions and deployed academic polysyllables, Jeff would kick the back of my chair and Trink would say that he could not understand the question. Over the course of the monologue—one could hardly call it a dialogue—Jeff and I fell into an impromptu "good cop-bad cop" interview method with Jeff playing the heavy. Most of our questions were formulated to elicit Trink's ideas and opinions, not to engage him in debate; however, our desire to do so grew, as he became more comfortable with holding forth—especially when he analyzed a "bargirl's mind set" as solely dictated by income, and consistently asserted the absolute absence of AIDS from the heterosexual international sex industry as it manifests itself in such places as Patpong, Soi Cowboy, and Nana Plaza.

We arrived a bit early for our appointment, and he warily motioned for us to enter his office. He shared the space with several other writers for the paper, but the only one of these present was a fellow who slept at his computer through much of the conversation. Trink sat at his desk for most of the interview and stared at the wall directly in front of him; he rarely made eye contact. On the desk sat an ancient manual typewriter with yellowed paper stacked beside it and a sheet in the roller. A haphazard pile of books lay between the typewriter and a wall upon which a poster displayed photos of the city's famed nightlife.

Once we had finished, Trink said, "All I ask is don't make me sound stupid"; his views were based on a "hell of a lot" of experience. Additionally, he suggested I had not asked necessarily pertinent questions and that I should bear in mind the constraints inherent in the relative brevity of our conversation. This is why I have inserted quotations from the "Nite Owl" column to illustrate, modify, or question particular points that Trink himself made.

The Interview

Bishop What are the major changes in the bar scene that you have noticed over the years?

Trink The biggest change in the bar scene over the years since I've been covering it is that the most beautiful girls are no longer in the bars. They are working as "receptionists" in Japanese night spots. People ask me where have the beautiful girls gone? Second-class girls are the only ones there now. Japanese membership clubs offer more money than the bars.

Bishop Do the bars recruit women from the countryside?

Trink No, the bars are not brothels. They do not recruit like the brothels do. They have applications.

> *BIG BLUE I BAR (Soi Cowboy) run by Andy and "Canadian" Jim, is short of lasses and is willing to hire Go-Go dancers by the day. They'll pay 140 baht for those in costume, 170 for topless and 250 for those willing to go on stage in their birthday suits. Any comment would be superfluous* (9 December 1995).

Bishop Is the influence of the Vietnam War and its effect on Thailand regarding the sex industry overblown? *esagerato*

Trink No, not really. Numbers of bars opened then. Patpong itself was not originally a nightspot area. It was a business area. New Petchaburi Road was not a road in the mid-1960s. Then bars and massage parlors started to show up. There was a definite effect, but there was always prostitution in other areas. The clientele then and now was mostly Thai. The number of *farangs* was never enough to keep these places going, even during the war.

Bishop Can you tell us about some of the different kinds of bars?

Trink There are all sorts of bars catering to different clients. Thai and Thai-Chinese—not much distinction between them—have far more brothels catering to them.

Bishop And the transformation of bars into sex sites occurred during the war?

Trink There is a big difference between brothels and bars. Bargirls are free; they choose to work there. Brothels recruit. Only a minority of the families do not know that they are going to brothels.

Bishop The bars don't recruit? Don't the same bonded labor agreements with families for brothels exist for the bars?

Trink No, there is no recruiting for the bars. The girls come of their own free will.

Bishop Compare the spots that cater to *farangs* with those that cater to Thais, like on Suttisan.

Trink Except for a very few *farang* bars, they need Thais to survive. So, I don't think you can really make a distinction. Journalists concentrate on the *farang* areas and ignore the Thai. In 1972 the law stated that a bar must be registered in the name of a Thai or a Thai company. So, the *farang* bar owners need Thais to get their registrations. And every brothel, without exception, is owned and operated by Thais. No *farangs* at all. They were muscled out. The bars are a very small percent of the total industry and a small percent of the cash. Sex tourists and expat *farangs* do not contribute a great deal of revenue for the bars. Mostly Thais.

Bishop I have never seen any Thai clients in Patpong or Soi Cowboy. Any Thai I have seen was working there.

Trink The only bars where Thais are kept out are the ones with sex shows. If prostitution is illegal, the sex shows are more illegal. The sex shows can get closed by the police, so some of the owners are worried about Thais because they may be plainclothes policemen. In all the places for *farangs*, many Thais are there as clients. Many of these bars have many floors, and you may not see them. For example, Klymaxx bar in Patpong and Five Star in Soi Cowboy, the vast majority of their clients are Thais. And Patpong 2, the lounges there are 90 percent Thai.

Petry What are the best books on the bar scene?

Trink None of them are any good.

Petry Why don't you write one then?

Trink Many people have asked me about this. I consider my column an ongoing book.

Petry What about Jack Reynolds's *A Woman of Bangkok*?

Bishop And its presentation of the bar-girl subjectivity?

Trink What?

Bishop Their attitudes and feelings.

Trink Yes, he got that right. It is over thirty years old, though. I knew Reynolds. I interviewed him once. He is the only person I ever interviewed who asked me to pay him for the interview.

Bishop What do you consider your role to be?

Trink I provide inside information about the bars, even to the bar owners. Many of them read the column to keep current. I also provide a vicarious experience of what the bars are like. Lots of people would not be caught dead at any of these places, but they want to know about it. And—I don't like these people who want to "help" the bargirls, like this group called EMPOWER. EMPOWER is bullshit. So, I tell the bar owners to treat the girls well. I recommend they get one day a week off. Right now they get two days a month. I've intervened to help bar girls with things like fines from the bar owners for tearing a costume, days off, and medical exams—about who pays for them. I try not to have the owners nickel-and-dime the girls to death. *Mamasans* read the column, too. I tell them don't let the girls work overseas. People lie to them and throw them into brothels. The girls want to get wealthy, but they can't overseas. I tell the customers to wear condoms. They need to protect themselves.

Bishop So is AIDS a big problem?

Trink Well, AIDS is not sex-related. You can't get it through sex—only anal sex and drugs. If you read books written by doctors, drugs lower the immunization [*sic*] systems. If the system is screwed up, then AIDS can enter it.

Bishop Let's talk about the transfer from the wartime R&R bar scene to the tourist one. What are your thoughts on that changeover?

Trink The number of bars has gone down.

Bishop Down?

Trink Yes, tourism has reduced the number of bars, not increased it. Also, the number of *farangs* after the war went down. Not nearly as many here now as then.

> *A night spot proprietor who has been around a while and isn't doing the business he used to says [Thailand is no longer a good tourist destination]. "Bangkok used to be great. Beer was reasonably priced, the girls weren't greedy, rent was affordable, nonsensical closing times weren't imposed. Those days are gone forever and so are the tourists." To be sure there's some truth to this, but also a fair amount of exaggeration. . . . Another publican [says] "Where else can tourists see exotic temples in the morning and erotic shows after dark? It beats the South Seas, where drinking coconut milk is the highlight of the trip. This is a wonderful country and it's getting better all the time. Tourism will increase yearly. Mark my words"* (25 November 1995).

Petry I have one stupid question. Any of these women, do they remain unaffected by their experiences? Is sex different for them than for other women? Is it like, as the Thai saying goes, a mosquito bite?

Trink If you had been reading my column carefully, you wouldn't ask this question. Prostitution does something to a person, it changes a person. Prostitutes are different. You can take the girl out of the bar but you can't take the bar out of the girl [*spoken as if revealing a significant insight*]. Remember, these girls are free. They choose this profession, but it changes them.

Petry How long does that process take?

Trink Only a couple of months. After a couple of months very few can ever do anything else. Oh, they may get married and live lives elsewhere, but many of them come back to the bars. They can't help it.

Petry If they had different or better opportunities in the country, wouldn't they choose to stay there? If they could support their families?

Trink [*shaking his head*] They send very little money home.

Petry If rural conditions were better, how many would still come?

Trink Let me put it this way. Things would have to change a lot. Right now, a prostitute can earn—as long as she's not a dog [chuckling]—she can make 30,000 baht a month. What alternative would provide the same salary?

> *Freelancers have been particularly hard hit by the weather. For the first time in recent memory, they vastly outnumber the punters at the Marine Disco (on the Golden Mile). A resident related that one approached him in the street, but he rejected her proposition. Whereupon, she made him an offer he couldn't refuse—a night together in return for dinner and breakfast. Any comment would be superfluous (28 October 1995).*

Petry Well, what if they could do work that was more respectable, and be near their families and not have to work in Bangkok?

Trink [*again shaking his head*] They want the same salary.

Petry Why exactly the same?

Trink That's what they want. The realistic situation is they want that and more. You have to understand the mind set of a bar girl.

Bishop Where does this subjectivity come from?

Trink I don't understand.

Bishop This mind set? Where does it emerge from?

Trink Well, greed is inborn. Would you do another job if it paid less? And Buddhism plays a large role. There are virtually no Muslim bar girls. It is part of the culture, the religion—it's more tolerant. There is not very strong moral teaching in Buddhism.

Petry Then why aren't there more working in the profession? How many women do you think are working as prostitutes now?

Trink My own figure is around 300,000, which is 1 percent of the female population; 99 percent are not prostitutes, so I am only dealing with 1 percent of the population. The others take more respectable work. You have to understand that Thai women are not different from any other women.

Bishop Does the international press try to make Thailand a unique case?

Trink They concentrate on Thailand.

> *The kingdom continues to get a hammering from the sensational foreign media. The usual accusations—bars are brothels; child prostitutes are everywhere to be seen; AIDS is rampant in the Patpong area, local males are passing it on to their wives and the mothers of their unborn children. . . . To enhance these fairy tales, plane-loads of scriveners from as far afield as Europe and Australia are arriving. . . . to capture on film and videotape the activities of bar girls/GoGo dancers. . . . . Publicans, aware of their intentions from past experience, refuse to allow them inside the boites with their equipment. . . . Their pleas of "only giving a balanced account" of our night life are ignored, taken for the lies that they are* (23 March 1996).

Trink It's always overlooked that Thailand gets pointed out. I ask, isn't there prostitution in New York and Los Angeles?

Bishop Yes, certainly. But women in New York or L.A. have more choices, more options available to them for other work. If given the opportunity, don't you think most of the women in the bars would choose otherwise?

Trink Some go back to the bars even when they have good situations. They like being desired and the atmosphere. Some of them enjoy the exhibitionism of the work. Thailand gets singled out, but the percentage of prostitutes here is virtually the same as in any other country.

Petry But in the U.S. the availability is different. If I am in Lebanon, Pennsylvania, and want to find a prostitute, it would be hard. I would have to go to New York. Whereas here, I could find a prostitute in any village, regardless of the size. [*Prostitutes can, of course, be found in small U.S. towns, but it may be more difficult than finding them in Thai villages.*]

Trink I don't know about that. You haven't asked me about or mentioned foreign prostitutes here, *farang* prostitutes.

Bishop Are there any?

Trink Sure, mainly from East European countries.

Bishop And who are their clients?

Trink Mostly Thais.

Bishop Wouldn't these women—as in a place like Kenya or the Caribbean, too— be caught in the same globalization processes, the same development strategies and need for cash, that the women here are?

Trink I would say they needed money, they need cash. I don't know about those other places except that they have prostitutes just like everywhere else.

Bishop Earlier you said you don't like groups that claim to help the women in the bars, like EMPOWER, that EMPOWER is a bullshit operation. Why?

Trink They're good at building themselves up, but they concentrate on the conditions and situations of the women, not what they actually do. To help them you have to look at the bars and know the bar business. A few years back they went around putting on a kind of kindergarten-level play about condom use. When they did that, fine, but that's all they did. When I asked them what else they do, they said they teach English so that the girls can bargain better. A year ago they stopped that, and now they are working on AIDS discrimination, especially for hospitals to open AIDS wards for infected patients and to protect them from discrimination, which is fine, but it doesn't help the women. For them it is only money. The only thing that would move them out is a job that pays as well. The only jobs like that are acting or modeling. It's like this American who has come here wanting to be the Dr. Schweitzer of AIDS in Thailand. He's full of BS. He claimed to have found two women with HIV over two years. He is an example of helping but not really helping.

Bishop The only real help is money?

Trink Right.

> BUMBLE BEE BAR *has been renamed* After Skool *(Soi Cowboy). Run by Roger and Sun, lasses in schoolgirl abbreviated costumes dancing A-Go-Go is the format. . . . A visit is in order. . . . . Not the least reason Nana Entertainment Plaza is picking up is that Patpong demimondaines demand 2,500 for short-time (though some will settle for 2,000 baht, while making it clear they are unhappy about receiving less). Their NEP counterparts ask 1,000 for short-time (many settling for 700 baht with good grace). Cases of "TIT" (This Is Thailand)* (16 December 1995).

Trink Do you know that there has not been one AIDS case in Patpong, not one?

Bishop I saw on a documentary that the Kings Group [*a large company that owns several bars in Patpong*] has reported cases in the clinics they have for their bars.

Trink It's their clinic. They test the girls every three months. But there is not a single AIDS case there.

> Unless and until the three HIV-positive girls are pulled out, I'll no longer attest that the Patpong area is AIDS free. . .I have never trivialized AIDS and I'm not going to start now* (2 December 1995).

Petry What if I told you that a friend of mine got HIV from a prostitute whom we both know?

Trink I'd have to know a lot more about them. Did she have anal sex? Did she use drugs?

Petry I wasn't there every time she serviced a client, but she was very dry at the moment of the act and he opened a place on his member—

Trink [*shaking his head*] You know all those doctors and nurses who cut themselves all the time? Do you know one case of a person who died of AIDS from that?

Bishop Actually, I—

Trink You don't.

Bishop Okay.

Trink You know why?

Bishop No, why? Tell me.

Trink I am telling you.

Petry That it is not sexually transmitted?

Trink That it is not sexually transmitted.

Bishop You mentioned some sources about this. Can you recommend one?

Trink [*standing up, rebuckling his trousers and belt, which were undone (we hadn't noticed while he was sitting at his desk) and retrieving a tome from a cabinet*] Here.

He handed me *Deadly Deception*, by Robert Willner M.D. and Ph.D., from Peltec Publishing Company, a book not widely respected in the AIDS research community. (A knowledgable commentator on AIDS research characterizes the author as a crank.) While I scanned it, Jeff asked him about Cleo Odzer's book *Patpong Sisters* (1994); he described it as "pathetic." Jeff asked if he wanted to know about Odzer's homepage on the Internet and her inclusion of him in an interactive cyberspace game about the Bangkok bar scene. Trink was not interested. He conveyed the caveats regarding the brevity of the discussion and my inadequate questioning. We then left.

More from the "Nite Owl"

We see in Trink's writings and interview statements the alienated sexual subjectivity that fuels the international sex industry. Certainly, differences between the expat and the one-time (or some-time) tourist mentality exist, and Trink occupies a uniquely liminal position between them: an expat—but not a "sexpat" —communicating to tourists and Bangkok residents alike. Although we do not wish to posit monolithic, static structures for either, we are generalizing about psychological phenomena created by variegated combinations of histori-cal, cultural, and textual traditions interacting with market forces. And Trink sees himself as a major player in the scene where these phenomena manifest themselves.

A number of Patpong area publicans are pleasantly surprised that their girls living in Thon Buri aren't using the flood as an excuse to stay away from work. "They wade through water twice a day and show up a little late, but considering the cir-cumstances, I wouldn't dream of cutting their pay" (4 November 1995).

There is a general misconception that the lasses leaving their upcountry villages to seek their fortune in the cities are wholesome, then lose their virtue to pimps who force them to sell their bodies in watering holes. The theme of many books, movies and TV dramas, there is some truth to this stereotype abroad but hardly any in the Land of Smiles. The actual scenario here is that girls in the provinces tend to give up their virginity early and move in with their boyfriends while still in their teens, registering their marriages at local amphurs, a formality more than a few dispense with. Legal wives or not, they give birth to one or more children. There are the usual fights over money, the men drinking and visiting brothels. Resigned to their fate, the lasses assume that this is all life has to offer them. Patient, hoping they won't be beset by sickness, they look forward to an occa-sional new dress. Perhaps a telly on which to watch soap operas and see things advertised they could never afford to buy. Friends migrate to the cities and write of earnings made in the nitery entertainment field, but such a life isn't for them.

Then her husband brings home a minor wife and her secure world collapses. She has no say in the matter. Her protests are met with slaps, her tears with punches. She is told to cook for and wash the clothes of the newcomer, who is encouraged to treat her as a servant. There is a new dress, but it goes to the *mia noi* [minor wife]. If she claims that the arrangements are insufferable, she is told to get out. Adding injury to insult, he gives her a parting kick. Where can she go?

Remembering the letters from her friends she heads for Pattaya, Phuket, Hat Yai, etc. [at] 20 or thereabouts, reasonably attractive apart from stretchmarks, she looks up one or more friends to take her in. Brought to the oasis where they work, she applies for and gets a job. The publican spells out that her wages will depend on what she is willing to do to earn them. It is up to the knowledgeable mamasan to take her in hand. If shy, she'll start out as a doorgirl. Then she'll be brought inside as a bargirl, cadging lady drinks from which she gets a percentage. Noting that a Go-Go dancer gets a higher salary, she may ask to become one. Those will-ing to go topless get more and the birthday suit girls still more. Quite likely she'll go that route.

The real money comes from being bought out, making her a full-fledged demi-mondaine. But this is the long way. A number shorten the process by omitting the doorgirl and bargirl steps. And if she applies herself to servicing customers, her earnings soar. Whether or not she enjoys the sex, she likes the feeling of being in demand.

Now that she's in the chips, she has an unexpected and unwelcome visitor. Her husband shows up, oozing congeniality and requesting a reconciliation. He assures her that he realised his mistake as soon as she left, dumped the other woman and is prepared to live happily ever after with her. In fact, he'll handle her earnings and will buy a bigger house with them. He asks her to think of the children, their needs and wants, always uppermost in his mind. She may fall for it—if she doesn't he may well do her an injury—but keep in mind that very many demimondaines in the Realm have this background. Sad but true (28 October 1995).

LOLLIPOP (NEP) reopens today, inside and outside. It features the Mermaidium, which should be as interesting as the shower show at the G spot. Hit it! (9 December 1995)

The Pearl S. Buck Foundation will soon be holding a summer camp for mixed-race children who have been abandoned by their fathers. Many of the children feel isolated, as they may be the only mixed-race child in their village or neighbourhood (16 March 1996).

When saloonkeepers raise the price of bar fines, they have two reasons. One is to make more money (greed, if you will). The other is to try to keep at least some girls in the bars until closing. When all of the girls are bought out, customers tend to go elsewhere where there are girls. . . . Which is why a tavern never has enough girls. If it has 25, the night spot owner wants 50. If it has 50, he wants 75 and so on. That's the way it is (18 November 1995).

In a slightly warped sense, Trink represents the ethnographic participant-observer that virtually every anthropological fieldworker is trained to aspire to become. Such a researcher attempts to integrate him- or herself into the culture being studied to such an extent as to feel a member of the group while simultaneously maintaining an objective, observational mind-set. In theory, one does not alter the cultural interaction by one's presence but, blending into the scenery, as it were, simply becomes privy to what otherwise might not be observed. In the 1960s, as ethnographers increasingly felt that such a presence inevitably changes the events observed, some anthropologists began more active intervention into the site of inquiry, particularly when they believed that their actions could benefit indigenous peoples under threat of obliteration by international processes, development strategies, and national policies, including "modernization." The pitfalls and naïveté operative in the participant-observer scenario, whether one "intervenes" or not, are fairly obvious.

This harrowingly scant overview of a debate that has been played out in the discipline for decades is invoked here simply to continue an analogy of this sort of fieldworker with Trink. Trink, however, does not attempt to fade into the background of cultural/social inquiry. By dint of his occupation, he must stand out a bit from the crowd. Moreover, he has played a significant role in the construction of the industry upon which he reports, and his livelihood depends on its perpetuation. Trink has lived in the industry he reports on for about as long as that industry—that is, the international sex industry important to tourism—has been in operation. (Ironically enough, this time frame parallels and is synchronous with the debate in anthropology regarding fieldwork practices.)

He is, he claims, an interventionist. Even though his interview statements speak primarily of how he aids the sex workers in the industry (more so than EMPOWER does), his column generally addresses the plight of these women en masse but the problems of employers and clients individually. It cannot be denied that he actively serves the interests of the latter two groups more frequently and readily than he does the former. To him, and to the many clients of the sex workers, this work is simply work—better-paid work than these uneducated and unskilled women can expect to find anywhere else.

Trink reinforces the assumption that the vast majority of the men bring to the site: that they are doing these women a favor, or helping them out. Thus, whether client or bar owner, one must be aware of scams, shifty hookers, price changes, laziness, robberies, and so on—all the ways these men can be exploited while exploiting others. The chance that one of these little vixens will get more than her "fair share" and the client less than his is ever present and falls to those who are caught off guard. Trink provides numerous warnings about clip joints, prices individual workers charge in different parts of the city, and numerous accounts of nefarious behavior on the part of the sex workers. Forewarned is forearmed, as the following passage from his column reveals:

> A punter picked up a freelancer at 11 p.m. and she promised faithfully to spend 10 hours with him, for which he agreed to give her 1,000 baht. However, after an hour she asked if it would be all right for her to go as she remembered her girlfriend was having a birthday party. "I don't mind at all," he said and handed her 100 baht. She refused to take it. "Be fair," he said. "We agreed on 1,000 baht for 10 hours. That comes to 100 baht an hour. Stay the 10 and you get the 1,000." She stayed. The moral of the story is never pay in advance. Cases of "MANURE" (huMAN natURE) (2 December 1995).

The myth of reciprocity, as discussed in the previous chapter and in this one, obviously operates here. Under such a rubric, the women have choices and the clients have choices. Each gets what he or she wants from the marketplace, itself a completely natural, naturalized, and self-regulated/regulating system. No sense of historical factors, international forces, or inequitable power relations operates in such an analysis of the situation. Hence, Trink, like the Internet author of "Sex in Thailand: The Basics" (1994), feels he is deploying his expertise for the common weal. The moves of self-deception and self-legitimation in explanation of his activities find analogy with those proffered by expat and tourist clients alike. They are operative in Moore's characters, in the multiple anonymous postings on the Internet, in the men one meets on Patpong or Soi Cowboy. The power of these dominant discursive practices cannot be overestimated, for it is the nature of dominant discourses to "go without saying"; their presence is defined as the "social impossibility of [their] absence" (Terdiman 1985, 61).[3] Bordieu has called the naturalization and universalization that follow from and constitute dominant discourses "genesis amnesia," for its origins—its material, cultural, historical, and linguistic genealogies—are necessarily forgotten in the social apparatuses that deploy them.

Interview with Nong

The bar scene is such an amnesiac site for its clients, but is probably not so for its sex workers, as my conversation with Nong (August 1996) reveals.

In her early thirties, Nong wears her hair cut very short, which adds a pixieish quality to her high-voltage persona. She has worked as a freelancer for over ten years; thus, when she enters the German Beer Garden or the Thermae, she is greeted warmly and often by regular sex workers and clients. Having been married to a Dutch native with whom she communicated in English, she is remarkably fluent. Her language skills have led to many offers for other work, but none that would pay as much as she can earn in the bars, and certainly not enough to support her son or her parents. Working in the profession for a long time has allowed Nong to create a clientele of regulars, and as a result, she only occasionally has to freelance in the bars. Through a mutual friend, we met at the German Beer Garden around ten o'clock on a typically hot, sticky Saturday night as the place was in full swing.

Leaning over a beer and shouting over the general din, I asked her, "Would you prefer to do another kind of work?"

"Of course. Who wouldn't?"

"Some *farangs* say that many, if not most, of the women love the bars: the men, the drinking, the dancing, the money, the attention. They say all this gets in the women's systems. Then, if they try to do another type of work, or simply get out of this job and go home, they can't do it."

Shaking her head, Nong responds, "No, I don't think so." She blows a plume of smoke into the air. "Maybe some do, but most don't. Most are here because they have no education and no real choice. How can you live on 6,000 baht ($240) with a family? In Bangkok?"

"You can't," I agree. "But is the money *that* much better in the bars?"

"Not really, no. The extra 3,000 to 5,000 baht a month makes a real difference though."

"So, just a few women like the work."

Nong nods in agreement.

"What percent, would you say?" I ask.

"Maybe two or three percent—at the most."

"Are you ever afraid to go with a man?"

Her eyes widen. "Sure! All the time. Every time. You never know what he's going to do," she says, clutching her throat, "One guy tried to strangle me and I hit him with the ashtray. Now I always look for the ashtray when I go with a man I don't know."

"Is that often now?"

"No. I have a pretty steady group of men who are nice to me, which is why I go with them. But some months, the rent is due and my son's school needs to be paid—no money in the bank—so I go here [GBG] or the T-room. I don't know if you've ever, you know, been starving or scrambling for food for your child. You do some crazy things. That's when I have to smile sweetly at guys who are really shit, you know. Each time, too, there's that fear along your back, near your spine—fear of losing that guy's attention and money, fear of not getting enough money, fear that he might hurt me. If I have some money, I can tell the guys I don't like to fuck off. If I don't, then it's smiling at this shithead who's grabbing me all over my body," she moves her hands in illustration.

"Do most of the women dream of doing something different?"

"Yeah, sure. A house with children, you know. A good husband, food every day, maybe some maids," she laughs. "Of course, who wouldn't want that?"

"Do they want a lot—I mean, a *big* house, electronic equipment, new cars, power?"

Nong nods and draws on cigarette, "Yeah, yeah. Sure."

"Where do they get the desire for all this? Most of them come from villages where people barely survive. So where does this come from? TV or friends or magazines? Where?"

"TV, for sure."

"Like the *lakhon* [*popular nighttime soap operas*] shows?"

"Yeah, TV. It's really a big problem. They all watch it and think that they can be the people on TV. Even the commercials!" she laughs.

"But day after day," I respond, "their dreams are confronted by reality, right? They step outside, after maybe watching some TV; they step out into the heat, pollution, the garbage and shit in the *sois*—the men in the bars and the lousy pay, don't these affect their dreams?"

"No. They think 'Today may be bad, but tomorrow, you know, will be better. Something will save me.' Really. They think that. Or, they start doing Horse Pills. That really messes them up. Then they don't know what they think. They still dream. Some are messed up to begin with, but the drugs really just take their mind."

"Would you have done things differently if you'd known what the life in the bars is really like?"

Nong's eyes mist over a bit as she looks up and away. She pauses for a second and pulls on her cigarette. "I never planned, you know, to do this. First, I worked in the German restaurant here. Then, the pay was so much better out here—or I thought it was—and I had a child, so I came out to this part of the bar. Everyone would like to change some things in their lives. I have a few, some big things. Mostly, I'm happy, I guess, but I don't much like my work."

"What do *you* dream of?" I ask her.

"A bookshop, you know. One that sells coffee, too. Maybe some music playing lightly in the background—quiet and cool. People could rent the books, too. They wouldn't even have to buy them."

The After Hours Spot: "Why Do You Think God Made the Thermae?"

When Jeff and I venture out to sample "the nightlife" further, we do not head to Nana Entertainment Plaza, where one venue touts "The Wall of Flesh." Nor do we go to Patpong, where customers of Crazy Jack's Shadow Bar receive a souvenir keychain of "Genuine Pubic Hair" encased in plastic. Instead, our goal is the haunt that Moore's "hardcores" find so friendly. The most infamous of Bangkok's nightspots and almost completely off limits to female *farang*, the Thermae gets widespread attention on the Internet. Calling it "HQ," among other names, Moore's descriptions wonderfully evoke this site and the clients, the "hardcores," who frequent it. Likening the Thermae to a 1950s North American rec room, Moore writes, "HQ was an elaborate replica of that basement; the handyman job performed by your father and a couple of neighbors back in the 50's. . . . Throw in a wet bar with plastic covered benches and a television set on a shelf at the far end, a hundred whores, and you're back but not where you started. Everyone's thirteen again, but this time they are flush with money for tits and ass" (Moore 1991, 31). Nostalgia and arrested adolescence blended with the myth of reciprocity permeate this bar beneath street level and just below a massage parlor.[4]

The most common entrance is the back door, which opens from a parking lot. One enters through a unisex, open lavatory leading directly to a narrow hallway that drops down into the main bar area. The Thermae does not have dancers, and no one directly controls the women—ranging from freelancers to loosely formed cliques organized by a *mamasan*—who work there, although the unspeakable rumor everyone knows maintains that the police own and run the establishment. Against the far wall to the right as one steps into the main bar space is a row of tables and chairs occupied by freelancers who are much older, heavier, sicker, and more scared than the young (17 to 25) crowd that also works the place. They sit, talk, eat, argue, and try to catch clients who have not yet linked up with anyone else when the place slows down around four or five in the morning. A much wider continuum of ages exists in the Thermae than in the Soi Cowboy, Patpong, Nana Plaza establishments, where women over twenty-five are usually relegated to bar work, recruiting or managing dancers, and hawking. In the Thermae, I saw a woman with a very fit body who appeared to be in her sixties, who was clearly looking to be taken out, and was not managing other workers. In the central space of the sitting area, a cluster of forty women who would be classified by Soi Cowboy standards as "past their prime" (that is, around thirty or so) vie with the intimidating younger freelancers who take money out of their pockets and food out of their mouths. However attractive, these "older" women know they can't really compete—for the brutally meager earnings—with the younger workers.

When Jeff and I enter around eleven o'clock, five potential clients—compared with more than fifty sex workers—casually drink and flirt with the women. The small number of people makes the place look empty. After we choose a table in the central sitting area and order drinks, the "older" workers gathered near us begin to make eye contact and motion at the jukebox. I punch in a couple of songs and return to my seat. The women continue to smile at us, gesture with their eyes or head to come over and talk, and they move a bit to the music. This activity continues until a younger, more brash and confident freelancer comes flying into the room. As the younger woman surveys the scene and sweeps through the place examining potential customers, hope visibly drains from the faces of the older women. When we remain seated, and neither of us goes for the hotter property, however, hope returns. This cycle of expectation, frustration, and renewed possibility occurs many times during the first hour we are there. It continues until I strike up a conversation with a worker who has walked over to sit at a booth near me to stake her claim. Throughout this hour, more men and women slowly file into the room; there is no single large influx, but eventually all the tables, booths, and standing spots in the place are filled. Jeff says, "It must be after midnight." I glance at the digital clock by the bar; it reads 00.10.

By this time, I have entered into a conversation with the startling young woman who has moved across the room to sit behind me. She has unusually large, luminous eyes and wears a blue tie-dyed shirt. At her table she was drinking warm tea with milk and looking very bored and discontented. Her air of ennui or despair may have been an honest display of her feelings; or it could have been a part she liked playing to attract a certain clientele. The more I talk with her, however, the more I believe the former to be the case.

Straightaway, I tell her, "I'm married, and I'm not interested in buying you out for the evening"—this despite the fact that I have been making eye contact with her in the hope of getting to talk to her (and thus, in essence, leading her on). She shows disappointment when I tell her that I only want to talk. "I know you're working, so I want to pay you, but just to talk. I'm doing research on tourism and the men who come here on vacation." I hand her a hundred-baht ($4) note, but she places it on the table.

A dry sense of humor colors much of her conversation with me—carried out in bits of combined Thai and English. "How old are you?" I ask. "Sixteen," she replies, which seems plausible.

"How long have you been working in the Thermae?"

She says "Seven years—which answer do you believe?"

After ordering more tea, we talk about her situation. She is a freelancer who works the Thermae and a few other bars. Because she lives far from Sukhumvit, in a notorious slum, she does not work every day. "I make most of the money for my family. My father and brother work some, but they can't get much money. When I come into town, I have to find at least one client each night I work. It's too far. Costs too much to come in."

"Do you like doing this?" I ask.

She shakes her head no. "It's terrible, but the money is good—much more than doing anything else. And my family depends on me. Without my money, no food, no house, nothing."

"What do you think about the men? Do you like them? Are they nice to you?"

"Once I felt love—for a young man from the Netherlands. He took me to the beach for two, three weeks. We did not have sex. I wanted to—the only time I ever wanted to. After we got back to Bangkok, he left. He promised to write me, but nothing. He was very gentle, very kind. He had a good heart—cared about me, what I felt, what I needed."

She never mentions money during our conversation unless I bring it up. She asks some questions about my research. While we speak, she often runs her hands though her hair and strokes my hands.

I cut short our conversation. "It's 1:00 A.M. on a Monday. I know you have to work, but I liked talking to you very much. Here's some money for your time." I give her 500 baht ($20), which is about what she would earn for a "short-time" with a client. At first, she refuses the money. "Please take it. You're working, and I took your time."

She finally accepts the money and holds the note in her hand. "I want you to buy me out for tonight. Will you? I want to go with you," she asks. I decline. Her pleading eyes cut me to the quick. Even knowing I was not interested in sex, she probably knows it would be much nicer to sleep in a hotel than at home. Also, despite my protestations to the contrary, she must assume that since I am a male, I could probably be persuaded into procuring her services, should we spend the night together, and thus increase her chance of revenue enhancement. Still, I decline. She pushes the money back toward me as I stand up.

I return to the table where Jeff is engaged in conversation with several workers. They are laughing a great deal and having a good time, especially because Jeff's Thai is very good. We confer for a bit and decide to leave. About this time, a *farang* male who had earlier captured everyone's attention reenters the bar. His AIDS-emaciated frame and face make him appear like a manifestation of the Grim Reaper *sans* scythe. He looks over the crowd, speaks loudly to himself, and leaves the room. We leave, too, but Jeff stops at the bathroom on the way out. As I stand in the parking lot waiting for him, the young sex worker with whom I had spoken for more than an hour hovers near the doorway, casting importunate glances in my direction. Then the skeleton reappears in a faint shaft of light; he drums his fingertips together and mutters to himself as he gazes at the moon. From around the corner, the chastising banter of a sex worker remarkably skilled at various English-language accents, especially Australian, echoes across the dark space. I stand there in the parking lot among prostitutes growing increasingly desperate (the imploring gaze of one boring right through me), taxi drivers sleeping on the hoods of their cars awaiting fares, the skeleton speaking nonsense into the night sky, and former prostitutes turned food vendors jeering at this AIDS-crazed ghost of clients past.

7

THE UNSPEAKABLE

Knowledge is not itself power, although
it is the magnetic field of power. Ignorance and opacity collude or compete
with it in mobilizing the flows of energy,
desire, goods, meanings, persons.
—Eve Kosofsky Sedgwick,
"Privilege of Unknowing"

Paulo Freire invented the term "the culture of silence" to describe the condition in which the impoverished majority
of the world's people are living—power-
less, and with little access to means of
communication.... There is also the
silence and ignorance in which the
affluent minority of the world is kept.
—Guy Brett, *Through
Our Own Eyes*

In the societies of which we are speaking, ... areas of avoidance or repression have typically included questions
of race and sex.... Out of personal

avoidance comes the possibility of
political repression.
—Ranjit Chatterjee, "After Privacy:
Linguistic Reflections on the
Personal and the Political"

There is no binary division to be made
between what one says and what one
does not say; we must try to determine
the different ways of not saying such
things.... There is not one but many
silences and they are an integral part
of the strategies that underlie and permeate discourses.
—Michel Foucault, *The History
of Sexuality*

If the external representations of the nightlife in Bangkok and the tourists'
experience of this nightlife are characterized by abundance, including discursive
abundance, then paucity best describes the internal discourse about the sex
industry. Two anecdotes in Chapter 1, however, provide rare instances in which
the silence was broken. One recounted the reportage of a young prostitute's
murder in the south of the country, and the trial and conviction of police officers
implicated in the crime. The other told of an incident that occurred at a conference in Pattaya, at which a highly placed academic at one of the major public
universities criticized current Thai university curricula for ignoring contemporary issues. In particular, this scholar questioned why students learn ancient
Thai history in detail but are kept ignorant of policies, strategies, and systemic
forces that have cohered in such a way as to make Pattaya, the site of the conference, one of the major destinations in the international sex industry. Both
instances arouse our interest in what is speakable in public discourse and what is
not, leading us to speculate about what happens when various phenomena cannot be addressed in the public forum and what happens when they can be.

The murder of a sex laborer in a nation so dominated by prostitution, though
horrific, did not come as much of a surprise. The surprise came when the story
was widely reported in the national media and the crime tracked from investigation to sentence. Shockingly, the story did not get lost in the void of silence that
surrounds the sex industry in both its international and indigenous dimensions.
The fact that public discourse was able to address this particular incident led
directly to the prosecution and conviction of the two policemen involved in the
murder, along with two others convicted of the crime. Similarly, in the summer
of 1994, four teenaged prostitutes in Hat Yai police custody drank poison and
committed suicide to avoid being sent home; again the Thai papers covered this
story. So, such stories about the plight of sex workers have recently entered the

national debate and political discussions—albeit to a small degree—and shed unaccustomed light on how willed unknowing and silence can allow abuses to be perpetuated. Hundreds, perhaps thousands, of similar incidents in the past were quietly kept out of public discourse through the shroud of silence and conspiracy of denial that operate with regard to the exploitation of rural women by the sex industry. Perhaps most important, these particular occurrences reveal what happens when an event moves from the constricted areas of the unspeakable to that of the speakable.

When the noted scholar stood up at the Pattaya conference and declared that students in Thailand don't learn why the resort we were in is known outside the nation primarily for prostitution, he spoke publicly about issues that are usually denied, ones considered unspeakable according to most contemporary Thai social norms. That he did so in English and at a conference on current directions in *American* Studies is significant. Speaking in English allowed him the latitude to articulate what cannot be spoken in Thai. His assertion hinted at what Eve Kosofsky Sedgwick (1988) calls the "privilege of unknowing," a privilege built into the educational system, which largely serves those who have profited, no matter how minimally, from policies aligned with international development strategies. That historical inquiry generally breaks off prior to the modern era means that students are allowed—in fact, encouraged—to cultivate an "ignorance" with regard to certain factors that operate in the country's development policies.

This ignorance creates the conditions necessary for the emergence of what we call "cultural aphasia," a willed inability within a culture to allow for the articulation of certain ideas, the loss of a discursive or linguistic center for addressing particular issues. In no way are we limiting these occurrences to Thailand; indeed, we would argue that in all cultures and nations this will-to-ignorance allows certain social and economic relations and interactions to be continued. Cultures vary widely, however, as to what falls into these discursive voids, and at the conference the ability to use English in a forum at which U.S. scholars and writers were engaged in critical evaluation of their own national, cultural, and institutional practices gave the courageous academic the impetus and the "cover" to speak about the constitution of "institutional ignorance" and some of its consequences within his own nation.

Those anecdotes help us frame other stories and theoretical positions and to raise questions addressed in this chapter: What is unspeakable at any given moment within a culture and why? How is the unspeakable constituted as such? What are the effects of the unspeakable on a given culture? What are the relationships between the unspeakable and public discourse, especially in regard to globalization processes and issues of power and tradition? What happens when the unspeakable eventually enters public discourse as speakable? How do the gaps between unspeakable and speakable, as well as private and public discourse, manifest themselves at any given moment? How does the unspeakable emerge as "cultural aphasia," and what are its effects? How does the unspeak-

able interact with the "privilege of unknowing," or "ignorance," as an epistemological site operative within a culture?[1]

Modernization and Public Discourse in Thailand

It may be useful at this point to remember the powerful vectors of "modernity,"
"modernization," and "development" of the nation-state that have dominated
public discourse in Thailand—a push toward Westernization begun in the middle of the nineteenth century with King Mongkut (who hired Anna Leonowens). During the age of modernization, particularly from 1947 on, virtually
anything tending toward Western, capitalist, democratic nationhood (including
industrialization and technological achievement) has been held as almost universally good. As with the projects of colonization and modernization in other
parts of the world, the discourse of development in Thailand often included
notions of leaving behind what Anne McClintock calls "anachronistic space,"
the "prehistoric, atavistic, and irrational" that are "inherently out of place in the
historical time of modernity" (1995, 40). Traditional values were often cast as
occupying this space, and Western ideas of industrialization and capitalism
became equated with modernization.

Only minimal critiques of the abstractions of development emerged, and
these came from Buddhism and Marxism. Those derived from Buddhism were,
for the most part, respectfully ignored; those from Marxism were demonized—
profitably so—by the various military dictators in the post–World War II years.
The brief moments in which public critiques of these processes were possible
(between 1955 and 1958 and again from 1973 to 1976) invariably ended in massive right-wing retaliation and violence. As a result, the discursive space that
questioned these international and national forces was constantly assaulted,
traumatized, and erased.

The post-1947 era saw Thailand swing from wartime support of Japan to
complete acceptance of and desire for American hegemony in the region during
the Cold War. As a result, the public discourse of development and modernization was dominated by the Cold War mentality and its attendant binarisms:
democracy versus communism, freedom versus totalitarianism, free market
economics versus state control of economic forces. These were respectively
considered ultimate goals and ultimate evils, with little contradiction, until the
mid-1970s. Just as the Cold War opposition to Communism in the U.S. had little
to do with Marxist theory, ideology, or economics, the official Thai response cast
Communism as "the enemy of the Nation, Religion (Buddhism), and Monarchy"; it was "Enemy Number One of Thainess" (Winichakul 1993, 69). The
United States aided this discourse ideologically, financially, and materially as it
increasingly cast Thailand as a bulwark of "the Free World" in a region rife with
unrest. During the Vietnam War the nation became a "landlocked aircraft carrier" for the United States. As noted in Chapter 4, the infusion of U.S. military

personnel and support set the stage for the urban, Western boom of the latter part of this century. But the foundation for this massive social sea change was laid—legally, discursively, and intellectually—much earlier.

The reign of King Vajiravudh (Rama VI), 1910–25, ushered in an era of new (Western) literary genres—particularly the political essay—led by the Oxford-trained king who himself published a wide array of articles, essays, plays, and morality tales under numerous pseudonyms. The theme that dominated his writings was "modernity . . . encouraging, even exhorting, people to act and live as modern people in the West did" (Wyatt 1982, 228). King Vajiravudh's vision of the "Thai Nation" intimately connected itself with the drive to Westernization. He formulated the trinity of "nation, religion, and monarchy"—each with its own Western ideological avatar—that has so dominated Thai public discourse and political "common sense" throughout this century, a trinity consistently invoked by any dictator or group seeking to seize and hold power (Wyatt 1982, 224–307; Anderson 1985, 12–40). After changing the name of the country from Siam to Thailand ("land of the free") in 1939 for nationalistic reasons, the media-savvy prime minister Phibun issued a series of Cultural Mandates "aimed at uplifting the national spirit and moral code of the nation and instilling progressive tendencies and 'newness' into Thai life" (qtd. in Wyatt 1982, 255). In these mandates, "progress" and "newness" were narrowly defined as those Western ideals being exported for consumption abroad. Amidst the Cold War *Zeitgeist* that dominated the second Phibun government and the brutal Sarit regime, the 1952 anti-Communist Law—a return of similar but ineffective laws passed in 1933—codified the rhetoric of the era and gave the government wide powers to suppress any oppositional voices (Girling 1981,187–230). The rationale behind this act—modeled on un-American activities legislation, so Thongchai Winichakul argues—"was that Communism is un-Thai in its ideas and ways of life" (1994, 6). With this law, any criticism of Western ideals (no matter their local application or effect on the population) became legally unspeakable, punishable by prison, torture, or death. Such lessons about linguistic practice and their social consequences over an extended period of time are not easily shed; they become an integral part of the discursive landscape and political-social-cultural mentality.

The main goal of Sarit's autocracy (1959–63) was to attract foreign (read, American) capital. To this end, besides instigating the anti-Communist Law, he banned all labor union activities and strikes, heavily censored the press, and allowed tax-exempt purchases of land by foreign companies. Girling calls this shift in governmental resources "the task of developing *public* infrastructure for the use of *private* enterprise" (1981, 81). The period thus witnessed a massive disjunction between the language of development for the many and the materialization of wealth for the few. Coming as it did after a brief period of relative openness in which there had been a momentary proliferation of literature aimed at social issues and the problems resulting from development, the years Sarit occupied the office of prime minister came to be known in Thailand as *Yuk*

Thamin, or "the cruel, violent times." So complete was the erasure of oppositional voices, Benedict Anderson argues, that at this time "a kind of cultural
amnesia overtook Thai intellectual life" (1985, 19). This amnesia wiped out the
discursive ability to critique what was happening to the nation and helped instill
the "cultural aphasia" that continues largely to define and delineate current
public debate in the kingdom.

Sarit's legacy long outlived him. His Anti-Communist Law was reinvoked
during the repressive 1976 response to the three-year period of cultural openness that saw students and intellectuals leading the way toward a substantial
reevaluation of the nation's direction in the wake of the American shift in policy
with regard to the region. In response to these challenges to what had been
unquestionable for so long, the right-wing *Nawaphon* (New Force movement)
emerged. Under the frequently invoked banner of "nation-religion-monarchy,"
this group characterized students, rural peasants (who had never shared in the
wealth of development), factory workers (again, a largely excluded community),
and anyone with socialist or communist leanings as enemies of the commonweal
and the trinity of ideals necessary for Thailand to remain free. As a result, students were burned to death and opposition leaders hanged from Democracy
Monument by right-wing paramilitary groups, including the National Border
Police. Famous Thai activist Sulak Sivaraska, whose left-wing bookstore was
destroyed in the violence, comments on this moment: "Up until 1973, we were
told we were the last of free lands. We had to fight the communists and believe
in Americanism and consumerism. . . . In 1976, the military came back to power
with the blessings of the Americans and the Japanese and began killing our students" (qtd. in Titmuss 1993, 160–61). The traumas that can cause aphasia manifested themselves in actions and in laws. After the suppression of critical voices
in 1976, prosecutions for *lèse-majesté* began in earnest as yet another means of
legally controlling public discourse.

During the 1973–76 period of national reevaluation and upheaval, various
groups previously excluded from the public discussion of the nation and its
direction attempted to reformulate the vocabulary, tropes, and rhetoric for discussing the state that had been firmly in place from King Vajiravudh on. Their
linguistic practices of dissent questioned all that the public at large had been led
to believe held the nation together. As Benedict Anderson remarks, "One must
imagine Thai students discussing in their parents' presence a Siamese nineteenth century *not in terms* of the great King Rama V, but of the commercializa-
tion of agriculture, the growth of compadre communities, foreign penetration,
bureaucratic aggrandizement, and so forth. Simply to *use a vocabulary* of social
processes and economic forces was to refuse the centrality of Thai monarchs as
heroes in or embodiments of national history"(Anderson 1977, 22, emphasis
added). But in 1976, the discursive practices of national critique were cast into
the black hole of cultural aphasia illustrated by the pendulum-like movements
of the lynched bodies swaying from Democracy Monument.[2]

In the face of the massive incursion of U.S. military personnel, infrastructure support, and capital that occurred in the 1960s—"the proliferation of hotels, restaurants, movie houses, supermarkets, night clubs, and massage parlors generated by the torrential flow of white businessmen, soldiers, and tourists" (Anderson 1977, 15)—denigrating such apparent wealth and growth, and what *caused* it, would have been tantamount to insanity, if not treason. Not only did massive U.S. aid affect local, village-level economies, but the influx of capital worked inversely on a national scale; imagine the local, immediate impact played out severalfold at the national level. This infusion of cash, though, created the reality of wealth for a few while also generating a desire for, along with a belief in the realization of, such wealth for the many. Modernization came to highlight money, wealth, and materialism in Thai society to such an extent that sociologists Sawai Simekarat and Somsak Sivaluk have argued, "The Thai people perceive money and all other forms of wealth and property . . . as the most important and desirable aspects of life" (qtd. in Girling 1986, 142). Hyperbolic though this assertion may be, it certainly reveals the sort of reception any alternative opinions were likely to confront. Lurking on the other side of this coin is the oppression received by the opposition, as Sulak Sivaraska reminds us: "In this country, consumerism came along with anti-Communism. If you use such concepts as communalism or communal farming, then you can be accused of being a communist" (qtd. in Titmuss 1993, 159), an accusation with severe legal ramifications. It is important to remember the historical reception of oppositional voices within the nation over the last century and a half—the reception of any criticism of the specific notions of development and modernization proffered by the state—and to realize the aphasia that swallowed any attempts at the articulation of dissent.

Benedict Anderson has proposed that partly because of a common colonial past, "most Southeast Asian countries have inherited a political vocabulary and rhetoric that is essentially radical-populist, if not left-wing, in character. It is very hard to find anywhere, except perhaps the Philippines, a calm, self-confident conservative ideology: indeed, since the nineteenth century, conservative ideology has been in epistemological shock and on the political defensive, its nationalist credentials deeply suspect. In Siam, mainly because the country escaped direct colonial control, the situation had been, until recently, almost exactly the reverse" (Anderson 1977, 20–21).[3] If Anderson's assertion is correct, and we think it is, then the discourse of critique in Thailand has been absent from the start, incapable of being articulated, much less heard. Or so it seems, especially if one refers to the bulk of Thai historical studies. The oppositional forces would have to be the masses against the elite, not the colonized against colonizers. This is the rub. As a strictly intranational phenomenon, resistance discourse of this ilk could not materialize according to received notions of "Thainess" (cf. Winichakul 1994; Reynolds 1991). Thais, being Thais, would not criticize the nation or the ruling elite. The domestic discourse about the modern nation-state does not allow it. If a Thai *should* critique national policy—that is, disrupt or reconsider the juggernaut of narrowly defined modernization—then the ideas are attributed to outside forces (Winichakul 1994; Reynolds 1991). The attribution to external forces reveals this mode of cultural aphasia as trauma, enforced by a battery of laws and attendant social beliefs. Because no Thai *would* articulate the unspeakable, no Thai *could*. To attempt such an articulation is to risk being taken for the social dysfunctionals as which aphasics are cast.

Perhaps no one better embodies the unspeakable than the radical poet-historian Jit Poumisak, whose mysterious death in 1965 and magnificent critiques of contemporary Thai politics and economics made him an outlaw hero of the 1970s student movement. The recouping of Jit led left-wing intellectuals to pursue information about his shadowy and elusive life. At Chulalongkhorn University, from which Jit had been expelled, researchers for an early biography were not allowed to refer to him by name but only by his various pseudonyms and the third-person pronoun *khao*. The text's editors in response highlighted this unspeakable name, or rather the unspeakability of the name, by printing the pronoun in large, boldfaced type (Reynolds 1987, 16). Suchat Sawatsi argues that the 1970s opposition forces gave Jit a privileged place in their intellectual lineage because of the mystery surrounding him and the censored knowledge his name represents. As late as 1987, Jit's poem "Mother" could still not be published in its entirety, leading Craig Reynolds to claim that "authority still uses the author Jit Poumisak to determine what can and cannot be said" (1987, 17).[4]

Theatricality and Cultural Aphasia

Though we have been speaking primarily about the discursive practices of what may seem like direct political critique, the unspeakable, as hinted above, in fact extends well into other areas of cultural behavior, and Thailand certainly is not alone in this regard. To critique virtually any aspect of modernization as defined by monetary wealth and materialism is to risk uttering the unspeakable. In this sense of the term, the unspeakable operates as social decorum and appropriateness, as well as reputation or face saver. In particular, and this may be partially due to decades of media censorship, most evocations of any issue that reflects negatively on the Thai nation are met with refutation or outright denial. Particularly taboo are the monarchy and the sex industry.[5] Although Thais often gossip about both in small groups of intimates, these same people will deny the validity of such utterances in larger groups, especially those composed of their colleagues or people of higher social rank. As might be expected, the government strongly encourages such discursive deceptions: hence the perpetuation of cultural aphasia. Speaking the unspeakable draws attention to "a hidden order underlying industrial modernity: the conquest of the sexual and labor power of colonized women" (McClintock 1995, 3) which the nation wants its citizens to ignore.

In contrast with what followed the events that open this chapter, when the unspeakable became speakable, the standard public discursive response to any external mention of the sex industry in Thailand is to relegate it to the unspeakable.[6] Sedgwick argues that "in the theatrical display of an already *institutional-ized ignorance* no transformative potential is to be looked for" (1990, 78). The response to these external references to the sex industry on the part of the government (read here as "institutional ignorance") is nothing if not theatrical, in that the gestures are grand and the language bombastic. Ironically, the official Thai response casts as unspeakable that which is most egregiously speakable in international public discourse about the nation: the sex industry. Two very recent events neatly exemplify this point: the response by the Tourist Authority of Thailand (TAT) to postings on the Internet, and the response by the Kingdom's chargé d'affaires in the United States to the Don't! Buy! Thai! campaign initiated by Andrew Vachss.

A story from the *Nation* (Bangkok), 21 April 1995, tells that Thailand, like many countries, is listed on the World Sex Guide (WSG)—a website that includes some of the materials we have cited in this book, and the TAT, thinking there was only one, identified as the author a particular individual who had actually never posted anything on the WSG. Niti Khongrut, the director of TAT, issued a public request that this material be removed from the net and that the author be officially classified as persona non grata by the Interior Ministry. Thus categorizing the alleged author made it possible for immigration authorities to arrest him should he try to enter the country. Simple repression is bad enough, but it becomes ridiculous when applied to the wrong person. Niti stated that the Foreign Ministry, the National Security Council, and Internal Security Organizations Command would "blacklist writers of work" that has negative impact on the country's image or security. Niti claimed that although prostitution does exist, the venues trick the TAT by fronting as restaurants or karaoke bars or barbershops. (There is a certain irony in having TAT officials provide a list of the very venues that supposedly trick them, and the irony becomes greater when the TAT is apparently still unable to locate them.) Nevertheless, under the scenario outlined by Niti, it remains possible for the government to silence by force of law those who speak about the unspeakable, reminding one that the ghost of Sarit still haunts governmental practice.

Vachss's movement, Don't! Buy! Thai! (D!B!T!), initiated in 1995, attempted to link national social policy directly to international economic policy by urging a boycott of goods made in Thailand because, in his estimation, the Thai government refused to intervene adequately in child prostitution. He held this opinion despite the Chuan administration's attempt to make this particular aspect of the sex industry an explicit target. According to Vachss, the boycott would exert pressure on the Thai government to implement existing laws against child prostitution. The bill toughening these laws and the penalties on procurers, brothel operators, and parents who sell their children into sex slavery, passed in April 1996 by the Thai Lower House of Parliament, showed the efficacy of this pressure—if only in prompting the passage of legislation and creating the appearance of doing something. But Vachss's movement, aided by his Batman novel (1995) and comic books, was loudly and publicly condemned by the Thai chargé d'affaires in the U.S. He claimed that Vachss had unjustly focused on Thailand for this practice and that his movement would adversely affect the economy of the nation. In reference to the David Hechler article (1995) on child sex tourism that serves as the coda for Vachss's novel and is included in the comic book, the chargé d'affaires wrote that "Mr. Hechler is also reinforcing very offensive, damaging and untrue stereotypes about Thai women and girls whose status and role have always been recognized and honored in Thai history and culture" (ctd. on the D!B!T! homepage). Official Thai response once again largely followed the lines of public denial and accusations that the international popular media were demonizing the country.

The same claims were made against a recent edition of the Longman dictionary, a new version of a CD-ROM encyclopedia, and a Japanese how-to manual about the Thai sex industry. In each case, the Thai government invoked the epistemological space of "ignorance" to perpetuate a situation in which dialogue about a given issue is unsustainable. In fact, it could reasonably be argued, especially given the glacial pace of most legislative processes that concern sensitive matters, the recent get-tough laws on child prostitution had much more to do with the several-year attempt by the Chuan administration to make the unspeakable practice of child prostitution something to be discussed in the public arena. The effort of that administration forced Thais to speak about a problem that they had hitherto been prohibited from addressing. When an issue is moved from the unspeakable to the speakable, "institutional ignorance" becomes increasingly difficult to maintain, and the possibility of transformation is created.

Still, when *The Longman Dictionary of Language and Culture* (1993) defined Bangkok as "famous for its temples and other beautiful buildings" but also mentioned it as a place where there are a lot of prostitutes, it brought cries of outrage from the Thai government and in the Thai media, accompanied by attacks on the integrity of the dictionary's main editor. Meanwhile, the most recent version of the *Microsoft CD-ROM Encyclopedia* described Bangkok as a flesh trade center, and the Japanese book *Thailand Night Zone Guidebook* provided prospective Japanese sex tourists with all the information they would need to exploit the industry's offerings fully during their stay. The publishers of all three received official protests from the Foreign Ministry, accusing them of spoiling the image of Thailand and banning their sale in the country. About the Japanese book, however, Naiyana Supapung, a lawyer at the Friends of Thai Women Workers in Asia (FOWIA), said, "It's not as if no one here knows about the sex industry. Approaching the issue [in the government's] manner makes us blind to the problems that actually exist in this country. . . . What the book says is true" (*Bangkok Post*, 3 February 1995, international edition). The FOWIA spokesperson explicitly points out the "institutional ignorance" operative in the governmental response, as well as its result: a blindness or an aphasia, a space unthinkable because it cannot be spoken of.

On 10 February 1996 the international edition of the *Bangkok Post* ran an editorial chastising the government for its standard response, saying that the state was using the foreign media as scapegoats invoking national dignity rather than addressing the country's problems: "How many more times will the Government have to issue protests to defend the country's honour? And for how long will the public tolerate the continued farce perpetrated by members of the Government in falling back on national dignity as a means of avoiding the real issue of the flesh trade?"

Although the theatrical display of "institutional ignorance" is certainly operative here, we see that it operates in select areas. Not all possible offenses to the nation's dignity are necessarily objected to and castigated. The editorial pointed out that the encyclopedia also invokes AIDS, pollution, traffic problems, and urban congestion as threats to Bangkok's well-being and the encyclopedia attributes these problems to "the lack of commitment on the Government's part in a rush towards becoming an industrialised country. The Kader toy factory fire [in which many employees died because of unsafe working conditions] was also mentioned as an indicator of the Government's lack of concern towards the safety of factory workers. It is interesting to note that the Government has only picked up on the problem of the flesh trade to use in its protest against the Microsoft encyclopedia." It is very interesting, indeed, but hardly surprising. The connection between nationhood and womanhood—the nation-state as a feminine figure, especially one that embodies purity—has long been a part of the modern nation's store of rhetorical tropes (see Chatterjee 1993; McClintock 1995; and Spurr 1993, among others). Like those of women in the sex industry, though, the working conditions of laborers have long been unspeakable, as the repression of unions that has sporadically operated in the nation and the lack of coverage of these conditions in the Thai media make evident—yet the administration did not express outrage at the encyclopedia's placing blame for those problems squarely on the government's shoulders, instead offering indignant scorn for the supposed tarnishing of Thai women's reputation. This response allows governmental culpability in the manifold problems besetting the nation to lapse into "ignorance."

Additionally, the TAT rarely mentions in its literature the realities of Bangkok that make the logistics of movement (not to mention breathing) very difficult. No external representations of these problems irritates the government nearly as much as the representation of the nation as the world's brothel, even though both issues are connected with "pollution" of one kind or another. And although it may be understandable why the latter appellation creates official anxiety and negative reactions, the government has nonetheless actively promoted the sex industry and helped create the conditions necessary for its proliferation, as Vice-Prime Minister Booncha Rajanasthian's statement encouraging "disgusting and embarrassing" acts "related to sexual pleasure" for the good of tourism (cited earlier) exemplifies. Displays of denial, to the extent of banning authors and books that report what everyone knows to be true about the culture and nation, point to a deeper problem: cultural aphasia. If certain issues are made unspeakable, and any articulation of these issues (even by legal fiat or vio-

lence) denied, the situation cannot possibly change. The unspeakable allows for
the perpetuation of inequitable if not abusive treatment of some while permitting those who directly or indirectly benefit from the exploitation to live in privileged ignorance. Although ignorance has a connotation of passivity, to ignore
something is not a passive act; it requires volition.

The Unspeakable and Cultural Aphasia

The Greek term *aphasia* means not only dysfunctional language use—that is,
the loss of the ability to articulate ideas in ways understandable to others, the
loss of a linguistic "center" shared by a larger community—but also by extension of its verbal form, it also means the unspeakable. Etymologically, then, the
linguistic dysfunctions of aphasia are related to—sometimes the equivalents of
—that which is denied discursive enunciation. We have been speaking of a
metaphorical "cultural aphasia" that bears strong resemblance to literal aphasia,
as defined by psycholinguists, psychologists, and neurolinguists. This cultural
aphasia embodies the aspects of cultural practice that are unspeakable and
manifest themselves as such at both cultural and individual levels. Un-
speakablity emerges for multiple reasons—politeness, notions of privacy, and
political or legal censure among them. In one respect, as illustrated earlier with
Anderson's hypothesis, the language to express the unspeakable simply does
not exist in Thai culture, hence its unspeakability. Yet in another respect the
language to express the unspeakable does exist but is not understandable by the larger discursive community, itself both defining and defined by various social relations. Therefore one who utters the unspeakable risks being
labeled linguistically (and thus socially) dysfunctional, if not being directly
ostracized. Whether or not the articulation of the culturally unspeakable is
actually understandable by the larger discourse community becomes a salient
issue because if it is understandable—only interpreted as not being so—then it
allows the "privilege of unknowing" and "ignorance" as an epistemological site
to prevail.

The prevalence of the will-to-ignorance complements the macroeconomic
schizophrenia operative in capitalist relations based on both international and
local exploitation of labor, as manifested in factory, domestic, and construction
work. Privilege emerges from the power to ignore exploitation, and exploitation
occurs because of the ability (and privilege) of ignorance. Cultural aphasia ren-
ders enunciations about exploitation, or abuse, impossible, and it perpetuates
the inequitable power relations operative in "ignorance." The inability to speak
about something makes it all the more difficult to think about that phenomenon
or, to put it another way, makes it easier *not* to think about it. The vectors of
modernity and modernization as they have emerged and continue to operate in
modern Thailand have helped construct and maintain a fiction of orientalist sexuality which has become too lucrative to relinquish. Likewise, then, the interna-

tional sex industry operates within the unspeakable space of cultural aphasia, for to speak of this industry would be to question—and perhaps threaten—the narrowly defined discourse of modernization adopted by the nation. It should come as no surprise that the unspeakable complements and cooperates with the eminently speakable discourses of progress and development. But the extent to which cultural aphasia causes the unspeakable to determine and become the unthinkable, in *any* culture at any moment, should give us pause, for it reveals the extent to which ignorance—perhaps even more than knowledge—determines our cultural topography and the social traffic within it.

The space of ignorance—institutional, societal, or individual—that we have been invoking owes a great deal to the theoretical work of Eve Kosofsky Sedgwick, who attempts to place ignorance in a relation to knowledge and power very different from the one that our inherited "common sense" normally dictates. Rather than understanding ignorance as some dark jungle of the mind or of a culture which needs to be overcome by the valiant efforts of the learned, or as a vast void to be filled by knowledge, Sedgwick argues that ignorance is "a weighty and occupied and consequential epistemological space" (1990, 77). As such, ignorance and silence operate hand in glove with knowledge and (or as) power. Sedgwick explains what follows from such a reconsideration of ignorance:

> If *ignorance* is not—as it evidently is not—a single Manichean, aboriginal man of darkness from which the heroics of human cognition can occasionally wrestle facts, insights, freedoms, progress, perhaps there exists instead a plethora of *ignorances*, and we may begin to ask questions about the labor, erotics, and economics of their human production and distribution. Insofar as ignorance is ignorance of a knowledge (a knowledge that may itself, it goes without saying, be seen as either "true" or "false" under some regime of truth), these ignorances, far from being pieces of the originary dark, are produced by and correspond to particular knowledges and circulate as part of particular regimes of truth (1988, 104).

Obviously, then, ignorances are ignorances about systemic forces at play in a given culture at a given moment in history. Ignorance as an epistemological site relates to cultural aphasia inasmuch as that which one does not think about cannot be articulated, and vice versa. The ideology of language and discursive practices results from their usage in the public sphere. Individuals who live within these linguistic codes learn them from the discourse communities they are part of. Likewise, the linguistic code—as Nietzsche, Wittgenstein, and Merleau-Ponty, among others, have argued—emerges historically from past "successful" uses of language. "This places crucial emphasis on the role of memory—both individual and 'collective'— . . . for the successful production of meaning in utterance" (Holland 1993, 33). Given the historical trajectory of modernization in Thailand delineated in this chapter, one punctuated by violence and trauma at moments in which systemic critique attempted to enter the public discursive arena, and given the powerful—indeed, hegemonic—discourse of modernity, it seems quite understandable that Thai culture should become aphasic with regard to language and concepts critical of the nation. The "collective" memory of successful speech allows for certain types of articulation and not others. In accord with this situation, and as both its cause and effect, ignorances become institutionalized to perpetuate particular cultural practices under the guise of ideological certainties, such as the nation's embrace of development, progress, tradition, religion, the market. The dramatic displays of denial and finger-pointing that have become the Thai government's typical *modus operandi* in responding to external articulations of the sex industry can be more easily understood when placed within these contexts.

In what has been presented above, we have already begun tracing the questions about "the labor, erotics, and economics" of the "human production and distribution" of ignorances, as Sedgwick suggests (Sedgwick 1988, 104). To complement these questions, we can return to one of our own: What happens when the unspeakable becomes the speakable? This is the crucial question. In the North American context, where some twenty-five years ago spousal or child abuse could not be spoken of in the public sphere, targets of this abuse suffered in silence and isolation while those who inflicted it were protected by the institutional ignorance and cultural aphasia that cast such actions as "private matters" not speakable in polite society. Once these private acts were forced into the public arena and could be spoken about there, those who suffered from them found increasing institutional support and help. As Ranjit Chatterjee argues, "The linguistic ideology of privacy provides the grounds, the unconscious justification, for unethical actions, those one wants to hide or [is] ashamed of" (1994, 14). Thus, a government may respond to external critique by claiming that the matters criticized are internal matters (public within the nation, but private within an international context). Such institutional ignorances invoking right to privacy and emerging as unspeakable phenomena, can lead to social exclusion, suppression, and repression. Sedgwick asserts that "it is only with this understanding that the political concept of a fight against sexual ignorance can make sense: a fight not against originary ignorance, nor for originary innocence, but against *the killing pretense that a culture does not know what it knows*" (1988, 121; emphasis added). "This killing pretense," "this privilege of unknowing," this will-to-ignorance, this cultural aphasia leads to the rather unremarkable claim that we are making about unspeakability and what it allows through containment and concealment: the exploitation, if not outright abuse, of others. Rendering the unspeakable speakable makes such exploitation more difficult to maintain.

Speaking the Unspeakable: Two Counterdiscursive Texts

To test this assertion, we can turn to two textual attempts at articulating the unspeakable within the Thai context of modernization. One is a novel from the late 1930s, and the other is a 1990 collection of investigative articles. Both texts, written by women, speak openly about the social conditions of the underclass during moments of hypermodernization.

As a small girl in the first decades of the twentieth century, Kanha Watana-phat watched the flow of human traffic in and out of a brothel that stood across from her home and behind a famous Bangkok temple.[7] Like Anna Leonowens in the century before her, Kanha resolved to write a book that would describe the "tragic lives" of the women who lived and worked there. Thus, in 1937, during the early stages of the Westernization and modernization period of the Phibun regime, Kanha, under her pen-name K. Surangkhanang, offered pub-lishers her third novel, scandalously titled *The Prostitute* (*Ying khon chua*). The title alone was enough to cause outright rejection by many, certain that the book must contain immoral and pornographic content. Scandalized that a woman from a "good" family would write such a book, some publishers advised Kanha to follow the tradition of didactic poetry for young women, as exemplified by *Suphasit son ying*, which teaches modesty and female subservience to males. Others suggested that she write "cookery books or manuals on child care" (Smyth 1994, vi). Anticipating such objections on the part of the larger reading public, Kanha wrote in the introduction to the first edition of the novel, "Why should I have to write a story about people who are always praised as being good when goodness, even if it is difficult to find among prostitutes, has not yet com-pletely disappeared?" (qtd. in Smyth 1994, vi). Phibun's modernization plans, replete with its Cultural Mandates, did not anticipate the textual practice of someone like Kanha.

The novel tells the tale of Reun, a young woman lured from a rural area by a brothel procurer. The young man professes love and uses the same seductive arguments about the difference between rural and urban life that are deployed today. Just as with rural women in contemporary Thailand, Reun is faced with limited choices that do not match the rewards promised by the public discourse of modernization and development. Placed in bonded servitude to pay back room and board fees with massive interest, Reun becomes a prostitute. One of her clients, Wit, hails from an aristocratic family; they fall in love and plan to marry. Before this can occur, Wit is sent by his family to study abroad. Unknown to him, Reun is pregnant with his child. Work in the brothel thus becomes impos-sible for her, and she finds employment as a domestic. Driven from that job after being recognized by a former client who visits the family that has hired her, she moves in with her friend from the brothel, and they try to raise the child together. Increasingly desperate for cash, they return to their former business. The friend dies, forcing Reun to pay an elderly couple to rear her child while she plies her trade as much as she can. Her health declines and, as her own demise approaches, she accidentally meets Wit, who has married a woman of his own class and at first does not recognize his former and much transfigured love. In a paean to the ineluctable power and truth of patrilineal eugenics, Kanha has Wit's wife recog-nize the biological imperative of male lineage, and the couple takes the child to rear as their own, creating a "happy ending": the young girl is rescued from crush-

ing poverty, and Reun—the tragic prostitute with the heart of gold—can die
peacefully, knowing that she has done the best she could for her child.

The piece certainly reads today like a flirtation with predictable melodrama.
In the Thailand of the 1930s and 1940s, however, this "gripping story," as one
reviewer called it, shocked the public by its open evocation of prostitution. Both
then and now, what might astound readers is the largely unflinching way Kanha
writes about sexual labor as a reality in a market economy, and as a type of work
not morally but socially tainted. (Kanha even visited a brothel with her husband
to get an ethnographic sense of the conditions under which the women worked
and lived, and apparently the oral history of one of the prostitutes there provided the basis for the novel.) Even more astounding was her exposure of the
hypocrisy of Thai culture with regard to its public moral pronouncements and
actual private practices. Kanha asserts that moral character does not necessarily
match social stratification. In her introduction she makes the observation, still
largely opposed in Thai society, that "high-class women may have base minds
just as low-class women may be noble-minded" (qtd. in Smyth 1984, vi).
Indeed, a character in the novel who has the highest official status a woman outside the royal family can possess, that of *khunying* (awarded by the monarch for
individual contributions to bettering society), is depicted as carousing at night
with crowds of young men and as having been a prostitute herself at one time. In
these ways, Kanha publicly spoke not only about an unspeakable industry but
about the hypocritical positions that the unspeakable encourages in the social-
cultural relations of economics, labor, and sexuality.

In fact, the story of Reun and Wit begins with a frame tale in which two
upper-class males, both friends of Wit, meet by accident on a train and discuss
his being in love with a prostitute. Hurtling through space on an international
train and talking of past and present involvements indicative of their class, the
two men are paradigms of the modern Thai male in the Phibun era. Their conversation reveals the distance between appearance and reality, however, as their
moral and ethical positions show them for who they are and reveal how they
must function in the culture. The novel is didactic, though not in the way publishers might have expected or wanted, and the notion of education enters it.
About Wit's frequenting prostitutes, one of the men says, "Everything in life is
an education. Going to prostitutes is one of the lessons" (Surangkhanang 1994,
8). The comment reveals Kanha's thesis that all actions in life provide lessons,
but class dictates and public pronouncements give value to some and not to others—indeed force engagement with some and negate interactions with others—
while simultaneously providing the basis necessary for the upper echelon to
appear morally superior to the lower classes.

The author warns her readers to look for lessons they would not ordinarily
expect from characters not stereotypically laudable in either their textual or cultural tradition. This point emerges straightaway as the two men discuss the falli-
bility of monks and their cynical abuse of the temple as an institution. Both the

monastic order and the temples they run are unquestionably "good" forces in polite, public social discourse, one of the men reminds the other, and such comments might offend people. When his interlocutor responds that he has only been speaking the truth, a warning of discursive censure is the other's reply: "I wasn't arguing about the truth of what you were saying, but truth can cause offense these days" (8–9). The near pairing of prostitutes and monks as conversational topics displays the inversions of social assumptions that Kanha wants to perform. Moreover, she exposes the operations of cultural aphasia by declaiming that the truth about social practices may cause offense and therefore cannot be uttered. In other words, under the prevailing discursive regime, the truth is unspeakable.

Kanha provides social critique at every turn. The brothel's madam proves to be a fine mother with an intelligent son whose education she supports financially and emotionally. Prostitutes turn out to be mostly victims of societal views of women and chastity, as well as victims of exploitative individuals who prey upon the lack of choices available to rural women; they are not, for the most part, immoral and loose as they are popularly portrayed. That a child's fate is determined by social constructs and not by divine ordination is exemplified by Reun's child: if identified as part of her father's family, she will be provided all the benefits allowed the gentry, but as her mother's daughter she is labeled "bastard" and child of a whore. Larger society forgives brothel clients through the silence their actions receive, whereas the women who meet the private demands of these clients are tarred with the brush of public scorn. In each of these cases and many others, the novel throws a wrench into rigid social hierarchies that presume a moral correspondence with class status.

Such cultural presumptions are borne out in the love interest at play in the novel. Reun and Wit have a real love but one socially forbidden, and Reun articulates her position within the culture by asking her love, "But what about other people? . . . They despise me and think I am disgusting." Wit's response tells what cannot be said about sex workers: "Even if you think you're bad and others say you are, that's up to them. Whoever wanted to be a prostitute because they thought selling sex was fun and profitable?" (22). Wit's question forces readers to examine the systemic forces operative in the choices people have and make. It further demands that readers question the all too easy explanations society provides and search for other, not easily articulated or thinkable, explanations.

The brothel becomes the site at which the hypocrisy of social pronouncements and practices is most explicitly revealed. Kanha discusses in detail and publicly speaks about the social elites who not only obtain the services of prostitutes but also set them up as minor wives or as part-time hookers, thus exploiting them in multiple ways. Reun sees royal princes with their princesses by their side being bowed to at public affairs and out on their own for "a bit of fun" the next night. A highly placed judge treated with "awe" by his family turns into a rollicking playmate of the prostitutes inside the brothel. Doctors whose "voices would tremble" as they spoke of "the horrors" of venereal disease prove to be daily customers (159–60). Such critique continues to strike sensitive chords in Thai society even today by articulating the unspeakable. Kanha reveals gaps in public discourse and tries to reinscribe the center erased by cultural aphasia, to expose "the killing pretense that a culture does not know what it knows" before that pretense proves terminal for that culture.

Despite these remarkably brave moves, Kanha remains much a product of her historical moment. Although she constantly emphasizes that the social and cultural nature of economic relations create prostitution—not fate or the inherent moral degradation of the prostitute herself—she undermines her own assertions somewhat by making genetics and the class divisions predicated upon them ultimately win the day. The problem Reun's child faces comes from being the offspring of both an aristocrat and a prostitute. The social condemnations placed on prostitutes will haunt the child, but the haunting will be all the more tragic and poignant if she does not receive her inherited aristocratic rights. Rhetorical and didactic contradictions appear in the story itself (as when the "natural" genetic father-daughter bond appears the moment the two meet), but part of the contradiction emerges from Kanha's own resignation to the importance that Thai society places on paternal bloodlines. That inherited discursive practices and their cultural manifestations prove difficult for even the most aware critics to discern and shake off is attested to by the status of this novel as a document: it has been around for sixty years, and its topic remains largely unspeakable in Thai society today.

The second text, Sanitsuda Ekachai's investigative journalistic articles collected in *Behind the Smile: Voices of Thailand* (1990) examines the effects of development strategies on rural people in Thailand near the end of the twentieth century. During the thirty-some years that have elapsed since the advent of "the American era" in the country, rampant industrialization, land speculation, and resource exploitation have occurred. Sanitsuda's book provides insights into some of the specters that lurk behind the smile of development and economic growth. In essence, she tells stories that run counter to the official versions of the "Thai Economic Miracle," stories usually relegated to cultural aphasia. First published in the *Bangkok Post*, these articles examine the effects of industrialization and tourism on the environment and the rural poor; the working conditions of the factory labor force; the mass exodus of youth from the villages to Bangkok; the impact of land speculation on farmers and government policies on forest use; the changing relationships between rural Thais and the various traditions that have sustained them; and, of course, the effects of the sex industry, particularly on the northern region of the country.

In her introduction to the section of the book titled "Invasion of the North," Sanitsuda delineates the various problems faced by rural communities, often composed of non-Thai minority groups (1990, 125–29). Subsistence farmers confront land shortages that are due to tourism speculation and the growth of agro-industry. Almost half the farming families in the region are forced to cultivate in protected areas, engage in illegal logging, hire themselves out by the day for manual labor, or pursue any means they can to survive in the expanding cash-dominant economy. Village cohesion and cooperation in everything from planting and harvesting to ceremonies such as weddings have become increasingly fragmented as families break up and necessity forces people to find survival opportunities elsewhere. "Northern communities face increasing debt problems because of decreased self-sufficiency, medical bills, consumerism, and investment in modernised agriculture. . . . The debts can only be paid off by sending youth to work in the cities, the young men as hired labourers or construction workers, the women as household servants or prostitutes. Prostitution is a common occupation among young women from certain areas of the North. It has become a major source of income and 'the key to survival' in the modern era" (Ekachai 1990, 128).

Two articles—" 'Go South' Young Girl" and "I Didn't Sell My Daughter"— provide contemporary stories about the sisters of Kanha's Reun, Sudham's Salee, and the women who populate Moore's novels, as well as of the real women encountered in the bars of Bangkok and tourist resorts. The stories of the women from the North parallel those of rural women from all over Thailand. In " 'Go South' Young Girl," one village, Baan Srijomjaeng, stands for rural villages throughout the country. Sanitsuda tells how most of the young girls in the village leave after grade six, around the age of twelve, and head south to major centers of the sex industry—generally with their parents' permission, because the parents have received payment or a loan for their daughters' labor. "The tragedy lies in the fact that Baan Srijomjaeng is no exception. It is just a typical village among thousands in the North" (168). Sanitsuda asks what causes this to occur—is it hunger, poverty or greed? Her article indirectly answers that it is all three, plus many other factors. Prostitution, she explains, provides virtually the only viable means for rural women to keep their families from starving and to purchase some of the amenities that urban dwellers take for granted. Such sacrifice is now considered an act of virtue by many in villages with few prospects: "The houses, paid for by the girls' remittances, are evidence of a daughter's virtue: her readiness to sacrifice herself, her gratitude to her parents, and, more importantly, her success" (171). Throughout the nation, at any place in or near a village where new houses are springing up amid the decay, Sanitsuda claims there is "no need to ask where the money came from" (171).

Nonetheless, she does ask, and she asks a man named Guan in Baan Srijomjaeng. Guan is initially shocked by this insolent question from a stranger about such "a private matter" (172). He and his wife explain that their daughter left at the age of fifteen, the first girl in the village to do so. Her mother claims that she suffered not only constant worry about her daughter's safety but massive anxiety brought on by the communal scorn of the village. "Money stopped the gossip," however; the daughter has now provided many modern accouterments of wealth, including a TV, a refrigerator, and a stereo besides the requisite concrete house.

[Guan] was once a landless peasant, one of those who sat in the back row at village meetings. Now he sits at the front. At social gatherings, he is the one who pays for the drinks.

"Having money is definitely good," [he says]. "It means we don't have to go about asking people for loans. We don't have to go through all that humiliation. . . . Money is definitely good," he reaffirms. His wife nods. In the deadening silence that follows, no one dares contradict him (173).

Not only in the "deadening silence" but also in the aphasic gaps of the larger discourse of modernization would virtually no one, except Sanitsuda, dare contradict Guan's declaration.

She presses her point in the next article, Moon Wonglah's story in "I Didn't Sell My Daughter." As part of the Lua hill-tribe minority, Moon and the others in her village are routinely subjected to racial prejudice and exploitation by corrupt officials. Because they are often unable to make their rice farms pay enough to ensure subsistence, many of the men engage in illegal logging (mostly for influential officials who profit from this enterprise), and young women are encouraged to "go south"—a euphemism for entering prostitution—to help their families out of crushing poverty. Across the North "it takes a girl or two to break the rigid cultural taboo," but "when everyone sees the immediate improvement in living standards that the girls bring to their families, all hell breaks loose, and everyone wants to go" (177). Commodities replace traditional values, as the discourse of development and progress dictate they should.

When Moon's husband was arrested and tossed into prison for illegal wood-cutting, the mother-in-law of a brothel owner living in the village suggested that Moon send her daughter south. Moon breaks down as she tells Sanitsuda of her plight. Operating out of denial, she claims not to have sold her daughter, but only to have accepted a loan, and declares her daughter is washing dishes at a resort. This is why, she claims, she borrowed only 2,000 baht ($80) despite being offered 10,000 baht for the girl. She says the smaller amount was all she needed to buy rice for her other children, and she did not want her daughter to have to work a long time to pay off the money. With the interest charged on such loans, however, 2,000 baht is just as unpayable as 10,000, so the brothel owners always win in these arrangements.

Moon's denial differs substantially from the institutional ignorance that produces cultural aphasia and its exploitive practices. Hers is a defense against a horrific reality; the other is a refusal to accept culpability in the profit-taking that occurs because of that horrific reality. The former aids the latter, however, just as the latter causes the former. The purpose of Sanitsuda's reportage is to explain and expose both, to give voice to those upon whom development does not smile but from whom and at whose expense it receives its ever widening grin. The Land of Smiles is so only for a very few, many of whom are not citizens of the nation, and the smiling mouths seem incapable of speaking about the systemic forces that have made it so only for the very few. What is perhaps most surprising, though, is that Sanitsuda tells the secret—the long-ignored secret that everyone knows but does not admit—not only that prostitution is the "key to survival in the modern era" for many rural families (which is to say, for about 85 per cent of the population) but that woman's-body-as-natural resource has become *the* commodity necessary for the survival of the nation's economy as a whole. The 1993 income from the export of women, according to a Chulalongkorn University study, totaled $20–23 billion, some two-thirds of the Thai national budget (*Bangkok Post*, 15 April 1996). And as the single largest source of foreign currency, tourism provides the nation the means to procure the much-needed fuel resources that keep the engine of industrialization humming. Tourists, as Michele Zack reminds us (1996, 49) "including the unsavory but economically significant sex tourists," contribute significantly to the foreign exchange ledgers.

The texts by Kanha and Sanitsuda speak, in McClintock's terms, about the "abject peoples . . . whom industrial imperialism rejects but cannot do without," who occupy "abject zones" such as red light districts and slums. "In inhabiting the cusp of domesticity and market, industry and empire, the abject returns to haunt modernity as its constitutive, inner repudiation: the rejected from which one does not part" (1995, 72). The subjects of these two texts, the subjects of their unspeakable textual transgressions, are the abject peoples who dwell in the nation's institutional ignorance and cultural aphasia as the rejected results of narrowly delineated modernization policies.

Sanitsuda's book provides open, public contradictions to blanket statements and mechanistic mutterings of the national discourse that pass as unassailable truths. Obviously, this is not to say that she thinks rural people should not have access to wealth and objects that urban Thais expect. Rather, she asks what forces at work in the nation determine that this access can be achieved almost solely through the bonded sexual labor of their daughters. Why is it, she queries, that few if any alternatives exist? Why has modernization, for most of the century, meant that rural women's only chance to partake even minimally in national economic growth has been the sex industry? Such questions cannot be uttered much in the public sphere, which is why it is important to note that Sanitsuda Ekachai's articles and book appeared in the English-language press. Much as it did for the scholar who spoke about the failure of current academic curricula to address the factors that have made Pattaya a site of the international flesh trade, English provided her a means, if not a cover, for speaking about the issues that suffer from cultural aphasia in Thai society and public discursive practices.

On the basis of these two textual attempts at articulation of the unspeakable, we can claim only marginal verification of our thesis that the move from the unspeakable to the speakable makes exploitive situations more difficult to perpetuate. Clearly, no simple causal relationships exist in such a complex situation, and no true predictability can be asserted. Kanha's novel did little, if anything, to alleviate the plight of sex laborers or change their relative status within the culture. In fact, some thirty years after the appearance of her novel, the international aspect of the sex industry exploded onto the scene. Sanitsuda's book, stressing the damaging aspects of development, has had more impact but chiefly in the English-speaking community, which has at least some semblance of cultural/national critique as part of its discursive practices. Her text appeared about the same time that the international community began to discuss AIDS and child prostitution as problems resulting from a laissez-faire approach to the international sex industry. Simultaneously, the Chuan administration admitted in 1995 that prostitution was a serious problem in the nation and promised that the government would take action to curb child prostitution as one means of addressing the larger problems of the sex industry. That the murder of a young prostitute made national news during the time Chuan was in office is indicative, it seems to us, of the power of institutional ignorances and cultural aphasia and the possibly transformative result of moving issues from the unspeakable to the speakable.

The Chuan administration attempted to make speakable the onerous practice called *tok khiew*. This phrase translates literally as "green harvest" but came to mean "pledging a green paddy," and for decades it symbolized the plight of rice farmers. When farmers did not have enough food or money to support their family, they would pledge a paddy not yet ready for harvest to a local rice miller, who paid about half the value of the grain up front to secure the crop at a bargain price. Now, though, *tok khiew* refers to the destitute farmers' pledge for cash of another unripe resource: their prepubescent daughters. Beginning in February 1994 the Chuan administration had branches of the government cooperate with nongovernmental organizations (NGOs) to create public awareness about the issue and to produce possible solutions for it. A television program devoted to social issues brought together politicians, academics, and activists to address the subject. Public policy statements about an unspeakable topic led to its being discussed in an open, popular media forum.

Given the years of secrecy about child prostitution and bonded labor, it is impossible to gauge what effect, if any, this change had on social practices. Clearly a distinction needs to be made between official public discourse and what the public at large feels can be addressed in social gatherings; a topic cannot be made speakable by fiat. Such leads by the government, however, hold promise, although the election of the old-guard Banharn Silpa-archa administration (1995) unfortunately sent the government back to earlier discursive positions. This administration has shown no desire to air the nation's dirty linen or engage in public gossip. From this perspective, both Khana and Sanitsuda *are* gossiping about their culture and nation; they've gone public with private topics and language. Much of the unspeakable circulates in private discourse but does so in the form of gossip. "Serious" gossip, as theorized by Patricia Meyer Spacks, bridges both public and private realms and the speakable and the unspeakable. Gossip traffics between these areas and linguistic practices in a way useful to our concerns here. Though sex and money are the paradigmatic topics of gossip, it also is stereotypically linked with female discursive practices, primarily because of the public disempowerment of women and the devaluing of their utterances. "Serious" gossip, though, creates intimacy and solidarity among subordinated people. "It violates the 'claims of civility,' but it incorporates the possibility that people utterly lacking in public power may affect the views of figures who make things happen in the public sphere" (Spacks 1985, 5–7). Cultural aphasia, in some instances, may be the result of decorum, as we've noted, and breaching the "claims of civility"—that is, speaking about what one is not supposed to speak about—can, in some situations, effect change in the civil, public arena.

Gossip "possesses a double valence: enemy and agent of desire. One explanation for gossip's two faces . . . is its liminal position between public and private" (Spacks 1985, 262). Kanha's and Sanitsuda's texts dwell in this liminal realm, too, by being uncivilly public about what everyone privately knows but publicly proclaims ignorance of. Both authors deploy their texts as enemies of destructive forms of desire by simultaneously being the agents of desire, though not the desire of the status quo. Both are nice girls from good families who have taken it upon themselves to say bad things about the society they live in, to shed the privilege of unknowing, and to gossip about the behavior of international and national policies in the daily lives of many of the country's women. Gossip, says Spacks, "speaks what needs to be said" (263), and perhaps their example can help others say what needs to be said. Spacks argues that gossip "embodies an alternative discourse to that of public life, and a discourse possibly challenging public assumptions. . . . A rhetoric of inquiry, gossip questions the established" (46). The rhetoric of inquiry and critique has often been unspeakable in the development of the Thai nation-state as a modern entity. The gossip of these two texts offers alternatives to the public discourse of modernity that has historically led, in Thailand, to a crushing cultural aphasia about the lived realities of modernization and the sex industry.

SEXUAL THEORY AND ITS DISCONTENTS

A reader (not a publican) takes exception to my ... [statement] that bar
girls/Go Go dancers are exploited.
Among the points he makes ... [is
that] prostitutes who feel they are
being cheated or inhumanely treated by
their employer ... can quit their jobs at
a moment's notice and work elsewhere. Hardly the dictionary definition
of exploitation.
—Bernard Trink "Nite Owl," *Bangkok
Post* (2 March 1996)

Am receiving more letters from readers
disputing that hookers are exploited:
... isn't it the man who is exploited
when he becomes infatuated with a
demimondaine and weds her, whereupon she takes him for everything he's
got? Good points.
—Bernard Trink "Nite Owl," *Bangkok
Post* (9 March 1996)

> Progressive movements currently artic-
> ulate a public and oppositional dis-
> course that inserts the elements of
> history, cultural ideologies, and power
> relations into any analysis of sexuality.
> It is the next challenge for them to cre-
> ate the space for individuals to deter-
> mine how the personal might be
> political in their sex lives.
> —Janice M. Irvine, *Deviant Bodies*

> These men who are involved with pros-
> titution are not nice men. I'll say it just
> like that: every man who goes to a
> prostitute is not a nice man.
> —Ariane Amsberg, Dutch writer and
> sexologist, in *Live Sex Acts*

> If they're old enough to bleed, they're
> old enough to "butcher."
> —Reported U.S. Marine Corps saying
> about young Filipina prostitutes

"The world's oldest profession." Most of the time, prostitution is casually, unthinkingly characterized this way. The effect is supposed to be at once euphemistic and humorous, a wry assertion that commercial sex is so long-established a practice that it constitutes the first known instance of exchange for value received. But not far below the surface of the weary witticism lurk assumptions that are central to the way our culture constructs that market—in general and in its manifestation as sex tourism. Reference to the purportedly ancient origins of prostitution supports the idea that it is ingrained in human behavior—if not, indeed, a natural activity. It is seen as deeply rooted because men's need for sex, a *thing* with which women can supply them, is so powerful that it drove our long-ago ancestors to establish commerce itself to accommodate it. Notions of "nature" and "human nature" meld in this conception to suggest that anyone calling for change is at best quixotic, at worst fanatic.

Although the so-called "temple prostitution" intrinsic to ancient religious practice in many parts of the world bears no relationship to commercial sex (as either entrepreneurial cottage industry or big business), and although most commentators agree that polygamy and concubinage should also be distinguished from true prostitution, both traditions are often adduced to "explain" that exotic others have an approach to sex different from that of one's own culture—a freer and less puritanical attitude. In the case of Thailand, this version of history complements the First World notion that buying and selling sex is "natural" and that Thai culture is thus a lot more "natural" in this respect than ours. When Pasuk Phongpaichit, a vocal academic opponent of the contemporary sex industry, declares that it originated in a "culture of male domination in which polygamy and concubinage played a significant role" (1982, 2), she is attempting to turn the argument around, demonstrating that the industry is the latest manifestation of a gendered system of privilege in which wealth and rank carried sexual entitlements. Modernization extends the privilege by decreeing, essentially, "every man a king (of Siam)." Pasuk's contribution is to point out that the tradition and its dissemination are unfortunate social developments, not normal human behaviors.

Similarly, it is our contention that prostitution is neither natural nor inevitable, but rather that it institutionalizes the alienated sexuality constructed by current economic and social forces. Whether those forces are characterized as postcolonial, neocolonial, or imperialist, it is undeniable that the globe is their literal sphere of operation, so it is not surprising that there should be an international dimension to contemporary sexual alienation. If treating prostitution as a little joke about our human and animal nature obstructs critical analysis, then recognizing that it is socially constructed should open the way to understanding it as a form of sexual culture. But as we pointed out in our discussions of framing the issue (Chapter 2) and on the political economy of the sex industry (Chapter 4), existing studies of sex tourism as a part of international economic planning, national development strategies, or the vagaries of the labor market for young women virtually ignore the special nature of the "commodity" that is traded on the sex market. For this reason, they have little to say about the commodificaton of sex itself as part of the economy and the culture of global capitalism. In this chapter we examine contemporary sexual theory and discourse, as well as recent debates over prostitution as both sex and labor, in an effort to bring the sexual specificity of Thai sex tourism into our understanding of the phenomenon.

Feminism and the Body of Knowledge

We chose the five epigraphs that head this chapter because they not only represent different points on the chart of attitudes toward sexuality and prostitution but express them in such radically different discourses. The Bangkok bar scene and the sexual encounters that it fosters take place in a world in which Trink, their official amanuensis, can let his readers in on new sex bargains, warn against "rip-offs," publicize a party at which even the bar fines (for purchasing a prostitute's time) are prepaid, and simultaneously conduct an ongoing debate—complete with inane recourse to "dictionary definitions"—about whether the sex workers are exploited. On an only somewhat lower level, U.S. military personnel take for granted their right to sexual services in exchange for minimal amounts of cash, while deploying "to butcher" as both a synonym and a grotesque euphemism for "to fuck." Yet it is also a world in which members of "progressive movements," admittedly further removed from the bright lights, having situated sexuality in its full social context, seek to apply to their own intimate lives the insights obtained from this theoretical move. And where a Dutch sexologist can categorically state that commercial sex customers are "not nice men."

Such a discrepancy in the way diverse segments of the First World population—with their different experiences of work, money, power, leisure, and reflection—think and talk about sex is not in itself surprising. In fact, it is to be anticipated, as the range of other life experiences and the expectations to which they lead encounter the universal human experience of sex. The contradictions do have to be confronted, however, because nearly all statements about sex, however much they may acknowledge and even celebrate subjectivity and diversity, are normative, meant to apply to a common reality: Sex *is* this, it *is not* that and (perhaps) watch out if it borders on the other.

We are hardly exempt from this tendency ourselves. Indeed, it is almost impossible to write about the Bangkok bar scene without conveying a sense of what one thinks sex "really" is or can be and how commercial sex expands on or limits the definition. One of us has even gone so far as to maintain, in a published meditation on her own subject position while engaged in writing about the industry in Thailand, "I see the activity of the sex trade . . . as somehow *unreal,* imitating or miming desire, rather than partaking in it" (Robinson 1996,186). The first draft of "In the Penile Colony" concludes with a description of the author, the only *farang* woman in the go go bar, wearing a lei of orchids and, feeling rather like a prize ox, watching dancers mime a sexuality they've never actually felt, and thinking, "I have more erotic knowledge in my little finger than these beautiful children do in their whole bodies." So we not only generalize, we make statements that would astonish and baffle the patrons of the Bangkok bars as we take *their* sexual subjectivity as *our* discursive subject.

But it is not just the discourse that is universalizing. It is the experience itself. The bodily basis of sexual acts and their relation to our physical commonality seem to dictate phenomenological generalizations. And the involvement of the body in other experiences, such as work and power, which are informed by larger economies, suggests that the sexual experience of the body may also belong to a system. The implication of sex tourism in global systems of dominance suggests, further, that the sexual as well as the economic aspects of the industry may be global in nature—in terms not necessarily of the universalizing statements they generate but because of the global *effects* that contribute to creating a worldwide sexual economy—whether as metaphor or as material fact.

If generalization and globalization bring out the differences among various perspectives on the peculiar institution of prostitution as practiced in Thailand, there is at least one place where they overlap.[1] That is in the notion of transgression and the value placed on it in both reflective and nonreflective, liberatory and "dominative" approaches. (Well, how would *you* characterize that line about bleeding and butchery? "Nonreflective" is the least value-laden term available.)

Sexual theory employs the word and the concept of transgression quite openly; at the same time, within the world of sex-tourism, transgression is encoded in expressions like "naughty boy" and "you couldn't do this at home." The only customers who behave as if the prostitution transaction were a publicly sanctioned one are those Germans who, contemplating a trip to Thailand, naively and methodically write to the embassy or the Goethe Institute to reserve a nice, clean girl for their use on arrival (*Documentation* 1983, 7–8). They know that what they have in mind is transgressive at home, but their secure faith in the existence of rule leads them to assume that the boundaries have merely been shifted, not removed, in the exotic locale and that official diplomatic and cultural institutions from the metropolis will be in charge of implementing an entitlement that derives, after all, from their national identity. This "limiting case" makes it clear that for most foreigners—even, probably, for most Germans—the freedom they enjoy in Bangkok is precisely the freedom to transgress, albeit under the benign protection of the kindergarten cops who patrol Patpong. (Of course, it could be argued that if, as every guidebook assures you, the local police are there to keep tourist-transgressors safe, why not the representatives of one's own country? In which case, what is remarkable is not an essentially different relation to transgression but only the incongruity of asking the upright and uptight Goethe Institute to pimp.)

On the sex tourists' side of the equation, there is a great deal of sexual discourse, much of it in a transgressive mode, but no sexual theory. (Unless, indeed, one accepts Christopher Moore's assumption, that the relative quality of towel service in two short-time hotels is a "concept.") Samples of that discourse may be found in Chapter 6 on the bar scene, and in our recurring references to the sex chat on the Internet's World Sex Guide. It should be pointed out, in fact, that of all the countries whose sex trade is represented in the WSG segment on Prostitution, only the contributors to the Thailand rubric have established a pattern of describing in detail what happened to the writer in a bar or massage parlor. Typically, a national listing provides legal information—status of prostitution laws, age of consent, and so on—along with current prices for various services, sometimes indicating which services are not customary in that country. In only a few cases (homosexual encounters in East Africa, Vietnamese massage parlors in San Francisco) are personal narratives also supplied. By contrast, the Thailand heading is continually updated with narratives of exactly who did what to whom. Except for a few entries like "Sex in Thailand—the Basics," the virtual instruction manual that we discuss in Chapter 5, these narratives are written in the first person. For many sex tourists, apparently, part of the experience is coming home and writing one's own story, which follows convention to produce a story that is exactly like all the others, as if the genre and the experience had become inextricably linked and causally related.

In any event, these narratives may help motivate a critical analysis of the segment of the Thai sex industry geared for tourists, but, for this very reason, they are not part of the critique. We draw on them from time to time as a kind of ground bass to the themes provided by contemporary constructions of sexual theory. Although they are absolutely untheorized—indeed, they usually reflect no sense that sexuality can be a source of questioning and speculation—the narratives of sex tourists do provide access to a heterosexual male perspective that is almost entirely absent from vanguard sexual theory.

Both sexology as an empirical science and sex therapy as its applied praxis tend to focus on male heterosexual experience, particularly in its most mechanical aspects (Tiefer 1994). In fact, it is not clear to observers whether the fields evolved as they did in response to a cultural context that takes male heterosexuality as the human norm, or whether the study of male sexuality and the therapeutic establishment that defines and attempts to heal its ills have informed the impersonal, clinical nature of that definition. Either way, sexology and sex therapy are straight-male-centered. It is those marginalized by such definition—which is to say, all women (bisexual, heterosexual, and lesbian) and gay men, who are responsible for the cutting-edge theory that has endeavored to make bodily, intellectual, and political sense of sexuality by generating contemporary theory.

The rebirth of First World feminism in the long shadow cast by the sexual revolution of the 1960s made it inevitable that women would seek in the movement we were creating the freedom promised but withheld by the changes in the surrounding sexual culture.[2] That freedom had two faces, expressed most simply as freedom *from* (objectification, alienation, rape, and abuse) and freedom *to* (develop and experience full sexual subjectivity). For most of us, this move and the theoretical writing that accompanied it were based in immediate experience, especially the experience of a sexual revolution that did not overturn enough established conditions to make us participants *in* liberation rather than the means *to* it.

But, near the very beginning of the process, Juliet Mitchell established a central role for sexuality in emergent left feminist theory. Mitchell identifies four structures as forming the "complex unity" of women's lives—Production, Reproduction, Sex, and Socialization of Children. While recognizing that "each separate structure may have reached a different 'moment' at any given historical time," she asserted that it was sexuality that was undergoing the "most rapid evolution" in the mid-1960s (Mitchell, 26). Although Mitchell's essay also warned that the liberatory potential of sexuality might be short-circuited as capitalism concocted "new forms of reification . . . which may void sexual freedom of any meaning" (48–49), it served, nonetheless, to authenticate *as political strategy* the critique we were enacting, a critique whose simultaneous targets were the sexual repression imposed by prevailing societal values and the passivity and alienation enforced by male power within relationships that had been liberated from the repression but not from male dominance.

Nearly twenty years earlier Simone de Beauvoir had pointed out the fundamental contradiction in the concept of sexual relationships: that they are not, or at least are not necessarily, relational. Since the woman "is object, any inertia on her part does not seriously affect her natural role. . . . It is even possible to copulate with a dead body. Coition cannot take place without the male's consent and male satisfaction is its natural termination" (1961, 350). Yet Beauvoir asserted that, although differently for male and female subjects, sexuality possesses a uniquely integrative capacity: "The erotic experience is one that most poignantly discloses to human beings the ambiguity of their condition; in it they are aware of themselves as flesh and as spirit, as the other and as subject" (378).

Beauvoir's woman as Other is not *primarily* other because of her role in heterosexuality, which is a site of her otherness only because of the way it is apprehended. In an effort that Judith Butler (1990, 12) was to decry as uncritically replicating not only the Cartesian mind-body split but the "phallogocentrism" of every major male thinker in the West from Plato to Sartre, "Beauvoir proposes that the female body ought to be the situation and instrumentality of women's freedom." As well as missing the radicalism of Beauvoir's theoretical project, Butler misses its resonance with postmodern sexual theory. For, when Beauvoir asserts that "to *make* oneself an object, to *make* oneself passive is a very different thing from *being* a passive object" (1961, 355, emphasis in original), she is playing with the same boundaries between essence and will that are at the heart of much contemporary theory—including Butler's own contributions—about "performing" gender and sexuality.

To remain for a bit longer, though, in the "pre-postmodern" moment, feminists of the 1960s and 1970s, caught up in Mitchell's "rapid evolution" of sexual values and behaviors, concentrated Beauvoir's call for an existential subjectivity into a demand for sexual subjectivity. At its most basic level this meant not being or being regarded as an object—of contempt, of violence, *or of impersonal, alienated desire.* It meant not being an object, a thing, period. And, beyond that, it led to a recognition that sexuality itself is not a thing, either. Sexuality may have been naïvely conceptualized as "some type of inner essence, available for self-expression, something separate from what you do when you have sex" (Segal 1994, 34), but it was not a thing in the sense that it could be acquired, traded, bought, or sold. Whether or not anyone else was listening at that point, we were attempting in this way to redefine our common understanding not only of specifically female sexuality but of sex itself.

Thus, feminist sexual theory posits the operations of power within and through sexuality. For Beauvoir, the penetration entailed in heterosexual intercourse, the common male-superior position, the male's deciding on positions and frequency, even the common phrasing "he *takes* his pleasure with her" and "he *gives* her pleasure" (361; original emphasis) are expressions of power that may derive their meanings from domination in extra-erotic experience—for there is no intrinsic reason that penetration or being on top has to signify an exercise of power—but she considers that connection only in the (sexual) site of its occurrence. Extending that perspective, "second-wave" feminism introduced the notion of "politics" into the bedroom. Kate Millett (1970, 22) defines it as referring "to power-structured relationships, arrangements whereby one group of persons is controlled by another," and locates such politics, initially, in literary representations of erotic scenes that enact on the ground of the female body patterns of domination and conquest originating in *social* relations.

Apparently bringing together feminist rejection of an objectified, essential sexuality and the theoretical construction of sexual practice within that rejection, Judith Butler argues that if sexuality "is culturally constructed within existing power relations, then the postulation of a normative sexuality that is 'before,' 'outside,' or 'beyond' power is a cultural impossibility and a politically impracticable dream, one that postpones the concrete and contemporary task of rethinking subversive possibilities for sexuality with the terms of power itself . . . [so that] within the terms of feminist sexual theory, it is clear that the presence of power dynamics within sexuality is in no sense the same as the simple consolidation or augmentation of a heterosexual or phallogocentric power regime" (1990, 30–31).

What is new in this restatement and the reason why Butler's bringing together of earlier feminist formulations is only apparent, is this introduction of the discursive element, the displacement into "phallogocentrism" of power relations that had previously been defined as the result of material forces. In fact, for Butler, "'(m)ateriality' appears only when its status as contingently constructed through discourse is erased, concealed, covered over. Materiality is thus the dissimulated effect of power" (1993, 251 n. 12). This displacement matters to our argument because, whereas it is possible to apprehend the sexual transactions that define Thailand's sex tourism as a literalization on the international and interracial level of the gender politics adumbrated by Beauvoir and Millett, the effect becomes considerably more abstract when an influential postmodern feminist thinker confines materiality between quotation marks and calls the resulting prisonhouse "discourse." The old theory, whatever its limitations, usefully described the sexual event, whereas the current and virtually hegemonic theory is saying something about the experience of sexuality that leaves the observer of the Bangkok bar scene wondering just whose sexuality in that scene—the women's or the customers' or something they unconsciously create together— we can possibly be talking about. And if the answer is "none of the above," what becomes of the universal claims made in the name of theory?

Teresa Ebert locates Butler's popularity among those whom she denominates "ludic feminists" in precisely this dispersion of the notion of power. Butler, she maintains, "provides an analytic of power in which we do *not* have to confront the global relations and systematicity of power; in which we do *not* have to deal with the most serious consequences of power operating in dialectical relation to the mode of production and division of labor—the consequences . . . of exploitation. By construing power as immanent in all processes, as operating *as* discourse, as citationality . . . and thus a 'reiterative acting' divided by differences-within, this ludic logic constitutes power as reversible, as generating its own resistance" (214, original emphasis). When applied to a particular instance of exploitation in a global context, Butler's vision of power is revealed as essentially metaphorical, even metaphysical, in character. To the extent that there is room in her theory for a concrete example—such as the sexuality enacted in the tourist bars of Bangkok—it would have to admit the existence of parallel narratives, one detailing the political economy of the sex industry and the other recounting the story about sexuality and power as always immanent, as if the international commercial exchange had nothing to do with the conjoint unit sex-and-power, because it has nothing to do with sex-and-power *as conceptualized in Butler's analysis.*

Butler's principal contribution to sexual theory is by way of her theory of performance. Gender, she pronounces (in italics), "is not a noun, but neither is it a set of free-floating alternatives, for . . . the substantive effect of gender is performativity produced and compelled by the regulatory practices of gender coherence" (1990, 24). She becomes even more specific about performance when she argues that gender "is the repeated stylization of the body, a set of repeated acts within a highly rigid regulatory frame that congeals over time to produce the appearance of substance, of a natural sort of being" (1990, 33). Thus, for example, "what is 'performed' in drag is . . . the *sign* of gender, a sign that is not the same as that which it figures, but that cannot be read without it" (1993, 237). Within that rigid structure of regulation, Butler finds the most interesting performative moves to be those that call the entire structure into question by setting performance *against* (apparent) nature, transgressing boundaries that are thereby revealed as fluid in their very rigidity. Some of these moves involve literal style: walk, gesture and mannerism, costume. But some of them necessarily entail sexual acts.

Once again, it is Ebert who offers a lucid reading of the ludic imperative. Butler, she maintains, offers a "discursive logic of agency as reiteration . . . a notion of *agency as invention,* which she variously calls performativity or citationality" (209, original emphasis). Insisting on the distinction between performativity and "mere" theatricality (Butler 1993, 234) results, according to Ebert (1995, 211), in the "meaning of performativity . . . [sliding] into a kind of speech act that repeats or cites the norms of sex."

But the "repetition" that matters to Butler is, as we have indicated, the one that goes against the grain: the drag queen or the butch lesbian. What about the performativity of those who, apparently taking the path of least resistance, *deliberately* choose vanilla? And, more to the point, what about those whose gender definition and sexual activity seems not to be deliberate, who are following a script whose existence *as* a script is not something they have ever consciously acknowledged, much less challenged? The Bangkok sex tourists are prime examples of this category, and it is fair to wonder, given the universalizing tone of Butler's description, whether they too can be said to be performing their gender and sexual identities. The same question may be even more strikingly posed with respect to the prostitute as gendered (and hence performative) subject.

Lenore Manderson's reading of the actual sex performances in Patpong bars addresses these issues. Some of the bar acts involve public display with a partner or partners; while others use the solo performing body as a set of almost autonomous genitalia capable of effecting, through muscular control, actions usually performed by the mouth ("blowing" a whistle) or the hands ("serving" a Ping-Pong ball) and taking apparent risks with delicate parts (extracting a string of razor blades). Manderson (1992) interprets these initially theatrical acts as "performative" in the Butlerian sense, since they reiteratively act out statements about gender and sexual norms as well as expressing contempt for the customers. But if the woman is still saying nothing about her own gender definitions or desire, and if no one in the audience except a *farang* woman anthropologist "gets" the double-edged message—so that the usual phenomenology of the event is not as Manderson describes it but as the male sex tourists do—can even the bold reversal really tell us anything about the sex in the sex industry?

One way out of the quagmire that results when high theory confronts eccentric but undeniable facts from the nontheoretical universe is through the notion of transgression. Because the performative moves on which Butler places value are those that deliberately transgress normative gender boundaries, this focus has little to say about the "undeliberate" sexualities of sex tourists, who also transgress established behavioral boundaries, but not gender codes. And it completely elides the sexuality of the prostitutes, who are the object of the journey but whose "performance" is an all-too-literal enactment of *someone else's* subjectivity. Their sexuality is not interrogated any more than that of the furnishings in the rooms where their sexual "performance" is, in fact, constituted as labor.

Theorist Gayle Rubin accords the politics of sexual transgression a wider range, for her emphasis, once her analysis conceptually divided sex and gender, has been on erotic behavior rather than gender definition. And the behaviors in which she terms "erotic variety" involve the gender and number of partners, types of relationships, sites of sexual activity, and specific actions (Rubin 1984, 278–82; see also Rubin 1975). So it is possible to include—or at least to consider including—the sexual behavior of *farang* tourists to Thailand within Rubin's framework. According to Rubin, the hierarchy of transgression, for which she provides an actual diagram (1984, 281), originates chiefly in religious and medical or psychiatric ideologies and is promulgated chiefly by means of popular culture. Rubin explicitly politicizes the hierarchies of sexual values when she maintains that they "function in much the same ways as do ideological systems of racism, ethnocentrism, and religious chauvinism. They rationalize the well-being of the sexually privileged and the adversity of the sexual rabble" (1984, 280).

The two lists accompanying Rubin's circular chart make up, respectively, "The Charmed Circle: Good, Normal, Natural, Blessed Sexuality" and "The Outer Limits: Bad, Abnormal, Unnatural, Damned Sexuality." Counterposed on the chart's "inner circle" with the category "free," there appears "commercial" sex, which is also labeled sex "for money." This suggests that the transgression consists in *taking* money for sex, and, indeed, elsewhere in her essay, Rubin lists prostitutes—along with such sexual transgressors as homosexuals, transvestites, and practitioners of sadomasochism—as victims of social and legal oppression because of their "sexuality." But even in the First World, prostitution is not usually "a" sexuality. Although it certainly entails sexual behavior, it is not (or not primarily) apprehended in progressive late twentieth-century theory as an expression of a *desire* that is condemned by harsh sexual law. As one study of prostitution reminds us, "many people are defined by their occupations, but with prostitutes it is the 'deviant' aspect of their work which defines them" (Perkins and Bennett 1985, 215). This definition is predicated on the "assumption that prostitutes behave in the same way sexually at work and in private life ... [that they are] 'deviants' by profession ... [and] go in for distasteful or 'kinky' acts in private life" (223).[3]

As for the sex customers, *their* transgression is apparently not included in Rubin's "commercial sex" category at all but is rather subsumed under one or more of the other rubrics on the "sin" list: unmarried, promiscuous, nonprocreative, casual, cross-generational sex—even, in a sense, sex carried out "in public," as contrasted with "at home." Since this accounts for more than half the "bad sex" list, the sex customers must really *be* and not just be called "naughty boys," which is to say, in Rubin's taxonomy, outlaws, heroic front-line fighters, victims of a repressive social apparatus, whose sexual behavior is at once the rationale for their exclusion and the site of their resistance.

Since hardly anyone would think of them in this way, the problem must reside in Rubin's construction of a politics in which, by analogy with more generally recognized forms of oppression, the power of the "sexually privileged" is opposed to that of the suffering "sexual rabble." By positing a transcendent "lust" as a motive force prior to and surviving beyond the other bodily needs, which traditionally belong to political analyses based in production, Rubin moves sexuality out of the realm of power as defined by exploitation and into that of power as defined by the mean, narrow-minded people who possess both that power and the institutional means for dissemination and enforcement of their meanness. In addition to the larger analytic problems generated by this positing of lust as a "strategy of crisis management in late capitalism" and of the "free subject as an excessive (autonomous) agent" (Ebert 1995, 51, see also 52–53, 64), it falls apart at its first contact with the basic situation presented by the Thai sex industry. For here, the desiring subject is not only a sexually needy "lacker" but is at the same time someone privileged by gender, nationality, and class, one who is invested in a global economic system in which the power is in his own hands—or at least in which he is on the side of the power —and where the varieties of "transgression" he commits are actively and institutionally solicited. There would apparently be no difference in Rubin's analysis, as there is not in Jeremy Seabrook's (1991) between Seabrook's gay and straight "sexpatriates," although the former are fleeing a sexual system that frowns on and often criminalizes intergenerational same-sex relations, while the latter are fleeing their countrywomen's self-assertion, which they denominate "feminism." The one is unquestionably transgressive, the other is not. Moreover, as the sex industry itself constructs the customer's role, he is not a swashbuckling transgressor, but a law-abiding citizen of a world system designed to privilege him.

Coming to Terms

> The whole thing probably takes about two-and-a-half minutes. Men's sexuality is totally unbelievable, and the worst part is that they come back again and again.
>
> —Eva, a Norwegian prostitute interviewed in *Backstreets*

If Western sexual theory "fits" so awkwardly over relations between Thai sex workers and foreign men, it is possible that there is more to be learned by turning the telescope around: building theory out of what we do know about the sexual aspect of prostitution and the debates over sex work. From this perspective, personal narratives from the Thai situation, whether by sex workers or their customers, provide a basic framework and some clues about how to proceed.

Interviews with Thai sex workers rely a great deal on euphemism. The women speak of pain and fear in their first encounters, of experiences of violence and the haunting fear of its recurrence, and of mentally distancing themselves from their actions. One such narrative is that of the woman Pasuk Phongpaichit calls "Taew." In six and a half pages devoted to this masseuse and her family—their history, relationships, and finances before and after the daughter's move to Bangkok—her prostitution experience is summarized in a few lines: "When she started at the massage parlor, Taew was still a virgin. At first she gave only a regular massage and got 18 baht (72 cents) per customer. Eventually, she was persuaded to sell her virginity. The client paid B8,000, of which Taew got B2,000 ($80). She sent the money home to build a well for drinking water. Taew did not like it a bit. She cried for several days afterwards, and had to see a doctor" (1982, 52). The Burmese women imported to work in Thai brothels tell Asia Watch's interviewers (1993) stories in which rape is the dominant motif: as the means of recruitment and a form of labor control, as well as a description of the initiatory and subsequent transactions.

In *Hello My Big Big Honey*, the range of what are characterized as problems with foreign customers is succinctly summarized by a *mamasan*: "Maybe have some sadist. Maybe he fuck too much. . . . And crazy maybe. Some hit her. Some sadist. And like to do her ass. Something like that. Or in her mouth" (Walker and Ehrlich 1992, 171). The active prostitutes interviewed use almost the same words to describe "crazy guy." Only the details differ: "He told me, 'Lady from Europe like a man hurt she.' I don't know, but I see . . . in photo, he don't know I see in his open locker. Wow! Picture he do with lady. He make lady hurt sex. Photo him hurt her with belt and tie her hands down. I see in his room the long whip" (66). Speaking of their initiation to "normal" sex on the job, these bar workers sound much like Pasuk's masseuses: "In the beginning I feel a little bit scared. Afraid of a man I never know before. I go with him. . . . How can you have a feeling when you don't know the man? . . . For sure it's bad but it's for the money. Bad for the body. Bad for the heart" (151). Asked what she thinks about when "making love" with a customer she doesn't like, one interviewee says, "I think, finish quickly, please finish quickly" (154).

Cleo Odzer's *Patpong Sisters* (1994) fills in some of the lacunae left by the decorum of Pasuk's study and the language gap between interviewers and subjects in *Hello My Big Big Honey.*[4] At the Rose Bar, Odzer chats with Dang, who seems to be on an amphetamine high and who says she used to love her English lessons with EMPOWER. Then,

> when three *farang* men came up the stairs, Dang moved me to the couch against the wall. . . . Two blow jobs commenced. One man sat at the far corner of the bar. A hostess, with the top of her dress pulled down, unzipped his pants and bent over to take his penis in her mouth. Her head pumped up and down and the hand that held his penis moved vigorously. The man frequently looked down to watch her. Then he'd gaze casually at the bar. The hostess worked without breaking stride, slowing down, or changing position for seventeen minutes. I wondered if my presence made it take longer than usual. When the man ejaculated, she unrolled a few sheets of toilet paper from the many rolls that lined the bar and cleaned him up. Then she refastened her dress (53).

Odzer also describes a live sex show, viewed in company with a *farang* doctor who claimed to be part owner of the club.

> In truth the male-female show was unerotic. Looking bored, the participants were clearly not enjoying themselves. The man performed cunnilingus for about ten seconds, then the woman fellated him for the same length of time. At one point the man craned his neck to fix his hair in a mirror across the room. The couple had intercourse in every position possible but the man only thrust two strokes in each. When the couple stopped moving, the bartenders applauded signalling the end of the show. The man pulled out and left the stage holding his erection.
>
> "The guy never comes," commented David, as if noting the impossibility of getting a repairman to fix the phone.
>
> "How many shows does he do a night?"
>
> "Two here, but they work several bars. Maybe six to eight shows a night" (36–37).

A work of Thai fiction that is exceptionally explicit about the sex in sex work describes precisely such a scene from the viewpoint of the male participant. Kon Krailat's short story, "In the Mirror" (1985) focuses on a young man who, like the archetypal female prostitute, has come to Bangkok from the countryside and been unable to find work outside the sex industry that would enable him to support himself and send money home to his family. The most powerful moment in the story details his thoughts as he engages in sexual intercourse with a partner whose husband calls for her nightly after work, just as he might with any other job. It is a scene of stunning alienation: his mind is occupied by thoughts of his parents and the shame they would feel if they knew how he earns his living, of his own self-disgust, and of his hopeless economic situation, while his body has to maintain a level of excitation that allows him to achieve and sustain an erection and (unlike the performer Odzer watched) eventually ejaculate.

These descriptions complement and contradict the accounts on the Internet or the advice given by Bishop's expert informant, cited in Chapter 6, on negotiating the bar scene. Although the women's voices sometimes suggest that there are also better sexual experiences, there is no indication of what they are or what sexual subjectivity on the women's part they denote. Told from the perspective of Thai women participants, a *farang* woman observer, or a sensitive Thai fiction writer, the story is essentially the same as the clients', although its *affect* is considerably bleaker. The customers' more positive approach to the event (many of them say that either the entire trip to Thailand or some portion of it was the greatest sexual experience of their lives) is enhanced by the enormous amount of detail they provide. Much of this detail is mechanical. When it's good, it's about the tightest little organ, the finest oiled breasts against the back, the body-to-body massage; when it's not good, the focus is the "dumb" masseuse who didn't know that muscles, not bones, get massaged or the blow job so inept that the narrator couldn't even get an erection (WSG, July 1995).

Most descriptive literature about the sexual aspect of prostitution comes from sources outside Thailand, from studies of sex work as it is carried on and experienced within countries that also generate sex tourists. This material provides information in two areas that have particular resonance for the Thai situation: the motivations of the customers and the sexuality of the prostitutes. Interviewed for *Being Prostitutes*, "Lee," a Sydney sex worker, says that customers' explicit requests "can go from good old-fashioned straight-out sex to swinging from the chandeliers." And "Maggie" tells of men who "were saying 'I've heard about this and that and would like to try it.' They mightn't like it but were willing to try it; they thought they might be missing something." The Australian prostitutes explain the compulsion of men who buy the opportunity of being the "bottom" in sadomasochism as a way of compensating, as "Kelly" puts it, for "too much power and authority in their own life. I guess they want to feel what it's like on the other end" (Perkins and Bennett 1985, 229).

Other studies, by contrast, mention the crude and aggressive behavior of Japanese sex tourists in Southeast Asia, quoting these businessmen as claiming that it is precisely because "they work so hard in Japan and never have time for sex there" (Sano 37). The explicit impersonality they want when purchasing sexual services in their own country is heightened, when they deal with women in other Asian countries, by "racial and nationalistic arrogance, a tendency to sexualize hierarchical relationships that these Japanese assume exist between their country and other Asian nations" (Allison 1994, 186, 140; Sano 1981, 63). Anne Allison also cites a Japanese study whose thesis is that the men's "desire is

not so much for a woman whose desires are sexual and female as for the type of
woman who, for money, is willing to indulge the man in in the expression of his
desires (construed therefore as being manly). To allow the men the expression
of these desires which, while legitimate, are still socially constituted as dirty, ani-
malistic, and base [acts where] a woman is degraded" (186).

Norwegian researchers and their informants agree with the Australian and
Japanese sources that the customers are ordinary men from all walks of life
(Hørigård and Finstad 1992, 55). And a French prostitute cited in the same
Norwegian study, *Backstreets*, agrees with the challenge to the dominant theoretical position on transgression: "When it comes down to it, men need to feel that
sex is dirty, forbidden, in order to enjoy it. Anyway, promiscuity, dirt and sex are
the same thing for them. . . . When a guy asks for 'specialties,' he . . . blames
himself for asking; he blames the woman for agreeing to it" (56–57).

Backstreets actually includes a section titled, in so many words, "What the customer wants from prostitution." The findings, here, confirm the Australian
experience that for many men it is particular acts, often ones they've heard or
read about, that "aren't necessarily very deviant or special . . . [but] that very
many would see as common elements in a varied sex life" (93). The pleasures of
variety itself, and of a woman whom they regard as highly sexed, may be part of
the package, along with the noncommitted and one-sided nature of the arrangement (94–96). On this last point, "Jack," a Norwegian john, says "'cause she's a
prostitute I dared to let myself flow . . . with the sexual energy. I didn't need to
pretend to like anything *or be considerate to her*. . . . I wasn't the one who was supposed to give her something" (96; emphasis added). "Arne" adds that the
absence of doubt, the absolute availability is also a factor. The sex worker is willing, "you can get a hold of her . . . you know you have her" (96). Similarly, "the
possibility of being rejected is partly what Japanese men pay to avoid" in the
hostess bars at home. "Their money assures that the woman will say yes to the
figurative dance" (Allison 175).

Despite the desire expressed by some customers in the First World for an
impersonal transaction, they may also hold on to the conviction—and apparently
need to do so—that the transaction whose economic aspect frees them from the
demands of mutuality is also satisfying and even meaningful to the woman. The
Internet contributors' obsession with prices and with the ever present threat of
being cheated, of possibly having to spend too much, likewise coexists with
expressed triumph at locating a prostitute who behaves "like a girlfriend" rather
than a slot machine: "The girls are beautiful, and treat you very good. As they
say, 'like a boyfriend'" (WSG, 26 April 1996).

According to *Backstreets*, most customers "are searching for something that
resembles regular intercourse. Then the sexual act is reduced to a one-sided
release—his. But if this becomes too blatantly clear, it affects his ability and
desire" (Hørigård and Finstad 1992, 90). This study's male informants go to
absurd lengths to make sure their experience is *not* so affected, stating their
belief in the mutuality of the experience. "Hugo" thinks "it's wonderful to feel

that a woman is coming. . . . I've had the experience twice that they've said they didn't want to. Otherwise they probably have. . . . I don't think I'm . . . easily fooled that way." "Ingmar" allows a moment of doubt: "I don't know, they wail a little, but whether they come, I don't know. . . . Yes, I'd say that most do." And "Tore" adds, "I feel she's enjoying herself, but I don't actually know what is faking and what is reality. But right then I don't think about it. . . . I suppose that she's feeling it." "Ragnar" sums it up: "Yeah, you can never be totally sure. . . . Women's orgasms—that's something men can't really understand. . . . It *can't* be just for economic reasons, there *must* be other things that come into it, too, that they have strong sexual drives and want experiences" (90–92).

By contrast, the most common term used by the very prostitutes these men frequent is that the man is "emptying himself." "Jane" considers it "totally crazy" that some men want to pay more in order to satisfy her sexually. Besides, it can't be done, "Hanna" says, because "the customers are basically assholes. . . . I don't feel anything sexually" (Hørigård and Finstad 1992, 51–52). The remark that serves as an epigraph for this section, about the two-and-a-half-minute average, is echoed on the other side of the world, by "Lee" in Sydney: "Anyone with a little bit of nous will realise that it takes longer for a female to turn on than a male, and seeing as most of your clients are three-minute wonders it is going to take a little longer than that to warm someone up" (Perkins and Bennett 1985, 224). The consensus among the women is that they just can't, and even if they could, they couldn't.

This is, by the way, one of the areas about which the sex tourists recently returned from Thailand have the most to say. "Southeast Asia Diary," a single posting, but a very long one (WSG, 29 September 1996), includes the following remarks: "We make love three times during the night, Goolop as passionate and practiced in this art as . . . others. At one point the stereotype of the secret sexual passion of oriental girls comes to mind, her being the embodiment" (1).[5] "She seems able to almost get off on just nipple sucking alone" (2). "She's a passionate lover, generally the case with the older ones in my experience, and I'm able to make her come through penetration alone. . . . Though I'm clearly a 'cheap charlie' relative to the rest of the farang, I must have some added value, for even at 300 baht she's asking to see me again this evening" (3). "After rising and drying we go over to the bed where I first go down on her, bringing her to a throbbing orgasm, and then penetrate her to a second" (5). "I don't come as quickly or easily as I did a few years ago. This is all the better from the girl's point of view, though, as the period of conjugation has become sufficiently long for me to consistently bring them to vaginal orgasm" (6). "Overall she's a rather orgasmic chick, as I'm able to get her off both orally and vaginally" (11). Although this informant's painstakingly detailed experiences are virtually identical to those of the other Internet correspondents, including the belief that the transactions they purchase bring pleasure to the woman, he insists on this latter point far more than the others. On his final page the reason for this preoccupation becomes clear: "She's definitely on the shy side and not nearly as wildly orgasmic as the first girl

I had in Pattaya, but is responsive enough *for me to get it up over"* (12, emphasis added). This attitude is complemented by that of the correspondent cited above who picked a dud in the massage and blow job departments: he observes that in the midst of the bad oral scene, "I thought about helping her with thinking at something *really* nice, but then I thought 'what for do I pay?' After five minutes successless blowing . . . " (WSG, July 1995; original emphasis).[6]

Although we have no evidence from Thai prostitutes on either side of the question, a British sex worker observes, "The worst men are the ones who don't turn you on and think that all women have to have about six orgasms before they will penetrate them" ("Barbara" 1994, 18). She speculates that this expectation comes from watching pornographic films: "Women who work in porn have twenty minutes in between takes to relax, before faking again. But if you have to fake six on the trot, that's hard work! . . . So you have to do this dramatic, over-the-top fake. And they manage to really believe it. They really do. . . . But I don't fake all the time. Sometimes I do get turned on. . . . But if you were to have a real orgasm, they wouldn't believe you."

Nina Hartley, an American actress in "adult" films, explains, "You know, there's real sex and there's camera sex; my skill is fusing the reality of camera sex with the intensity of real sex" (qtd. in Chapkis, 33). These position are far more complex than the Norwegian prostitutes' utter skepticism at the possibility of any pleasure with a customer. But it is important to note that even the occasional experience of pleasure does not obviate the necessity of "faking" or of making the representation resemble the "real thing"—an experience that places the sex worker in a position to commodify her own as well as her client's pleasure as part of the economics of the transaction. Another of Chapkis's contributors, a nurse and former prostitute called Maryann, explains that

> In sex work, there's this real issue around having orgasms on the job. One of the things I realized was that those orgasms were mine. They didn't belong to any-body else. . . . It had nothing to do with who I was with; it wasn't about being so turned on by this guy instead of that one. It was about me. It really challenged the idea that orgasms are something a man "gives" you (85).

This statement disagrees with many of the others in several key areas, but it does not challenge the material basis of the exchange.

The economic meaning of the specific sexual event is underscored by an older Australian prostitute who recalls the addition of oral sex to her repertoire: "I found I was working all night and half the day just doing sex (intercourse), while the girls were spending half the time making the same doing half-french and sex, so I thought I've got to get with this. I found it hard at first but I got used to it" (Perkins and Bennett 1985, 225). Cleo Odzer's concern about whether the seven-teen-minute blow job she witnessed was taking longer than usual because of her presence takes on a new meaning in this context of comparing sexual time to cash received.

The Norwegian prostitutes endow one commonly circulated story with the status of an urban legend: "The customer . . . would tell you about a friend or a friend of a friend, who contacted a prostitute. Then the prostitute . . . [fell] so deeply in love with him that he'd gotten it for free. It's incredible the number of men who came up with that exact same story" (Hørigård and Finstad 1992, 52). In fact, we find variations of it in the illusions of relationship that motivate the letter writers in *Hello My Big Big Honey*, as well as in a Net posting like this one:

> One thing I'll never forget . . . is my last night. I had specifically sought out one of the "Miss Thailands" I had spotted the previous evening and spent my last entertainment money on her. Afterwards, I returned to the bar of my previous night's carnal delights and ran into my "Sweetie" from . . . last night. Well, she just insisted about 1:00 am that we return to my hotel. When I explained about no $$$, she replied, "No plo-blem, you fl-end, you no pay!" I am sure it's not a first, but getting a freebie from a beautiful Patpong bar girl ranks way up there on my list! It also filled the time until my 5:00 am taxi to the airport (WSG, April 1996).

Tony Eardly, writing originally in the pro-feminist British men's magazine *Achilles Heel,* and genuinely trying to understand the duality in male desire and in the notion of transgression, concludes: "The attraction of the prostitute is that with her we can buy entry to a controlled environment, a playroom . . . where we . . . can purchase complicity in an elaborate simulation of love unshackled by domestic realities. But the prostitute must remain excluded from society. . . . Not just to maintain our illusion, but also because . . . seen too clearly, the purely economic nature of the contract with her may expose the same reality which exists, mystified, in marriage or romantic love" (Eardly in Seidler 1992, 138). If, on one level, this statement recasts the belief of Christopher Moore's Bangkok "hardcore" that all sex has its price, on another level it is a call, rare in this literature, for resistance and change, based on recognition that the conventions of male sexuality represent a dysfunction in our common humanity.

Debating It

If the prostitutes of Australia, Japan, Norway, and Britain offer insights into the experience of the sex trade in Thailand, the debate over sex work among North American feminists should add another dimension to the picture. It does, but one that is by no means consistent in itself or with the empirical studies. Gail Pheterson argues, for instance, that prostitution "may offer some women more freedom than other forms of labor available to them and they may prefer a situation that promises greater liberty over . . . unpaid labor—even at the risk of increased exposure to male violence" (1996, 18).

Another element of the debate offers a different perspective on prostitutes' relationship to the sexual commodity in which they trade. When sex workers are interviewed by journalists or social scientists, the resulting reports of sexual experience are all negative. The similarity of the voices making these statements, whether in *A New Form of Slavery*, *From Peasant Girls to Bangkok Masseuses* and *Hello My Big Big Honey*, or in *Being a Prostitute* and *Backstreets*, enhances the impression that they do reflect lived experience. Nonetheless, when activist prostitutes speak of their own sexuality, they sometimes have a more positive story to tell. (Such activists are inclined to be skeptical about the bias built into the focus and formulation of most studies, while many other sex workers and those conducting research in the area tend to consider the activists non-representative.) For example, the book *Good Girls/Bad Girls* (L. Bell 1987) reprints the proceedings of a 1985 conference in Toronto which, as the subtitle announces, brought "feminists and sex trade workers face to face." (That this face-off is often problematic is reflected in the expostulation of one of Pheterson's informants, who maintained, "I'd rather walk any street in the middle of the night than face a group of feminists" [62]). Peg Miller, founder of the Canadian Organization for the Rights of Prostitutes (CORP), offered an early intervention from the floor. Attacking feminists who, she claimed, may respect prostitutes' need to earn a living but nevertheless deny dignity to the particular work, she asked,

> What is so terrible about fucking for a living? I like it. I can live out my fantasies. . . . I represent many others out there, . . . lots of whores . . . who, despite the terrible legal and social environment, enjoy our work. Who am I to you if I enjoy my job? (49)

An unnamed participant, who said she had been a prostitute for eight years, objected:

> Can you count how many tricks you have had? You mean you have that many fantasies? Isn't it about having money to survive? I know that's your opinion, you like it, but prostitution to me was degrading. . . . If I had had to fuck one more of them—boy, I would have killed him! (50)

Whereupon Miller backtracked part of the way:

> I wasn't saying I enjoyed every experience. When you're doing a fucking car date and you're in and out of there and it's dirty, that guy is a gungebag, I know that. But . . . I've seen what prostitution, as a trade, can be like at its best (50).

Rather more pragmatically, porn actress Nina Hartley's contribution to *Live Sex Acts* contains the observation that "[w]ork is work: you have good days and bad days, but my worst day at work is still better than the best day selling shoes at Kinney's" (qtd. in Chapkis, 34). And Marianne, now a staff worker at the Dutch prostitutes' organization Red Thread, says, "Working and using [heroin] wasn't always fun but it was never boring. And you can't say that about a lot of people's lives" (qtd. 198).

Most of *Good Girls/Bad Girls* is devoted to the legal and political issues surrounding prostitution and pornography, but there are a few other intriguing remarks on the topic of sexuality. For instance, Margo St. James, founder of the San Francisco prostitutes' organization COYOTE (Call Off Your Old Tired Ethics), recommends twenty-one as the minimum age for working commercially or having multiple partners, adducing reasons of physical health for this restriction. But she adds, "if we're going to do a mental thing, we'd choose twenty-five because we feel that a young person should find their own sexual self before they're subjected to a lot of commercial leering and lusting" (129). This suggests that once such subjectivity is located and embraced, it can be fulfilled in and through commercial exchanges, in what St. James calls "the right to fuck . . . to have as many partners as I choose" (130). From this perspective, commercial sex is equated with sexual freedom in general and, in particular, with consensual nonmonogamy.

The most open challenge, however, appears very close to the end of the volume, in the lengthy summing up by three CORP members. They assert that the heart of the debate, for them, is "the whole business of treating our sexuality . . . [with] the same kind of credibility and support as we would any of our other needs" (204). But this general statement is rapidly replaced by a defense of what they call anonymous sex, by which they apparently mean that it is not connected to love or an ongoing relationship:

> There are a lot of people who feel unwilling or reluctant or unable to expose a lot of pockets of their sexuality and their sexual needs unless it is with someone that they don't have to look at afterwards. There's an excitement that goes with a new person, a novelty. These are all things that are accepted when it's expressed in other areas. . . . As far as we're concerned, there are a lot of *women* who could use this kind of service. They've never had a good fuck in their life. They need the service, and it would be well worth the money to pay and have a good service and awaken their sexuality. . . . How can . . . [feminists] hear us when they can't even hear their own bodies? . . . The first step is getting a woman to understand that her sexual needs are what they are and they're valid (204–17; emphasis added).

The CORP representatives would apparently find it as hard to accept the assertion that many women do not value impersonal sex *in our bodies* as such women find it to accept the idea that a commercial transaction has the capacity to meet female sexual needs on the physical level. More generally, the statement effects a slippage among three discrete categories: the prostitute's own sexual pleasure, the social value of the "service" she performs, and the desirability of a situation in which women would have equal access to commercial sexual services and the means to afford them.

All three categories center on a concept that is a touchstone of debates about prostitution in the West: power. As Shannon Bell (1994) outlines the positions of various contending "prostitutes' rights" groups, she attempts "to present prostitute discourse as a contested terrain that reproduces the dichotomization of the prostitute as a powerful sexual being and disempowered sexual victim" (135). Bell's overview of the discourses of prostitution climaxes (almost literally) with her discussion of six postmodern prostitute performance artists whose theatrical tropes she sees as a way of entering and controlling a discourse that has hitherto been carried on *about* but not *through* prostitutes' bodies. She maintains that "those, such as prostitutes, previously coded as merely 'obscene' and contained as carnivalesque transgression can reconstitute themselves in the performance medium as living embodiments of resistance, remapping, recodifying, and reclaiming the deviant body, the body of the sexual outsider and social outcast" (138). Bell's prostitute-performers are clearly drawing their maps of resistance on turf initially surveyed by Butler and Rubin.

Bell earlier cites René LeBlanc, founder of Prostitutes Anonymous—a twelve-step organization that conceptualizes prostitution as an addiction—as (nonetheless) stating categorically, "Telling me to give up my prostitution is telling me to give up my power" (133). But LeBlanc never states wherein this power resides. Others have envisaged the exercise of the profession as an exercise, as well, of an *ironic* power over men, a form of specifically sexual control that counterbalances the physical, social, and economic power that males possess and wield over women in general and over prostitutes in particular. But the power claimed in the performances Bell describes is a discursive power, the assertion of an alternative image of the prostitute body and, through it, the prostitute identity. Bell's position is that this representation tends toward both integration and destabilization. As integration, it resolves the artificial polarities between sacred and profane ("sluts" and "goddesses"), feminists and whores, therapists and prostitutes, good girls and bad girls, "porn stars and ordinary women" (183). The destabilization acts not only on the representation but also on "what has traditionally been considered theater and what is still considered theoretical engagement," broadening both "to include new areas of life and new political subjects" (184).

Although Bell also speaks about the performances as a way of creating a "subject position from which to address the social" (138), this position is also and exclusively a discursive one. For that matter, the concept of the "social," as it appears here, is itself a representation. That is, the nearest thing to a social arena into which performance art can enter is a theatrical event meant as a social intervention, such as street rally or demonstration. But just as there is a crucial distinction between a "Take Back the Night" demonstration (Bell highlights Scarlot Harlot's performance at one) and women's taking back any night other than the one on which the march is held, there is a difference between enacting power *at* the social realm and actually achieving it there.

Bell takes at face value the claim that the prostitute runs the sexual event because she says she does—and *by* saying she does. As a work of cultural criticism, her study need not consider what interactions there are between the world of the performance and the one in which prostitutes ply their trade. (For surely she does not believe that the trade itself is restricted to its performative aspects?) But as a work of feminist theory or philosophy—two of the three intellectual or disciplinary categories into which the cover indicates that the publisher has slotted this book—it does have a responsibility to consider and possibly even to take a place in a social constellation in which discourse is only part of the whole. And in which power—in the long run, life and death power—is wielded not by women, but by men.

A few of Chapkis's prostitute-contributors confirm a sense of power outside of the performance experience. Maryann states that "an important part of prostitution for me was realizing that sex didn't have to be about intimacy. There is great power in the realization that you are, in fact, in control" (84). She does not take this control, however, beyond the sense of being in charge of her own pleasure. Vision, who often works with Annie Sprinkle, explicitly denies the economic exchange, as she maintains, "It was important to me that it wasn't just sex for money. It wasn't really even about sex: it was about healing and giving men the opportunity to be in the presence of goddess energy" (87).

In the course of planning and writing this book, we have been challenged a number of times about our right as *farangs*—one of us a male, to boot—to "speak for" the prostitutes of Thailand. The reiterated challenge has forced us to define our (individual and common) subject positions with some care and to be scrupulous in explaining that, although our scholarship clearly advocates a stance *vis-à-vis* the sex workers, we are far from constituting ourselves their representatives. On one occasion, early on, this challenge was articulated by a member of a lecture audience, who insisted that the only person who did have a right to speak on the topic would be a "Thai Annie Sprinkle." The implication was that the chief difference between a Thai prostitute spokeswoman and the American prostitute performer would be their visible ethnicity (Robinson 1996, 184). The cultural chauvinism involved in such a statement, although probably unconscious, seems to us more questionable than our attempt to describe the world of the Bangkok bars, especially as constructed by First World financial, corporate, ideological, and sexual interests.

Thai sex workers do not yet have a spokeswoman from within their ranks, but they *have* engaged in educational performances, through the musical produced by EMPOWER. Although also concerned about both self-acceptance and popular myths defining them and their work, the kind of consciousness-raising Bangkok bar girls do through that musical is on another level from the statement(s) being made by the North American prostitute performers. Some differences, of course, reside in cultural traditions, but others have to do with different understandings of "the social" and how best to interpret or intervene in it. Superficially simpler, the EMPOWER show never loses sight of the relation between historical forces and the fate of any individual, a fate that—despite the organization's emphasis on language lessons, self-help, and mutual aid—the performers never confuse with matters of discourse or believe is theirs to control. Does that mean that the Thai bar girls who are culturally and personally unable to perform in-your-face celebrations of their prostitute identity and the sexuality it entails are censoring themselves? Or does the denial of material conditions in the North American sex goddess/true therapist performance-identities constitute a suppression of certain key facts?

The Thai prostitute, whether sold into bonded labor, recruited out of rural poverty, or selecting sex work over the low pay and horrific working conditions of a sweatshop or domestic service, can never speak about her life without placing its economic reality at the center. She may not know about the big bosses who run international lending institutions or who plan Thailand's tourist industry, and she may not dare to criticize bar owners or the police, but she knows that her family is desperately poor and depends on her. Every sexual event is thus predicated on an original monetary transaction and on its daily repetition through her labor. The truth of her own body is one that she can apprehend only in and through these transactions. Even if she scornfully believes that *farang* men flock to Thailand because of the shortcomings of their own country-women—"after married get fat," "have skin like frog, . . . hole is very big," "not take care" (Walker and Ehrlich 1992)—she has no illusions that this turns *her* body-as-commodity into a spiritual or therapeutic artifact.

Such mythologizing belongs to the subjectivity of the sex tourist, not that of the myth's object. Relying on yet another theatrical correlative, Laurie Shrage introduces her discussion of "Erotic Exotica" as fantasized by First World men with a reference to David Henry Hwang's *M. Butterfly*. Citing Dorinne Kondo's observation (1990, 25) that "if the Orient is a woman, in an important sense women are also the Orient," Shrage moves in and out of the myth, as well as in and out of ironic mode:

> If the Asian woman is constructed in Western culture as super-feminine and hyper-hetero-sensual, then it is not difficult to see why she is desired as a sex provider. . . . A relationship with her promises greater sexual, gender, and racial *complementarity*, and thus it almost guarantees *romance*. For the non-Asian men for whom other avenues of social access to her may be rare, sex trading provides perhaps the easiest path to her sexual services. This path may also be attractive because the customer can satisfy his racialized sexual fantasy without having to confront racial hostility itself. More significantly, we should infer from the globally dispersed construction of Asian womanhood that the sexual desires and fantasies that propel the customer to the Asian prostitute are shaped by global racial politics rather than a universal male biology. . . . Johns who cross national and racial barriers for Asian prostitutes are typically acting upon principles that position Easterners as inferior to Westerners (Shrage 1994a, 152–53; emphasis added).

One indication of the limits of this approach is the absence of any speculation about the Asian woman's fantasies. Her subjectivity is not represented as sexual at all, because the "complementarity," by definition, does not extend that far. (A less mystified way of speaking of "complementarity," of course, is to reject any implication of reciprocity by calling it structural inequality.) She does not embrace the sensual, "hyper-feminine," inferior identity in its political or sexual dimension, but rather apprehends the *farang* in terms of relative kindness, openness to her, and readiness to spend.

Although Shrage goes on to characterize the fantasy and the sex industries to which it gives rise as "oppressive to all Asians, and especially Asian women" (153), her observations about "Exotic Erotica and Erotic Exotica" are offered in support of a legalized, regulated sex trade that she believes could serve as a model of humane socialist and feminist business practice. Needless to say, the very "global racial politics" that the customers' desire is enacting would mean that the Thai woman at home would not benefit from regulation of the First World sex trade. The labor market, including sex work, may be global, but the Third World sex worker would benefit from improvement in metropolitan conditions only in the way and to the extent that sweatshop workers may be said to "benefit" from runaway shops.

Shrage is an active participant in the feminist debate over prostitution, which foregrounds ethical and legal questions as well as sexual ones. This debate is, of course, also understood by the protagonists and the First World feminist movement generally as political. It remains curiously ethnocentric, however, drawing, where appropriate, on information about prostitutes of color in the metropolis or the situation of the sex trade in the Third World to bolster an argument, while apparently feeling no responsibility to construct either a theory or a program that takes account of the international dimension of sex work. Thus, Christine Overall (1992), surveying the philosophical and activist literature on the issue, concludes against prostitution because it is a manifestation of "capitalist patriarchy" without citing that manifestation of late capitalism known as imperialism, or interrogating the impact of this globalization of the system on the institutions of patriarchy.

Shrage's reply to Overall relies on opportunistic references to women in postcolonial situations. She correctly points out that Overall's argument is based entirely on First World conditions, but her counterargument uses race and class issues within various Third World sex industries as identity markers, rather than expressions of social forces. So she believes that a useful critique of Overall's conclusion can be derived from the fact that prostitutes and customers in Kenya "belong" to the same "indigenous, dislocated, and impoverished colonized adult population," or that, in the colonial period some prostitutes in Nairobi were self-employed petty bourgeois, not "sex *workers*." Without examining "a greater variety of cultural contexts," she argues, Overall "has no grounds to claim that . . . [prostitution] is inherently or essentially anything." While praising

Overall for listening to and basing her analysis on the testimony of prostitutes in our own society, she states that these histories also point the way to opening the debate to prostitute women in other societies (Shrage 1994b, 567, 569). The problem with Shrage's approach is not only that her reference to other cultures is intermittent but, more important, that even using the discourse of postcolonialism, she represents other cultures as somehow discrete and even autonomous, evading questions of international or interracial dominance aside from those that are the product of cultural myths and private fantasies.[7]

Wendy Chapkis's *Live Sex Acts* is one of the very few Western defenses of First World prostitution that gives consideration to the conditions facing Thai sex workers in constructing generalizations about prostitution. This consideration, however, occupies far too perfunctory a place in the overall analysis, as Chapkis moves, in rapid succession, from citing Wendy Lee's assertion that only "about ten per cent of prostitutes in Thailand are deceived or forced into the profession" (qtd. 47), confusing the issue somewhat by suggesting that this figure may actually apply to Thai prostitutes working in Europe (48), adding that "it is disingenuous at best to portray a stigmatized sexual practice as inevitably coercive," agreeing that "[e]ven using low estimates, the reality remains that many thousands of women and children are involved in commercial sex against their will," but concluding that "[t]his . . . is a different set of claims than the argument that commercial sex is inevitably a form of slavery" (49).

In contrast to both these theorists, Kathleen Barry, in *The Prostitution of Sexuality*, does not so much participate in the feminist debate over prostitution as attempt to marginalize it. From her point of view, the central fact of what she calls the industrialization of prostitution on a global scale is that it has become the source and the model for all (hetero)sexual relations. Although recognizing the role that international prostitution, including sex tourism, plays in national development strategies, Barry reads the resulting oppression of women entirely in terms of gender inequality. Even the flawed analytic category "capitalist patriarchy" would detract from her focus on the second of those terms. Capitalism itself, she seems to believe, could be cleaned up, were it not for the patriarchal structures that force women in Third World countries away from the "mainstream" of the development process. That this mainstream is polluted, constituting the "horror within which the horror of sex tourism is contained" (Robinson 1995, 13), is elided in her arguments. It is implicitly recognized, however, in the Convention against Sexual Exploitation, which was drafted for submission to the UN by the Coalition against Trafficking in Women (which Barry cofounded) and which calls upon states . . . "to reject policies and practices of economic development that channel women into conditions of sexual exploitation. . . . They shall insure that economic development policies provide for the full economic development of women through their integration into dignified paid labor at a decent standard of living. . . . Therefore they shall prohibit sex tourism and penalize those who organize it . . . in both the countries from which customers travel and the countries to which they go for sex tourism" (Barry 1995, 306–35).

Although this proposal's stipulation of "dignified paid labor at a decent standard of living" suggests an awareness on the authors' part of the current absence of alternatives outside the sex industry that can meet basic human needs, it expresses an entirely unwarranted faith in the capacity of the global market to function in this way. Part of the problem is Barry's denial of an economic definition—or even an economic dimension—of exploitation. She is of course aware that monetary exchange is at the root of the prostitution experience, but she makes "exploitation" synonymous only with "rape," "assault," and "abuse," not with the labor process itself.

For this reason, Barry also rejects the term and the concept of "sex work." We are among those who welcomed the introduction of the term into feminist discourse precisely because it makes possible, without either sentimentality or moralizing, thinking about prostitution and allied jobs as labor. Being a prostitute (or a stripper, porno film performer, or "exotic" dancer) can thus stand in contrast not to being a "good girl" but rather to being a chambermaid, grocery bagger, or waitress, the comparative availability, wages, and working conditions of the various jobs permitting a focus on a context constituted by the labor market (Robinson 1996, 184). Consideration of the special nature of the labor and the "product" is necessary, but does not alter the economics of the situation. The authors of *Casting Stones*, however, focus on the special nature and thus argue that to "use the term 'work,' as if selling one's body for sexual use were the equivalent of typing someone's letter or serving someone food, masks too much to be useful much of the time" (2).

Barry considers the notion of "sex work" part of the conspiracy to normalize prostitution and thereby to prostitute sexuality as a whole. Noting that many sexual activities formerly relegated to the commercial world are now practiced within marital or dating relationships prompts her to claim that the pro-prostitution opinions held by non-prostitutes are motivated by the desire to reinforce "the distinction between prostitute and nonprostitute [*sic*] women, especially as it becomes indistinguishable in the sexual acts through the prostitution of sexuality. . . . Knowing those women who do 'sex between consenting adults' as 'sex workers' protects other women from being seen as whores when they are doing the same sex in their marriages, in dating, or in anonymous, unpaid liaisons" (Barry 1995, 70–71). In contrast to the many First World women who are demanding (or even deploying) the right to sexual subjectivity, up to and including explorations on Gayle Rubin's "outlaw" list, and the few for whom this means actually claiming a "prostitution identity" (69), Barry returns to the posture of nineteenth-century feminism. Whereas, for most contemporary feminists, rape has replaced prostitution as the "quintessential sexual terror," Barry restores a newly industrialized prostitution to that place. Historians Ellen DuBois and Linda Gordon (1984, 32–33) record their astonishment that feminists in the nineteenth century deemphasized rape itself, "as if the norms of legal sexual intercourse were in themselves so objectionable that rape did not seem that much worse." To be able to eliminate that "as if," Barry has to erase the distinction between choice and coercion in all sexual contacts. Even though this essentially amounts to erasing female desire, it is a step she does not hesitate to take. It is one that makes it difficult to pass from the powerful anecdotes and statistics she supplies to an analysis that can bring together the sexual and economic, the psychological and material aspects of the prostitution transaction.

Barry's attempt to represent prostitution relations as the prevailing world system falters under the very weight she assigns it. In her analysis, prostitution replaces all other forms of sweated labor as the archetype of exploitation, at the same time as it subsumes all contemporary heterosexual relations and is the ultimate source of other crimes against women, such as pornography, rape, and domestic violence. Long before Barry pulls the lugubrious Patricia Hearst card out of her sleeve, devoting an entire chapter (pp. 250–75) to the claim that the mid-1970s abduction and alleged rape of the heiress is the "prototype of female sexual slavery," most readers will have rejected the causalities and conspiracies she posits. Yet in *The Prostitution of Sexuality* Barry not only collects a great deal of information about the abuse of women around the world—including some devastating material on the Thai sex industry—but does infer from the mass of data the existence of a global *system* of exploitation, one that defines the lives of women in the First World as well as in developing nations. Unfortunately, she assumes that the "sexual slavery" she identifies is itself a world system, independent of anything else that we might know (or, she would probably interject, that we think we know) about global systems of exploitation.

A similar—and, it would seem, similarly deliberate—blind spot mars Cynthia Enloe's original and provocative *Bananas, Beaches, and Bases*, which does bring together the worldwide sexual *and* economic exploitation of women and which considers cultural as well as material evidence. (Her reading of the manufacture of "exotic" female icons from Pocahontas to Carmen Miranda is an intellectual *tour de force*.) From a perspective informed by these various strains in her argument, Enloe points out that in order to succeed, "sex tourism requires Third World women to be economically desperate enough to enter prostitution; having done so it is made difficult to leave. The other side of the equation requires men from affluent societies to imagine certain women, usually women of color, to be more available and submissive than the women in their own countries. Finally, the industry depends on an alliance between local governments in search of foreign currency and local and foreign businessmen willing to invest in sexualized travel" (1990, 36–37). With specific reference to Thailand, she goes on to point out that sex tourism "is now part of the domestic and international system" (37). But she does not otherwise identify that system or connect the sexual fantasies nurtured by First World cultures to the economics of dominance (Robinson 1991, 229).

Conclusion: The Value(s) of a Dollar

> I want fair for women, everything fair.
> Maybe fair more than men.
> —A twenty-three-year-old bar girl
> in *Hello My Big Big Honey*

In *The Prostitution Prism,* Pheterson describes the "mixture of . . . contempt, compassion, support and opposition" that prostitutes typically encounter from radicals, considering that, basically, "prostitution is likely to be a confusing and unsettling issue within progressive movements" (63). So the challenge for us, as we conclude, is to avoid this mixture as we try to see whether Barry's sense that there is a global sexual order, conditioned by the impersonality that character-izes prostitution encounters (Barry 1995, 20–48), can be joined with our analyses of the relation of sex tourism to the global economic order and the cultural and historical specificity of the Bangkok bar scene. One entirely unexpected clue about how to join them is provided by those repetitious World Sex Guide post-ings that we have indeed tended to cite with an uneasy combination of hilarity and scorn. As we have indicated, the travel reports follow one of two patterns: they either offer a sex tourism guide or present a journal of the author's own trip. There is remarkably little interchange among contributors: those who offer advice often seem unaware that the same comparisons of Patpong, Soi Cowboy, and Nana and the same recommendations of bars, clubs, massage parlors, restau-rants, and hotels already exist on the Net to be confirmed or emended. Similarly, the sexual diaries follow a set of conventions that govern how the sexual encounter is to be depicted and what is to be related—usually without acknowl-edging the other postings and the genre to which they all contribute.

In surveying published guidebooks and travel articles, we have called atten-tion to the concern—amounting at times to obsession—with getting the best bargains and not being cheated. Trink's column frequently chimes in with laments from the expat point of view about the bar owners he calls poor busi-nessmen because they "short-sightedly" engage in price gouging (though the majority of their customers are transients in any case). *Casting Stones* cites a pirated copy of the underground guide *Bangkok Back Streets,* which advises:

> Don't pay if they don't deliver. The only reason they try such *stupid* tactics is that some guys feel so guilty about wanting sex that they'll pay even for not getting any. *Generosity here is foolish and just spoils the field for the next guy* (qtd. 167, emphasis added).

The context makes it easy to miss the significance of the same preoccupation in the Internet narrators, those who set themselves up as alternative guides as well as those who rehash their own sexual vacations. The do-it-yourself guides are, of course, following the conventions of this branch of travel writing, but they go further by making the money aspect a key element in sexual judgments. The girls on Patpong or in a particular establishment there are said to ask too much money; the ones in Nana Plaza, who are cheaper, have a "better attitude." Sex shows are not merely rated according to the pleasure they afford; that pleasure itself is given a cash value, so the establishment is or is not a "waste of money."

The obsession becomes a compulsion in the personal narratives. Since all the minutiae of the trip are recorded, the payments for ground transportation from the airport, hotel rooms, and souvenirs are often part of the account—but so is the price of each sexual encounter with details of the particular services purchased. At the height of ecstasy—experienced or recollected in virtuality—these guys remain aware of how much it cost and whether each ejaculation was a rip-off, a relative bargain, a wise investment, or a splurge that paid off big time.

This is the context in which the man cited earlier can relate his refusal to participate in his own arousal—even to the extent of refusing to conjure up erotic images in his mind—because, after all, "what for do I pay" if not for the prostitute to do all the work? (And take all the blame when the encounter fails.) It leads to narratives in which the loss of a credit card and the wait for its replacement become a suspense-enhancing motif, and in which romance is destroyed and "heartbreak" ensues when a prostitute gets "greedy"—that is, when she tells the *farang* she has been seeing "steadily" for several days that according to her roommate 1000 baht, not 500, should be the price for an all-night session. It is only fitting that the diary posting dated 19 September 1996, the one that celebrates the narrator's ability to bring any number of sex workers to orgasm, is headed "The following is a true account of my trip to Thailand; Note: $1 = 25 Baht."

Cleo Odzer expresses sympathy for the economic plight of her prostitute subjects, yet her account, like those on the World Sex Guide, is larded with references to exactly how much she is spending for what. More to the point, although she is supposedly willing to pay her subjects for their time and is sometimes generous with those she befriends (taking them on research trips to their home villages and vacations to Ko Samet or Pattaya), she becomes readily exasperated at the way their families and boyfriends avail themselves of her ability to pay for things. Moreover, the prostitutes themselves often seem to her to be out for whatever they can get. (Why, they act like whores!) And when Odzer becomes involved with Jek, the Patpong tout, the issue of his repayment of her 500-baht ($20) loan to him acquires the same dramatic significance as the Internet account of the girl who spoiled a beautiful relationship by unexpectedly raising her price. Odzer has no compunction about sharing her bed with Jek, losing herself "in a blend of East and West" (1994, 116), but both before and after they have sex for the first time, she asks, "Did I trust him in the apartment with my computer and other electronic gadgets? Not really" (110). Although she spares no detail of the emotional "price" she pays as this relationship runs its course, it is only after Odzer has reclaimed her sense of *farang* entitlement that she takes on the full sex-tourist mentality. Thus, in her memories of that romantic night with the trekking guide, she relates the "flirty looks" they exchanged the next day, as he poled the raft around "perilous turns and protruding rocks," recalling, "He'd promised to take me on a *free tour* of Chiang Mai on his motorbike that night" (305; emphasis added). The aphrodisiac delights of getting something for nothing must never be underestimated. And all this time, Odzer is the one complaining that the denizens of Patpong just don't know how to sustain an authentic, noncommercial human relationship!

Perhaps the most vivid conflation of monetary and sexual values is provided by the regular client we call "Peter," whose monologue of advice is included in our account of the bar scene (Chapter 6). From the moment he suggests getting serviced at the hotel immediately upon arrival, so as to shoot "your pre-wad," he is constantly adding to the bank account of ejaculations, yet always holding out—deferring gratification even while being satisfied—for the big score that always remains in the future. At the German Beer Garden "we're looking to take the edge off . . . not get fucking married. . . . Take the edge off, bro, so you're not drooling later and do something foolish like spend too much." Later, Peter's disciple in applying the Protestant ethic to new terrain will "get a massage, a manicure, pedicure, haircut, and BJ somewhere. . . . You're being treated like royalty from top to bottom at twenty bucks a throw." And remember, the intelligence or wit or personality of the bar girl doesn't matter, because if you're only in town "for a day or two, *talk is not what you're after.*"

The moments when the narrator, whether Odzer or a sex tourist, routinely links sexual and emotional gratification to the financial particulars and those when monetary matters take on affective meanings are equally suggestive. In these passages—and, clearly, in the consciousness of the writers—sexuality is commodified not simply by being susceptible of being bought or sold but by being fetishized. According to Karl Marx, commodity fetishism is intrinsic to the culture of capitalism, occurring when the boundary between the human and everything else—whether inanimate or ideational—dissolves. It is a phenomenon, in short, whereby "the productions of the human brain appear as independent beings endowed with life and entering into relations both with one another and the human race" and in which, at the same time, a human relationship can assume "the fantastic form of a relation between things" (1867, 77).[8]

The commodity fetishism that characterizes these sexual descriptions occurs at the nexus between the material and psychological meanings of "alienation." Sex work is alienated labor—that is, labor whose value is appropriated—and it is also alienated in the emotive sense: that is, separated and *causing* separation from authentic feelings, giving rise to isolation and revulsion. The record of the customers' fetishized mentality makes clear that it is not only the prostitutes who experience the transaction as alienated but the clients as well, whether they are praising the quality of the product they have purchased or convincing themselves that, unlike the other purchasers, they have established a *true* relationship.

From this point of view, consider these passages of a letter from a *farang* (nationality unspecified) to a woman in Bangkok:

My work has been very boring since I got back, but this week I will soon be very busy. But I don't mind, when I am busy I can forget about being in here and the days are shorter when I'm working.

I am pleased to hear you're are [*sic*] working as a waitress. I hate to see so many beautiful girls pretending to have fun with horrible farangs!

But things in Thailand are so different, believe me, I do not make any judgements, because I have no right to do so, I don't understand your life and your situation, the only thing I do understand is your honesty and your love (Walker and Ehrlich 1992, 42).

Given what we know about the nature of sex tourism's sexual exchanges, it is not easy to tell whether this writer is uniquely perceptive or uniquely alienated from the implications of his own insights.

The first night we two went to Soi Cowboy together, one of our *farang* companions gestured around the bar and exclaimed, "Look at these guys: they're so obviously the losers of the Western world!" Or, as one bar girl expresses the same view, "When they're in their country they can't get a girl friend. They're very lonely. Work, work, work and come back here" (Walker and Ehrlich 1992, 153). By contrast, what has always struck us was the *ordinariness* of the men crowding the bars; it requires no stretch of the imagination to transport almost any of them, mentally, to a restaurant table in his own country, facing a non-commercial companion of his own age and nation. They are "losers" only because they prefer a game with even fewer rules and with guaranteed certainty as to the result. They prefer the sexual event as a transaction, even if some of them are also capable of mystifying the commercial aspects.

The bar girl is also right when she connects their "loser" status to "work, work, work." Sex tourism is as much a part of their working lives as the routine in which a busy week is welcomed because it makes the time go faster. Thanh-Dam Truong points out the "interplay between leisure policy and leisure industry" and the way "the economic value of leisure and 'free time' as unoccupied time . . . [has been] incorporated into the logic of production and consumption" (1990, 98). Moreover, leisure, like sexuality, possesses an existential, a social, and an economic dimension and, like sexuality, has to be analyzed in terms of changing forms of production and reproduction (95). Industrialized sexuality as a form of industrialized leisure can thus be understood as intrinsic to the system in which work is defined and carried out—a system, in other words, of *totalizing alienation*. That sex tourism builds on an infrastructure established for military R&R and extended through corporate recreational contracts underscores this totality of the work-leisure institution.

Seeing the system as one of international sexual alienation offers a perspective on the kind of sexuality that the sex industry trades in, and recognizes it as part of the global system of exchange, domination, and exploitation that functions on the economic level. Thus, while ignoring Marx's economic definition of alienation, Brock and Thistlethwaite focus on the other sorts of alienation, arguing that capitalism "tends to make the person unstable as a social, discursive, somatic, and psychic entity . . . [T]he lack of congruity between life and work, what Marx called alienation, is characteristic of . . . (capitalist) societies. This alienation is an important mechanism of power that supports prostitution, because the body must be regarded as a commodity in order for the sex industry to obtain workers" (1996, 108). They go on to point out that one of the most important ways in which capitalism enables the sex industry to function "is the reduction of the human body to property" (110). This also helps make material sense of the moral imperative that Kathleen Barry enunciates: "*When the human being is reduced to a body, objectified to sexually service another, whether or not there is consent, violation of the human being has occurred*" (1993, 23, original emphasis). Seeing it as sexual alienation means placing this violation in the context of all the other violations inherent in a system in which work is performed by "labor power"—a dehumanized but not disembodied quality possessed by human beings who are sometimes identified as "hands"—and in which the same alienation envelops those who manage and (even) those who profit.

Recognizing sexual alienation as part of a totalizing system makes it hard to accept easy answers about what is to be done about sex tourism, because all are, at best, partial solutions. Cynthia Enloe has faith in the combined action of official nationalism in developing countries, allied feminist groups in the First and Third World, and the fear of AIDS (1990, 37). Kathleen Barry works through pressure on the United Nations (1995, 276–344). Andrew Vachss (1995) calls for a boycott of Thai exports.[9] Laurie Shrage (1994a) posits a humane, regulated industry and Shannon Bell calls for further exploration of the power of the performative prostitute body and of all expressions of female sexual subjectivity (1994, 185–89). Each of them, like the activist movements at work within Thailand, acknowledges only a part of the problem and pursues a solution based on that perception.

But to say that none of these is enough is also not enough. Solutions have to be sought that are on the scale of the problem, however daunting it may appear. They have to be sought with our eyes open to the full dimensions of the complex reality.

AFTERWORD

Our book is done—and suddenly the true nature of the Thai "economic miracle" is being exposed in the international media as far from miraculous. All that loudly and widely proclaimed economic boom has rapidly become all that economic fall. The failure of more than fifty major financial firms in the kingdom led to runs on banks, rumors of coups and very wobbly legs for the Chavalit administration, and finally capitulation to an IMF austerity plan that included a bailout to the tune of 16 billion dollars, for starters.

The agreement signed on 11 August 1997 calls for a $4 billion loan from the IMF itself, a form of international indebtedness that Thailand had successfully avoided hitherto, supplemented by loans from Japan and other nations. For the first time in decades, the baht has been allowed to float against other major currencies, and a value-added tax has been levied, meaning that the burgeoning middle class and the poorest consumers will probably suffer more in the belt-tightening than they had ever benefited from its much-ballyhooed loosening. All this is happening, moreover, just a few months after the Clintons visited the country and, while the First Lady praised efforts to eradicate the national taint of child prostitution, the President joined the multinational chorus of financial experts celebrating the kingdom's prosperity.

More important, from our perspective, than asking the obvious questions about how the current crisis emerged so rapidly and massively, is asking how Thailand will cope with the bust and at whose expense it will attempt to regain its status at the table of international economic players. Even though Finance Minister Thanong Bidaya has asked everyone in the nation "to endure the pain," we may legitimately inquire who will be required to endure the most and which sectors of the economy will provide the salve. One possible answer may be found in the kingdom's falling back on what it knows best, deploying again what has been successful before; to that end, the already planned and publicized Tourist Authority of Thailand's 1998 extravaganza, "Amazing Thailand," seems as good a place as any to start.

Tourism has always proved a reliable source for hard currency and, with the kingdom's racking up so much unforeseen debt in such currency, the travel industry will surely factor into the recovery equation. Likewise, financially strapped countries always offer good value to tourists who keep their eyes peeled for travel bargains. This crisis occurs just as it had begun to appear as if the greater poverty of Vietnam and Cambodia might attract some of Thailand's sex-tourism dollars. If our study shows anything, it shows that a sizable bunch of prospective tourists ever-sensitive to the needs and conditions of the Thai tourist industry are ready to travel at a moment's notice. So a bumper crop of visitors may well be in the offing for "Amazing Thailand Year."

And what will so amaze the tourist to "Amazing Thailand '98"? Precisely what did so before—certainly in greater abundance and very likely at even lower prices. Think of Spalding Gray's riff on the "amazing" Thai pussy in his performance film *Swimming to Cambodia* (1987): "pussies" that shoot darts, play Ping-Pong, drink through straws, smoke cigarettes, service the tourist to new ecstatic heights, do everything, in fact, but (re)produce and bring forth babies! If tourism is to be as central to Thailand's economic recovery as it was to the kingdom's boom-time development—and it can hardly be otherwise, since the planned bailout entails no new industrial or agricultural directions—sex will continue to be essential to tourism and hence to the nation's economic rescue. Thailand's "miracle" was built on the backs of women working on *their* backs; the reconstruction process will doubtless make use of the same means.

Despite their economic salience, however, the sex industry and its personnel have once more become invisible in official accounts and in media coverage of the crisis. In a report released by the Public Health Ministry just a week before the crash (28 July 1997), the number of sex workers was placed at 64,886—not the two million reported by an unnamed NGO (*Bangkok Post*, 29 July 1997). The timing of the report is as interesting as the incredibly low and surprisingly specific number claimed by the ministry. Hard currency revenue from the "illegal" industry would be invisible, in any event, to IMF overseers because it does not officially exist. But even if it did exist, the ministry's report seems to indicate that it is too small to count or be counted.

For the media, these days, the "real" story, the only one, is about the declining baht and troubled financial institutions, and the only voices to be heard are those of banking experts, finance ministry spokesmen, and international lenders. In a grotesque extension of the "personal interest" lead-ins we've discussed, an AP story dealing exclusively with macroeconomic issues is illustrated by a photo of an impoverished mother and child seated on a sidewalk. The caption reads: "A Thai woman begs in downtown Bangkok, where poverty has increased as family debt burdens soared" (Associated Press, "IMF Forges Bailout for Thailand," *Raleigh News and Observer,* 12 August 1997, 11A).

Although the article itself makes no reference to what "the world's second-largest economic rescue plan" will do for the plight of women begging in the streets, it does not take much imagination to figure out what it means for the sex workers in the bars and those who will join their ranks in the months to come. If the boom was fueled by national and international development policies that deliberately functioned to impoverish certain regions of the country, in order to maintain a heavy flow of age- and gender-specific workers for low-paid unskilled jobs, including those in tourism, rural conditions can only grow grimmer as the boom fizzles out. This means more desperate families, more and younger women recruited to prostitution, and worsening labor conditions (greater competition, smaller incomes, and more menacing health conditions, as safe sex becomes a luxury fewer girls can afford to insist on).

We originally planned for *Night Market* to tell the story of the Thai "miracle" as manifested in venues from girlie bars to international banks. The book as written is the story of the boom. It turns out that we also seem to have written the story of the bust.

—RB and LSR
13 August 1997

NOTES

Chapter 1: Points of Departure: Catalysts and Contexts

1. "London's" last four lines, with the "marriage hearse" and the "harlot's curse," also provide the epigraph of a recent book on prostitution elsewhere in Asia. See Carolyn Sleightholme and Indrani Sinha, *Guilty Without Trial: Women in the Sex Trade in Calcutta* (1997).

Chapter 2: Naming the Problem

1. The authors' attitude toward (male) sexuality can best be epitomized in their admiring accounts of the legendary prowess of the dictatorial former prime minister, Sarit Thanarat, and their quotation of Mechai Viravaidya, Thailand's "Mr. Condom," who claims that "the Thai male propensity to consume sex is immense" (Kulick and Wilson 1992, 126–127). In a similar vein, their only paragraph on the growth of tourism, which cites the well-known statistics about number of tourists, dollar amounts spent, and the industry's relation to the balance of payments, is followed by a paragraph approximately twice as long praising two tourist attractions, the Oriental Hotel and the Queen Sirikit Conference Center. With tourism as with sex, as far as they are concerned, nothing succeeds like excess.

2. In this regard, it should be noted that Thongchai Winichakul's provocative analysis of "Thai-ness" argues that certain commonly held beliefs about Thai essence have resulted in Western scholars' fetishizing their Thai colleagues. Often these Thai scholars, Winichakul claims, are products of a system of privilege that has made university education an aristocratic right, thus making "Thai-ness" a concept that supposedly transcends class but is in fact wholly class-defined. This situation has occasionally resulted in an "uncritical intellectual cooperation by pro-indigenous Western scholars who have tended to accept the established views of the Siamese elite as *the* legitimate discourse about Thailand" (1994, 7). Even those persons outside the elite, including famous activist-scholar Sulak Sivaraksa and members of the early manifesta-

tions of the Communist Party of Thailand, have not argued against the ontological status of "Thai-ness."

3. Interestingly, none of Pasuk's subsequent work that we are aware of cites Truong's book.

4. Although the subtitle of Truong's study refers to Southeast Asia as a whole, the text concentrates on Thailand and, to a lesser extent, the Philippines.

5. It may appear disingenuous of us to place the studies that do consider the politics of sexuality and of prostitution in another chapter, the last one in this book, and then fault the sexless approach of the scholars discussed here. But the sexuality-based studies, which tend to ignore economics much as Pasuk and Truong ignore sexual theory, generate their analysis almost exclusively from First World experiences and hence make no contribution to the process of naming and framing the issues around the sex trade in Thailand.

6. Readers interested in a critical literature review of tourism studies should see Crick's "Representations of International Tourism in the Social Sciences: Sun, Sex, Sights, Savings, and Servility" (1989). Those interested in a lively discussion of the various issues at play in tourism studies should consult the introduction to Hitchcock, King, and Parnwell, *Tourism in Southeast Asia* (1993).

7. Marcus and Fischer's foundational work *Anthropology as Cultural Critique* (1986) proposes using the discipline of anthropology as a self-reflexive tool for evaluating one's own culture and suggests that ethnographies may reveal more about the mentalities of the representer than of the represented. The move to self-critique makes it likelier, in theory, for significant cross-cultural dialogue to occur. Like the Hobsbawm and Ranger (1983) and the Clifford (1988) texts, Marcus and Fischer detail a useful heuristic tool for tourism studies. This is a point made by Robert Wood (1993) in "Tourism, Culture and the Sociology of Development."

8. The long discursive relationship linking colonialism, tourism, and sexuality is explored at length in Chapter 5.

9. Lengthier discussions of Truong, Cohen, Odzer, and others appear in later chapters. The evocation of them here is meant to illustrate academic approaches to this topic, not to provide any detailed critique of their arguments.

10. For a more extended discussion of the Anna-in-Siam tradition (or industry), centering on Anna Leonowen's own books, see Chapter 5.

11. At that time, *Weekend* aired monthly, replacing *Saturday Night Live* every fourth week.

Chapter 3: Languages of Tourism

1. Erik Cohen (1993, 36–39) posits a more detailed schematic for reading tourism's images, particularly those of "native people." He offers seven areas of examination: (1) who represents (2) whom (3) for whom, (4) how, (5) in what medium, (6) under which sociological circumstances of native people, and (7) under which prevailing sociopolitical relationships.

2. An excellent and thorough analysis can be found in Graham M. S. Dann's *The Language of Tourism: A Sociolinguistic Perspective* (1996). The earlier chapters neatly provide various sociolinguistic schemata and theories for interpreting tourist promotional literature, ranging from the convergent and divergent properties of the language of tourism to the ways this language infantilizes the tourist and acts as a form of social control. The later chapters provide an encyclopedic typology of "pretrip," "ontrip," and "posttrip" examples of tourism's language in a wide array of media.

Chapter 4: A Very Political Economy

1. For eloquent testimony to the power of this dream, see the interviews in *"Hello My Big Big Honey!": Love Letters to Bangkok Bar Girls and Their Revealing Interviews* (Walker and Ehrlich 1992). The letters reflect the complementary fantasy on the part of certain customers.

2. Phongpaichit and Baker (1995,148) states that tourism did not achieve this dominant economic role until 1985; Muscat (1990, 2) situates it in 1987.

3. This reasoning seems to work; Leheny (1995, 372) points out that male travelers represent roughly 70% of Thailand's arrivals, which is higher than expected, even taking into account business travelers who are predominantly male. Although Leheny is trying to demonstrate the drawing power of sex tourism, he certainly does not mean to imply that the categories "business traveler" and "sex-industry client" never overlap.

4. See Sanitsuda Ekachai, *Behind the Smile: Voices of Thailand* (1990), for vivid descriptions of farming and fishing villages whose source of livelihood has been deliberately eroded or eliminated.

5. The 1989 *Country Study* edited by Barbara Leitch LePoer—which looks like a sequel or companion volume but was published under the imprint of the U.S. Department of the Army, in its Area Handbook series—does index several items under "Prostitution."

6. In the same passage (Phongpaichit 1982, 11) Pasuk cites the penalties stipulated in the 1960 Prostitution Act for anyone, including the owners of establishments, found guilty of engaging in the trade: imprisonment of three months to one year or a fine of 1,000 to 2,000 baht. It is not clear whether higher fines have replaced these now derisory sums (amounting, respectively, to $40 and $80), but if the fines are almost never imposed it hardly matters.

7. Uli Schmetzer (1993) provides no source for his figure of 2 to 3 million prostitutes, a third of them children, although he implies that some Thai officials recognize a prostitute population on this scale.

8. The narrator's voice in the Patpong musical *This Is Us* calls the prostitute "the daughter of the land," suggesting one level of the family tie, and adds that the women "are also mothers who sacrifice their bodies so their children would have a better chance in this society" (EMPOWER np).

9. It seems legitimate to use figures provided by a young man in this case, since there is no indication that the economics of the situation is substantially different for male sex workers, and this was the most recent figure available.

10. It goes without saying that Mitani's characterization of Buddhist values is crudely inaccurate.

11. For discussion of this phenomenon with respect to Hawaii, see Ferguson and Wilson-South, "The Feminization of Hawai'i: Occupation of a Nation, Dialogue between Haunani-Kay Trask and Lillian Robinson" (1989–90). The longstanding association of the land to be despoiled and the vulnerable female body is explored in such studies as Annette Kolodny's work on representations of the American frontier, *The Lay of the Land* (1975).

Chapter 5: Imagining Sexual Others

1. We are indebted to John Nguyet Erni for this conceit and for his comments on earlier drafts of this chapter.

2. In the introduction and first chapter of *Imperial Leather* (1995), Anne McClintock does an excellent job of tracing important connections between colonialism, sexuality, capital, and race. In so doing, she presents a solid argument for the construction of "dangerous classes," including indigenous peoples and prostitutes, in need of paternalistic control. Also useful is her discussion

of how Africa and the Americas, to which we would also add Asia, became a "porno-tropics for the European imagination—a fantastic magic lantern of the mind onto which Europe projected its forbidden sexual desires and fears" (22). For a slightly different take on gender, sexuality, and colonialism—particularly how they affected European women in colonial sites—see Ann Laura Stoler's "Carnal Knowledge and Imperial Power: Gender Race, and Morality in Colonial Asia" (1991). Particularly useful in this article is a discussion of concubinage that has some relation to our study of John Stedman later in this chapter.

    3. Homi Bhabha also notes the paradoxical nature of colonial discourse. His notion of the "ambivalence" of the stereotyped Other as "an object of derision and desire" (1986, 313) over-laps with our concept of "schizoid othering." However, Bhabha's concern is primarily with psychoanalytic ramifications of representation with regard to race and colonial subject formation through which the stereotype becomes a fetish justifying colonial rule. (McClintock 1995 discusses in detail the link between colonial discourse and fetishism.) Also, Edward Said, in his important text *Orientalism* (1978), talks about the vacillation operative in the discourse of Otherness and how the structure of the literature about the Orient shapes the encounter between East and West.

    4. This is a trajectory inspired by Malek Alloula's *The Colonial Harem* (1986). He provides one such transition, and we have modified and expanded it.

    5. Michel Foucault (1978) argues this point at length in his discussion of the "hysterization of women's bodies."

    6. For an excellent account of these biographical refashionings, as well as a provocative reading of this text, see Morgan's introduction to Leonowens (1992). Also, we should emphasize that we are not attacking Anna Leonowens herself so much as the residual interpretive equipment that she replicates in various ways.

    7. All quotations from the creators of the show and the lyrics come from the *Miss Saigon* homepage at: rsjdfg@clark.net—one of two such homepages.

Chapter 6: The Bar Scene

    1. For an excellent study of the political, social, legal and empirical situations of Burmese women and girls in Thailand, see *A Modern Form of Slavery*, by the Asia Watch Women's Rights Project (1993). Information about Thai women in Japan can be found in Kazuko Watanabe's "Trafficking in Women's Bodies, Then and Now" (1995).

    2. As with the genealogy of representations that contextualizes this site and its interactions, past events provide analogies for the contemporary bar scene. Writing of the phenomenon known as "the Masque" in early eighteenth-century England, Terry Castle (1988) cites Richard Steele; "The being in disguise takes away the usual checks and restraints of modesty, and consequently the beaux do not blush to talk wantonly, nor the belles to listen; the one as greedily sucks in the poison as the other industriously infuses it" (*The Guardian*, no. 142, 24 August 1713). In many senses, the eighteenth-century masque reemerges in the "contact zone" of the late twentieth-century Thai bar. At the masquerades, revelers could explore sexual and social roles unavailable to them in a daily life circumscribed by rigid moral parameters; that is, they could move easily up or down the class hierarchy and—beneath the umbrella of anonymity provided by the artifice of costume—engage in sexual experimentation, rubbing shoulders, not to mention other body parts, with members of social classes different from their own. This situation finds analogy in the social and class artifice of international tourism, especially international sex tourism, given the appearance (if not the reality) of wealth necessary for such travel and the anonymity possible in being elsewhere. The freedom from moral constraints regarding sexual

behavior in "proper" eighteenth-century English society is also mirrored in international sex tourism, especially if, as described in Chapter 5, the culture being visited is represented as qualitatively and quantitatively different with regard to sexual mores. Further, the masque's promise of promiscuity was realized by the general availability of large numbers of prostitutes in attendance (as depicted by William Hogarth in *The Harlot's Progress*), much as this promise is fulfilled in Bangkok bars. The prostitutes at the masque, like their Thai *doppelgängers*, played the role of autonomous, willing sexual companion and indulged in the artifice of the site which allowed those involved to ignore the economic necessity that drove the women to this particular place. As at the masques, in the Thai bars some women involve themselves to express and enact their own sexual subjectivity, but these are very few in number. The vast majority place themselves there for economic gain, which, though meager, is unattainable elsewhere in the economy. Class aspirations, class divisions, and economic disparities create sites for sexual satisfaction for some under the guise of free choice on the part of the participants and for endless play plus pleasure and fulfillment for those with economic and social clout.

For an excellent examination of the eighteenth-century masquerade in English culture and society, see Terry Castle's "The Culture of Travesty," in the collection *Sexual Underworlds of the Enlightenment* (1988). Castle's fine article served as inspiration for this analogy and supplied much of the information for our analysis.

3. The introduction to Richard Terdiman's *Discourse/Counter Discourse* (1985) discusses the history of symbolic resistance that emerges from the philosophy of language.

4. The Thermae described in this piece was closed in July 1996, but it is the one most familiar to those who know anything about the sex tourism scene in Bangkok. Bishop, however, also visited the new Thermae, a few doors down from the previous establishment, shortly after it opened. It is larger and cleaner than the original site, but many regulars find the new spot "impersonal," "lifeless," and "antiseptic." A large, S-shaped bar splits the room, with clients and workers perched on both sides of it. A line of high-backed booths, interrupted by a CD jukebox, traces one wall, and a counterlike bar with tall stools runs the length of the opposite wall. The booths, the regulars complain, make it difficult to get a good view of the room and the interactions taking place there. A set of tables in the back can be used for eating. Access to the bar, as in the old place, can be gained from the street or the parking lot. Although the regulars complain, most say that they will become accustomed to the new space. The continuity of the same nononsense waiters and privileged police relations should help make the transition easier.

When the original Thermae closed, the *Bangkok Post* ran an elegy of sorts (14 July 1996): it told the history of the establishment, its ability to convert easily from R&R clientele to postwar tourists, and its capacity to survive "prevailing political and economic winds." The article stated that in this site, mostly Western males met mostly Northeastern (Thai) females, and declared (in the language of the sex tourism business) that their "intercultural interaction varied from a shorttime to a lifetime." Among those interviewed for the piece was Christopher Moore, who "found inspiration in the Thermae for a series of novels."

Chapter 7: The Unspeakable

1. Although we have modified the way she applies them, we are indebted to Sedgwick (1985) for the phrase "privilege of unknowing" and the idea of ignorance as an epistemological site.

2. The information about the 6 October 1973 violence and coup has necessarily been sketchy for the purposes of this chapter, so we will briefly fill in some details here. In 1971, as the Vietnam War dragged on and doubts about U.S. commitment to the region were exacerbated by

reestablished American relations with China, Thailand found itself in a difficult position. Forces on the left and right began to draw their ranks together, and the military settled matters in November 1971 with a right-wing coup that abolished parliament, banned political parties, suspended the constitution, and imposed martial law. The regime's authority was questioned by rural groups and left-wing intellectuals. In 1973, just when it seemed that full-blown civil violence might erupt, the king named a new government, forcing the coup leaders to flee. A glorious moment of democratic rule, international autonomy, and national self-reflection followed. But as the left pushed further and faster with political and constitutional reform, the right and the military grew increasingly twitchy. When the two coup leaders returned from exile in September 1976, students took to the streets in protest, and the situation grew tense. The lynching of two labor leaders by the right led a group of Thammasat University students to stage their own mock lynchings of various right-wing leaders on 5 October. The military-controlled media, which had been denouncing students' activities for a couple of years, pounced on this photo op and broadcast nationwide their condemnation of the students' sacrilege. The next day a combination of military, police, paramilitary, and private citizens turned into an angry, well-armed mob and unleashed their anger on the students: firing on the unarmed youth, lynching many, dousing some with gasoline and setting them on fire, and rounding up more than fifteen hundred for general arrest. A new military group toppled the democratic government and reinstituted the provisions imposed in November 1971. (For more details on this series of events, see Anderson 1977, Girling 1981, Prizzia 1985, and the *Far Eastern Economic Review* and *Bangkok Post* for the period concerned.)

3. The operative qualities, in Anderson's assessment, are "calm" and "self-confident." The Thai national ideology certainly was not the only conservative one in Southeast Asia but may have been the only "calm" and "self-confident" one.

4. The material on Jit comes from Craig Reynolds's excellent study *Thai Radical Discourse: The Real Face of Thai Feudalism*, whose subtitle is borrowed from one of Jit's most influential works. Reynolds provides his own translation of this text and a wonderful contextualization of it within Thai radical thought and English-language histories of Thailand.

5. The popular music genre *phleng luk thung* , discussed in Chapter 2, does, of course, explicitly address the sex industry in a mass media form. But, in a sense, it too remains unspeakable, or rather unhearable, due to class and ethnicity constraints. The central Thai middle class and Bangkok urban elite would not listen to this genre. Their domestic servants might tune it in on their transistor radios, but they themselves would tune it out. Once again, a will to ignorance would overwhelm the articulation of unpleasant or contradictory information.

6. The sex industry for Thais is unspeakable because it denigrates the nation by airing private secrets in public. This kind of loss of face is called *Kai na*. If a *farang* or other external source discusses the sex industry, the Thai wonder how this group knew what should have been their secret. The loss of face in this situation is called *Sia na*. The difference between the two terms is one of transitivity: with *Kai na*, you cause yourself to lose face, whereas with *Sia na*, someone else causes you to lose face.

7. Much of the biographical information about Kanha comes from the brief but useful introduction by David Smyth to his translation of the novel (Surangkhanang 1994). All quotations from the text are from the Smyth translation.

Chapter 8: Sexual Theory and Its Discontents

1. We are aware, of course, that the term "peculiar institution" was initially coined to describe chattel slavery in the antebellum American South. Carrying both connotations of

"peculiar"—at once strange and familiar—into the discussion of the Thai sex industry is an intentional move on our part.

2. As noted in our preface, whichever one of us is writing, the subject "we" usually feels comfortable. But just as Ryan necessarily had recourse to the singular when he described his experiences as a *farang* male in the Bangkok bars, I—Lillian—find it impossible to say "they" about the feminist movement's quest for sexual definition in the late 1960s and early 1970s; I've tried to keep it as unconfusing as possible, but the "we" of the rebirth of feminism is Lillian-and-her-sisters, not Lillian-and-Ryan.

3. Perkins and Bennett (1985) distinguish between male and female prostitutes in this regard, which suggests that Rubin, whose own anthropological studies focus on gay "leather-men," draws her conclusions about female prostitutes from observations of males. As homosexuals, however, these men would figure somewhere on the "outlaw" list whether or not they engaged in sex for money, whereas female prostitutes are often transgressive solely because of the commercial nature of their activity. The situation in Thailand is even more complex, because, as transvestites or transsexuals, some male prostitutes fit the "bad list" categories; others who service male clients professionally are heterosexual in their private lives.

4. Since these books focus primarily on issues of the sex trade other than the actual sex, discursive and translation issues are central only in those few passages that do look at the sexual relations.

5. Page numbers of the printout are provided because this is such an unusually long entry, as is the guide cited at length in Chapter 5.

6. Although English is the common language of the World Sex Guide, it is clearly not the native tongue of all correspondents.

7. Overall's reply (1994) to Shrage's comments reflects a better grasp of materialist philosophy—particularly in her sense that power is about relationships, not fixed categories—but it continues to ignore the international implications of her analysis.

8. Marx's meditation (1867) on the cultural, psychological, and emotional meanings of gold is also instructive with regard to the nature of the exchanges occurring in Thailand.

9. The pages following the fictional text in Vachss's 1995 *Batman: The Ultimate Evil* are unnumbered. The list of organizations fighting child prostitution—including the boycott group Don't!Buy!Thai!—appears on what would, if numbered, be page 214.

WORKS CITED

Aiken, Peter. 1980. "Into the Heart of Thailand." *Travel-Holiday*, November, pp. 43–47.

Alleman, Richard. 1983. "The Lure of Living Lavishly—at Bangkok's Oriental Hotel." *Vogue*, June, pp. 135–36.

Allison, Anne. 1994. *Nightwork: Sexuality, Pleasure and Corporate Masculinity in a Tokyo Hostess Club*. Chicago: University of Chicago Press.

Allman, T. O. 1989. "Jewel of the Chao Phraya." *Gentleman's Quarterly*, January, pp. 160–63, 193–94.

Alloula, Malek. 1986. *The Colonial Harem*. trans. Myrna Godzich and Wlad Godzich. Minneapolis: University of Minnesota Press.

Anderson, Benedict R. O'G. 1977. "Withdrawal Symptoms: Social and Cultural Aspects of the October 6 Coup." *Bulletin of Concerned Asian Scholars* 9 (3): July–September pp. 13–31.

————. 1985a, "Introduction" to *In the Mirror: Literature and Politics in Siam in the American Age*. pp. 9–41, Bangkok: DK Books.

————. 1985b. and Ruchira Mendiones. trans. *In the Mirror: Literature and Politics in Siam in the American Age*. Bangkok: DK Books.

Asia Watch Women's Rights Project. 1993. *A Modern Form of Slavery*. New York: Human Rights Watch.

Atcheson, Richard. 1973. "Electric Chiang Mai, Town of 100 Wat," *Holiday*, March, pp. 36–37, 62–63.

Baldwin, W. Lee and W. David Maxwell. 1975. *The Role of Foreign Financial Assistance to Thailand in the 1980s*. Lexington, Mass.: Lexington Books-Heath.

Ballhatchet, C. 1980. *Race, Sex and Class Under the Raj: Imperial Attitudes, Policies and their Critiques*. London: Weidenfeld and Nicolson.

Bangkok Post, International Weekly Review. 1995. "Government Bans Nightlife Guide." 7 (5): 3 February, 1.

———. 1995. "Protests to Foreign Media Ignore the Real Problem." 7 (6): 10 February, 8.

"Barbara." 1994. "It's a Pleasure Doing Business with You." *Social Text* 11 (3): 13–22.

Barbour, John. 1993. "Slavery Still Blights All Races, Nations." Associated Press, *Roanoke* (Virginia) *Times and World-News*, 12 September, pp. B1, B5.

Bardhan, Kalpana. 1986. "Women's Work, Welfare and Status: Forces of Tradition and Change in India." *South Asia Bulletin* 6 (1): 3–16.

Barnathan, Joyce. 1993. "The AIDS Disaster Unfolding in Asia." *Business Week*, 22 February, pp. 52–53.

Barry, Kathleen. 1995. *The Prostitution of Sexuality*. New York: New York University Press.

Beauvoir, Simone de. 1961. *The Second Sex* (1949). trans. H. M. Parshley. New York: Knopf, 1953, Bantam ed.

Bell, Laurie, ed. 1987. *Good Girls/Bad Girls: Feminists and Sex Trade Workers Face to Face*. Seattle, Wash.: Seal Press.

Bell, Shannon. 1994. *Reading, Writing, and Rewriting the Prostitute Body*. Bloomington: Indiana University Press.

Berger, John. 1972. *Ways of Seeing*. London: BBC and Penguin Books.

Bhabha, Homi K. 1992. "The Other Question: The Stereotype and Colonial Discourse." In *The Sexual Subject*. pp. 312–21. London: Routledge.

Bishop, Ryan, and Lillian S. Robinson. 1995. Review of *Patpong Sisters*, by Cleo Odzer. *Z Magazine* 8, September, pp. 68–70.

———. 1996. "Batman goes to Bangkok," review of *Batman: The Ultimate Evil*, by Andrew Vachss. *Nation*, 29 January, pp. 34–35.

———. 1998. "Genealogies: The Night Market in the Western Imagination. In *Gender and Sexuality in Modern Thailand*, eds. Nerida Cook and Peter Jackson. Chiang Mai: Silkworm Books.

Bock, Carl. 1986. *Temples and Elephants: Travels in Siam in 1881–1882*. (1884). Singapore: Oxford University Press.

Bordieu, Pierre. 1977. *Outline of a Theory of Practice*. trans. Richard Nice. Cambridge Studies in Social Anthropology. Cambridge: Cambridge University Press.

Bounds, Elizabeth M. 1991. "Sexuality and Economic Reality: A First World and Third World Comparison." In *Redefining Sexual Ethics*, ed. S.F. Dunes and E. H. Haney. pp. 131–43. New York: Pilgrim Press.

Brett, Guy. 1986. *Through Our Own Eyes: Popular Art and Modern History*. London: GMP Publishers.

Briggs, Walter L. 1949. "Thailand: Peace and Prosperity." *The New Republic*, 31 October, p. 15.

Brock, Gail Nakashima and Susan Brooks Thistlethwaite. 1996. *Casting Stones: Prostitution and Liberation in Asia and the United States*. Minneapolis: Fortress Press.

Brookhiser, Richard. 1989. "The Authors' Lounge." *American Spectator*, December, p. 46.

Brown, Phyllida, and David Concar. 1991. "HIV Epidemic Threatens Asia's Developing Nations." *New Scientist*, 22 June, p. 18.

Burge, Frederica, ed. 1981. *Thailand: A Country Study*. Washington, D.C.: American Universities Foreign Area Studies.

Busch, Noel. 1955. "Letter from Bangkok." *The New Yorker*, 3 December, pp. 193–200.

Butler, Judith. 1990. *Gender Trouble: Feminism and the Subversion of Identity*. New York: Routledge.

———. 1993. *Bodies that Matter: On the Discursive Limits of "Sex."* New York: Routledge.

Castle, Terry. 1988. "The Culture of Travesty." In *Sexual Underworlds of the Enlightenment*, ed. G. S. Rosseau and Roy Porter. pp. 156–80. Chapel Hill: University of North Carolina Press.

Chapkis, Wendy. 1997. *Live Sex Acts: Women Performing Erotic Labor*. New York: Routledge.

Charasdamrong, Prasong, and Subin Khuenkaew. 1993. "A Post Enquiry." *Sunday Bangkok Post,* 17 January, pp. 18–19.

Chatterjee, Partha. 1993. *The Nation and its Fragments.* Princeton: Princeton University Press.

Chatterjee, Ranjit. 1994. "Riflessioni linguistiche sul personale e sul politico." *Parolechiave,* nuova serie di "Problemi del Socialismo," 5, pp. 79–91.

Chu, Valentin. 1968. *Thailand Today: A Visit to Modern Siam.* New York: Crowell.

Clark, Blake. 1950. "Siam: Land of Smiles." *Reader's Digest,* August, pp. 125–30.

Clarke, Henry. 1965. "The Golden Court of Thailand." *Vogue,* 5 February, pp. 82–91.

Clement, Harry G. 1961. *The Future of Tourism in the Pacific and the Far East.* Washington, D.C.: United States Department of Commerce.

Clifford, James. 1988. *The Predicament of Culture: Twentieth Century Ethnography, Literature, and Art.* Cambridge: Harvard University Press.

Cohen, Erik. 1982. "Thai Girls and Farang Men: The Edge of Ambiguity." *Annals of Tourism Research* 6 (1): 18–35.

———. 1984. "The Dropout Expatriates: A Study of Marginal Farangs in Bangkok." *Urban Anthropology* 13 (1): 91–114.

———. 1986. "Lovelorn Farangs: The Correspondence Between Foreign Men and Thai Girls." *Anthropological Quarterly* 59 (3): 115–27.

———. 1987. "Sensuality and Venality in Bangkok: The Dynamics of Cross-Cultural Mapping of Prostitution." *Deviant Behavior* 8: 223–34.

———. 1988. "Tourism and AIDS in Thailand." *Annals of Tourism Research* 15 (4): 467–86.

———. 1989. "'Primitive and Remote': Hill Tribe Trekking in Thailand." *Annals of Tourism Research* 16: 30–61.

———. 1993a. "Open-ended Prostitution as a Skillful Game of Luck: Opportunity, Risk and Security Among Tourist-Oriented Prostitutes in a Bangkok Soi." In *Tourism in South-East Asia.* eds. Michael Hitchcock, Victor T. King, and Michael J. G. Parnwell, 155–77. London: Routledge.

———. 1993b. "The Study of Touristic Images of Native People: Mitigating the Stereotype of the Stereotype." In *Tourism Research: Critiques and Challenges.* ed. D. Pearce and R. Butler. pp. 36–69. London: Routledge.

Cohen, Jon. 1995. "Search for the Ideal Cohort." *Science* 270, 10 November, p. 905.

Crick, Malcolm. 1989. "Representation of Tourism in the Social Sciences: Sun, Sex, Sights, Savings, and Servility." *Annual Review of Anthropology* 18: 301–44.

Cummings, Joe. 1994. "Thailand." In *Southeast Asia: A Lonely Planet Shoestring Guide.* Hawthorn, Victoria, Australia: Lonely Planet.

———. 1995. *Bangkok: A Lonely Planet City Guide.* Hawthorn, Victoria, Australia: Lonely Planet.

D!B!T! (Don't Buy Thai) Homepage, members.aol.com/dbtlori/dbtl

Dann, Graham M.S. 1996. *The Language of Tourism: A Sociolinguistic Perspective.* Wallingford, Oxfordshire, U.K.: CAB International.

deKadt, Emanuel. ed. 1979. *Tourism—Passport to Development?* New York and London: Oxford University Press, for the World Bank and UNESCO.

Derrida, Jacques. 1974. *Of Grammatology.* 1969, trans. Gayatri Chakravorty Spivak. Baltimore: Johns Hopkins University Press.

Devi, Mahasweta. 1995. *Imaginary Maps,* trans and intro. Gayatri Chakravorty Spivak. London: Routledge.

Diderot, Denis. 1991. "Supplement to Bougainville's *Voyage*" (1773) in *This is Not a Story and Other Stories.* trans. and intro. P. N. Furbank. pp. 60–112. Columbia: University of Missouri Press.

DuBois, Ellen Carol and Linda Gordon. 1984. "Seeking Ecstasy on the Battlefield: Danger and Pleasure in Nineteenth-Century Feminist Sexual Thought." In *Pleasure and Danger: Exploring Female Sexuality*. ed. Carole S. Vance. pp. 31–46. Boston: Routledge & Kegan Paul.

Durdin, Peggy. 1955. "Bangkok: One Capital That Doesn't Worry." *New York Times Magazine*, 3 July, pp. 9–11.

Eastlake, William. 1966. "Dragon Train to Singapore." *Nation*, 16 September, pp. 283–84.

Ebert, Teresa L. 1995. *Ludic Feminism and After: Postmodernism, Desire, and Labor in Late Capitalism*. Ann Arbor: University of Michigan Press.

Economist. 1989a. "Thailand: AIDS Homes In," 4 February, p. 37.

———. 1989b., "Protecting the Tarts of Thailand." 25 February, p. 30.

———. 1990a. "AIDS? What AIDS?" 24 March, p. 36.

———. 1990b. "Thailand: Cops and Rubbers." 10 November, p. 40.

———. 1991. "AIDS in Thailand: The Debut of Safe Sex." 19 January, p. 34.

———. 1992. "Thailand: Sense About Sex." 8 February 1992, pp. 32–33.

———. 1993. "Termites in the Basement." 18 September, p. 42.

———. 1995. "AIDS: Counting the Cost." 23 September, pp. 26–27.

Ekachai, Sanitsuda. 1990. *Behind the Smile: Voices of Thailand*. Bangkok: Thai Development Support Committee.

———. 1994. *Seeds of Hope: Local Initiatives in Thailand*. Bangkok: Thai Development Support Committee.

Ellerbee, Linda. 1986. *"And So It Goes": Adventures in Television*. New York: Berkeley Books.

EMPOWER (Education Means Protection of Women Engaged in Re-Creation). 1987. *Patpong Musical: This is Us*, written and directed by Aurapin Dararatana.

Enloe, Cynthia. 1990. *Bananas, Beaches and Bases: Making Feminist Sense of International Politics*. (1989). Berkeley, University of California Press.

———. 1992. "It Takes Two." In *Let the Good Times Roll: Prostitution and the U.S. Military in Asia*, ed. Saundra Pollock Sturdevant and Brenda Stolzfus. pp 22–27. New York: The New Press.

Erlanger, Steve. 1991. "A Plague Awaits." *New York Times Magazine*. 14 July, pp. 25–26, 49, 52.

Erni, John Nguyet. 1997. "Of Desire, the Farang, and Textual Excursions: Assembling 'Asian AIDS.'" *Cultural Studies* 11 (1): 64–77.

Fairclough, Gordon. 1994. "No Bed of Roses: Government Tries to Uproot Prostitution from Economy." *Far Eastern Economic Review* 157, 15 September, p. 30.

———. 1995. "Doing the Dirty Work: Asia's Brothels Thrive on Migrant Labour." *Far Eastern Economic Review* 158, 14 December, pp. 27–28.

Fanon, Frantz. 1974. *The Wretched of the Earth*. (1961), Harmondsworth, U.K.: Penguin Books.

Febas Borra, J. 1978. "Semiología de lenguaje turistica." *Estudios Turisticos* 57–58: 17–203.

Ferguson, Kathy E. and April Wilson-South. 1989–90. "The Feminization of Hawai'i: Occupation of a Nation. A Dialogue Between Haunani-Kay Trask and Lillian Robinson." *Voices: The Hawaii Women's News Journal* 3 (3): 4–16.

Flaherty, Gloria. 1988. "Sex and Shamanism in the Eighteenth Century." In *Sexual Underworlds of the Enlightenment*. ed. G. S. Rosseau and Roy Porter. pp. 261–80. Chapel Hill: University of North Carolina Press.

Fockler, Shirley. 1977. "Pacific Places: Far East." *Travel/Holiday*, December, pp. 36, 39.

Fodor's Guide to Thailand. 1991. New York: Fodor.

Foucault, Michel. 1978. *The History of Sexuality*, vol. 1. trans. Robert Hurley. New York: Pantheon-Random House.

———. 1984. "Nietzsche, Genealogy, History." In *The Foucault Reader*. ed. Paul Rabinow. pp. 76–100. New York: Pantheon-Random House.

Fowler, Roberta. 1995. "Bountiful Bangkok: A Buyer's Paradise." *Travel-Holiday*, August, pp. 61, 63, 107.

Gardiner, Harry W., and Ormsin Sornvoonpin Gardiner. 1991. "Women in Thailand." In *Women in Cross-Cultural Perspective*. ed. Leonore Loeb Adler. New York: Praeger.

Gillies, John. 1994. *Shakespeare and the Geography of Difference*. Cambridge: Cambridge University Press.

Girling, John L.S. 1981. *Thailand: Society and Politics*. Ithaca, NY: Cornell University Press.

Gooi, Kim. 1993. "Cry of the Innocents." *Far Eastern Economic Review* 152, 9 September, pp. 36–37.

Gordon, David G. 1984. "Tongue Thai'd in Bangkok: The Beguiling Flow of Thailand." *Travel-Holiday*, October, pp. 52–57.

Gray, Paul and Lucy Redoit. 1995. *Thailand: The Rough Guide*. 2nd. edition. London: Rough Guides.

Grayman, Jesse, Andrew Williams, Pai E. Young, and Amy E. Yeager. 1996. *Let's Go: The Budget Guide to Southeast Asia*. New York: St. Martin's.

Greenwood, Davyyd J. 1989. "Culture by the Pound: An Anthropological Perspective on Tourism as Cultural Commoditization." In *Hosts and Guests*. ed. Valene Smith. pp. 171–85. Philadelphia: University of Pennsylvania Press.

Grogan, David, and Cinia Tamaki. 1990. "Let Half a Billion Condoms Bloom: Thailand's Mechai Thrives as the Barnum of Birth Control and Safe Sex." *People*, 24 September, pp. 91–92.

Grove, Noel. 1996. "Thailand." *National Geographic* 89 (2): February, pp. 82–104.

Gubernick, Lisa. 1989. "Somerset Maugham Did Not Sleep Here." *Forbes*, 11 December pp. 290–92.

The Hague Declaration on Tourism. 1989. The Hague: Inter-Parliamentary Conference on Tourism.

Hall, John. 1996. "The Party's Over at the Thermae." *Bangkok Post*, 14 July.

Hamilton, Annette. 1991. "Rumors, Foul Calumnies and the Safety of the State: Mass Media and National Identity in Thailand." In *National Identity and Its Defenders: Thailand 1939–1989* ed. Craig Reynolds. pp. 341–79. Chiang Mai: Silkworm Books.

Handley, Paul. 1989. "The Lust Frontier." *Far Eastern Economic Review*, 2 November, pp. 44–45.

———. 1990. "Dangerous Liaisons." *Far Eastern Economic Review*, 21 June, pp. 25–26.

———. 1992a. "Catch if Catch Can." *Far Eastern Economic Review*, 13 February, pp. 29–30.

———. 1992b. "An Ounce of Prevention." *Far Eastern Economic Review*, 13 February, pp. 30–31.

———. 1992c. "Invisible Hand: AIDS at Work." *Far Eastern Economic Review*, 12 March, p. 48.

Hechler, David. 1995. "Child Sex Tourism." In Andrew Vachss, *Batman: The Ultimate Evil*. New York: Warner.

Henderson, John, et al. 1972. *Area Handbook for Thailand*. Washington, DC: United States Government Printing Office.

Hill, Catherine. 1993. "Planning for Prostitution: An Analysis of Thailand's Sex Industry." In *Women's Lives and Public Policy: The International Experience*. eds. Meredeth Turshen and Briavel Holcomb. pp. 133–44. Westport, Conn.: Greenwood Press.

Hitchcock, Michael, Victor T. King, and Michael J.G. Parnwell. eds. and intro. 1993. *Tourism in Southeast Asia*. London: Routledge.

Hitchens, Christopher. 1983. "Minority Report" column. *Nation*, 29 November, p. 598.

Hobsbawm, Eric, and Terence Ranger. eds. 1983. *The Invention of Tradition*. Cambridge: Cambridge University Press.

Hodges, Luther. 1961. "Foreword" to *The Future of Tourism in the Pacific and the Far East*, by Harry G. Clements. Washington, D.C.: United States Department of Commerce.

Holder, Peter, Jürgen Horleman, and Georg Friedrich Pfafflin. eds. 1983. *Documentation: Tourism Prostitution Development*. Bangkok: Ecumenical Council on Third World Tourism.

Holland, Eugene W. 1993. *Baudelaire and Schizophrenia: The Sociopoetics of Modernism.* Cambridge: Cambridge University Press.

Hørigård, Cecilie, and Liv Finstad. 1992. *Backstreets: Prostitution, Money, and Love.* trans. Katherine Hanson, Nancy Sipes, and Barbara Wilson. (1986). University Park, Penn.: Pennsylvania State University Press.

Hornblower, Margot. 1993. "The Skin Trade." *Time*, 21 June, pp. 45–51

Hulme, Peter. 1986. *Colonial Encounters.* London: Methuen.

Insor, D. 1963. *Thailand: A Political, Social, and Economic Analysis.* New York: Praeger.

Irvine, Janice M. 1995. "Regulated Passions: The Invention of Inhibited Sexual Desire and Sexual Addiction." In *Deviant Bodies: Critical Perspectives on Difference In Science and Popular Culture.* pp. 314–37. eds. Jennifer Terry and Jacqueline Urla. Bloomington: Indiana University Press.

Iyer, Pico. 1980. "The Smiling Lures of Thailand." *Time.* 17 October, pp. 84–86.

———. 1988. *Video Night in Katmandu.* New York: Knopf.

Jacobs, Norman. 1971. *Modernization Without Development: Thailand As an Asian Case Study.* New York: Praeger.

Kahn, E. J., Jr. 1964. "Letter from Bangkok." *New Yorker*, 5 December, pp. 163–82.

Kaye, Dena. 1986. "Thai High." *Vogue*, December, pp. 221. 224.

Kayr-Win, Mary, and Harold E. Smith. 1995. *Historical Dictionary of Thailand.* Lanham, Md.: Scarecrow Press.

Kearney, Robert P. 1983. "Poppy Tours." *Harper's*, September, p. 27.

Kelly, Neil. 1991. "Counting the Cost." *Far Eastern Economic Review* 153, 18 July, p. 44.

Keyes, Charles F. 1987. *Thailand: Buddhist Kingdom as Modern Nation-State.* Boulder, Cob.: Westview Press.

Kolodny, Annette. 1975. *The Lay of the Land: Metaphor as Experience and History in American Life and Letters.* Chapel Hill: University of North Carolina Press.

Kondo, Dorinne. 1990. "M Butterfly: Orientalism, Gender, and a Critique of Essentialist Identity." *Cultural Critique* 16: 5–29.

Krailat, Kon. 1985. "In the Mirror." In *In the Mirror: Literature and Politics in Siam in the American Age.* Trans. and intro. by Benedict R. O'G. Anderson and Rachira Mendiones. Bangkok: DK Books.

Kristof, Nicholas D. 1996. "Asian Children Sacrificed to Prosperity's Lust." *New York Times*, 14 April, pp. 1, 6.

Krongkaew, Mehdi. 1992. "Poverty and Income Distribution." In *The Thai Economy in Transition*, ed. Peter G. Warr. pp. 401–37. Cambridge: Cambridge University Press.

Kulick, Elliott, and Dick Wilson. 1992. *Thailand's Turn: Profile of a New Dragon.* New York: St. Martin's.

Landon, Margaret. 1944. *Anna and the King of Siam.* New York: John Day.

Leheny, David. 1995. "A Political Economy of Asian Sex Tourism." *Annals of Tourism Research* 22 (2): 367–84.

Leonowens, Anna H. 1953. *Siamese Harem Life.* 1873; rpt. New York: E. P. Dutton and Co.

———. 1991. *The Romance of the Harem.* (1873). rpt. ed. Susan Morgan. Charlottesville: University Press of Virginia.

LePoer, Barbara Leitch. ed. 1989. *Thailand, A Country Study.* Washington, D.C.: United States Department of the Army.

Levy, John, and Kyle McCarthy, eds. 1994. *Frommer's Comprehensive Travel Guide: Thailand.* 2nd ed. New York: Macmillan.

Lintner, Bertil, and Hseng Noung. 1992. "Immigrant Viruses" *Far Eastern Economic Review*, 20 February, p. 31.

MacCannell, Dean. 1989. *The Tourist: A New Theory of the Leisure Class* (1976), 2d ed. New York: Schocken.

McClintock, Anne. 1995. *Imperial Leather: Race, Gender, and Sexuality in the Colonial Contest.* New York: Routledge.

McIntosh, Robert W. 1977. *Tourism: Principles, Practices, Philosophies.* Columbus, Ohio: Grid Press.

Manderson, Lenore. 1992. "Public Sex Performances in Patpong and Explorations of the Edges of Imagination." *Journal of Sex Research* 19 (4): 451–75.

Marcus, George E., and Michael M.J. Fischer. 1986. *Anthropology as Cultural Critique.* Chicago: University of Chicago Press.

Marx, Karl. 1867. "The Fetishism of Commodities and the Secret Thereof." *Capital*, Vol. I. Moscow: Progress.

Matthews Harry G. 1978. *International Tourism: A Political and Social Analysis.* Cambridge, Mass.: Schenkman.

Michener, James. 1954. "Thailand—Jewel of Asia." *Reader's Digest*, December, pp. 57–66.

Millett, Kate. 1970. *Sexual Politics.* New York: Doubleday.

Mitani, Katsumi. 1968. "Key Factors in the Development of Thailand." In *Economic Development Issues: Greece, Israel, Taiwan, and Thailand*, ed. Committee for Economic Development. New York: Praeger.

Mitchell, Juliet. 1984. "Women: the Longest Revolution" (1966). rpt. *Women, the Longest Revolution: On Feminism, Literature and Psychoanalysis.* New York: Pantheon-Random House.

Moore, Christopher G. 1991. *A Killing Smile.* Bangkok: White Lotus Press.

———. 1993. *A Haunting Smile.* Bangkok: White Lotus Press.

———. 1995. *The Comfort Zone.* Bangkok: White Lotus Press.

———. 1996. *The Big Weird.* Bangkok: Siam Books.

Moore, Fred J. 1974. *Thailand: Its People, Its Society, Its Culture.* New Haven, Conn.: HRAF Press.

Moorehead, Alan. 1954. "Letter from Bangkok." *New Yorker*, 6 March, pp. 71–83.

Moreau, Ron. 1988. "Asia's New Economic 'Tiger.'" *Newsweek*, 11 July, pp. 52–53.

———. 1992. "Sex and Death in Thailand." *Newsweek*, 10 July, pp. 50–51.

Morgan, Susan. 1991. "Introduction" to *The Romance of the Harem*, by Anna Leonowens. rpt. Charlottesville: University Press of Virginia.

Muqbil, Irntiaz. 1989. *The Thai Tourism Industry: Coping with the Challenge of Growth.* Bangkok: THAI International.

Muscat, Robert J., 1990. *Thailand and the United States: Development, Security, and Foreign Aid.* New York: Columbia University Press.

Narula, Karen Schur. 1985. "On Bangkok's Waterways: Unveiling Life in Thailand." *Travel-Holiday*, pp. 59–61.

Nation (Bangkok). 1995. "TAT Seeks Internet Porn Clean-Up." 21 April.

New Republic. 1963. "Thailand: The Missing Balance." 28 December, pp. 11–12.

New Yorker. 1945. "Talk of the Town: Our Own Baedeker." 15 September, p. 7.

Newsweek. 1973. "Thailand: Paradise Lost." 5 February, p. 52.

Nimanthemindor, Sukich. 1956. "A Thai's Formula for Happiness." *New York Times Magazine*, 2 December, pp. 102–106.

Odzer, Cleo. 1994. *Patpong Sisters: An American Woman's View of the Bangkok Sex World.* New York: Blue Moon-Arcade.

O'Merry, Rory. 1990. *My Wife in Bangkok.* Berkeley: Asia Press.

Osborne, Christine. 1994. *Essential Thailand.* Lincolnwood, IL: Passport Books.

Overall, Christine. 1992. "What's Wrong with Prostitution? Evaluating Sex Work." *Signs: Journal of Women in Culture and Society* 17 (4): 705–24.

———. 1994. Reply to Shrage. *Signs: Journal of Women in Culture and Society* 19 (2): 571–75.

Parini, Jay. 1983. "Thailand Diarist: Anomalies." *New Republic*, 15–22 August, p. 43.

Passport's Illustrated Travel Guide to Thailand for Thomas Cook. 1992. Lincolnwood, Ill.: Passport Books.

Perkins, Roberta, and Garry Bennett. 1985. *Being a Prostitute: Prostitute Women and Prostitute Men*. Sydney: George Allen and Unwin.

Pheterson, Gail. 1996. *The Prostitution Prism*. Amsterdam: Amsterdam University Press.

Phongpaichit, Pasuk. 1982. *From Peasant Girls to Bangkok Masseuses*. Geneva: International Labour Organisation.

———. 1989. "The Economic Development Culture and the Environment." In *Culture and Environment in Thailand: A Symposium of the Siam Society*. pp. 337–48. Bangkok: The Siam Society.

———. 1993. "Services." In *The Thai Economy in Transition*, ed. Peter Warr. pp. 151–71. Cambridge: Cambridge University Press.

———. and Chris Baker. 1995. *Thailand: Economy and Politics*. Kuala Lampur: Oxford University Press.

Powell, Gareth. 1989. "Bangkok by Day and Night." *Sydney Morning Herald*. In *World Press Review*, August, p. 62.

Pratt, Mary Louise. 1992. *Imperial Eyes: Travel Writing and Transculturation*. London and New York: Routledge.

Prizzia, Ross. 1985. *Thailand in Transition: The Role of Oppositional Forces*. Honolulu: University of Hawaii Press.

Purcell, Carl. 1982. "'The Land of Smiles': A Nice Place to Visit—Over and Over Again." Traveler's Camera column, *Popular Photography*, 89: April, pp. 58, 152.

Reeves, Gayle. 1993. "Asian AIDS Epidemic Holds Threat of Disaster." Knight-Ridder Tribune News Service, *Austin American-Statesman*, 1 May.

Reisender, Walter. 1985. "Exotic Bangkok." excerpted from *South China Morning Post* in *World Press Review*, November, p. 62.

Reynolds, Craig. 1987. *Thai Radical Discourse: The Real Face of Thai Feudalism Today*. Ithaca, NY: Cornell Southeast Asia Program.

———. ed. 1991. *National Identity and Its Defenders: Thailand 1939–1989*. Chiang Mai: Silkworm Books.

Reynolds, Jack. 1986. *A Woman of Bangkok*. (1956). rpt. Bangkok: DK Books.

Rhodes, Richard. 1992. "Death in the Candy Store" *Rolling Stone*, 28 November.

Richter, Linda K. 1989. *The Politics of Tourism in Asia*. Honolulu: University of Hawaii Press.

Robertson, Archie. 1953. "Siam: No Chip on Its Shoulder." *Vogue*, 15 October. pp. 66–68.

Robinson, Lillian S. 1991. Review of *Bananas, Beaches, and Bases*, by Cynthia Enoe. *Mānoa* 3 (1): 227–29.

———. 1993. "In the Penile Colony: Touring Thailand's Sex Industry." *Nation*, 1 November, pp. 492–97.

———. 1995. "From Whorehouse to Our House," review of *The Prostitution of Sexuality*, by Kathleen Barry. *Women's Review of Books* 13 (1): October, 12–13.

———. 1996. "Subject/Position." pp.177–87 in *"Bad Girls"/"Good Girls": Women, Sex and Power in the 90s*. New Brunswick, NJ: Rutgers University Press.

Roth, Andrew. 1949. "Siam: Tranquillity and Sudden Death." *Nation*, 11 October, pp. 317–20.

Rubin, Gayle. 1975. "The Traffic in Women: Notes on the 'Political Economy' of Sex." In *Toward an Anthropology of Women*, ed. Rayna R. Reiter. pp. 157–210. New York: Monthly Review Press.

———. 1984. "Thinking Sex: Notes for a Radical Theory of the Politics of Sexuality." In *Pleasure and Danger: Exploring Female Sexuality*, ed. Carole S. Vance. pp. 267–319. Boston: Routledge & Kegan Paul.

Sager Mike. 1984 "Thailand's Home for Wayward Vets." *Rolling Stone*, 10 May.

Said, Edward. 1978. *Orientalism*. New York: Pantheon-Random House.

Sano, Shinichi. 1981. Sei no Okuku (Empire of sex). Tokyo: Bungeishinju.

Scriber, Charles. 1981. "Thailand's Treasures" excerpted from *The Australian*, in *World Press Review*, August, p. 63.

Schmetzer, Uli. 1992. "Pair's Odyssey, Escape," sidebar to "Across Asia, Slave Trade Prospers— Often for Child Labor or Sex." Knight Ridder Tribune News Service, *Austin American-Statesman* 23 February, pp. J1, J7.

Seabrook, Jeremy. 1991. "Cheap Thrills." *New Statesman and Society*, May, pp. 12–13.

Sedgwick, Eve Kosofsky. 1988. "Privilege of Unknowing." *Genders* 1: 102–24.

———. 1990. *Epistemology of the Closet*. Berkeley: University of California Press.

Segal, Lynne. 1994. *Straight Sex: Rethinking the Politics of Pleasure*. Berkeley: University of California Press.

Seidler, Victor, ed. 1992. *Men, Sex and Relationships: Writings from* Achilles Heel. London: Routledge.

Selwyn, Tom. 1993. "Peter Pan in South-East Asia: Views from the Brochures." In *Tourism in South-East Asia*, ed. Michael Hitchcock, Victor T. King, and Michael J.G. Parnwell. pp. 117–37. London: Routledge.

Serrill, Michael S. 1993. "Defiling the Children," *Time*, 21 June, pp. 53–55.

Shaplen, Robert. 1967. "Letter from Bangkok." *New Yorker*, 18 March, pp. 135–72.

Shenon, Philip. 1992a. "After Years of Denial, Asia Faces Scourge of AIDS." *New York Times*, 8 November, pp. 1, 12.

———. 1992b. "Brash and Unashamed, Mr. Condom Takes on Sex and Death in Thailand." *New York Times*, 20 December, Week in Review, p. 11.

Shrage, Laurie. 1994a. *Moral Dilemmas of Feminism: Prostitution, Adultery, and Abortion*. New York: Routledge.

———. 1994b. Comment on Overall's "What's Wrong with Prostitution? Evaluating Sex Work." *Signs: Journal of Women in Culture and Society* 19 (2): 564–70.

Simms, Peter. 1969. "Siam-by-the-Sea." *Saturday Review*, 8 March, pp. 86–88.

Sleightholme, Carolyn, and Indrani Sinha. 1997. *Guilty Without Trial: Women in the Sex Trade in Calcutta*. (1996). New Brunswick, NJ: Rutgers University Press.

Smith, Griffin. 1979. "A Night on the Siamese Express." *Saturday Review*, 17 March, pp. 49–50.

Smith, Valene, ed. 1989. *Hosts and Guests*. 2nd ed. Philadelphia: University of Pennsylvania Press.

Smyth, David. 1994. "Introduction" to *The Prostitute*, by K. Surangkhanang. (1937). rpt. Kuala Lampur: Oxford University Press.

Spacks, Patricia Meyer. 1984. *Gossip*. New York: Knopf.

Spierenburg, Pieter. 1991. *The Broken Spell: A Cultural and Anthropological History of Preindustrial Europe*. New Brunswick, NJ: Rutgers University Press.

Spurr, David. 1993. *The Rhetoric of Empire: Colonial Discourse in Journalism, Travel Writing and Imperial Administration*. Durham, NC: Duke University Press.

Stedman, John Gabriel. 1988. *Narrative of a Five Years Expedition against the Revolted Negroes of Surinam*. ed. Richard Price and Sally Price. (1790). Baltimore: Johns Hopkins University Press.

Stevenson, Adlai. 1953. "Stevenson Report." *Look*, 16 June, pp. 49–51.

Stocking, George W. 1987. *Victorian Anthropology*. New York: Free Press.

Stoler, Ann Laura. 1991. "Carnal Knowledge and Imperial Power: Gender, Race, and Morality in Colonial Asia." In *Gender at the Crossroads: Feminist Anthropology in the Postmodern Era*. ed. Micaela di Leonardo, pp. 51–101. Berkeley: University of California Press.

Sudham, Pira. 1983. *Siamese Drama and Other Stories from Thailand*. Bangkok: Shire Books.

Surakhanang, K. 1994. *The Prostitute*. (1937), trans. and intro. by David Smyth. Kuala Lampur: Oxford University Press.

Tasker, Rodney. 1994. "Dirty Business: A Spate of Child Sex Cases Highlights a National Concern." *Far Eastern Economic Review* 157: 13 January, p. 23.

Terdiman, Richard. 1985. *Discourse/Counter-Discourse*. Ithaca, NY: Cornell University Press.

Thai Values: Incentive Travel to the Land of Smiles. 1995. Bangkok: THAI International.

Thailand in the 90s. 1991. Ed. Thienchai Srivichit, et al. Bangkok: National Identity Office of the Prime Minister.

Thailand Knopf Guide. 1993. 1st American Edition, New York: Knopf; Paris: Editions Nouveaux Loisirs-Gallimard.

Tiefer, Leonore. 1994. *Sex is Not a Natural Act and Other Essays*. Boulder, Colo: Westview Press.

Time. 1950. "Garden of Smiles." 3 April, pp. 28–31.

———. 1965a. "Thailand: The Rural Revolution." 28 May, pp. 37–38.

———. 1965b. "Thailand: Behind Every Successful Woman," 17 December, pp. 91–92.

———. 1970. "Gloom in the Land of Smiles." 17 July, p. 22.

———. 1971. "Thailand: Paradise Lost." 2 August, p. 60.

Titmuss, Christopher. 1993. *Spirit of Change*. Alameda, Calif.: Hunter House.

Todorov, Tzvetan. 1993. *On Human Diversity: Nationalism, Racism, and Exoticism in French Thought*. trans. Catherine Porter. Cambridge, Mass.: Harvard University Press.

Tourist Attractions in the North. 1995. Bangkok: Tourist Authority of Thailand.

TAT (Tourist Authority of Thailand) Homepage: (http://www.cs.alt.ac.th/tat/stable/history.html).

Trink, Bernard. 1995. Interview with Ryan Bishop and Jeff Petry, 8 August.

Truong, Thanh-Dam. 1990. *Sex, Money and Morality: Prostitution and Tourism in South-East Asia*. London: Zed.

Ty, Eleanor. 1994. "'Welcome to Dreamland': Power, Gender and Post-Colonial Politics in *Miss Saigan*." *Essays in Theatre/Essais théatrales*, 13 (1); 14–27.

Ungpakorn, Ji. 1994. "To Defeat AIDS, Stop Preaching," rpt. from *Nation* (Bangkok), *World Press Review*, June, p. 52.

United Nations. 1963. *Recommendations on International Travel and Tourism*. Rome: United Nations.

U.S. News and World Report. 1992. "Thailand: Selling Sex Does Not Pay." 27 July pp. 52–53.

Vachss, Andrew. 1995a. *Batman: The Ultimate Evil*. New York: Warner.

———. 1995b. Interview with Ryan Bishop. 17 November.

Van Beek, Steve. 1988. *Insight Guide to Thailand* (Hans Höfer, *Thailand*). Singapore: Apa.

———. 1991. *Insight Guide to Thailand* (Hans Höfer, *Thailand*). Singapore: Apa.

———. 1993. *Insight Guide to Thailand* (Hans Höfer, *Thailand*). Singapore: Apa.

van Lier, R.A.J. 1971. "Introduction," to *Narrative of a Five Years Expedition Against the Revolted Slaves in Surinam*, by Captain J. G. Stedman. (1790). Barre, Mass.: Imprint Society.

Vogue. 1989. "Paradise Lost—and Found." January, pp. 120, 123–24.

Vollmann, William T. 1993a. *Butterfly Stories*. New York: Grove Press.

———. 1993b. "Sex Slave." *Spin*, December, pp. 74–148.

Walker, Dave, and Richard S. Ehrlich, eds. 1992. *"Hello My Big Big Honey!": Love Letters to Bangkok Bar Girls and Their Revealing Interviews*. Bangkok: Dragon Dance.

Warr, Peter G. ed. 1993. *The Thai Economy in Transition*. Cambridge: Cambridge University Press.

Watanabe, Kazuko. 1995. "Trafficking in Women's Bodies, Then and Now: The Issue of Military 'Comfort Women.'" *Peace & Change* 20 (4): October, pp. 501–14.

Wilke, Renate. 1981. In *Der Uberbick*, April, excerpted in *Documentation: Tourism Prostitution Development*. ed. Peter Holder, Jürgen Horlemann, and Georg Friedrich Pfäfflin. Bangkok: Ecumenical Council on Third World Tourism, p. 41.

Wilson, Donald. 1994. "Prostitution in Thailand: Blaming Uncle Sam." Chiang Mai: Crescent Press Association, December.

Winichakul, Thongchai. 1994. *Siam Mapped: A History of the Geo-Reality of the Nation.* Chiang Mai: Silkworm Books.

Wood, Robert E. 1993. "Tourism, Culture, and the Sociology of Development." In *Tourism in Southeast Asia*, ed. Michael Hitchcock, Victor T. King, and Michael J. G. Parnwell. pp. 48–70. London: Routledge.

Wyatt, David K. 1982. *Thailand: A Short History.* New Haven, Conn.: Yale University Press.

Xin Ren. 1993. "China." In *Prostitution: An International Handbook on Trends, Problems, and Policies.* ed. Nanette J. Davis. Westport, Conn.: Greenwood Press.

Young, Sir G. 1973. *Tourism. Blessing or Blight?* Harmondsworth, U.K.: Penguin.

Zack, Michele. 1996. "Challenge from Within." *Far Eastern Economic Review*, 15 August, 49.

INDEX

The authors would like to thank Dennis Foster and the Department of English at Southern Methodist University for their financial support in constructing the index. To that end, we would also like to thank Chris Breding for his courageous work on the index.